An Annotated Guide to the Writings and Papers of Leonard Woolf

for Charis and William

AN ANNOTATED GUIDE TO THE WRITINGS AND PAPERS OF LEONARD WOOLF

*by Janet M. Manson
and Wayne K. Chapman*

© 2017 Clemson University Press
All rights reserved

Third Edition (revised)

ISBN: 978-1-942954-53-8

For information about Clemson University Press,
please visit our website at www.clemson.edu/press.

Typeset in Minion Pro by Wayne Chapman
with production and design specialist Charis Chapman.
Printed and bound in the USA by Ingram/Lightning Source.

Cover portrait: Leonard Woolf, October 1922,
as a Labour Party candidate for Parliament

TABLE OF CONTENTS

Introduction vii
   1. General Overview by Wayne K. Chapman vii
   2. Research Acknowledgments by Janet M. Manson xi

Part One: Signed Published Works by Leonard Woolf
   1. Authored Books and Monographs 2
      1.1 Autobiographies 2
      1.2 Correspondence and Diaries 3
      1.3 Drama and Fiction 4
      1.4 Literary/Social Criticism and History 4
      1.5 "Practical Politics" and International Affairs 6
   2. Edited Books and Monographs 9
      2.1 Works with Contributions by Leonard Woolf 10
   3. Journalism (in chronological sequence) 12
      3.1 *The Nation* 12
      3.2 *The Athenaeum* 13
      3.3 *The Nation & The Athenaeum* 13
      3.4 *The New Statesman* 72
      3.5 *The New Statesman and Nation* 74
      3.6 *The New Statesman* (after July 1957) 86
      3.7 *The Political Quarterly* 87

Part Two: Unsigned Published Writings by Leonard Woolf
   1. Articles 102
      1.1 *The Nation* 102
      1.2 *The New Statesman* 104
      1.3 *The Athenaeum* 110
      1.4 *The Nation & The Athenaeum* 110
      1.5 *The Political Quarterly* 166

Part Three: Selected Titles on Political Subjects from the Library of Leonard Woolf
   1. Books from Monks House, Rodmell, Sussex 172
   2. Books from 24 Victoria Square, London 180
      2.1 Items Belonging to or Presented to Leonard Woolf 180
      2.2 Miscellaneous—Some with Slight Association with
          Leonard Woolf 185
      2.3 Books with Notes and References on End Pages in
          Leonard Woolf's Handwriting 207

3. Index to Part Three (by Author, Subject, and Title): Selected
Titles on Political Subjects from the Library of Leonard Woolf 219

Part Four: Bibliographic Appendices
Appendix A: Notes on *The Nation and Athenaeum* Archival Records
(by Janet M. Manson) 254
Appendix B: Collaborative Reviewing by Leonard and Virginia
Woolf (by Wayne K. Chapman). 258
Appendix C: Virginia Woolf's Contributions to Anonymous,
Composite Reviews in *The Nation and Athenaeum*, 1924–1928
(by Wayne K. Chapman) 263
Appendix D: Grist and Rainbow (a review by Wayne K. Chapman) 270

Related Collections and Resources. 275

Introduction

1. General Overview—by Wayne K. Chapman
(September 2017)

By a fluke, which readers may relate to the lobes of the whale's tail in *Moby Dick*, this third edition of our little book on the estimable writings of Leonard Woolf turns technologically bad news into good after a complete reformatting of the core content of the second edition for another successful launch as an open-access e-book, the first two having occurred in 2005 and 2006. Notably, this one is the first edition to be typeset for display in the latest print format employed by Clemson University Press since university administration mandated adoption of Cascade for all websites. The new look necessarily abandons previous HTML features and coding, including hyperlinked matter, among the book's former strong points. Instead, the text is now fashioned, in compensation, to those specifications set out by Ingram's Lightning Source for the printing of inexpensive paperback copies on-demand. While content is still searchable in PDF, a printed copy may be purchased by credit card when an order is placed by following the link to CUP's online store (Marketplace). The loss of the old "SCROLL" website—including the established networks Virginia Woolf International, Ireland in the Arts and Humanities, African American Studies, and James Dickey Revisited—is a regrettable trade-off for the sake of institutional homogeneity. But rebuilding has begun. In this case, the most dramatic changes that will be noticed by anyone familiar with the book up to now are those incident to the shift away from hypermedia to long-scroll presentation, wherein former links to related texts and numerous collections in the US and the UK have been converted to citations and cross-references that are strategically located within the book, particularly at the end, where URL addresses are listed parenthetically according to the most recent date of access.

An Annotated Guide to the Writings and Papers of Leonard Woolf was originally designed for what was then called the Clemson University Digital Press. (That trademark changed in 2015 with omission of the word "Digital.") In 2001, the *South Carolina Review* On-Line Library (or SCROLL) came into being with "Virginia Woolf International," so-named after the themed issue of the journal (29.1 [fall 1996]), becoming, in effect, a repository of articles and monographs in that library. Hence the *Annotated Guide* joined a number of e-books and hypermedia anthologies published by the university press for more than a decade, including *Literature and Digital Technologies: W. B. Yeats, Virginia Woolf, Mary Shelley, and William Gass* (ed. Karen Schiff, 2003), the late Douglass W. Orr's *Virginia Woolf's Illnesses* and *Psychoanalysis and the Bloomsbury Group* (both edited by Wayne Chapman and published in 2004), and an emergent series of *Selected Papers* from the annual International Virginia Woolf conferences. The latter series continues in hardcover to this day, published by CUP in partnership with Liverpool University Press and with North American distribution by Oxford University Press.

The *Annotated Guide* was an on-going project at the digital press, with plans to publish notes on relevant archives in Sussex, Cambridge, and elsewhere. Its mission, overall, was to share with a global audience such vital information as concerns the location, nature, and extent of primary materials widely distributed in their physical state. Initially, the emphasis was on Leonard Woolf's signed and unsigned journalism as literary editor at *The Nation and Athenaeum* newspaper (London), based on extant files at City University, London, and selected titles of political works by other authors in his library. For context, brief accounts of these materials were (and still are) presented as appendices based on work by the authors in *Women in the Milieu of Leonard and Virginia Woolf* (ed. Chapman and Manson), in *Virginia Woolf and Her Influences: The Selected Papers from the Seventh Annual Virginia Woolf Conference* (ed. Laura Davis-Clapper and Jeanette McVicker), and in *The South Carolina Review* 31.1—each of these in 1998 and by courtesy of Pace University Press and Clemson University Press. Recommended, too, is Chapman's article on the Rowntree political monthlies, formerly located on the Virginia Woolf International website. Printed copies of the essay—"Leonard Woolf and the Rowntree Political Monthlies, 1916–1922: With the Irish Rebellion as a Case in Point," *The South Carolina Review* 34.1 (Fall 2001): 165–69—may be purchased by making request to the current editor of *SCR*.

For the second edition, citations for Leonard Woolf's books and monographs were added to **Part One: Signed Works**, as well as annotated entries for all of his signed pieces in *The Political Quarterly*. To **Part Two: Unsigned Articles**, we incorporated his unacknowledged editorial contributions to *The Political Quarterly*, as well. Internal links (now lost) were added to both Parts One and Two for greater ease in navigating these long, roughly chronological lists. We also made provision in the organization for "Other Periodicals"—that is, for bibliographic work to be grafted into later editions (as one may hope). Finally, in the Relevant Links section of the second edition (presently called **Related Collections and Resources**) we referred readers to the following useful websites: to that of King's College, Cambridge (Modern Archives); to the John Maynard Keynes Papers, King's College, Cambridge; to the Virginia Woolf and Lytton Strachey collections at the Harry Ransom Humanities Research Center, University of Texas Libraries; to the Archives of the Hogarth Press (1917–1955), University of Reading; and to the Location Register of 20th-century English literary manuscripts and letters, University of Reading Libraries—an increase from 11 to 17.

In a way, we aimed to provide on Leonard Woolf the kind of bibliographic information one finds in the pages of *Woolf Studies Annual* on Virginia Woolf.

Not only does the *Annotated Guide* include a finding aid to collections of Leonard Woolf's papers, but it already augments and improves several such tools available elsewhere, such as WSU's unindexed *Short Title Catalog* and the slightly indexed but incomplete account of Leonard Woolf's journalism, compiled by Leila Luedeking and Michael Edmonds in the "C" section of *Leonard Woolf: A Bibliography*.

After reading this "Introduction," one might make a study of the problems inherent in defining the Leonard Woolf *oeuvre* by scrolling through **Appendices A–D**. One will find that two of them are recommended as references in the headnotes of **Parts One and Two**. However, the reader might prefer to begin with **Part One**, reviewing the extensive lists of "Authored Books and Monographs," "Edited Books and Monographs," and "Journalism" acknowledged to be Woolf's because of an attached by-line. Reading or browsing **Parts One, Two**, and **Three** sequentially might be best overall. We are grateful to Stuart Clarke for being the first scholar, so far as we know, to take up the challenge I set down in 1998, that one should delve into the missing volumes of the *Nation and Athenaeum* for additional unsigned reviews and paragraphs by Virginia Woolf between April 1923 and February 1930. (See **Appendix C**.) For example, in the May 2005 issue of the *Virginia Woolf Bulletin*, Clarke established her authority for a 1927 "Books in Brief" review of *The Life of Jenny Lind* and reprinted the review. Certainly, the time has come for specialists to read up on these bibliographic issues and to join in the hunt for "unidentified contributions" to the *Nation and Athenaeum* by *both* Leonard and Virginia Woolf, writing singularly or together. (See **Appendices B–D**.)

Part Two of the *Guide* is directed at the unsigned writings of Leonard Woolf during his term as literary editor. We recommend that you use your browser to view **"About the Athenaeum" (at the address provided)** to obtain a picture of a column written before the *Nation* and the *Athenaeum* merged. The author's name is inscribed at the end of the piece, and the record was of value to management because it related to payment rendered per the column inch and to the person who earned his or her shillings paid out by the accountants. Naturally, editors drew a lot of minor donkey work and were thus frequently recorded for their contributions of the sort, unsigned and soon forgotten but the stuff on which such periodicals were made and still are made today. Hundreds of these short writings of a paragraph or more were penned by Leonard Woolf and are now identified (though sometimes equivocally) in a six-volume partial set at City University, the rest, presumably, having been destroyed or lost in the war during the London blitz.

Before joining the faculty at Clemson University, I provided a preliminary list to WSU librarian Leila Luedeking in 1990; I made copies of all signed and unsigned journalism by Leonard in WSU open stacks, and I began corresponding with Brownlee Kirkpatrick, who was then working on the finishing touches, with Stuart Clarke, to the fourth edition of *A Bibliography of Virginia Woolf*, published in 1997 after she reprinted 45 unrecorded *Times* and *TLS* reviews by Virginia Woolf in a delayed special issue of *Modern Fiction Studies* (38.1 [Spring 1992]; pub. January 1993). Naturally, Brownlee was more than merely interested in our findings and the mystery of the missing volumes. Moreover, she is almost certainly the person most responsible for starting negotiations with management at the *New Statesman and Society* offices to save rather than pulp its older archives. For, today, as you will find in one of the listings in **Related Collections and Resources**, the *New Statesman* archive has moved to the University of Sussex Libraries. Brownlee had examined the *Nation and Athenaeum* marked files and helped to judge authority in equivocal cases, and she had filled in the blanks for us on over fifty partial citations, both of signed and unsigned writings, which we had obtained during our Fulbright year at the University of London. Sadly, the Luedeking/Edmonds bibliography appeared while all of this cross-checking was going on. Up on ladders, down on knees chasing so-called "official" and unofficial marked copies in the basement of the *New Statesman and Society* offices at Great Turnstile, Brownlee was inspiring, as her professionalism continues to inspire. Thus, we hope to have created something both useful and accessible to Bloomsbury scholars of various disciplines. While freely given, it does still depend on the internet and on browsers such as Internet Explorer, Firefox, and Chrome for navigating word searches.

In **Part Three** of the *Annotated Guide*, we have tried to do something new by building on an old friend, the archival annotated copy of WSU's *Catalogue of Books from the Library of Leonard and Virginia Woolf* (Holleyman and Treacher Ltd., 1975), though in cross-section. As Stuart Clarke and William Baker have said in their reviews of the printed edition of *The Library of Leonard and Virginia Woolf: A Short-Title Catalog*—respectively, in *Woolf Studies Annual* and the *Papers of the Bibliographical Society of America*—nothing serves so well as a good index. In **Part Three**, we have the clumsy but still useful Holleyman and Treacher inventory of books sold to WSU Libraries after the death of Leonard Woolf, with the exception of books sold by Sotheby's to the University of Texas, as noted by Elizabeth Steele, and other minor exceptions. Given our interdisciplinary interest in Leonard Woolf's ideas on international issues, we have drawn together a selection of notes on political books identified by Holleyman and Treacher as derived from either the Monks House (Sussex) or Victoria Square (London) locations and associated with Leonard Woolf rather than with Virginia or her father, Sir Leslie Stephen. WSU's *Short-Title Catalog* is not indexed, nor organized by association. However, viewing its online edition is recommended when using **Part Three** of the Manson/Chapman *Annotated Guide*, thereby supplementing our notes, on occasion, with full citations.

Since presenting the *Annotated Guide* at the fifteenth Virginia Woolf Conference in Portland, Oregon, we added to the second edition nearly 300 titles to the 467 that were in our first posting. We also created an author-subject-title index for **Part Three** as keyed to the Monks House and Victoria Square designations that were assigned in the original Holleyman and Treacher inventory. The rest of Leonard's share of the library may be built into the system eventually. At present, our selection on politics would not even constitute half of the books that are associated with Leonard Woolf in the library as a whole, as 1,755 items (or titles) for 2,163 volumes are thus associated, by far most of the books in the Leonard and Virginia Woolf Library at Washington State. The relevant sections of Holleyman and Treacher are as follows:

- **Monks House (MH), III**—Items belonging to or presented to Leonard Woolf
- **Monks House (MH), IV**—Items belonging to or presented to Virginia and Leonard Woolf
- **Monks House (MH), V**—Miscellaneous, some with slight association
- **Monks House (MH), VI**—Books with notes and references to text and on end papers in the hand of Leonard Woolf
- **Victoria Square (VS), III**—Items belonging to or presented to Leonard Woolf
- **Victoria Square (VS), V**—Miscellaneous, some with slight association with Leonard Woolf
- **Victoria Square (VS), VI**—Books with notes and references to text and on end papers in the hand of Leonard Woolf

Finally, a number of **useful addresses** have been arranged for your convenience in the **Related Collections and Resources** section of the *Annotated Guide*. For example, Washington State University Libraries's online catalog is there, as well as the *Short-Title Catalog* by Julia King and Laila Miletic-Vejzovic, in addition to guides and conspectuses to the important collections in Sussex, New York, London, Cambridge, and elsewhere, including site addresses for the International Virginia Woolf Society, Pace University Press, and Clemson University Press. We welcome suggestions as we may not be through building the *Annotated Guide* with this third iteration of fall 2017.

2. Research Acknowledgments—by Janet M. Manson
(September 2017)

Many of us are aware that Leonard Woolf was a prolific writer and that he championed liberal causes in many of his published and unpublished pieces. But we still have much to learn about him as a writer. I began work on the *Annotated Guide to the Writings and Papers of Leonard Woolf* by compiling entries of Woolf's signed and unsigned pieces that were published in *The Nation*, *The Athenaeum*, *The Nation and The Athenaeum*, *The Nation and Athenaeum*, *The New Statesman*, and *The New Statesman and Nation*. The *Annotated Guide* expands the work started by Leila Luedeking and Michael Edmonds in *Leonard Woolf: A Bibliography* in that the *Annotated Guide* provides information not included in the Luedeking-Edmonds volume, most especially fuller descriptions for all entries. The online publication of our research tool will make Leonard Woolf's work more accessible to scholars and globally to members of the general public, thereby creating the opportunity for these individuals to build on our knowledge of Woolf and his work.

The *Annotated Guide* is a product of the research on Leonard Woolf that I began with Professor Wayne K. Chapman in the late 1980s. Thus, we created the *Annotated Guide* from materials that we have gathered at many archives and libraries, including the Leonard Woolf Papers, the University of Sussex; the Library of Leonard and Virginia Woolf, Washington State University; the British Library; Senate House, the University of London; and City University, London. We have worked in consultation with a number of scholars and experts on Leonard Woolf, including Diane F. Gillespie, Leila Luedeking, B. J. (Brownlee) Kirkpatrick, Cecil Woolf, Jean Moorcroft Wilson, S. P. Rosenbaum, Elizabeth Inglis, and others.

There is, of course, more information out there on Leonard's signed pieces. But even with the resources of the Library of Leonard and Virginia Woolf, Washington State University, there is much detective work to be done tracking down the articles themselves. Yet scholarly detective work becomes all the more important in tracking down the unsigned pieces—a task that Leila Luedeking urged us to take on in the late 1980s—as we finished up our dissertation projects on other topics.

As luck would have it, the subject came up in 1990 over wine and snacks in a London pub in the excellent company of seasoned academic sleuths Warwick Gould and his partner in life, Deirdre Toomey, *Yeats Annual* Editor and Research Associate, respectively. Warwick's institution at that time, the Royal Holloway and Bedford New College of the University of London, was then hosting our work on "Leonard Woolf, Bloomsbury Ethics, and the Proscription of War" as Visiting Scholars in the Fulbright Collaborative Research Program. Warwick turned to me at one point in the conversation and said, "Marilyn, you must ask Deirdre to tell you about the marked files of *The Nation and Athenaeum* at City University." The ensuing conversation was the first of many wonderful detective stories that they shared with us that afternoon.

Deirdre described the marked files as tightly bound volumes of the journal that the editors used for book-keeping purposes to keep track of the authors of unsigned columns. The editors, including John Maynard Keynes and Leonard

Woolf, used the files to keep track of authors such as Leonard and Virginia Woolf, who were paid for their writing by *The Nation and Athenaeum*, the marked files being the only record of authorship for the most common and ephemeral writing that they did for the newspaper.

Deirdre advised me to call Pamela Lighthill to make an appointment to work in City University Special Collections. Warwick interrupted her description of the collection to ask: "Deirdre, you did see articles that were written by Leonard and Virginia?" Deirdre nodded as she raised her glass and said that she had seen a lot of articles that the editors of *The Nation and Athenaeum* had identified as being written by them. She was researching another author, W. B. Yeats, in the time of H. Massingham's editorship of *The Athenaeum*, and so she hadn't made notes on the Woolfs.

A partial set of *The Nation and Athenaeum* marked files (Vol. 35, 5 April–27 September 1924; Vol. 37, 4 April–26 September 1925; Vol. 38, 3 October 1925–27 March 1926; Vol. 43, 7 April–29 September 1928; Vol. 45, 6 April–28 September 1929; and Vol. 47, 5 April–27 September 1930) were temporarily moved to City University when *The New Statesman* offices no longer had space for them. Subsequently, the marked files have apparently found a permanent home there, in as much as they are now listed on the City University web site under "*The Nation and Athenaeum*" in Special Collections (https://library.city.ac.uk/record=b1201193).

My journey to City University was just as Deirdre had described it: a short tube ride from King's Cross station on the Northern Line to Angel station and then a nice walk by small shops and restaurants down St. John Street to City University on Northampton Square. Special Collections was located in a small room on one of the lower floors of the library. A library staff person was there to greet me as I entered and then to escort me to the locked, glassed-in, bookcases where the marked files were kept. I immediately began looking for the file cabinets that Deirdre had said were located across from the bookcases. I asked whether the short, cream-colored, file cabinets on the other side of the long library table contained *The New Statesman* correspondence files. The staff person looked puzzled and said that she would have to consult a colleague about that. A short time later, she came back with the colleague who discussed the files with me. Few people knew that Special Collections had them; no one used them; and staff members wanted to move them out to make room for other materials—news that no dedicated researcher wants to hear. I encouraged the archivists to find a new home for the files. I believe I suggested that they contact the University of Sussex to see what might be worked out.

After working with the correspondence files, I turned to the marked files, which thankfully took up much less space—a factor, undoubtedly, in City University's decision to retain them. Like so many older, tightly-bound volumes, they are too fragile to be photocopied. So researchers such as Deirdre and myself (and, later, Brownlee Kirkpatrick) must have spent hours and hours going through them carefully and making notes.

After John Maynard Keynes and others gained a controlling interest in *The Nation* and merged it with *The Athenaeum* in March 1923, Keynes asked Leonard to become the paper's literary editor. As many of you know, Leonard had done quite a bit of reviewing for both journals, and he had filled in as the political editor for *The Nation* in 1920 and then took over that post in 1922.

He began to do even more reviewing for *The Nation and Athenaeum* after he became the literary editor. For example, Woolf wrote signed pieces for "The World of Books" column, starting on 5 May 1923; and most of the unsigned pieces identified by entries from the marked files are review columns. (His last "World of Books" column appeared on 15 February 1930.) Unsigned columns included "Books in Brief," "From Alpha to Omega," and "Things to see or hear in the coming week," "On the Editor's Table," "New Gramophone Records," and short items in the "Reviews" section of the journal.

In short, Woolf reviewed a wide-range of books, plays, concerts, performances, and events, and records. In his unsigned pieces, we see instances in which he reviewed books or discussed topics that were close to his heart. For example, he reviewed his sister Bella Sidney Woolf's book *From Groves of Palm* on 30 January 1926. He also plugged Sigmund Freud's *The Future of Illusion* (Hogarth Press) in the "On the Editor's Table" column of 21 July 1928. And Woolf critiqued a performance of George Bernard Shaw's play *Caesar and Cleopatra* in the ubiquitous column "From Alpha to Omega" on 2 May 1925. Moreover, he took special interest in political subjects such as the Native Reserves in Kenya. See "Naboth's Vinyard" (9 June 1928), "The Word of Elijah" (5 July 1930), and "Sir Edward Grigg" [colonial governor of Kenya] (23 August 1930). Although it seems more Bloomsbury writers and their works are treated in Woolf's signed pieces, his unsigned writings are also indicative of this rich intellectual habitat.

To reaffirm one of the conclusions of *Women in the Milieu of Leonard and Virginia Woolf* (1998), the first monograph that we published from the discoveries we made on the work of Leonard Woolf in 1990, *The Nation and Athenaeum* very much bore the Bloomsbury stamp during the years of Leonard Woolf's literary editorship. It was an influential organ in the dissemination of both his ideas and those of like-minded intellectuals and creative people in London between 1923 and 1930. And so it continues to occupy an important place in this book, the latest iteration of *An Annotated Guide to the Writings and Papers of Leonard Woolf* (third edition, revised).

PART 1

SIGNED PUBLISHED WORKS BY LEONARD S. WOOLF

Works cited in Part One are arranged according to the following structure:

1. Authored Books and Monographs
2. Edited Books and Monographs
3. Journalism in *The Nation, The Athenaeum, The Nation & The Athenaeum, The New Statesman, The New Statesman and Nation, The Political Quarterly*, and Other Periodicals. (Articles are listed in chronological sequence as noted:)
3.1. *The Nation* (7 Aug. 1915–27 Aug. 1921)
3.2. *The Athenaeum* (18 Apr. 1919–30 Apr. 1920)
3.3. *The Nation & The Athenaeum* (21 Apr. 1923–21 Feb. 1931)
3.4. *The New Statesman* (7 June 1913–2 Oct. 1920)
3.5. *The New Statesman and Nation* (28 Feb. 1931–12 May 1956)
3.6. *The New Statesman* (4 Jan. 1958–31 May 1968)
3.7. *The Political Quarterly* (1930–1969)

For context on the journalism acknowledged below in sections 3.1–3.7, see Appendix A, pages 254–57, below: "Notes on *The Nation and Athenaeum* Archival Records," by Janet M. Manson, from *Women in the Milieu of Leonard and Virginia Woolf.*

1. Authored Books and Monographs by Leonard Woolf

1.1. Autobiographies

Beginning Again: An Autobiography of the Years 1911 to 1918. London: Hogarth Press, 1964. This volume covers the early years of Leonard and Virginia Woolf's marriage; the beginning of Leonard's new career as a writer, editor, and political activist in the Fabian Society and in the Labour Party; and Leonard's and Virginia's establishment of the Hogarth Press in 1917.

Downhill All the Way: An Autobiography of the Years 1919 to 1939. London: Hogarth Press, 1967. This volume covers Leonard Woolf's professional and private life during the period between the world wars. Both Leonard and Virginia led very productive lives as writers and publishers during this period. They expanded production at the Hogarth Press. Leonard also served on the editorial board of journals such as the *Nation* and the *Political Quarterly* and on Labour Party committees such as the Advisory Committee on International Questions.

Growing: An Autobiography of the Years 1904–1911. London: Hogarth Press, 1961. This volume covers Leonard Woolf's life as a civil servant in Ceylon (present-day Sri Lanka) from 1904 to 1911. In 1911, Woolf left a promising career in the colonial service to marry Virginia Stephen and to become a writer.

The Journey, not the Arrival Matters: An Autobiography of the Years 1939–1969. London: Hogarth Press, 1969. This volume covers the last couple of years of Virginia Woolf's life and the last three decades of Leonard Woolf's private and professional life. Leonard continued his career as a writer, editor, publisher, and political activist into the 1960s.

Sowing: An Autobiography of the Years 1880 to 1904. London: Hogarth Press, 1960. This volume covers Leonard Woolf's childhood in London; his education at St. Paul's Preparatory School from 1894 to 1899; and his education at Trinity College, Cambridge from 1899 to 1904 when he left Cambridge and entered the British colonial civil service. Woolf's fellow students at Cambridge included John Maynard Keynes, Lytton Strachey, Thoby Stephen, and Clive Bell.

1.2. Correspondence and Diaries

Diaries in Ceylon, 1908–1911: Records of a Colonial Administrator. London: Hogarth Press, 1963. The official diaries of Leonard Woolf that he kept when he served as Assistant Government Agent of Hambantota, Ceylon (present-day Sri Lanka), August 1908 to May 1911.

Letters of Leonard Woolf. Ed. Frederic Spotts. New York: Harcourt Brace Jovanovich, 1989. The selected letters of Leonard Woolf gleaned from important collections, especially the University of Sussex Library. Frederic Spotts has grouped this volume of letters into the following categories: Woolf's education at Cambridge University 1901–04; his service in Ceylon (present-day Sri Lanka) 1904–11; his marriage to Virginia Stephen 1911–41; his career as an editor and publisher 1917–68; and his later life 1941–69. The last category, Woolf's later life, deals with correspondence about Virginia's and Leonard's writings and with Leonard's personal relationships, including the relationship with Marjorie Tulip (Trekkie) Ritchie Parsons. This volume contains few letters that touch on Leonard Woolf's political activities in the Labour party, the Fabian Society, or other political organizations.

Love Letters: Leonard Woolf & Trekkie Richie Parsons 1941–1968. Ed. Judith Adamson. 2001; London: Pimlico, 2002. A collection of 372 letters of the correspondence between Leonard Woolf and Trekkie Richie Parsons from 1941 to 1968. The letters are divided as follows: October 1941–July 1943 (letters 1–72); August 1943–15 July 1944 (letters 73–194); July 1944–January 1947 (letters 195–215); June 1949–October 1950 (letters 216–46); 2–12 July 1951 (letters 247–59); September 1953–spring 1957 (letters 260–81);

September–October 1957 (letters 282–85); July–August 1958 (letters 286–300); and April 1960–October 1968 (letters 301–72).

1.3. Drama and Fiction

The Hotel. A Play about the Horror before World War II. London: Hogarth Press, 1939.
Woolf's only play. A number of the major characters have extreme political views such as communism or fascism.

Stories of the East. Richmond: Hogarth Press, 1921. "A Tale Told by Moonlight"; "Pearls and Swine"; and "The Two Brahmans". These short stories are all set in colonial Ceylon (present-day Sri Lanka) and are a product of Leonard Woolf's observations as a colonial civil servant there.

[With Virginia Woolf.] *Two Stories.* Richmond: Hogarth Press, 1917. The stories are "Three Jews" by Leonard Woolf and "The Mark on the Wall" by Virginia Woolf.

The Village in the Jungle. London: Edward Arnold, 1913. Woolf's literary masterpiece about the complexities of life in a traditional Ceylonese village during British colonial rule. Woolf drew on his own observations and experiences as a British civil servant in writing the novel. In an annotated edition of the original version of *The Village in the Jungle*, Professor Yasmine Gooneratne observes that "[t]he novel holds a central place in the English literature of Sri Lanka as the first great (if not the first) work of creative art to emerge in modern times from the experience of local living" (2). *The Village in the Jungle by Leonard Woolf: Revised and Annotated with the Original Manuscript*, edited by Yasmine Gooneratne. Lewiston, New York; Queenston, Ontario: The Edwin Mellen Press, 2004.

The Wise Virgins. A Story of Words, Opinions and a few Emotions. London: Edward Arnold, 1914. Woolf's second novel contrasts Jewish middle class differences with those of a non-Jewish, upper, middle class family. Some of the main characters are loosely based on some of the Woolf and Stephen family members. See *Letters of Leonard Woolf.* Ed. Frederic Spotts, esp. pp. 195–200, for correspondence about the novel.

1.4. Literary/Social Criticism and History

After the Deluge: A Study of Communal Psychology. Vol. 1 [About Democracy.] London: Hogarth Press, 1931. Woolf discusses communal psychology and how it relates to democracy. He especially focuses on the influence of the French philosophes, the values and ideals of American democracy, and the influence of the French Revolution.

After the Deluge: A Study of Communal Psychology. Vol. 2: 1830 & 1832. [History of the purpose of democracy.] This work focuses on the English Reform Act of 1832 and the French Revolution of 1830. London: Hogarth Press, 1939.

Barbarians at the Gate. London: Victor Gollancz, 1939. "The World We Live in;" "Anatomy of Civilization;" and "The Choice before Us." Historical essays about the threat to civilization and its fundamental values posed by Italian and German fascism.

Essays on Literature, History, Politics, Etc. London: Hogarth Press, 1927.

ESSAYS ON LITERATURE: "Ben Jonson" A shorter version of this essay appeared in *The Nation & The Athenaeum*, 23 June 1923: 396. "Hazlitt," reprinted from *The New Statesman*, 15 December 1917. "An Englishman" A version of this essay appeared in *The Nation & The Athenaeum*, 25 August 1923: 662. "Herbert Spencer," reprinted from *The New Statesman*, 10 March 1917: 541–2. "The Fall of Stevenson" A version of this essay appeared in *The Nation & The Athenaeum*, 5 January 1924: 517. "Samuel Butler" A shorter version of this essay appeared in *The Nation & The Athenaeum*, 17 November 1923: 276. "Joseph Conrad" A version of this essay appeared in *The Nation & The Athenaeum*, 9 August 1924: 595. "A Traveler in Little Things" A shorter version of this essay appeared in *The Nation & The Athenaeum*, 18 August 1923: 638. "Lord Morley" A version of this essay appeared in *The Nation & The Athenaeum*, 13 October 1923: 55. "Mr. George Moore and the Critics" A version of this essay appeared in *The Nation & The Athenaeum*, 16 February 1924: 702. "The Modern Nightingale" draws on material in "World of Books" columns, *The Nation & The Athenaeum*, 18 April 1925: 76, 15 August 1925: 598, and 5 December 1925: 354. "The First Person Singular" This is an expansion of part of a "World of Books" column, *The Nation & The Athenaeum*, 3 November 1923: 188; and "Winged and Unwinged Words," reprinted from *The New Statesman*, 6 July 1918: 272–73.

ESSAYS ON HISTORY AND POLITICS: "The Pageant of History" This is an expansion of a "World of Books" column, *The Nation & The Athenaeum*, 19 January 1924: 574. "A Civilized Man," reprinted from *The Nation & The Athenaeum*, 21 June 1924: 381; "International Morality"; "Statesmen and Diplomatists" A version of this essay appeared in *The Nation & The Athenaeum*, 13 June 1925, and it draws on material in "World of Books" columns, *The Nation & The Athenaeum*, 31 January 1925 and 13 June 1925. "The Two Kings of Jerusalem" An earlier edition of this essay appeared in *The New Statesman*, 28 April 1917: 85–87. "Please, Sir, It Was the Other Fellow" draws from "World of Books" columns, *The Nation & The Athenaeum*, 24 October 1925 and 26 June 1926; "Politics in Spain," reprinted from *The Nation & The Athenaeum*, 21 April 1923: 74–75; and "John Bright and Liberalism," reprinted from *The Nation & The Athenaeum*, 18 July 1925: 489.

ESSAYS ON ET CETERA: "The Aristocratic Mind" A version of parts of this essay appeared in "World of Books" columns, *The Nation & The Athenaeum*, 20 December 1924: 444 and 17 January 1925: 553. "The Anatomy of Old Age" A version of this essay appeared in *The Nation & The Athenaeum*, 7 July 1923: 456. "Look Up, There With Me!" reprinted from *The Nation & The Athenaeum*, 29 November 1924: 331; "Discarnate Spirits," reprinted from *The Nation & The Athenaeum*, 23 January 1926: 585; and "The Gentleness of Nature," reprinted from *The New Statesman*, 6 January 1917: 326–27.

Fear and Politics: A Debate at the Zoo. The Hogarth Essays [first series] no. 7. London: Hogarth Press, 1925. An essay about the nature of government and the role of the people in choosing their own governments. Woolf also uses these issues to discuss international relations and the need to maintain peace.

Hunting the Highbrow. Hogarth Essays, second series, no. 5. London: Hogarth Press, 1927. A satirical essay on popular and elite tastes in literature and the arts. For example, Woolf compares the appeal of popular writers such as Gilbert Frankau, Hall Caine, and Ella Wheeler Wilcox to that of Vergil, Shakespeare, Dante, Jane Austin, and others.

Principia Politica: A Study in Communal Psychology. [The third volume of *After the Deluge*.] Woolf continues his discussion of communal psychology, in part, by drawing on personal experiences. This volume focuses on authoritarianism, including European fascism. London: Hogarth Press, 1953.

Quack, Quack! [Essays on unreason and superstition in politics, belief and thought]. London: Hogarth Press, 1935. The book has two chapters: "Quack, Quack in Politics" and "Intellectual Quack, Quack". Woolf uses the title *Quack, Quack!* to examine quackery in politics and in the dissemination of political ideas. This approach enables him to discuss various aspects of demagoguery and its application, particularly in European fascism.

1.5. "Practical Politics" & International Affairs

The Control of Industry by the People. Papers for Guides. London: Women's Co-operative Guild, 1915.

Control of Industry by the People through the Co-operative Movement. [N.p.]: Co-operative League of America, 1920. Woolf explores what is meant by control of industry by the people. He examines democratic principles and representation in this type of economic system.

Co-operation and the Future of Industry. London: Allen & Unwin, 1918. Woolf focuses on the objectives and role of the Co-operative Movement, especially "its development into a great democratic industrial system." This piece was written in light of the Co-operative Union's decision at its October 1917 conference to create a political party.

Co-operation and the War. I. Effects of War on Commerce and Industry. Papers for Guides. London: Women's Co-operative Guild, 1915.

Co-operation and the War. II. Co-operative Action in National Crises. London: Co-operative Printer's Society, [n.d.].

Economic Imperialism. Swathmore International Handbooks. International Relations series 5. London: The Swathmore Press; New York: Harcourt, Brace & Howe, 1920; rpt in New York (H. Fertig), 1970. Woolf examines European economic imperialism in Africa and Asia. He utilized some the research conducted for *Empire & Commerce in Africa: A Study in Economic Imperialism* in producing *Economic Imperialism*.

Education and the Co-operative Movement. Papers for Guides. London: Women's Co-operative Guild, 1914.

Empire & Commerce in Africa: A Study in Economic Imperialism. Report for a committee of the Labour Research Department, Fabian Society. Westminster: The Labour Research Dept.; London: George Allen & Unwin, 1920. [Also editions in New York (Macmillan 1920) and London (Hogarth Press 1925); rpts. in London (Allen & Unwin) and New York (H. Fertig), 1968.] Woolf relied on his wife, Virginia, and on Alix Sargant-Florence (later Mrs. James Strachey) for research assistance in producing this book. He critically examines European economic and colonial policies in much of Africa, especially Algeria; Tunis and Tripoli; Abyssinia and the Nile River basin; Zanzibar and East Africa; and the Belgian Congo.

[With Charles Buxton for the Imperial Advisory Committee of the Labour Party.] *The Empire in Africa: Labour's Policy*. London: Labour Party Publications, [n.d.; but c. 1920]. Memorandum prepared by the Advisory Committee on International Affairs. The memorandum recommends reform of economic and political policies to reflect Labour Party principles of "equal economic opportunity and industrial democracy." The memorandum addresses the following issues: land, the labor system, the governmental system, and education.

Foreign Policy: The Labour Party's Dilemma. Foreward by Harold Laski. With a critical comment by W. N. Ewer. Fabian Research Series no. 121. London: Fabian Publications and Victor Gollancz, 1947. The objective of the pamphlet is to provide the Labour Party with foreign policy options for its consideration. The Fabian International Committee chose Woolf to describe the Committee's differing views on foreign policy and to formulate a policy that might serve as a basis for consensus within the Committee. It also requested that W. N. Ewer provide a comment in order to foster a broader debate. Woolf discusses British policy objectives and the difficulties of forging an effective foreign policy given the realities of the Cold War and the U.S.-Soviet superpower rivalry.

The Future of Constantinople. London: George Allen & Unwin, 1917. Woolf analyzes the causes of international conflict over Constantinople and the straits and explores proposals for a postwar settlement for the area.

Imperialism and Civilization. London: Hogarth Press, 1928. Woolf focuses on 19th century imperialism, particularly in Africa and Asia. He examines imperialism as "an aspect of the conflict of civilizations."

International Co-operative Trade. Fabian Tract no. 201. [London: The Fabian Society, 1922]. Woolf saw the opportunities for developing international cooperative trade after the war and sought to clarify key issues in order to foster the movement. He focuses on three objectives: the development of international cooperative trade; the promotion of an effective international relationship between agricultural movements and consumers'movements; and the development of financial institutions to support international cooperative trade.

The Labour Party: International Economic Policy. [London: Labour Party Publications, 1919]. Woolf considers the following issues: protectionism and free trade; economic policy and the empire, colonial possessions, dependencies, etc.; "the economic League of Nations"; and international cooperative trade and industry.

International Government: Two Reports...Together with a Project by a Fabian Committee for a Supernational Authority that Will Prevent War. London: III Fabian Society, 1916; Westminster: Fabian Society, 1916. [Also published in New York, 1916, and translated and published in Paris, 1916, and Stockholm, 1917—rev. American edition in 1923.] The book is divided into three parts: Part I: An International Authority and the Prevention of War; Part II: International Government; and Part III: The Supernational Authority that Will Prevent War. (Part III was drafted by a Fabian Committee and contains the blueprint for an international collective security organization. Leonard Woolf and Sidney Webb were the primary authors.) Drafts of Parts I and III were published as supplements to *The New Statesman* in July 1915. [For more information, see Wayne Chapman, "'L.'s Dame Secretaire': Alix Strachey, the Hogarth Press and Bloomsbury Pacificism, 1917–1960" in *Women in the Milieu of Leonard and Virginia Woolf: Peace, Politics, and Education*, Eds. Wayne K. Chapman and Janet M. Manson (New York: Pace University Press, 1998), 36.]

The International Post-War Settlement. London: Fabian Society Research Series no. 85. [London]: Fabian Publications with Victor Gollancz, 1944. A draft policy statement on the international post World War II settlement written for the Labour Party.

The League and Abyssinia. Day to Day Pamphlets no. 31. London: Hogarth Press, 1936. In the pamphlet, Woolf provides a critical analysis of the Abyssinia crisis, and of the response of the League of Nations, and of British policies.

Mandates and Empire. [League of Nations Union publication] London: British Periodicals Ltd, 1920. Woolf examines the League of Nations mandate system as set forth in the Covenant. Moreover, he discusses the administration of the mandates, particularly in Africa, and makes recommendations for implementing the League objective of administering mandates for the "'well-being and development' of the native population."

In Savage Times: Leonard Woolf on Peace and War. Four pamphlets by Leonard Woolf. Ed. Stephen J. Stearns. New York and London: Garland Publishing, Inc., 1973. The pamphlets are: *Fear and Politics: A Debate at the Zoo* (1925); *The Way of Peace* (1928); *The League and Abyssinia* (1936); and *The International Post-War Settlement* (1944).

Scope of Mandates under the League of Nations. London: C. F. Rowarth, [n.d.].

Socialism and Co-operation. Independent Labour Party: Social Studies series, Vol. 4. London & Manchester: L. Parsons, 1921. This work builds on the earlier *Co-operation and the Future of Industry* (1918). The focus of *Socialism and Co-operation* is the role of the co-operative system in a socialist society. By 1921, the Co-operative Party had become established and had elected members to the House of Commons.

Taxation: 1. What it Is; 2. Methods and Uses; 3. Principles. London: Women's Co-operative Guild, [n.d.].

The War for Peace. London: Routledge, 1940. Woolf makes the case for establishing an international collective security organization to succeed the League of Nations after World War II.

The Way of Peace. Self and Society Booklets no. 10. London: Ernest Benn, 1928. Woolf discusses international economic competition and the cooperative movement, particularly the international cooperative movement.

"What Is Politics?" *Current Affairs* no. 99. London: Bureau of Current Affairs, 1950: 3–14. This article is the first in a series of three articles by different authors that the Bureau of Current Affairs published before the February 23rd election. The purpose of the series was to inform the general public about the importance of politics and how citizens can make informed decisions when voting. In "What Is Politics?" Woolf discusses why politics is necessary; its scope; and political values, especially liberty and authority.

2. Books and Monographs Edited by Leonard Woolf

Fabian Essays on Co-operation. London: The Fabian Society, 1923. This volume is one in a series of Fabian tracts "dealing with the principal problems which confront the Consumers' Co-operative Movement." Woolf is the series editor. The "Preface" is by Leonard Woolf. The pamphlets in this volume are:

"International Co-operative Trade" by Leonard Woolf; "The Constitutional Problems of a Co-operative Society" by Sidney Webb; "The Need for Federal Re-Organisation in the Co-operative Movement" by Sidney Webb; "The Position of Employees in the Co-operative Movement" by Lilian Harris; "Co-operative Education" by Lilian A. Dawson; and "The Co-operator in Politics" by Alfred Barnes. Woolf's essay in this collection is a reprint of *International Co-operative Trade*. Fabian Tract no. 201. See entry for this item above.

The Framework of a Lasting Peace. London: G. Allen & Unwin, 1917. "Introduction" by Leonard Woolf. The book contains schemes for an international political organization to prevent war drafted by the following groups or organizations: League to Enforce Peace; the Central Organization for Durable Peace, the Hague; The League of Nations Society; Lord James Bryce's Group; The Fabian Society; The Community of Nations; and A Dutch Committee. [The "Introduction" was originally published in the March 1917 issue of *War & Peace*.]

Hitler's Route to Bagdad. Prepared for the International Research Section of the Fabian Society. London: G. Allen & Unwin, [1939]. "Introduction" by Leonard Woolf with sections on Eastern European countries: "Yugoslavia" by Barbara Ward; "Rumania" by Barbara Buckmaster; "Bulgaria" by Clare Hollingworth; "Greece" by Vandeleur Robinson; "Turkey" by Lilo Linke; and Maps by J. F. Horrabin.

The Intelligent Man's Way to Prevent War. London: Victor Gollancz, 1933. A collection of essays: "Introduction" by Leonard Woolf; "The International Anarchy" by Norman Angell; "Revision of the Peace Treaties" by Gilbert Murray; "The Problem of Russia" by C. M. Lloyd; "Inter-continental Peace" by Charles Roden Buxton; "The League as a Road to Peace" by Viscount [Lord Robert] Cecil; "Arbitration, Security, Disarmament" by William Arnold-Forster; "Educational and Psychological Factors" by Norman Angell; and "The Economic Foundations of Peace" by Harold J. Laski. Appendix: The Covenant of the League of Nations.

2.1. Works with Contributions by Woolf

Adams, Mary, ed. *The Modern State*. [A symposium.] Ed. Mary Adams. London: Allen & Unwin, 1933. A collection of essays based on the British Broadcasting Corporation (BBC) symposium, "The Changing World". The collection is divided into three parts: Part I: "Can Democracy Survive?' with essays by Leonard Woolf and Eustace Percy; Part II: "Social Institutions" by Beatrice (Mrs. Sidney) Webb; and Part III: "World Government" by Arthur Salter.

Part I contains the following essays by Leonard Woolf: "What is Democracy?" pp. 15–27. A discussion on people's attitudes toward democracy since 1900: the extension of suffrage in democratic countries as well as the rise of communist and fascists states. "Happiness", pp 28–39. A discussion on "the democratic ideal of happiness." "Equality", pp. 40–51. A discussion of the "meaning of democratic equality" and how perceptions of equality have changed in the last thirty years. "Liberty", pp. 52–63. A discussion of the "democratic idea…of liberty or freedom." "Gods or Bees", pp. 64–75. A discussion of democratic values and ideals and the economic system that requires specialized trade and professional skills. And "Citizens of the World", pp. 77–86. A discussion about national identity and the international community of nations.

Hinden, Rita. *Kenya: White Man's Country?* Report to the Fabian Colonial Bureau. With a Preface by Leonard Woolf. Research Series no. 78. London: Fabian Publications and Victor Gollancz, 1944. Woolf summarizes the objectives of the pamphlet which are to examine British colonial policies in Kenya and to recommend policies that will advance the interests of all Kenyans. Dr. Rita Hinden gathered the materials used in drafting the pamphlet which focuses on the economic and political relations between white settlers and native Kenyans.

New Fabian Research Bureau. *Labour's Foreign Policy*. Proposals for Discussion Put forward by the International Section of the Bureau under the Chairmanship of Leonard Woolf. No. 18. London: Victor Gollancz and the NFRB, 1934. The pamphlet is the product of two 1934 Labour Party Conferences and provides foreign policy proposals for discussion. These proposals deal with the League of Nations and the challenges posed by Germany, Italy, and Japan.

——. *Population Movements: A Study in Migration*. By Louis Ginsburg. With an introduction by Leonard Woolf. No. 37. London: Victor Gollancz Ltd. and The New Fabian Research Bureau, 1937. The pamphlet deals with recent emigration from Britain, Europe, and Asia and issues concerning the control of migration.

——. *Revision of Treaties and Changes in International Law*. A Report of the International Section of the Bureau under the Chairmanship of Leonard Woolf. No. 14. London: Victor Gollancz and the NFRB, [n.d.; but c. 1934]. An examination of international law on the revision of treaties and avenues for peaceful change. The pamphlet also deals with the 1919 Treaty of Versailles and provisions of the League of Nations Covenant.

——. *When Hostilities Cease: Papers on Relief and Reconstruction Prepared for the Fabian Society*. With a Foreword by Philip Noel-Baker. "Introduction" by Leonard Woolf. London: Victor Gollancz Ltd., 1943. A collection of essays based on conference papers of the International Bureau of the Fabian Society Conference, Oxford, December 1942. The essays: "Relief and Reconstruction" by Julian Huxley; "The Machinery of International Relief" by Harold J. Laski; "International Controls" by William Arnold-Forster; "Food for Starving Europe" by John Marrack; "Post-War Medical Relief in Europe" by Aleck Bourne; "Relief Measures for Agriculture" by John Hammond; and "The Re-establishment of Displaced Peoples" by Kenneth G. Brooks. The essay collection is meant to promote knowledge of important issues for the general public.

The Royal Institute of International Affairs. *The Future of the League of Nations: The Record of a Series of Discussions Held at Chatham House*. New York: Oxford University Press, 1936. The Council of the Royal Institute of International Affairs sponsored a symposia to examine the future of the League and the possible revision of its Covenant. The symposia was held, from May 29 to July 7, prior to the Assembly meeting in September 1936 where the issue of reforming the League Covenant probably would be considered. Current events brought this issue to the fore. Symposia participants included Norman Angell, Arnold J. Toynbee, Arthur Salter, Harold Nicolson, G. M. Gathorne-Hardy, Lord Lothian, Lord Ponsonby, H. G. Wells, and Leonard Woolf

Woolf, Leonard. "The Political Advance of Backward Peoples," *Fabian Colonial Essays*. Ed. Rita Hinden. With an Introduction by Arthur Creech Jones. London: George Allen and Unwin Ltd., 1945: 85–98. Woolf examines the future of colonial peoples, primarily those in Africa.

3. Signed Articles by Leonard Woolf

3.1. THE NATION

The Nation was established in 1907 by the Rowntree family whose members belonged to the Liberal party. Henry William Massingham, a Liberal who drifted into the Labour party by 1922, served as editor from 1907–23. Leonard S. Woolf became the acting political editor in 1920 and then took over that position in 1922.

"The International Mind," "Reviews" column, *The Nation* (7 August 1915): 614. Review of J. A. Hobson's *Towards International Government* (Allen & Unwin).

Letter to the Editor, *The Nation* (21 August 1915): 675–76. On J. A. Hobson's conceptions of government. L.W. possibly is commenting on some of the material from Hobson's book on international government.

"A Break in the Clouds?" Letter to the Editor, *The Nation* (2 December 1916): 325. Comments on the German Chancellor's speech. Woolf calls on Britain and Germany to define peace terms.

"The Fog of History," "Life and Letters" column, *The Nation* (27 August 1921): 761–62. Review of *The Evolution of World Peace* edited by F. S. Marvin (Milford).

3.2. The Athenaeum

The Athenaeum was established in 1828. Liberal M. P. Arnold Rowntree acquired it after World War I. Due to declining circulation, *The Athenaeum* was joined with *The Nation* in 1921. (See www.newstatesman.com/nsabout.htm.)

"Righteous Quaker," *The Athenaeum* (18 April 1919): 207–08. Review of *Joseph Sturge: His Life and Work* by Stephen Hobhouse (Dent).

"Lost and Other Causes" "Reviews" section, *The Athenaeum* (3 October 1919): 971–2. Review of *My Diaries: Being a Personal Narrative of Events, 1888-1914, Part One: 1888–1900* by Wilfrid Scawen Blunt (Secker).

"Lord Grey's Foreign Policy," *The Athenaeum* (10 October 1919): 999. Review of *How the War Came* by Earl Loreburn (Methuen).

"Far Eastern Politics," *The Athenaeum* (21 November 1919): 1223. Review of *The Mastery of the Far East* by Arthur Judson Brown (Bell).

"Social History," *The Athenaeum* (16 January 1920): 75–76. Review of *The Skilled Labourer, 1760–1832* by J. L. Hammond and Barbara Hammond (Longmans).

"Woe for the Kings Who Conquer!" *The Athenaeum* (13 February 1920): 210. Review of *My Diaries: Being a Personal Narrative of Events, 1888–1914, Part Two: 1900–1914* by Wilfrid Scawen Blunt (Secker).

"Going in for God," *The Athenaeum* (19 March 1920): 365–66. Review of *William Booth, Founder of the Salvation Army*, 2 vols., by Harold Begbie (Macmillan).

"Charles Bradlaugh and General Booth" "Correspondence" section, *The Athenaeum* (2 April 1920): 458. Letter to the Editor regarding the use of a quotation from *William Booth, Founder of the Salvation Army*, 2 vols., by Harold Begbie that Woolf used in his review of the work. See "Going in for God," *The Athenaeum* (19 March 1920): 365–66 above.

"The Vision of Lord Kitchner," *The Athenaeum* (30 April 1920): 571–2. Review of *Life of Lord Kitchner*, 3 vols., by Sir George Arthur (Macmillan).

3.3. The Nation & The Athenaeum

By 1923. John Maynard Keynes bought a controlling interest in *The Nation* from the Rowntree Trust. (According to Leonard S. Woolf, The Rowntrees, who were Liberals, decided to sell *The Nation* because of Henry William Massingham's Labourite editorial policies. See *Down Hill All the Way*, 92, 96-97.) The journal appeared as *The Nation & The Athenaeum* under Keynes' management. Woolf served as the literary editor from 1923 to 1930. Hubert Henderson replaced Massingham as editor and held the post until 1930.

"Politics in Spain," *The Nation & The Athenaeum* 33 (21 April 1923): 74–75. L.W.'s observations about Spanish society and politics, including the war in Morocco, based on the Woolfs travels there in April 1923.

"The World of Books" column, *The Nation & The Athenaeum* 33 (5 May 1923): 157. Review of a reprint of *Men of Letters* by Dixon Scott (1916) with the original introduction by Max Beerbohm and a new essay on Whitman. This book is the first volume in The Bookman Library series (Hodder & Stoughton).

"The World of Books" column, *The Nation & The Athenaeum* 33 (12 May 1923): 196. Review essay on *On the Margin* by Aldous Huxley (Chatto & Windus).

"Lord Northcliffe Round the World," "The World of Books" column, *The Nation & The Athenaeum* 33 (19 May 1923): 226. Review of *My Journey Round the World* by Alfred, Viscount Northcliffe (Lane).

"The Russians," "The World of Books" column, *The Nation & The Athenaeum* 33 (26 May 1923): 271. Reviews of *The Plays of Leo Tolstoy*, translated by Louise and Aylmer Maude (World's Classics, Milford); *A Russian Gentleman* by Serghei Aksakoff, translated by J. D. Duff (World's Classics, Milford); *December the Fourteenth* by Dimitri Merezhkovsky, translated by N. A. Duddington (Cape); and *The Diary of Nellie Ptaschkina*, translated by Pauline de Chary (Cape).

"Poetry and Malaria," "The World of Books" column, *The Nation & The Athenaeum* 33 (2 June 1923): 304. Review essay on *Memoirs* by Sir Ronald Ross (Murray).

"Mr. Drinkwater's Difficulty: Oliver Cromwell at His Majesty's," "The Drama" column, *The Nation & The Athenaeum* 33 (9 June 1923): 342. Review of a play about Oliver Cromwell.

"From Hickey to Hardman," "The World of Books" column, *The Nation & The Athenaeum* 33 (16 June 1923): 367. Reviews of the third volume of *Memoirs of William Hickey* (Hurst & Blackett) and *A Mid-Victorian Pepys* (the letters and memoirs of Sir William Hardman), edited by Mr. S. M. Ellis (Cecil Palmer).

"Ben Jonson," "The World of Books" column, *The Nation & The Athenaeum* 33 (23 June 1923): 396. Review of a full edition of *Heads of a Conversation betwixt the famous Poet Ben Jonson, and William Drummond of Hawthornden, January 1619*, edited by Dr. Patterson (Blackie & Son).

"London Town," "The World of Books" column, *The Nation & The Athenaeum* 33 (30 June 1923): 427. Reviews of *Historic Streets of London* by L. & A. Russan (Simpkin); *London and Westminster in History and Literature* by W. Marston Acres (Fisher Unwin); *Queer Things about London* by Charles

G. Harper (Palmer); *The London of Dickens* by Walter Dexter (Palmer); and *London, Its Origin and Early Development* by William Page (Constable).

"**The Anatomy of Old Age,**" "The World of Books" column, *The Nation & The Athenaeum* 33 (7 July 1923): 465. Review essay on *A Green Old Age* by Professor A. Lacassage (John Bale, Sons & Danielsson) and a translation of Cicero's *De Senectute* (Heinemann).

"**Books for a Holiday,**" "The World of Books" column, *The Nation & The Athenaeum* 33 (14 July 1923): 489. Reviews of *Primitive Mentality* by Professor Levy-Bruhl (Allen & Unwin); *Companionable Books* by Henry Van Dyke (Hodder & Stoughton); *Masters and Men* by Philip Guedalla (Constable); *The Man of Promise, Lord Rosebery* by E. T. Raymond (Fisher Unwin); *Adventures in the Near East, 1918–1922* by Colonel A. Rawlinson (Melrose); *In Many Places* by Clare Sheridan (Cape); and *Racundra's First Cruise* by Arthur Ransome (Allen & Unwin).

"**A Chronicle of Kings,**" "The World of Books" column, *The Nation & The Athenaeum* 33 (21 July 1923): 520. Review of *The Glass Palace Chronicle* [chronicle of Burmese kings], translated by Mr. Pe Maung Tin and Mr. G. H. Luce (Milford).

"**An Ancient Codger,**" "The World of Books" column, *The Nation & The Athenaeum* 33 (28 July 1923): 548. Review essay on *Tales of Nasr-ed-Din Khoja*, translated from Turkish by Henry D. Barnham (Nisbet).

"**Dryden,**" "The World of Books" column, *The Nation & The Athenaeum* 33 (4 August 1923): 575. Review essay on *Dryden and His Poetry* by Allardyce Nicoll, the Poetry and Life series (Harrap) and *Dryden's Heroic Plays* by B. J. Pendlebury (Selwyn & Blount).

"**A Traveller in Little Things,**" "The World of Books" column, *The Nation & The Athenaeum* 33 (18 August 1923): 638. Review essay on reprints of W. H. Hudson's *Far Away and Long Ago*, *Idle Days in Patagonia*, and *A Traveller in Little Things* (J. M. Dent and Sons).

"**An Englishman,**" "The World of Books" column, *The Nation & The Athenaeum* 33 (25 August 1923): 662. Review essay on works by William Cobbett: William Cobbett's *Rural Rides*, in the Blackie's English School Texts series, edited by Dr. Rouse (Blackie). And *Cobbett*, a book of selections with an essay by Hazlitt and notes by Mr. A. M. D. Hughes (Clarendon Press).

"**Herman Melville,**" "The World of Books" column, *The Nation & The Athenaeum* 33 (1 September 1923): 688. Review of the Jonathan Cape, Library Edition series, of five of Herman Melville's books: *Moby Dick*, *Typee*, *Omoo*, *White Jacket*, and *Mardi*.

"**The Pilgrimage of Fa-hsien,**" "The World of Books" column, *The Nation & The Athenaeum* 33 (8 September 1923): 715. Review of a new translation of

The Travels of Fa-hsien or Record of the Buddhistic Kingdoms, translated by Professor Giles (Cambridge University Press).

"Ruskin," "The World of Books" column, *The Nation & The Athenaeum* 33 (22 September 1923): 777. Review essay on *Selections from Ruskin* by Mr. A. C. Benson (Cambridge University Press).

"Charming Memories," "The World of Books" column, *The Nation & The Athenaeum* 33 (29 September 1923): 808. Review essay on *Early Memories: Some Chapters of Autobiography* by John Butler Yeats (Cuala Press).

"The Man with the Nose," "The World of Books" column, *The Nation & The Athenaeum* 34 (6 October 1923): 15. Review of Cyrano de Bergerac's *Voyages to the Moon and Sun* translated by Richard Aldington (Routledge).

"Lord Morley," "The World of Books" column, *The Nation & The Athenaeum* 34 (13 October 1923): 55. Review of Lord Morley's *Politics and History* (Macmillan)—Morley's complete works.

"Lord Curzon's Travels," "The World of Books" column, *The Nation & The Athenaeum* 34 (20 October 1923): 120. Review of Lord Curzon's Tales of Travel (Hodder & Stoughton).

"Arabia Deserta," "The World of Books" column, *The Nation & The Athenaeum* 34 (27 October 1923): 155. Review of *Wanderings in Arabia* by Charles Doughty (1908; reprint Jonathan Cape and the Medici Society); (1908; reprint Duckworth) and *Travels in Arabia Deserta* by Charles Doughty (1888; reprint Jonathan Cape and the Medici Society); (1888; reprint Duckworth). Doughty published two different accounts of his travels, and both accounts were reprinted by two publishers.

"The First Person Singular," "The World of Books" column, *The Nation & The Athenaeum* 34 (3 November 1923): 188. Review essay on a new edition of *The Diary of Samuel Pepys* by Mr. Wheatley (G. Bell & Son); *Myself When Young* by Alec Waugh (Grant Richards); and *The Luck of the Year* by E. V. Lucas (Methuen).

"The Lost Flute, "The World of Books" column, *The Nation & The Athenaeum* 34 (10 November 1923): 222. Reviews of *The Temple and Other Poems* by Arthur Waley (Allen & Unwin) and *The Lost Flute and Other Lyrics* by Gertrude Laughlin Joerissen

"Samuel Butler," "The World of Books" column, *The Nation & The Athenaeum* 34 (17 November 1923): 276. Review of Jonathan Cape's *Canterbury Settlement and Other Early Essays* and *Erewhon* (Shrewsbury Edition)—the works of Samuel Butler.

"The Journalessayist," "The World of Books" column, *The Nation & The Athenaeum* 34 (24 November 1923): 314. Review essay on the jounalessayist that deals with the following: *Fantasies and Impromptus* by James Agate (Collins); *The Blue Lion* by Robert Lynd (Methuen); *Sparks from the Fire* by Gilbert Thomas (Chapman & Hall); *Pencillings* by J. Middleton Murray (Collins); *I for One* by J. B. Priestley (Lane); *Streams of Ocean* by Aubrey de Selincourt (Heinemann); and *Life and I* by C. Lewis Hind (Lane).

"The Daydream," "The World of Books" column, *The Nation & The Athenaeum* 34 (1 December 1923): 346. Review of *The Daydream: A Study in Development* by George H. Green (University of London Press).

"Mr. Conrad's Rover," "The World of Books" column, *The Nation & The Athenaeum* 34 (8 December 1923): 377. Review essay on Joseph Conrad's *The Rover* (Fisher Unwin) and volumes 13, *Twixt Land and Sea*, and 14, *Chance*, (Dent) of Conrad's complete works.

"Gossip and History," "The World of Books" column, *The Nation & The Athenaeum* 34 (15 December 1923): 431. Reviews of John Beresford's *Gossip of the Seventeenth and Eighteenth Centuries* (Cobden-Sanderson) and *The Diary of Lady Anne Clifford*, edited by Vita Sackville-West (Heinemann).

"W. H. Hudson," "The World of Books" column, *The Nation & The Athenaeum* 34 (22 December 1923): 463. Review essay on W. H. Hudson's *Nature in Downland, Hampshire Days*, and *The Land's End* (Dent) and *153 Letters from W. H. Hudson*, edited by Edward Garnett (Nonesuch Press).

"The Fascination of Crime," "The World of Books" column, *The Nation & The Athenaeum* 34 (29 December 1923): 490. Review of Sir John Hall's *The Bravo Mystery and Other Cases* (Lane); Charles Kingston's *Dramatic Days at the Old Bailey* (Stanley Paul); John C. Goodwin's *Insanity and the Criminal* (Hutchinson); and *Trial of Frederick bywaters and Edith Thompson*, edited by Filson Young (Hodge).

"The Fall of Stevenson," "The World of Books" column, *The Nation & The Athenaeum* 34 (5 January 1924): 517. Review of the first ten volumes of *The Complete Works of Robert Louis Stevenson* (Heinemann); Rosaline Masson's *Life of Robert Louis Stevenson* (Chambers); and *Selected Essays of Robert Louis Stevenson*, edited by H. G. Rawlinson (Oxford Press and Milford).

"A Seventeenth-Century Barber," "The World of Books" column, *The Nation & The Athenaeum* 34 (12 January 1924): 546. Review of *Master Johann Dietz* (Allen & Unwin)—a translation of the autobiography of Meister Johann Dietz edited by Dr. Ernst Constentius.

"The Pageant of History," "The World of Books" column, *The Nation & The Athenaeum* 34 (19 January 1924): 574. Review of a new edition of R. B. Morgan's *Readings in English Social History*.

"The Buccaneers," "The World of Books" column, *The Nation & The Athenaeum* 34 (26 January 1924): 607. Review of Esquemeling, the *Buccaneers of America, A True Account of the Most Remarkable Assaults Committed of Late Years upon the Coast of the West Indies by the Buccaneers of Jamaica and Tortuga, Both English and French. Written Originally in Dutch by John*

Esquemeling, One of the Buccaneers Who Was Present at These Tragedies (Amsterdam, 1678; English translation, 1684; recent edition published by Routledge with an introduction by Andrew Lang).

"Rabindranath Tagore," "The World of Books" column, *The Nation & The Athenaeum* 34 (9 February 1924): 669. Review of Rabindranath Tagore's *Gora* (Macmillan).

"Mr. Moore and the Critics," "The World of Books" column, *The Nation & The Athenaeum* 34 (16 February 1924): 702. Review of George Moore's *Conversations in Ebury Street* (Heinemann).

"Butler's 'Fair Haven,'" "The World of Books" column, *The Nation & The Athenaeum* 34 (23 February 1924): 735. Review of Samuel Butler's *Fair Haven* and *Life and Habit* (Cape).

"Tolstoi's Plays," "The World of Books" column, *The Nation & The Athenaeum* 34 (1 March 1924): 766. Review of *The Dramatic Works of Lyof N. Tolstoi*, translated by Nathan Haskell Dole (Harrap).

"Confessions," "The World of Books" column, *The Nation & The Athenaeum* 34 (8 March 1924): 798. Review of *The Chinese Confessions of C. W. Mason* by C. W. Mason (Grant Richards).

"The Harvest of Spring," "The World of Books" column, *The Nation & The Athenaeum* 34 (15 March 1924): 834. List of recently published books:

NOVELS: E. M. Forster's *Passage to India* (Arnold); David Garnett's *A Man at the Zoo* (Chatto & Windus); Mr. de la Mare's *Crossings* (Collins); *Wandering Stars* by Clemence Dane (Heinemann); *The House of Polyglot* by Mr. William Gerhardi (Cobden-Sanderson); Osbert Sitwell's *Triple Fugue* (Grant Richards); *Counterplot* by Hope Mirrlee (Collins); *Defeat* by Geoffrey Moss (Constable); *England My England* by D. H. Lawrence (Secker); *The Conscience of Gavin Blane* by W. E. Norris (Hutchinson); *The Dream* by H. G. Wells (Cape); *Gora* by Rabindranath Tagore (Macmillan); *To-morrow and To-morrow* by Mr. McKenna (Butterworth); *Unity* by Mr. Beresford (Collins); and *A Cure of Souls* by May Sinclair (Hutchinson).

BIOGRAPHIES: *Jane Welch Carlyle: Letters to Her Family*, edited by Leonard Huxley (Murray); *The Letters of Charles Greville and Henry Reeve* (Fisher Unwin); *The Fugger Newsletters* (Bodley Head); *Letters of Anne Thackery Ritchie* (Murray); *The Journal of the Hon. Henry Edward Fox* (Thornton Butterworth); Harold Nicholson's *Bryon, the Last Journey* (Constable); Desmond MacCarthy's *Byron* (Heinemann); *Byron in England* by S. C. Chew (Murray); *Sigmund Freud* by Wittels (Allen & Unwin); H. G. Wells' *The Story of a Great School Master* (Chatto & Windus); *Contemporary Personalities* by the Earl of Birkenhead (Cassell); *The Life of Dr. John Clifford* (Cassell); Wickham Steed's *Through Thirty Years* (Heinemann); *My Cricket Memories* by Jack Hobbs (Heinemann); *An Ambassador's Memoirs*, Vol. III, by M. Paleologue

(Hutchinson); *General Botha* by Earl Buxton (Murray); *W. H. Hudson* by Morley Roberts (Nash); and *Life of Olive Schreiner* by S.C. Cronwright Schreiner (Fisher Unwin).

TRAVEL BOOKS: *Man and Mystery in Asia* by Ferdinand Ossendowski (Arnold); *Wrangle Island* by Mr. Stafanson (Arrowsmith); and *In Quest of El Dorado* by Stephen Graham (Macmillan).

POETRY: *Secrets* by W. H. Davis (Cape); *Ding Dong Bell* by W. de la Mare (Selwyn and Blount); and *Mock-Beggar Hall* by Robert Graves (Hogarth Press).

CRITICISM AND ESSAYS: *Shelley and the Unromantics* by Lowen Ward Cambell (Methuen); *Southern Baroque Art* by Scheverell Sitwell (Grant Richards); *More Obiter Dicta* by Augustine Birrell (Heinemann); *The Right Place* by C. E. Montague (Chatto & Windus); *Literary Studies and Reviews* by Richard Aldington (Allen & Unwin); and *The Contemporary Theatre* by James Agate (Parsons).

HISTORY, ECONOMICS, SCIENCE, ETC.: *The Disinherited Family, a Plea for Family Endowment* by Eleanor Rathbone (Arnold); *Crime and Insanity* by W. C. Sullivan (Arnold); *The Electron in Chemistry* by Sir. J. J. Thomson (Chapman & Hall); *Einstein's Theory of Relativity* by Max Born (Methuen); *The Foundations of Einstein's Theory of Gravitation* and *The Theory of Relativity* by Professor Freundlich (Methuen); *New Theories of Matter and the Atom* by A. Berthoud (Allen & Unwin); *Psycho-Analysis and Gland Personalities* by Andre Tridon (Brentano); *Some Aspects of Psycho-Analysis* by Ernest Jones (Williams & Norgate); and *Rejuvenation—the Work of Steinach, Voronoff, and Others* by Dr. Norman Haire (Allen & Unwin).

"**Daedalus and Icarus,**" "The World of Books" column, *The Nation & The Athenaeum* 34 (22 March 1924): 890. Review essay on two books in Kegan Paul's "Today and Tomorrow" series: *Daedalus, or Science and the Future* by J. B. S. Haldane (Kegan Paul) and *Icarus, or the Future of Science* by Bertand Russell (Kegan Paul).

"**A Real Historian,**" "The World of Books" column, *The Nation & The Athenaeum* 34 (29 March 1924): 922. Review essay on Frederick Arthur Simpson's *The Rise of Louis Napoleon* (John Murray, 1909) and *Louis Napoleon and the Recovery of France, 1848–1856* (Longmans, 1923).

"**A Great Autobiography,**" "The World of Books" column, *The Nation & The Athenaeum* 35 (5 April 1924): 17. Review of *The Memoirs of Alexander Herzen, Parts I & II*, translated by J. D. Duff (Yale University Press), and *The Memoirs, My Past and Thoughts* by Alexander Herzen, translated by Constance Garnett (Chatto & Windus).

"**The Romance of a Drowned Parrot,**" "The World of Books" column, *The Nation & The Athenaeum* 35 (12 April, 1924): 51. Review essay on *The Conquest of the River Plate* by Cunninghame Graham (Heinemann).

"The Fall of Stevenson—II," "The World of Books" column, *The Nation & The Athenaeum* 35 (19 April 1924): 86. Review of the second ten volumes of the complete works of Robert Louis Stevenson, Tusitala Edition (Heinemann).

"Mr. Garnett's Second," "The World of Books" column, *The Nation & The Athenaeum* 35 (26 April 1924): 115. Review essay on David Garnett's *A Man in the Zoo* (Chatto & Windus).

"The Road to Immortality," "The World of Books" column, *The Nation & The Athenaeum* 35 (3 May 1924): 146. Review essay on *The Diary of a Country Parson: The Reverend James Woodforde, 1758–1781*, edited by John Beresford (Milford).

"Lawyers and Criminals," "The World of Books" column, *The Nation & The Athenaeum* 35 (10 May 1924): 178. Review essay on C. L. McCluer Stevens' *Famous Crimes and Criminals* (Stanley Paul); E. Bowen-Rowlands' *Judgment of Death* (Collins); and E. Bowen-Rowlands' *Seventy-two Years at the Bar, A Memoir* [memoir of Harry Bodkin Poland] (Macmillan).

"Mrs. Carlyle," "The World of Books" column, *The Nation & The Athenaeum* 35 (17 May 1924): 206. Review essay on *Jane Welsh Carlyle: Letters to Her Family, 1839–1863*, edited by Leonard Huxley (Murray).

"George Barrow," "The World of Books" column, *The Nation & The Athenaeum* 35 (24 May 1924): 262. Review of the Norwich Edition of *The Works of George Barrow*, edited by Clement Shorter (Constable).

"The Apotheosis of Toryism," "The World of Books" column, *The Nation & The Athenaeum* 35 (31 May 1924): 294. Review of *A History of the Tory Party* by Maurice Woods (Hodder & Stoughton).

"Patriotism and Literature," "The World of Books" column, *The Nation & The Athenaeum* 35 (7 June 1924): 322. Review of *Patriotism in Literature* by John Drinkwater (Williams & Norgate).

"Arch Beyond Arch," "The World of Books" column, *The Nation & The Athenaeum* 35 (14 June 1924): 354. Review of E. M. Forster's *Passage to India* (Arnold).

"A Civilized Man," "The World of Books" column, *The Nation & The Athenaeum* 35 (21 June 1924): 381. Review essay on Erasmus, especially the fifth volume of Erasmus's letters, *Erasmi Epistolae, Tom. V., 1522–1524*, edited by Dr. Allen (Clarendon Press); Charles Scribner's Sons' Great Hollanders Series' translation of the life and study of Erasmus by J. Huizinga; and *Erasmus and Luther* by R. H. Murray.

"Characters," "The World of Books" column, *The Nation & The Athenaeum* 35 (28 June 1924): 413. Review of *A Book of Characters*, compiled and translated by Richard Aldington (Routledge).

"The Classics," "The World of Books" column, *The Nation & The Athenaeum* 35 (5 July 1924): 442. Reviews of three volumes in the *Library of Greek*

Thought, edited by Ernest Barker (Dent): *Greek Literary Criticism* by J. D. Denniston; *Greek Historical Thought* by Arnold J. Toynbee; and *Greek Civilization and Character* by Arnold J. Toynbee. Three volumes in the *Our Debt to Greece and Rome* series (Harrap): *Euripides and His Influence* by F. L. Lucas; *Language and Philology* by Roland Kent; and *Catullus and His Influence* by K. P. Harrington. And *A Lexicon of the Homeric Dialect* by Richard John Cunliffe (Blackie); *M. Fabii Quintiliani Institutionis Oratoriae. Liber* I., edited by F. H. Colson (Cambridge University Press); and *Catullus*, translated by Sir William Marris (Clarendon Press).

"Egoism in Print," "The World of Books" column, *The Nation & The Athenaeum* (12 July 1923): 481. Reviews of a reprint of *The Life of Benjamin Franklin Written by Himself* in Milford's *World Classics* series; *The Book of My Youth* by Hermann Sudermann, translated by Wyndham Harding (Lane); and *A Russian Schoolboy* by Serghei Aksakoff, translated by J. D. Duff, Milford's *World Classics* series.

"Mr. Shaw's Saint Joan," "The World of Books" column, *The Nation & The Athenaeum* (19 July 1924): 511. Review essay on George B. Shaw's "Saint Joan" (Heinemann).

"Words," "The World of Books" column, *The Nation & The Athenaeum* (26 July 1924): 538. Reviews of Logan Pearsall Smith's pamphlet, *Four Words: Romantic, Originality, Creative, Genius* (Clarendon Press), in the series, the Society for Pure English Tracts; *Michael Neo Palaeologus, His Grammar* by his father, Stephen N. Palaeologus (Dent); and *The Philosophy of Grammar* by Otto Jespersen (Allen & Unwin).

"The Strange History of Education," "The World of Books" column, *The Nation & The Athenaeum* (2 August 1924): 566. Review of *A Survey of Education* by Helen Wodehouse (Arnold).

"Joseph Conrad," "The World of Books" column, *The Nation & The Athenaeum* (9 August 1924): 595. Review essay on Conrad's books, especially *Lord Jim* and *Heart of Darkness*.

"The Conspiracy Mania," "The World of Books" column, *The Nation & The Athenaeum* 35 (16 August 1924): 620. Review essay on *Secret Societies and Subversive Movements* by Nesta H. Webster (Boswell Publishing Co.).

"Non-Secret Societies," "The World of Books" column, *The Nation & The Athenaeum* 35 (23 August 1924): 644. Reviews of *Introduction to the Survey of English Place-Names* and *The Chief Elements in English Place-Names* by the English Place-Name Society (Cambridge University Press); a pamphlet issued by The Seafarers' Education Service describing its activities; and the annual report of The Cremation Society of England.

"The Making of Books," "The World of Books" column, *The Nation & The Athenaeum* 35 (30 August 1924): 667. Review essay on *The Net Book Agreement, 1899, and the Book War, 1906–1908* (MacLehose).

"Reprints," "The World of Books" column, *The Nation & The Athenaeum* 35 (6 September 1924): 693. Review of The Bodley Head Quartos reprints published by John Lane: *Daemonologie in Forme of a Dialogue by King James I*, together with *Newes of Scotland*; and pamphlets: Robert Greene's "The Blacke Bookes Messenger," together with "Cuthbert Conny-Catcher's The Defence of Conny-Catching."

"The Duke and Miss Jenkins," "The World of Books" column, *The Nation & The Athenaeum* 35 (13 September 1924): 721. Review of *The Letters of the Duke of Wellington to Miss J., 1834–1851*, edited by Christine Terhune Herrick, with an introduction by W. R. H. Trowbridge (Fisher Unwin).

"The Common People," "The World of Books" column, *The Nation & The Athenaeum* 35 (20 September 1924): 750. Review of *Mediaeval People* by Eileen Power (Methuen).

"Mumbo Jumbo," "The World of Books" column, *The Nation & The Athenaeum* 35 (27 September 1924): 778. Reviews of *Napoleon* by Elie Faure, translated by Jeffery E. Jeffery (Constable); *The Campaign of 1812 and the Retreat from Moscow* by Hilaire Belloc (Nelson); *Napoleon and His Court* by C. S. Forester (Methuen); and H. G. Wells' *A Short History of the World* (Labour Publishing Company).

"Poetry and Dreams," "The World of Books" column, *The Nation & The Athenaeum* 36 (4 October 1924): 18. Review of Robert Graves' *The Meaning of Dreams* (Palmer).

"The Harvest of Autumn Books," "The World of Books" column, *The Nation & The Athenaeum* 36 (11 October 1924): 54. List of recently published books: BIOGRAPHIES: *The Life of James Elroy Flecker* (Oxford); a translation of Paul *Cezanne* by Ambroise Vollard (Brentano); The Travel Diary of a Philosopher, by Count Herman Keyserling (Cape); Mrs. [Mary?] MacCarthy's *A Nineteenth Century Childhood* (Heinemann); *Memoirs of William Hickey*, vol. 4, (Hurst & Blackett); *Mazzini* by Edyth Hinkley (Allen & Unwin); *The Life of John Strutt, Third Baron of Rayleigh* by Robert John Strutt (Arnold); *Without Prejudice* by Margot Asquith (Thornton Butterworth); *John Keats* by Amy Lowell (Cape); *David Lloyd George, War Minister* by J. Saxon Mills (Cassell); *Life and Letters of Anton Tchehov* by S. S. Koteliansky and Philip Tomlinson (Cassell); *The Memoirs of Alexander Herzen: My Past and Thoughts*, Vols. III and IV, translated by Mrs. Garnett (Chatto & Windus); *Leigh Hunt* by Edmund Blunden (Cobden-Sanderson); *Mark Twain's Autobiography* (Harper); *The Life of Lord Wolseley* by Sir Frederick Maurice (Heinemann); *The River of Life* by John St. Loe Strachey (Hodder & Stoughton); *The Life of the Archpriest*

Avvakum by Himself, translated by Jane Harrison and Hope Mirrlees (Hogarth Press); *Life and Letters of Rt. Hon. George Wyndham* (Hutchinson); *Ben Kendim: A Record of Eastern Travel* by Aubrey Herbert (Hutchinson); *Politics from Within* by Rt. Hon. C. Addison (Jenkins); *Fugger News-Letters* (Lane); *Memorials of Albert Venn Dicey* (Macmillan); *Out of the Past* by Mrs. W. W. Vaughn (Margaret Symonds) (Murray); *Lord Minto* by John Buchan (Nelson); *Master Richard Quyny* by E. I. Fripp (Oxford University Press); *The Byron Mystery* by Sir John Fox (Grant Richards); *Memories of the Foreign Legion* by M. M. (Secker); *The Letters of Olive Schreiner* (Fisher Unwin); and *Recollections and Reminiscences* by Lord Hawke (Williams & Norgate).

NOVELS: *Sturly* by Pierre Custot (Cape); *Spring Sowing* by Liam O'Flaherty (Cape); *Innocent Desires* by E. L. Grant Watson (Cape); *Elsie and the Child: A Tale of Riceyman Steps* by Arnold Bennett (Cassell); The Old Men of the Sea by Compton Mackenzie (Cassell); *Tents of Israel* by G. B. Stern (Chapman & Hall); *The Polyglots* by William Gerhardi (Chapman & Hall); *Those Barren Leaves* by Aldous Huxley (Chatto & Windus); *Orphan Island* by Rose Macaulay (Collins); *Something Childish* by Katherine Mansfield (Constable); *A. O. Barnabooth* by Valery Larband (Dent); *The Nature of a Crime* by Joseph Conrad and F. M. Hueffer (Duckworth); *The White Monkey* by John Galsworthy (Heinemann); *The Grub Street Nights* by J. C. Squire (Hodder & Stoughton); *Seducers in Ecuador* by Vita Sackville-West (Hogarth Press); *People, Houses, and Ships* by Elinor Mordaunt (Hutchinson); *Arnold Waterlow* by May Sinclair (Hutchinson); *Pipers and a Dancer* by Stella Benson (Macmillan); *The Old Ladies* by Hugh Walpole (Macmillan); *The Roadside Fire* by Madeline Linford (Parsons); and *The Boy in the Bush* by D. H. Lawrence and M. L. Skinner (Secker).

CRITICISM, LITERATURE, AND ESSAYS: Published by Cambridge University Press: *A History of Early Eighteenth Century Drama, 1700–1750* by Allardyce Nicholl; and *A History of Persian Literature in Modern Times, 1500–1924* by Professor E. G. Browne. *John Donne: a Critical Study* by Hugh I'Anson Fausset (Cape); *Restoration Comedy, 1660–1720* by Bonamy Dobree (Oxford University Press); *Punch and Judy and Other Essays* by Maurice Baring (Heinemann); *The Peal of Bells* by Robert Lynd (Methuen); and *A Volume of Essays* by Rose Macaulay (Methuen).

HISTORY: *The Foreign Policy of Castlereagh, 1815–1822* by Professor C. K. Webster (Bell); *The Mediaeval Village* by G. G. Coulton (Cambridge University Press); *The Hittite Empire* by John Garstang (Hodder & Stoughton); *The History of the University of Oxford* by Sir Charles Mallet (Methuen); *Sidelights on the Thirty Years' War* by Hubert G. R. Reade (Routledge); and *Tudor Economic Documents*, edited by R. H. Tawney and Eileen Power (Longmans).

POLITICS AND SOCIOLOGY: *Conflict of Policies in Asia* by T. F. Millard (Allen & Unwin); *Germany and the World Tragedy* by Theodor Wolff (Benn); *Kenya* by Norman Leys (Hogarth Press); *Prison Reform at Home and Abroad* by Sir Evelyn Ruggles-Brise (Macmillan); *Labour, Social Reform, and Democracy* by Dr. A. S. Rappoport (Stanley Paul); and *Britain, Egypt, and the Sudan* by M. Travers Symons (Palmer).

OTHER BOOKS OF INTEREST: *Isvor, the Country of Willows* by Princess Bibesco, translated from French (Heinemann); *Tidemarks* by H. M. Tomlinson (Cassell); *Sunward* by Louis Golding (Chatto & Windus); *Selected Poems of Emily Dickinson*, edited by Conrad Aiken (Cape); Halliford Edition of the *Complete Works of Thomas Love Peacock*, 10 volumes (Constable); the works of R. L. Stevenson, 35 volumes, Tusitala Edition, pocket edition (Heinemann); the complete works of R. L. Stevenson, Skerryvore Edition (Heinemann); and the works of Samuel Butler, vol. 8, Shrewsbury Edition (Heinemann) [full set will be 20 vols.]. Fisher Unwin will publish the Atlantic Edition of Mr. Wells' works in 28 vols., and Nonesuch Press will publish Wycherley's works in 4 vols.

"The Lesser Fleas," "The World of Books" column, *The Nation & The Athenaeum* **36 (18 October 1924): 113.** Reviews of *Latitudes* by Edwin Muir (Melrose); *Contemporary Criticism* by Orlo Williams (Parsons); and *Fritto Misto* by E. S. P. Haynes (Cayme Press).

"Traveller's Tales," "The World of Books" column, *The Nation & The Athenaeum* **36 (25 October 1924): 155.** Reviews of the New Aldine Library translation of the Second Book of Herodotus' *History*, translated by George Rawlinson (Hopkinson); *Herodotus* by T. R. Glover (Cambridge University Press); *Simplicissimus the Vagabond* by Grimmelshausen, translated by A. T. S. Goodrick (Routledge, Broadway Translations); *Moritiz's Travels in England in 1782* by Moritz (Milford); *An Irish Peer on the Continent*, edited by Thomas U. Sadleir (Williams & Norgate); and *Memoirs of the Foreign Legion* by M. M., with an introduction by D. H. Lawrence (Secker).

"The False Step at Geneva," [letter to editor], *The Nation & The Athenaeum* **36 (25 October 1924): 148.** L. Woolf supports the Geneva Protocol that provided for the settlement of international disputes, and he criticizes the position taken by *The Nation & The Athenaeum* on the Protocol.

"Old News," "The World of Books" column, *The Nation & The Athenaeum* **(1 November 1924): 187.** Review of *The Fugger News-Letters* (Lane).

"Mark Twain," "The World of Books" column, *The Nation & The Athenaeum* **(8 November 1924): 217.** Review of *Mark Twain's Autobiography*, two volumes (Harper).

"Crime and Criminals," "The World of Books" column, *The Nation & The Athenaeum* **(15 November 1924): 267.** Reviews of the recent volume in the

Notable British Trials series, *Trial of Adolf Beck (1877–1904)*, edited by Eric R. Watson (Hodge); *Problems of Modern American Crime* by Veronica King (Heath Cranton); *Studies in Murder* by Edmund Lester Pearson (Macmillan); and *The Criminal as a Human Being* by George S. Dougherty (Appleton).

"Peacock," "The World of Books" column, *The Nation & The Athenaeum* 36 (22 November 1924): 298. Review of volumes II to V of the Halliford edition of Peacock's work (Constable).

"Look Up There, With Me!" "The World of Books" column, *The Nation & The Athenaeum* 36 (29 November 1924): 331. Review of *To the Unknown God* by J. Middleton Murry (Cape).

"Samuel Butler Again," "The World of Books" column, *The Nation & The Athenaeum* 36 (6 December 1924): 364. Reviews of two volumes in the Shrewsbury Edition of the complete works of Samuel Butler (Cape. 20 vols.): *Luck or Cunning?* and *Alps and Sanctuaries*; and a volume in the Road maker series: *Samuel Butler* by C. E. M. Joad (Parsons).

"Two Autobiographies," "The World of Books" column, *The Nation & The Athenaeum* 36 (13 December 1924): 414. Reviews of *Memoir of Thomas Bewick* by Thomas Bewick (Bodley Head); and *Marbacka* by Selma Lagerlof (Laurie).

"The Tower of Walburga, Lady Paget," "The World of Books" column, *The Nation & The Athenaeum* 36 (20 December 1924): 444. Review of *In My Tower* by Walburga, Lady Paget (Hutchinson).

"Swinburne," "The World of Books" column, *The Nation & The Athenaeum* 36 (27 December 1924): 472. Review of *Creative Spirits of the Nineteenth Century* [a collection of essays] by Georg Brandes (Fisher Unwin).

"Greek in English," "The World of Books" column, *The Nation & The Athenaeum* 36 (3 January 1925): 497. Reviews of *Aristophanes* with the English translation by Benjamin Bickley Rogers, Loeb Classical Library (Heinemann); *The Pastoral Loves of Daphnis and Chloe*, translated by George Moore (Heinemann); *The Symposium or Supper of Plato*, translated by Francis Birrell and Shane Leslie (Nonesuch Press); and *The Antigone of Sophocles*, translated by R. C. Trevelyan (University Press of Liverpool and Hodder & Stoughton).

"The Future of Woman," "The World of Books" column, *The Nation & The Athenaeum* 36 (10 January 1925): 526. Reviews of *Lysistrata, or Women's Future and Future Woman* by Anthony M. Ludovici, the To-Day and To-Morrow series (Kegan Paul) and *The Soul of Woman* by Gina Lombroso (Cape).

"Queen Victoria's Uncle," "The World of Books" column, *The Nation & The Athenaeum* 36 (17 January 1925): 553. Review of *Letters of the King of Hanover to Viscount Strangford*, with an historical note by E. M. Cox and an introduction by Charles Whibley (Williams & Norgate).

"The Novel," "The World of Books" column, *The Nation & The Athenaeum* **36 (24 January 1925): 584.** Review essay on George B. Shaw's *An Unsocial Socialist, The Irrational Knot, Love Among the Artists,* and *Cashel Byron's Profession* published by Constable and *Those Barren Leaves* by Aldous Huxley (Chatto & Windus).

"Castlereagh," "The World of Books" column, *The Nation & The Athenaeum* **36 (31 January 1925): 613.** Review of *The Foreign Policy of Castlereagh, 1815–1822* by C. K. Webster (Bell).

"Foreign Parts," "The World of Books" column, *The Nation & The Athenaeum* **36 (7 February 1925): 649.** Reviews of *The Coasts of Illusion* by Clark B. Firestone (Harper); *Lady Anne Barnard at the Cape of Good Hope, 1797–1802* by Dorothea Fairbridge (Clarendon Press); *The Shadow of the Gloomy East* by Ferdinand Ossendowski (Allen & Unwin); *The Vanished Cities of Arabia* by Mrs. Steuart Erskine (Hutchinson); and *To Lhasa in Disguise* by W. Montgomery McGovern (Thornton Butterworth).

"The Mind of a Chimpanzee," "The World of Books" column, *The Nation & The Athenaeum* **36 (14 February 1925): 681.** Reviews of The International Library of Psychology publication of *The Mentality of Apes* by W. Koehler [English translation] (Kegan Paul) and *The Growth of the Mind* by Professor K. Koffka (Kegan Paul).

"Chekhov's Letters," "The World of Books" column, *The Nation & The Athenaeum* **36 (21 February 1925): 717.** Review of *The Life and Letters of Anton Tchekhov* by S.S. Koteliansky and Philip Tomlinson (Cassell).

"The Life of Keats," "The World of Books" column, *The Nation & The Athenaeum* **36 (28 February 1925): 749.** Review of *John Keats*, 2 volumes, by Amy Lowell (Cape).

"The Bestseller," "The World of Books" column, *The Nation & The Athenaeum* **36 (7 March 1925): 777.** Reviews of *Arnold Bennett* by Mrs. Arnold Bennett (Philpot); *Arnold Bennett of the Five Towns* by L. G. Johnson (Daniel); *Sheila Kaye-Smith and the Weald Country* by R. Thurston (Palmer); and *Open Confession to a Man from a Woman* by Marie Corelli (Hutchinson).

"The Spring Books," "The World of Books" column, *The Nation & The Athenaeum* **36 (14 March 1925): 814.** List of recently published books:

BIOGRAPHIES, LETTERS, ETC.: *W. H. Massingham: Life and Writings,* edited by Harold J. Massingham (Cape); *The Letters of Sir Walter Raleigh* (Methuen); *Moberly Bell and His Times* by F. Harcourt Kitchen (Philip Allan); *What I Have Seen and Heard* by J. G. Swift MacNeill (Arrowsmith); *The Life of James Elroy Flecker* (Blackwell); *Places and Persons* by Margot Asquith (Thornton Butterworth); *Anatole France at Home* by Jean Jacques Bousson (Thornton Butterworth); *Tom Moore's Diary* (Cambridge University Press); *John Keats* by Amy Lowell (Cape); *The Life and Letters of Anton Tchekhov* by

S. S. Koteliansky and P. Tomlinson (Cassell); *The Letters of Anton Pavlovitch Tchekhov to Olga Knipper*, translated by Constance Garnett (Chatto & Windus); *My Reminiscences* by S. M. J. Woods (Chapman & Hall); *The Portrait of Zelide* by Geoffrey Scott (Constable); *Lenin* by Leon Trotzky (Harrap); *Doughty Deeds* by R. B. Cunninghame Graham (Heinemann); *Original Letters from India, 1799–1815* by Mrs. Fay, with notes by E. M. Forster (Hogarth Press); *Memoirs of William Hickey*, Vol. IV (Hurst & Blackett); *The Life and Letters of George Wyndham* (Hutchinson); *The Letters of Mary Russell Mitford* (Lane); *King Edward VII* by Sir Sidney Lee, Vol. I (Macmillan); *Memorials of Alfred Marshall*, edited by A. C. Pigou (Macmillan); *The Letters of Queen Victoria*, Second Series (Murray); *Out of the Past* by Mrs. W. W. Vaughan (Murray); *A King's Private Letters* by King Constantine of Greece (Nash & Grayson); *The Death of Christopher Marlowe* (Nonesuch); *Three Essays in Biography* by Bonamy Dobree (Oxford University Press); *Carlyle on Cromwell and Others, 1837–47* by D. A. Wilson (Kegan Paul); and *Early Letters from Sir Henry Campbell-Bannerman to His Sister Louisa* (Fisher Unwin).

NOVELS: *The Tale of Genji* by Lady Murasaki, translated by Arthur Waley (Allen & Unwin); *The Mother's Recompense* by Edith Wharton (Appleton); *Mr. Petre* by Hilaire Belloc (Arrowsmith); *An Affair of Honor* by Stephen McKenna (Thornton Butterworth); *High Noon* by Percy Lubbock (Cape); *The Informer* by Liam O'Flaherty (Cape); *Christina Alberta's Father* by H. G. Wells (Cape); *The George and the Crown* by Sheila Kaye-Smith (Cassell); *Tales of the Long Bow* by G. K. Chesterton (Cassell); *Thunderstorm* by G. B. Stern (Chapman & Hall); *Those Barren Leaves* by Aldous Huxley (Chatto & Windus); *The Sailor's Return* by David Garnett (Chatto & Windus); *Sixty-four, Ninety-four!* by R. H. Mottram (Chatto & Windus); *The Polyglots* by W. Gerhardi (Cobden-Sanderson); *The Monkey Puzzle* by J. D. Beresford (Collins); *Inner Circle* by Ethel Colburn Mayne (Constable); *Myrtle* by Stephen Hudson (Constable); *Piano Quintet* by Edward Sackville-West (Heinemann); *The Voice of the Dark* by Eden Phillpotts (Hutchinson); *The Rector of Wyck* by May Sinclair (Hutchinson); *Mrs. Dalloway* by Virginia Woolf (Hogarth Press); *Love* by the author of *Elizabeth and Her German Garden* (Macmillan); *St. Mawr* by D. H. Lawrence (Secker); *Death in Venice and Other Stories* by Thomas Mann (Secker); *Bring! Bring!* By Conrad Aiken (Secker); and *Tales of Hearsay* by Joseph Conrad (Fisher Unwin).

CRITICISM AND LITERATURE: *Charles Dickens and Other Studies* by Sir A. Quiller-Couch (Cambridge University Press); *Words and Idioms* by Logan Pearsall Smith (Constable); *Dostoieffsky* by Andre Gide (Dent); *The Common Reader* by Virginia Woolf (Hogarth Press); *The English Comic Characters* by J. B. Priestly (Lane); *Keats and Shakespeare* by J. Middleton Murry (Oxford University Press); *Ben Jonson*, 2 vols., edited by C. H. Herford and

Percy Simpson (Oxford University Press); *Poetic Unreason* by Robert Graves (Palmer); and *The Idea of Great Poetry* by Lascelles Abercrombie (Secker).

HISTORY: *English Life in the Middle Ages* by L. F. Salzman (Oxford University Press). Forthcoming new editions: Smollett in eleven volumes (Blackwell); Fonthill edition of William Beckford, nine volumes (Guy Chapman); Florida edition of Mark Twain, eighteen volumes (Chatto & Windus); Blake, *Writings*, 3 vols. (Nonesuch); and Burton's *Anatomy*, 2 vols. (Nonesuch).

SOCIOLOGY AND POLITICS: *Industry and Civilization* by C. Delisle Burns (Allen & Unwin); *British Government in India* by Marquis Curzon of Kedleston (Cassell); *English Judges* by the Earl of Birkenhead (Cassell); *The Public Life* by J. A. Spender (Cassell); *India as I Knew It* by Sir Michael O'Dwyer (Constable); *The Geneva Protocol* by P. J. Noel Baker (King); *The Austrian Revolution* by Otto Bauer (Parsons); and *The Menace of Colour* by J. W. Gregory (Seeley & Service).

"The Biography of Kings," "The World of Books" column, *The Nation & The Athenaeum* 36 (21 March 1925): 859. Review of *King Edward VII*, Vol. I, by Sir Sidney Lee (Macmillan).

"The Last Word in Crime," "The World of Books" column, *The Nation & The Athenaeum* 36 (28 March 1925): 889. Review of *The Crime and Trial of Leopold and Loeb* by Maureen McKernan (Allen & Unwin).

"Modern Poetry," "The World of Books" column, *The Nation & The Athenaeum* 37 (18 April 1925): 76. Reviews of *The Muse in Council* by John Drinkwater (Sidgwick & Jackson); *Troy Park* by Edith Sitwell (Duckworth); *Masks of Time* by Edmund Blunden (Beaumont); *Island Blood* by F. R. Higgins (Bodley Head); and *An Indian Ass* by Harold Acton (Duckworth).

"The Religion of A——," "The World of Books" column, *The Nation & The Athenaeum* 37 (25 April 1925): 106. Reviews of *What I Believe* by Bertrand Russell (Kegan Paul); *The Religion of a Darwinist* by Sir Arthur Keith (Watts); and *Science and Religion* by J. Arthur Thomson (Methuen).

"The Most Dangerous Trades," "The World of Books" column, *The Nation & The Athenaeum* 37 (2 May 1925): 137. Review essay on J. A. Spender's *The Public Life*, two volumes (Cassell).

"Falstaff to Micawber," "The World of Books" column, *The Nation & The Athenaeum* 37 (9 May 1925): 177. Review of J. B. Priestly's *The English Comic Characters* (Lane) and *The Novels of Fielding* by Aurelien Digeon (Routledge).

"Mr. Belloc," "The World of Books" column, *The Nation & The Athenaeum* 37 (16 May 1925): 207. Review of *The Cruise of the Nona* by Hilaire Belloc (Constable).

"The Death of Marlowe, "The World of Books" column, *The Nation & The Athenaeum* 37 (23 May 1925): 238. Reviews of the *Bible*, Vol. I, *Genesis to*

Ruth (Nonesuch) and *The Death of Christopher Marlowe* by J. Leslie Hotson (Nonesuch).

"Plays and Their Critics," "The World of Books" column, *The Nation & The Athenaeum* 37 (30 May 1925): 269. Reviews of *Glamour: Essays on the Art of the Theatre* by Stark Young (Scribner) and *The Contemporary Theatre, 1924* by James Agate (Chapman & Hall).

"H. W. M.," "The World of Books" column, *The Nation & The Athenaeum* 37 (6 June 1925): 296. Review essay on *H. W. M. (H. W. Massingham)*, edited by H. J. Massingham (Cape).

"Canning," "The World of Books" column, *The Nation & The Athenaeum* 37 (13 June 1925): 325. Review essay on *The Foreign Policy of Canning* by Harold Temperly (Bell).

"Anatole France," "The World of Books" column, *The Nation & The Athenaeum* 37 (20 June 1925): 370. Review of *Anatole France Himself: A Boswellian Record* by his secretary, Jean-Jacques Brousson, translated by John Pollock (Thornton).

"Cricket To-day," "The World of Books" column, *The Nation & The Athenaeum* 37 (27 June 1925): 401. Review of *Gilligan's Men* by M. A. Noble (Chapman & Hall).

"The End of Sensible Conversation," "The World of Books" column, *The Nation & The Athenaeum* 37 (4 July 1925): 430. Reviews of *Mary Hamilton*, edited by Elizabeth G. Anson (Murray); *The Journal of Clarissa Trant, 1800–1832*, edited by C. G. Luard (Bodley Head); *Tom Moore's Diary*, edited by J. B. Priestly (Cambridge University Press); *The Memoirs of Alexander Herzen*, Vol. IV, translated by Mrs. [Constance?] Garnett (Chatto & Windus).

"Plato the Dago," "The World of Books" column, *The Nation & The Athenaeum* 37 (11 July 1925): 460. Review of *The Greek Point of View* by Professor Maurice Hutton, University College, Toronto (Hodder & Stoughton). L. Woolf also comments on the following books in the Loeb Classics series: *The Iliad*, Vol. II, by Homer; *Scripta Minora* which includes *Hiero, Agesilaus,* and *The Lacedaemonians* by Xenophon; *Politicus, Philebus,* and *Ion* by Plato; *The Histories*, Books IX–XV, by Polybius; Lucian, Vol. IV; *The Stratagems* and *The Aqueducts of Rome* by Frontius; and *The Scriptores Historiae Augustae*, Vol. II.

"John Bright," "The World of Books" column, *The Nation & The Athenaeum* 37 (18 July 1925): 459. Review essay on *The Life of John Bright* by G. M. Trevelyan (Constable).

"Ben Jonson," "The World of Books" column, *The Nation & The Athenaeum* 37 (25 July 1925): 516. Review of *Ben Jonson*, Vols. I and II: *The Man and His Work*, edited by C. H. Herford and Percy Simpson (Clarendon Press).

"Every Man's One Good Book," "The World of Books" column, *The Nation & The Athenaeum* 37 (1 August 1925): 545. Review essay on *My Circus Life* by James Lloyd, with a preface by G. K. Chesterton (Noel Douglas) and *Fifty Years of Sport* by Lt.-Col. E. D. Miller (Hurst & Blackett).

"A Doctor's View of History," "The World of Books" column, *The Nation & The Athenaeum* 37 (8 August 1925): 571. Review of *Mere Mortals, Medico-Historical Essays, Second Series* by Dr. C. MacLaurin, University of Sydney (Cape).

"Modern Poetry," "The World of Books" column, *The Nation & The Athenaeum* 37 (15 August 1925): 598. Review of seven pamphlets: *Shelley, Keats, Hilaire Belloc, Rabindranath Tagore, Rupert Brooks, Edmund Blunden,* and *Robert Bridges* in the Augustan Books of Modern Poetry series (Benn).

"An Unfortunate Man," "The World of Books" column, *The Nation & The Athenaeum* 37 (22 August 1925): 623. Review of new edition of *The Life of Thomas Holcroft (1745–1809)*, 2 vols., by William Hazlitt, edited by Elbridge Colby (Constable).

"William Blake," "The World of Books" column, *The Nation & The Athenaeum* 37 (29 August 1925): 649. Review of *The Writings of William Blake*, 3 vols., edited by Geoffrey Keynes (Nonesuch Press).

"Literature and Revolution," "The World of Books" column, *The Nation & The Athenaeum* 37 (5 September 1925): 678. Review of Leon Trotsky's *Literature and Revolution* (Allen & Unwin).

"Lives of the Great," "The World of Books" column, *The Nation & The Athenaeum* 37 (12 September 1925): 706. Review of *Memoirs*, 2 vols., by Sir Almeric FitzRoy (Hutchinson) and *Courts and Countries After the War* by H. R. H Infanta Eulalia of Spain (Huchinson).

"Mr. Wells and the Immortals," "The World of Books" column, *The Nation & The Athenaeum* 37 (19 September 1925): 734. Review essay on *Christina Alberta's Father* by H. G. Wells (Cape).

"Mark Twain," "The World of Books" column, *The Nation & The Athenaeum* 37 (26 September 1925): 753. Review of *The Adventures of Huckleberry Finn*; *Tom Sawyer, Detective, & etc,* and *A Double-Barrelled Detective Story*; *The Prince and the Pauper*; *A Tramp Abroad*; and *The L1.000,000 Bank-Note*, 5 vols., by Mark Twain, The Florida Edition of Mark Twain series (Chatto & Windus). The completed series will have 18 volumes.

"The Last Conrad," "The World of Books" column, *The Nation & The Athenaeum* 38 (3 October 1925): 18. Review of *Suspense* by Joseph Conrad (Dent).

"The Harvest of Autumn Books," "The World of Books" column, *The Nation & The Athenaeum* 38 (10 October 1925): 56. List of recently published books: FICTION: *Christina Alberta's Father* by H. G. Wells (Cape); *The Sailor's Return* by David Garnett (Chatto & Windus); *The Informer* by Liam O'Flaherty (Cape); *The Sacred Tree* (originally, *The Tale of Genji*) by Lady Murasaki, translated by Mr. Waley (Allen & Unwin); *Cloud Cuckoo Land* by Naomi Mitchison

(Cape); *Suspense* by Joseph Conrad (Dent); *Tales of the Long Bow* by G. K. Chesterton (Cassell); *Mockery Gap* by T. G. Powys (Chatto & Windus); *A Moment of Time* by Richard Hughes (Chatto & Windus); *Broomsticks and Other Stories* by Walter de la Mare (Constable); *Odtaa, or Change for Threepence* by John Masefield (Heinemann); *Cats' Cradle* by Maurice Baring (Heinemann); *Turbott Wolfe* by William Plomer (Hogarth Press); *The Whole Story* by Princess Bibesco (Hutchinson); *Portrait of a Man With Red Hair* by Hugh Walpole (Macmillan); and *Simonetta Perkins* by L. P. Hartley (Putnam).

BIOGRAPHY: *The Diary of a Country Parson*, edited by John Beresford (Oxford University Press); *The First Napoleon: Some Unpublished Documents from the Bowood Papers*, edited by the Earl of Kerry (Constable); *The Later Correspondence of Lord John Russell*, edited by G. P. Gooch (Longmans); *The Correspondence of Samuel Pepys, 1679–1703*, edited by J. R. Tanner (Bell); *Twenty-five Years, 1892–1916*, by Viscount Grey (Hodder & Stoughton); *Letters on Literature by Anton Chekhov* (Bles); *The (Official) Life of Benito Mussolini* by Margherita G. Sarfatti (Butterworth); The Life and Letters of W. T. Stead (Cape); *The Diary of Princess Lieven* (Cape); *The Letters of Anton Pavlovitch Tchehov to Olga Knipper* (Chatto & Windus); *The Memoirs of Raymond Poincare* (Heinemann); *Joseph Conrad as I Knew Him* by Jessie Conrad (Heinemann); *A New Series of Intimate Biographies* (Cobbett, Savonarola, Stevenson, and Napoleon) by G. K. Chesterton (Hodder & Stoughton); *Disraeli: The Alien Patriot* by E. T. Raymond (Hodder & Stoughton); *Reminiscences of a Student's Life* by Jane E. Harrison (Hogarth Press); *The Confessions of a Capitalist* by Sir Ernest Benn (Hutchinson); *Disraeli and Gladstone* by D. C. Somervell (Jarrolds); *The Fugger News-Letters: Second Series* (Lane); *Henry Montagu Butler* by J. R. M. Butler (Longmans); *Letters of Sir Walther Raleigh* (Methuen); *More Changes, More Chances* by H. W. Nevinson (Nisbet); *Essays in Biography* by Bonamy Dobree (Oxford University Press); and *The Life of Racine* by Mary Duclaux (Fisher Unwin).

CRITICISM AND EDUCATIONAL STUDIES: *Dostoevsky* by Andre Gide (Dent); *Collected Essays of W. P. Ker* (Macmillan); *French Studies and Reviews* by Richard Aldington (Allen & Unwin); *Keats and Shakespeare* by J. Middleton Murry (Oxford University Press); *The Writing of Fiction* by Edith Wharton (Scribner); *Shakespeare: A Survey* by E. K. Chambers (Sidgwick & Jackson); *The Story of the Old Vic* by Lilian Baylis and Cicely Hamilton (Cape); *British Drama* by Allardyce Nicoll (Harrap); *Our Public Elementary Schools* by Sir Michael Sadler (Butterworth); and *Spiritual Values in Adult Education* by Basil Yeaxlee (Oxford University Press).

HISTORY, POLITICS, SOCIOLOGY, AND ECONOMICS: *The Cambridge Ancient History*, Vol. III and *The Cambridge Medieval History*. Vol. V (Cambridge University Press); *History of Ireland, 1798–1924* by Sir James

O'Connor (Arnold); *The Pioneers of the French Revolution* by M. Roustan (Benn); *The Other Side of the Medal* by E. J. Thompson (Hogarth Press); *The Rise of Modern Industry* by J. L. Hammond and Barbara Hammond (Methuen); *Mr. Secretary Walsingham and the Policy of Queen Elizabeth* by Conyers Read (Oxford University Press); *Mesopotamia* by Prof. L. Delaporte (Routledge); *International Anarchy* by G. Lowes Dickinson (Allen & Unwin); *Free Thought in the Social Sciences* by J. A. Hobson (Allen & Unwin); *England's Green and Pleasant Land* (Cape); *Unemployment: Its Causes and Cure* by J. L. F. Vogel (Chapman & Hall); *The Peril of the White* by Sir L. Chiozza Money (Collins); *The Intelligent Women's Guide to Capitalism and Socialism* by Bernard Shaw (Constable); *The Social Significance of Death Duties* by Prof. Rignano (Noel Douglas); *Financial Reconstruction in England, 1815–1822* by A. W. Acworth (King); *A Short History of the British Working Class* by G. D. H. Cole (Labour Publishing Co.); *Memorials of Alfred Marshall: Collected Papers* (Macmillan); *Religion and the Rise of Capitalism* by R. H. Tawney (Murray); *The History of Witchcraft* by Montague Summers (Routledge); *Fundamental Thoughts in Economics* by G. Cassel (Fisher Unwin); and *Germany's Industrial Revival* by Sir Philip Dawson (Williams & Norgate).

NEW EDITIONS: *Fonthill Edition of William Beckford* (Guy Chapman); *The Novels of Henry Fielding* (Blackwell); *The Novels of Tobias Smollett* (Blackwell); *The Works of the Earl of Rochester* (Nonesuch Press); and Burton's *Anatomy of Melancholy* (Nonesuch Press).

"Biographies," "The World of Books" column, *The Nation & The Athenaeum* 38 (17 October 1925): 117. Reviews of *Henry Montagu Butler* by his son, J. R. M. Butler (Longmans); *Monarchs and Millionaires* by Lalla Vandervelde (Butterworth); *Myself Not Least, Being the Personal Reminiscences of X* (Butterworth); *The (Official) Life of Benito Mussolini* by Margherita G. Sarfatti (Butterworth); and *Disraeli and Gladstone* by D. C. Somervell (Jarrolds).

"Viscount Grey," "The World of Books" column, *The Nation & The Athenaeum* 38 (24 October 1925): 151. Review of *Twenty-five Years, 1892–1916*, 2 vols., by Viscount Grey (Hodder & Stoughton).

"Crime," "The World of Books" column, *The Nation & The Athenaeum* 38 (31 October 1925): 183. Reviews of *Trial of Ronald True*, edited by Donald Carswell, Notable British Trials series (Hodge); *Murder, Piracy, and Treason, a Selection of Notable English Trials* by Raymond Postgate (Cape); *Tales of Bohemia, Taverns, and the Underworld* by Stanley Scott (Hurst & Blackett); *Dramatic Days at the Old Bailey by Charles Kingston*, The Library of Crime series (Stanley Paul); and *Famous Crimes and Criminals* by C. L. McCluer Stevens The Library of Crime series (Stanley Paul).

"A Painful Mystery," "The World of Books" column, *The Nation & The Athenaeum* 38 (7 November 1925): 217. Review of *Lions 'n Tigers 'n Everything* by Courtney Ryley Cooper (Cape). Mention of *My Friend Toto* by Cherry Kearton (Arrowsmith).

"Charlotte Bronte," "The World of Books" column, *The Nation & The Athenaeum* 38 (14 November 1925): 260. Review essay on *The Twelve Adventurers and Other Stories* by Charlotte Bronte (Hodder & Stoughton).

"Disraeli," "The World of Books" column, *The Nation & The Athenaeum* 38 (21 November 1925): 292. Review essay on *Ixion in Heaven* by Benjamin Disraeli (Cape); *Disraeli and Gladstone* by D. C. Somervell (Jarrolds); and *Disraeli: The Alien Patriot* by E. T. Raymond (Hodder & Stoughton).

"The Eighteen Century," "The World of Books" column, *The Nation & The Athenaeum* 38 (28 November 1925): 322. Review essay on *Lyme Letters, 1660–1760* by Lady Newton (Heinemann); *Lord Fife and His Factor* [letters, 1760–1800, of Lord Fife to his factor, William Rose] (Heinemann); *The Diary of Thomas Turner, of East Hoathly, Sussex (1754–1765)* by Thomas Turner (Bodley Head); and *The Canning Wonder* by Arthur Machen (Chatto & Windus).

"'Jug Jug' to Dirty Ears," "The World of Books" column, *The Nation & The Athenaeum* 38 (5 December 1925): 354. Reviews of *Human Shows: Far Phantasies: Songs and Trifles* by Thomas Hardy (Macmillan); *English Poems* by Edmund Blunden (Cobden-Sanderson); and *Poems, 1909–1925* by T. S. Eliot (Faber & Gwyer).

"The New Art of Biography," "The World of Books" column, *The Nation & The Athenaeum* 38 (12 December 1925): 404. Review essay on *Essays in Biography* by Bonamy Dobree (Oxford University Press) and *The Life of Florence Nightingale* by Sir Edward Cook, abridged edition (Macmillan).

"English Prose," "The World of Books" column, *The Nation & The Athenaeum* 38 (19 December 1925): 438. Review essay on *The Oxford Book of English Verse*, edited by Q and *The Oxford Book of English Prose*, chosen and edited by Sir Arthur Quiller-Couch (Clarendon Press).

"The Overbury Mystery," "The World of Books" column, *The Nation & The Athenaeum* 38 (26 December 1925): 470. Review of *The Overbury Mystery* by His Honour Judge Edward Abbott Parry (Fisher Unwin).

"The End of Hickey," "The World of Books" column, *The Nation & The Athenaeum* 38 (2 January 1926): 497. Review of *Memoirs of William Hickey*, Vol. 4, (Hurst & Blackett).

"Handwriting and Character," "The World of Books" column, *The Nation & The Athenaeum* 38 (9 January 1926): 525. Review of *The Psychology of Handwriting* by Robert Saudek (Allen & Unwin).

"Laurence Sterne," "The World of Books" column, *The Nation & The Athenaeum* 38 (16 January 1926): 554. Review of *The Life and Times of Laurence Sterne*, 2 vols., by Wilbur L. Cross (Milford).

"Are the 'Two Discarnate Spirits'?" "The World of Books" column, *The Nation & The Athenaeum* 38 (23 January 1926): 585. Review of *The Facts of Psychic Science and Philosophy, Collated and Discussed* by A. Campbell Holms (Kegan Paul).

"Who Caused the French Revolution?" "The World of Books" column, *The Nation & The Athenaeum* 38 (30 January 1926): 615. Review of *Pioneers of the French Revolution* by W. Roustan, translated by Frederic Whyte, The Library of European Political Thought (Benn).

"Mr. Pepys and Modernity," "The World of Books" column, *The Nation & The Athenaeum* 38 (6 February 1926): 647. Review of *Private Correspondence and Miscellaneous Papers of Samuel Pepys, 1679–1703, in the Possession of J. Pepys Cockerell*, 2 vols., edited by J. R. Tanner (Bell).

"A Moratorium for Poetry," "The World of Books" column, *The Nation & The Athenaeum* 38 (13 February 1926): 682. Review essay on *What's O'Clock* by Amy Lowell (Cape); *The Bridle-Way* by the Earl of Sandwich (Elkin Mathews); *Poems* by Mary E. Drinkwater (Simpkin); *Collected Poems* by Teresa Hooley (Cape); *Odes and Oddities* by A. G. Hamilton (Horseshoe Printing Co.); *Fairies and Fantasy* by A. T. Wynyard-Wright (Horseshoe Publishing Co.); *Poems* by Lewis W. Townsend (High House Press); *The Assaying of Brabantius* by C. S. Sherrington (Oxford University Press); *Nature Dialogues* by N. M. Copland (Claude Stacey); and thirteen volumes in the Augustan Books of English Poetry series (Benn).

"A Plentiful Lack of Wit," "The World of Books" column, *The Nation & The Athenaeum* 38 (20 February 1926): 717. Reviews of *Frederic Harrison, Thoughts and Memories*, by Austin Harrison (Heinemann); *James Leigh Strachan-Davidson, Master of Balliol* [memoir], by J. W. Mackail (Clarendon Press); *The Memoirs of Sir David Erskine of Cardross*, edited by Mrs. Steuart Erskine (Fisher Unwin); *Echoes and Memories* by Bramwell Booth (Hodder & Stoughton).

"Queen Victoria," "The World of Books" column, *The Nation & The Athenaeum* 38 (27 February 1926): 746. Review of *The Letters of Queen Victoria*, 2 vols., second series (Murray).

"Bad Dreams," "The World of Books" column, *The Nation & The Athenaeum* 38 (6 March 1926): 778. Review essay on *International Anarchy,1904–1914* by G. Lowes Dickinson (Allen & Unwin).

"The Promise of Spring," "The World of Books" column, *The Nation & The Athenaeum* 38 (13 March 1926): 810. List of recently published books:
POETRY: *The Bird of Paradise, and Other Poems* by Mr. Davies (Cape); *Confessio Juvenis* by Richard Hughes (Chatto & Windus); *Collected Poems* by Mr. [Edward?] Shanks (Collins); and *The Works of J. C. Squire* (Heinemann).

NOVELS: *The World of William Clissold* by Mr. [H. G.?]Wells (Benn); *The Silver Spoon* by John Galsworthy (Heinemann); *Odtaa* by Mr. [John?] Masefield (Heinemann); *Two or Three Graces* by Aldous Huxley (Chatto & Windus); *Crewe Train* by Rose Macauley (Collins); *The Wharf and Other Stories* by Walter de la Mare (Collins); *The Plumed Serpent* by D. H. Lawrence (Secker); *From Man to Man* by Olive Schreiner (Fisher Unwin); *How to Write Short Stories* and *Gullible's Travels* by Ring Lardner (Chatto & Windus); *The Job* by Sinclair Lewis (Cape); and *Appassionata* by Fannie Hurst (Cape).

SCIENCE: *Science and the Modern World* by A. N. Whitehead (Cambridge University Press); *The Quantum Theory of the Atom* by G. Birtwistle (Cambridge University Press); *Atomicity and Quanta* by J. H. Jeans (Cambridge University Press); *The New Heat Theorem* by Professor W. Nernst (Methuen); *Sex in Man and Animals* by John R. Baker (Routledge); and *The Origin of Birds* by Gerhard Heilman (Witherby).

BIOGRAPHY: *Life of Frederick William, the Great Elector of Brandenburg* by C. E. Maurice (Allen & Unwin); *Catherine the Great* by Katherine Anthony (Cape); *Henry Jackson, O. M.* by R. St. John Parry (Cambridge University Press); *Letters of Sir Walter Raleigh* (Metheun); *The Letters of Queen Victoria, Second Series, 1862–1878* (Murray); *My Apprenticeship* by Mrs. Sidney Webb (Longmans); *The Diary of a Country Parson*, Vol. II (Oxford University Press); *Mary Macarthur* by Mrs. Hamilton (Parsons); *The Life and Letters of Thomas Jefferson* by F. W. Hirst (Macmillan); *Jefferson and Hamilton* by C. G. Bowers (Constable); *The Intimate Papers of Colonel House* (Benn); *James Joyce* by Herbert S. Gorman (Bles); *Leon Trotsky* by Max Eastman (Faber & Gwyer); and *Seventy Years a Showman* by "Lord" George Sanger (reprint; Dent).

"Another Empress," "The World of Books" column, *The Nation & The Athenaeum* 38 (20 March 1926): 862. Review essay on *Catherine the Great* by Katherine Anthony (Cape).

"Preacher or Artist," "The World of Books" column, *The Nation & The Athenaeum* 38 (27 March 1926): 896. Review essay on *The Modern Ibsen, a Reconsideration* by Hermann J. Weigand (Dent).

"Havelock Ellis," "The World of Books" column, *The Nation & The Athenaeum* 39 (3 April 1926): 17. Review of *Impressions and Comments* (First and Second Series), *Affirmations*, and *The World of Dreams* by Havelock Ellis (reprint; Constable).

"Living Vicariously," "The World of Books" column, *The Nation & The Athenaeum* 39 (10 April 1926): 45. Reviews of *The Diary of a Country Parson*, Vol. II: *1782–1787*, by James Woodforde, edited by John Beresford (Milford); *Seventy Years a Showman* by "Lord" George Sanger, with an introduction by Kenneth Grahame (reprint; Dent); *Recollected in Tranquillity* by Janet E.

Courtney (Heinemann); *Naphtali* by C. Lewis Hind (Bodley Head); and *Hubert Parry*, 2 vols., by Charles L. Graves (Macmillan).

"Science and Scientists," "The World of Books" column, *The Nation & The Athenaeum* 39 (17 April 1926): 74. Review essay on *Why We Behave Like Human Beings* by George A. Dorsey (Harper); *Science and Poetry* by I. A. Richards, Psyche Miniature Series (Kegan Paul); *Aphasia* by S. A. Kinnier Wilson, Psyche Miniature Series (Kegan Paul); and *Evolution and Creation* by Sir Oliver Lodge (Hodder & Stoughton).

"Mutton and Sheep," "The World of Books" column, *The Nation & The Athenaeum* 39 (24 April 1926): 102. Review essay on the following paperback books in the Essays of Today and Yesterday series (Harrap): *Philip Guedalla*; *Andrew Lang*; *Basil MacDonald Hastings*; *James Agate*; *Barry Pain*; and *Alice Meynell*.

"Out of the Wilderness," "The World of Books" column, *The Nation & The Athenaeum* 39 (1 May 1926): 130. Review essay on *Abraham Lincoln*, 2 vols., by Carl Sandburg (Cape).

"The Art of Thought," "The World of Books" column, *The Nation & The Athenaeum* 39 (22 May 1926): 178. Reviews of *The Art of Thought* by Professor Graham Wallas (Cape) and *The Language and Thought of the Child* by Jean Piaget, International Library of Psychology, Philosophy, and Scientific Method series (Kegan Paul).

"Racial Fantasies," "The World of Books" column, *The Nation & The Athenaeum* 39 (29 May 1926): 209. Reviews of *To-day and To-morrow: the Testing Period of the White Race* by J. H. Curle (Methuen) and *Race and History, an Ethnological Introduction to History* by Eugene Pittard (Kegan Paul).

"From Talleyrand to Mr. Harriman," "The World of Books" column, *The Nation & The Athenaeum* 39 (5 June 1926): 250. Reviews of *The Romantic Diplomat* [Talleyrand, Metternich, and Chateaubriand] by M. Paleogue (Hutchinson) and *Dollar Diplomacy* by Scott Nearing and Joseph Freeman (Allen & Unwin).

"Rationalism and Religion," "The World of Books" column, *The Nation & The Athenaeum* 39 (12 June 1926): 279. Review essay on *Essays in Religion* by A. Clutton-Brock (Methuen); *The Dynamics of Religion* by J. M. Robertson (Watts, New Edition); *The Religion of an Artist* by the Hon. John Collier (Watts); and *Death-Bed Visions* by Sir William Barrett, F. R. S. (Methuen).

"George Meredith," "The World of Books" column, *The Nation & The Athenaeum* 39 (19 June 1926): 323. Review essay on *George Meredith* by J. B. Priestly (Macmillan).

"Please, Sir…," "The World of Books" column, *The Nation & The Athenaeum* 39 (26 June 1926): 355. Review essay on *The Memoirs of Raymond Poincare*, translated and adapted by Sir George Arthur, with a preface by the Duke of

Northumberland, K. G. (Heinemann); an English translation of *The Limitations of Victory* by M. Fabre-Luce (Allen & Unwin); and *Sarajevo* by Dr. R. W. Seton-Watson (Hutchinson).

"Queerish Talk in the Circumstances," "The World of Books" column, *The Nation & The Athenaeum* 39 (3 July 1926): 386. Review essay on Walter de la Mare's prose works, including *The Connoisseur* (Collins); *Memoirs of a Midget* (reprint; Collins); *Henry Brocken* (reprint; Collins); and *The Return* (reprint; Collins), as well as the assessment of Gerald Bullett in *Modern English Fiction* (Jenkins).

"English History," "The World of Books" column, *The Nation & The Athenaeum* 39 (10 July 1926): 418. Review essay on G. M. Trevelyan's *History of England* (Longmans).

"In the Cave," "The World of Books" column, *The Nation & The Athenaeum* 39 (17 July 1926): 446. Review essay on *Must Britain Travel the Moscow Road?* by Norman Angell (Noel Douglas) and *The Creed of a Tory* by Pierse Loftus (Philip Allan).

"The Hohenzollern Mind," "The World of Books" column, *The Nation & The Athenaeum* 39 (24 July 1926): 474. Review essay on *I Seek the Truth: a Book on Responsibility for the War* by the ex-Crown Prince Wilhelm of Germany (Faber & Gwyer).

"Fielding's Novels," "The World of Books" column, *The Nation & The Athenaeum* 39 (31 July 1926): 503. Review essay on Henry Fielding and his *The Life of Mr. Jonathan Wild the Great*, the Shakespeare Head Edition of Fielding's Novels (Blackwell).

"Sir Roger Casement and Charles Peace," "The World of Books" column, *The Nation & The Athenaeum* 39 (7 August 1926): 530. Review essay on the *Trial of Roger Casement*, edited by G. H. Knott, the Notable British Trials series (Hodge); *Scotland Yard* by Joseph Gollomb (Hutchinson); *Black Fame* by J. C. Ellis (Hutchinson); *Carlo Guesaldo, Musician and Murderer* by Cecil Gray and Philip Heseltine (Kegan Paul); and *The Rise and Fall of Jesse James* by Robertus Love (Putnam).

"Gotterdammerung," "The World of Books" column, *The Nation & The Athenaeum* 39 (14 August 1926): 558. Review of *The Decline of the West; Form and Actuality* by Oswald Spengler, authorized translation with notes by Charles Francis Atkinson (Allen & Unwin).

"The Apollinian Soul," "The World of Books" column, *The Nation & The Athenaeum* 39 (21 August 1926): 586. Review essay on the following books: These books in the Loeb Classical Library series: Plato's *Laws*, Books 1–6; Demosthenes' *De Corona* and *De Falsa Legatione*; Plutarch's *Lives of Aratus, Artaxerxes, Galba and Otho*; Epictetus' *Discourses*, Books 1 and 2; Josephus'

The Life and *Against Apion*; and Pausanias Books 3 and 4 (Heinemann). And a translation of *Hellenic Civilization* by M. Maurice Croiset (Knopf).

"The Art of Cricket," "The World of Books" column, *The Nation & The Athenaeum* 39 (28 August 1926): 614. Review essay on *Between the Wickets*, compiled by Eric Parker (Philip Allan), with a short list of other recent books on sports: *The Lawn Tennis Masters Unveiled* by B. H. Liddell Hart (Arrowsmith); *Better Golf* by Percy Alliss (A. & C. Black); and *The Art of Boxing* by Georges Carpentier (Harrap).

"Political Rationalism," "The World of Books" column, *The Nation & The Athenaeum* 39 (4 September 1926): 642. Review of *An Inquiry Concerning Political Justice and Its Influence on General Virtue and Happiness*, 2 vols., by William Godwin, edited and abridged by Raymond A. Preston (1793; Knopf).

"Mr. Galsworthy," "The World of Books" column, *The Nation & The Athenaeum* 39 (11 September 1926): 674. Review essay on John Galsworthy's works, including his latest, *The Silver Spoon* (Heinemann).

"Bogeys," "The World of Books" column, *The Nation & The Athenaeum* 39 (18 September 1926): 703. Review essay on *Essays on Nationalism* by Professor Carlton J. H. Hayes, Columbia University (Macmillan) and *The Twilight of the White Races* by Maurice Muret, translated by Mrs. Touzalin (Fisher Unwin).

"Mr. Wells v. Mr. Belloc," "The World of Books" column, *The Nation & The Athenaeum* 39 (25 September 1926): 735. Review essay on *Mr. Belloc Objects* by H. G. Wells (Watts) and on the "intellectual dogfight" between Hilaire Belloc and H. G. Wells.

"Whitewash," "The World of Books" column, *The Nation & The Athenaeum* 39 (2 October 1926): 766. Review of *George IV* by Shane Leslie (Benn).

"The Publishing Season," "The World of Books" column, *The Nation & The Athenaeum* 40 (9 October 1926): 24. List of recently published books:
BIOGRAPHY, MEMOIRS, AND LETTERS: *Life and Letters of Lord John Bryce* by H. A. L. Fisher (Macmillan); *The Early Life and Letters of John Morley* by F. W. Hirst (Macmillan); *Fifty Years of Parliament* by the Earl of Oxford and Asquith (Cassell); *The Life and Letters of Joseph Conrad* by P. Jean Aubry (Heinemann); *Joseph Conrad as I Knew Him* by Jessie Conrad (Heinemann); *Cummy's Diary* by Alison Cunningham [R. L.? Stevenson's nurse] (Chatto & Windus); *The Journals of Thomas Cobden-Sanderson* (Cobden-Sanderson); *Letters of George Gissing to His Family*, edited by Algernon and Ellen Gissing (Constable); *The Letters of Baron von Huegel* (Dent); *My Life and Times* by Jerome K. Jerome (Hodder & Stoughton); *Autobiography and Journals* of Benjamin Haydon, with a preface by Aldous Huxley (1853; reprint; Peter Davies); *The Life of Benjamin Haydon*, edited by Alexander Penrose (Bell); Autobiography of Benjamin Haydon, the World's Classics series (1853; reprint; Milford); *Napoleon* by Emil Ludwig (Allen & Unwin); *Disraeli* by D. L.

Murray (Benn); *Palmerston* by Philip Guedalla (Benn); *Certain People of Importance* by A. G. Gardiner (Cape); *Soldiers and Statesmen* by Field-Marshal Sir William Robertson (Cassell); *The Days of My Life* by Sir H. Rider Haggard (Longmans); and *My Early Life* by the Ex-Emperor of Germany (Methuen).

NOVELS: *Debits and Credits* by Rudyard Kipling (Macmillan); *The Silver Spoon* by John Galsworthy (Heinemann); *Lord Raingo* by Arnold Bennett (Cassell); *The World of William Clissold*, 3 vols., Mr. [H. G. ?] Wells (Benn); *A Wreath of Cloud*, the third part of *The Tale of Genji* by Lady Murasaki (Allen & Unwin); *Saviours of Society* by Stephen McKenna (Butterworth); *Mr. Gihooley's Mistress* by Liam O'Flaherty (Cape); *Crewe Train* by Rose Macauley (Collins); *Lud-in-the-Mist* by Hope Mirrlees (Collins); *The Casuarina Tree* by Somerset Maugham (Heinemann); *Daphne Adeane* by Maurice Baring (Heinemann); *The River Flows* by F. L. Lucas (Hogarth Press); *Good-bye Stranger* by Stella Benson (Macmillan); *From Man to Man* by Olive Schreiner (Fisher Unwin); and *Before the Bombardment* by Osbert Sitwell (Duckworth).

REPRINTS: *English Poems of Milton*, with Blake's Illustrations (Nonesuch Press); *Memories of My Grandson* by John Evelyn (Nonesuch Press); *The Lady's New-Year's-Gift or Advice to a Daughter* by the Lord Marquis of Halifax (Cayme Press); *The Metamorphosis of Pigmalion's Image* by John Marston (Golden Cockerel Press); *The Julian Shelley* (Benn); *The Works of Laurence Sterne* (Blackwell); and *The Bonchurch Edition of the Works of Algernon Charles Swinburne* (Heinemann). Noel Douglas will produce the 1609 edition of Shakespeare's Sonnets and the 1783 edition of Blake's *Poetical Sketches* as volumes in *The Noel Douglas Replicas* series.

HISTORY: *A History of the Ancient World*, Vol. I: *The Orient and Greece*, by M. Rostovtzeff (Oxford University Press); *The Gordon Riots* by J. Paul de Castro (Oxford University Press); *The History of Witchcraft and Demonology* by Montague Summers (Routledge); *The Letters of Marie Antoinette, Fersen, and Barnave* (Lane); and *Richard Cobden and Foreign Policy* by W. H. Dawson (Allen & Unwin).

CRITICISM AND ESSAYS: *On Writing and Writers* by Walter Raleigh (Arnold); *Transformations. Critical and Speculative Essays on Art* by Roger Fry (Chatto & Windus); *Fallodon Papers* by Lord Grey of Fallodon (Constable); and *Transition* by Edwin Muir (Hogarth Press).

ECONOMICS AND POLITICS: *Money* by Karl Helfferich (Benn); *Industrial Fluctuations* by A. C. Pigou (Macmillan); and *The Dying Peasant* by J. W. Robertson Scott (Williams & Norgate).

"Lord Raingo," "The World of Books" column, *The Nation & The Athenaeum* 40 (16 October 1926): 86. Review of *Lord Raingo* by Arnold Bennett (Cassell).

"The Power of the Ego," "The World of Books" column, *The Nation & The Athenaeum* 40 (23 October 1926): 114. Review essay on *Prison Memories of an Anarchist* by Alexander Berkman (Daniel); *A Great-Niece's Journals* [selections from the journals of Mrs. Wood, a great-niece of Fanny Burney], edited by Margaret S. Rolt (Constable); *The Days of My Life* by H. Rider Haggard (Longmans); *The Fire of Life* by Harold Spender (Hodder & Stoughton); and *My Reminiscences* by Victor Sampson (Longmans).

"Publishers and Old Books," "The World of Books" column, *The Nation & The Athenaeum* 40 (30 October 1926): 148. Review essay on *The Truth about Publishing* by Stanley Unwin (Allen & Unwin) and the following reprints: Five volumes of Jane Austin's works, edited by Mr. Chapman, published by Oxford University Press; facsimiles of the 1609 edition of Shakespeare's Sonnets and the 1783 edition of Blake's *Poetical Sketches*, *The Noel Douglas Replicas* series (Noel Douglas); *The Travels of Marco Polo*, with an introduction by Mr. [John?] Masefield (Dent); *The Life of Benvenuto Cellini*, translated by Anne Macdonnell (Dent); *Everybody's Pepys*, abridged and illustrated (Bell); *Moby Dick* by Herman Melville, abridged and illustrated (Cape); *A Selection of the Principal Navigations, Voyages, Traffiques and Discoveries of the English Nation* by Richard Hakluyt, illustrated by Laurence Irving (Heinemann); and *Irene Iddesleigh* by Amanda M'Kittrick Ros (Nonesuch).

"The All-Highest," "The World of Books" column, *The Nation & The Athenaeum* 40 (6 November 1926): 184. Review essay on *Kaiser Wilhelm II* by Emil Ludwig, translated from German by Ethel Colburn Mayne (Putnam) and *Chronicles of the Prussian Court* by Miss Topham [a governess at the Kaiser's Court] (Hutchinson).

"The Sum of All Villanies," "The World of Books" column, *The Nation & The Athenaeum* 40 (13 November 1926): 220. Review essay on *British Slavery and its Abolition, 1823-1838* by William Law Mathieson (Longmans).

"Sugar and Soap and Salt," "The World of Books" column, *The Nation & The Athenaeum* 40 (20 November 1926): 271. Review essay on *My Early Life* by William II, Emperor of Germany (Methuen); *Kaiser Wilhelm II* by Emil Ludwig, translated from German by Ethel Colburn Mayne (Putnam); *H. R. H., a Character Study of the Prince of Wales* by Major F. E. Verney (Hodder & Stoughton); *Demosthenes* by Georges Clemenceau (Hodder & Stoughton); *Rabindranath Tagore* by E. J. Thompson (Oxford University Press); *Havelock Ellis* by Issac Goldberg (Constable); and *Skin for Skin* by Llewelyn Powys (Cape).

"Mr. Roger Fry," "The World of Books" column, *The Nation & The Athenaeum* 40 (27 November 1926): 304. Review of *Transformations. Critical and Speculative Essays on Art* by Roger Fry (Chatto & Windus)

"Palmerston," "The World of Books" column, *The Nation & The Athenaeum* 40 (4 December 1926): 230. Review of *Palmerston* by Philip Guedalla (Benn).

"Faith and the Slave Trade," *The Nation & The Athenaeum* 40 (4 December 1926): 333. Letter to the editor. L. Woolf responds to an article by John Lee on the abolition of the slave trade. Woolf quotes from *British Slavery and its Abolition, 1823–1838* by William Law Mathieson (Longmans) which he reviewed on 13 November 1926. See "The Sum of All Villanies" above.

"Carlyle," "The World of Books" column, *The Nation & The Athenaeum* 40 (11 December 1926): 388. Review of *Thomas Carlyle* by Mary Agnes Hamilton, The Roadmaker Series (Parsons).

"Faith and the Slave Trade," *The Nation & The Athenaeum* 40 (18 December 1926): 418. Letter to the editor. L. Woolf responds to John Lee's comments on the abolition of the slave trade. See 4 December 1926 above.

"Cobden and Cobdenism," "The World of Books" column, *The Nation & The Athenaeum* 40 (18 December 1926): 424. Review essay on *Richard Cobden and Foreign Policy* by W. H. Dawson (Allen & Unwin).

"The Psychology of Methodism," "The World of Books" column, *The Nation & The Athenaeum* 40 (24 December 1926): 454. Review essay on *The Psychology of the Methodist Revival* by Sydney G. Dimond (Oxford University Press and Milford) and *Up from Methodism, a Study in Religious Intolerance* by Herbert Asbury (Knopf).

"Life That Is a Vision," "The World of Books" column, *The Nation & The Athenaeum* 40 (1 January 1927): 482. Review essay on Yeats' Collected Works (Macmillan); *Memoir of Jane Austen* by her nephew, James Edward Austen-Leigh (Clarendon Press); *The Passionate Pilgrim, or Eros and Aneros* by Francis Turner Palgrave, with and introduction by R. Brimley Johnson (Peter Davies); *The Adventures of Johnny Walker, Tramp* by Mr. W. H. Davies (Cape); *Osman Digna* by Mr. H. C. Jackson, Sudan Political Service (Methuen); and *My Fifty Years* by Prince Nicholas of Greece [brother of King Constantine] (Hutchinson).

"Disraeli the Novelist," "The World of Books" column, *The Nation & The Athenaeum* 40 (8 January 1927): 510. Review essay on *Vivian Grey*, *The Young Duke*, and *Popanilla and Other Tales* by Benjamin Disraeli, The Bradenham Edition (Peter Davies).

"Shakespeare and Machiavelli," "The World of Books" column, *The Nation & The Athenaeum* 40 (15 January 1927): 539. Review of *The Lion and the Fox, the Role of the Hero in the Plays of Shakespeare* by Wyndham Lewis (Grant Richards).

"Anthony Trollope," "The World of Books" column, *The Nation & The Athenaeum* 40 (22 January 1927): 565. Review essay on *The Warden* by Anthony Trollope (reprint; E. Mathews) and *Trollope, A Commentary* by Michael Sadleir (Constable).

"The Apotheosis of Journalism," "The World of Books" column, *The Nation & The Athenaeum* 40 (29 January 1927): 594. Review essay on *The Making of Modern Journalism* by Harold Herd (Allen & Unwin) and journalism.

"John Morley," "The World of Books" column, *The Nation & The Athenaeum* 40 (5 February 1927): 627. Review of *Early Life and Letters of John Morley*, 2 vols., by Mr. F. W. Hirst (Macmillan).

"British Genius," "The World of Books" column, *The Nation & The Athenaeum* 40 (12 February 1927): 663. Review of *A Study of British Genius* by Havelock Ellis, revised edition (Constable).

"Political Ideas and Political Delusions," "The World of Books" column, *The Nation & The Athenaeum* 40 (19 February 1927): 698. Review essay on *The Science and Method of Politics* by G. E. G. Catlin (Kegan Paul); *Notes on Democracy* by H. L. Mencken (Cape); and *Political Myths and Economic Realities* by Francis Delaisi (Noel Douglas).

"Detective Stories," "The World of Books" column, *The Nation & The Athenaeum* 40 (26 February 1927): 727. Review essay on *The Mystery of Belvoir Mansions* by Ben Bolt (Ward, Lock); *The Colfax Bookplate* by Agnes Miller (Benn); *The Big Four* by Mrs. [Agatha?] Christie (Collins); *The Three Taps* by Ronald A. Knox (Methuen); and *The Crime at Diana's Pool* by Victor L. Whitechurch (Fisher Unwin).

"Old Europe," "The World of Books" column, *The Nation & The Athenaeum* 40 (5 March 1927): 760. Review essay on *A Diplomatist in Europe* by Sir Arthur Hardinge, former Ambassador to Spain (Cape); *Under Three Emperors* by Baron von Reischach, former Master of the Horse or Controller of the Imperial Household, translated into English by Prince Bluecher (Constable); and *Disraeli* by D. L. Murray.

"The Promise of Spring," "The World of Books" column, *The Nation & The Athenaeum* 40 (12 March 1927):798. List of recently published books:

ART AND ARCHITECTURE: *Cezanne and His Circle* by Julius Meir-Graeffe (Benn); *Catalogue of the Eumorfopoulos Frescoes* (Benn); *Landmarks in Nineteenth-Century Painting* by Clive Bell (Chatto & Windus); and *Spanish Art* by R. R. Tatlock, Sir C. Holmes, et al. (Batsford).

BIOGRAPHY: *Napoleon* by Emil Ludwig (Allen & Unwin); *Revolt in the Desert* by Colonel T. E. Lawrence (Cape); *Trollope, A Commentary* by Michael Sadleir (Constable); *Letters of George Gissing to His Family*, edited by Algernon and Ellen Gissing (Constable); *Oscar Browning* by H. E. Wortham (Constable); *The Correspondence of Edmund Burke* (Faber & Gwyer); *Disraeli* by Andre Maurois (Lane); *Early Life and Letters of John Morley*, 2 vols., by Mr. F. W. Hirst (Macmillan); *The Life and Letters of John Bryce* by H. A. L. Fisher (Macmillan); *A Great Man's Friendship* [letters of the Duke of Wellington to Mary, Marchioness of Salisbury] (Murray); *The Life and Letters of Joseph*

Conrad by P. Jean Aubry (Heinemann); and *The Private Diary of Leo Tolstoy, 1853–1857*, edited by Aylmer Maude (Heinemann).

FICTION: *A Wreath of Cloud*, the third part of *The Tale of Genji* by Lady Murasaki (Allen & Unwin); *The Woman Who Stole Everything* by Arnold Bennett (Cassell); *Sister Carrie* by Theodore Dreiser (Constable); *To the Lighthouse* by Virginia Woolf (Hogarth Press); and *She Must Go* by David Garnett (Chatto & Windus). History: *The World Crisis, 1916–1918* by Winston Churchill (Butterworth); *Five Centuries of Religion*, Vol. III, by G. G. Coulton (Cambridge University Press); and *English Democratic Ideas in the Seventeenth Century* by G. P. Gooch (Cambridge University Press).

NEW EDITIONS: *The Complete Works of Walter Savage Landor*, edited by Earle Welby, 16 volumes (Chapman & Hall).

SOCIOLOGY: *English Local Government*, Vol. VII, by Beatrice and Sidney Webb (Longmans).

TRAVEL: *Mornings in Mexico* by D. H. Lawrence (Seeker).

MUSIC: *The Escape from Beethoven* by W. J. Turner (Benn); *Beethoven's Pianoforte Sonatas* by William Behrend (Dent); *The Unconscious Beethoven* by Ernest Newman (Parsons); and *Ludwig van Beethoven* by Harvey Grace (Kegan Paul).

CRITICISM: *A History of the Late Eighteenth-Century Drama* by Allardyce Nicholl (Cambridge University Press); *Charles M. Doughty* by Barker Fairley (Cape); *On the Poems of Henry Vaughan* by Edmund Blunden (Cobden-Sanderson); *Second Essays in Literature* by Edmund Shanks (Collins); *Dryden* by Montague Summers (Routledge); and four volumes in the English Men of Letters Series: *Hood* by E. V. Knox; *Peacock* by J. B. Priestly; *Horace Walpole* by Dorothy Stuart; and *Oscar Wilde* by H. C. Harwood.

NOVELS: *Twilight Sleep* by Edith Wharton (Appleton); *Bernard Quesnay* by Andre Maurois (Cape); *Elmer Gantry* by Sinclair Lewis (Cape); *Rogues and Vagabonds* by Compton Mackenzie (Cassell); *Decadence* by Maxim Gorki (Cassell); *The Tapestry* by J. D. Beresford (Collins); *I Speak of Africa* by William Plomer (Hogarth Press); *The Marionette* by Edwin Muir (Hogarth Press); *Your Cuckoo Sings by Kind* by Valentine Dobree (Knopf); *The Gallion's Reach* by H. M. Tomlinson (Heinemann); and *Mortal Image* by Elinor Wylie (Heinemann).

ECONOMICS: *Money* by Karl Helfferich (Benn); *An Economist's Protest* by Edwin Cannan (King); *Industrial Fluctuations* by A. C. Pigou (Macmillan); and *Official Papers* by Alfred Marshall (Macmillan).

PHILOSOPHY: *The Analysis of Matter* by Bertrand Russell (Kegan Paul) and *Modern Humanists Reconsidered* by J. M. Robertson (Watts).

POETRY: *Requiem* by Humbert Wolfe (Benn); *Poems* by Camilla Doyle (Benn); *Stuff and Nonsense* by Walter de la Mare (Constable); *Meleager* by

R. C. Trevelyan (Hogarth Press); *Rustic Edges* by Edith Sitwell (Duckworth); *The Cyder Feast* by Sacheverell Sitwell (Duckworth); and *Poems, 1914–1926* by Robert Graves (Heinemann).

PSYCHOLOGY: *The Development of Psychopathology* by Bernard Hart (Cambridge University Press); *The Ego and the Id* by Sigmund Freud (Hogarth Press); and *The Conduct of Life* by William McDougall (Methuen).

SOCIOLOGY: *Bolshevism, Fascism, and Democracy* by Francesco Nitti (Allen & Unwin); *The Conditions of Industrial Peace* by J. A. Hobson (Allen & Unwin); *Political Myths and Economic Realities* by F. Delaisi (Noel Douglas); *The Anatomy of African Misery* by Lord Olivier (Hogarth Press); and *Life and the Law* by the Earl of Birkenhead (Hodder & Stoughton).

"On Advertising Books," *The Nation & The Athenaeum* 40 (19 March 1927): 848–49. An essay on the role of advertising in the book trade.

"The Epic of the Modern Man," "The World of Books" column, *The Nation & The Athenaeum* 40 (19 March 1927): 857. Review of *Revolt in the Desert* by Colonel T. E. Lawrence (Cape). Woolf compares this book with *Arabia Deserta* by Charles Doughty.

"The Man Beethoven," "The World of Books" column, *The Nation & The Athenaeum* 40 (26 March 1927): 894. Review essay on *The Escape from Beethoven* by W. J. Turner (Benn); *The Unconscious Beethoven* by Ernest Newman (Parsons); *Beethoven: The Man* by M. Andre de Hevesy, translated by Mr. Flint (Faber & Gwyer); *Ludwig van Beethoven* by Harvey Grace (Kegan Paul); *Beethoven's Pianoforte Sonatas* by William Behrend (Dent); and *Beethoven* by Paul Bekker, [in translation] International Library of Books on Music series (Dent).

"The Armstrong Case," "The World of Books" column, *The Nation & The Athenaeum* 40 (2 April 1927): 927. Review of *Herbert Rowse Armstrong*, edited by Filson Young, Notable British Trials series (Hodge).

"The Eighteenth Century," "The World of Books" column, *The Nation & The Athenaeum* 41 (9 April 1927): 18. Review essay on three new books in The Broadway Library of Eighteenth-Century French Literature series: *Dialogues* by Denis Diderot, translated by Francis Birrell; *The Sofa: a Moral Tale* by Crebillon fils, translated by Bonamy Dobree; *Letters of Voltaire and Frederick the Great*, translated by Richard Aldington (Routledge); and on *Voltaire's Candide and Other Romances*, translated by Richard Aldington, with an introduction by Sir Edmund Gosse, Broadway Translations series (Routledge).

"Gulliver's Travels," "The World of Books" column, *The Nation & The Athenaeum* 41 (30 April 1927): 115. Review of the First Edition Club's reprint of *Gulliver's Travels* by Jonathan Swift (W. & G. Foyle).

"Old Books in New Covers," "The World of Books" column, *The Nation & The Athenaeum* 41 (7 May 1927): 152. Review essay on *The Shakespeare*

Head Edition of the Writings of Laurence Sterne, 7 volumes (Blackwell); The Baskerville Series volumes: *The Fountains* by Dr. Samuel Johnson and *Recollections of Charles Lamb* by George Daniel (Elkin Mathews); and *Domestic Manners in America* by Frances Trollope, with an introduction by Michael Sadlier (Routledge).

"Ancient Best Sellers," "The World of Books" column, *The Nation & The Athenaeum* 41 (14 May 1927): 186. Review of *The Light Reading of Our Ancestors* by Lord Ernle (Hutchinson).

"Edmund Burke," "The World of Books" column, *The Nation & The Athenaeum* 41 (21 May 1927): 218. Review of *Edmund Burke* by Bertram Newman (Bell).

"The Greatness of Great Men," "The World of Books" column, *The Nation & The Athenaeum* 41 (28 May 1927): 263. Review essay on *A Great Man's Friendship* [letters from the Duke of Wellington to Mary, Marchioness of Salisbury], edited by Lady Burghclere (Murray); *Cavour* [influential Italian statesman and politician] by Maurice Paleologue, translated from French (Benn); and *British Foreign Secretaries, 1807–1916* by Algernon Cecil (Bell).

"Crime and Punishment," "The World of Books" column, *The Nation & The Athenaeum* 41 (4 June 1927): 307. Review essay on *Capital Punishment in the Twentieth Century* by E. Roy Calvert (Putnam); *The Convict of To-day* by Sydney A. Moseley (Palmer); *The Psychology of Murder, a Study in Criminal Psychology* by Andreas Bjerre (Longmans).

"Nationality and Race," "The World of Books" column, *The Nation & The Athenaeum* 41 (11 June 1927): 339. Review essay on *National Character, and the Factors in its Formation* by Ernest Barker (Methuen).

"Man and —— ?" "The World of Books" column, *The Nation & The Athenaeum* 41 (18 June 1927): 371. Review of *John Sargent* [John Singer Sargent] by the Hon. Evan Charteris (Heinemann).

"Old Books, Old Authors, and Old Publishers," "The World of Books" column, *The Nation & The Athenaeum* 41 (25 June 1927): 416. Review essay on *Authorship in the Days of Johnson* by A. S. Collins (Holden) and *Shadows of the Old Booksellers* by Charles Knight, with an introduction by Stanley Unwin (Peter Davies).

"Ben Jonson," "The World of Books" column, *The Nation & The Athenaeum* 41 (2 July 1927): 447. Review of *Ben Jonson*, Vol. 3, edited by C. H. Hereford and Percy Simpson (Clarendon Press).

"One Day...," "The World of Books" column, *The Nation & The Athenaeum* 41 (9 July 1927): 480. Review essay on *Memories of an Eighteenth-Century Footman* (John Macdonald's Travels, 1745–1779), edited by John Beresford (Routledge); *Memoirs of Mary Wollstonecraft* by William Godwin, edited by W. Clark Durant (Constable); *The Living Links* by Etienne Dupont [the life of Chevalier Destouches, the Royalist of Granville in Normandy], translated by Captain N. Fleming (Hamilton); and Aloysius Horn, edited by Ethelreda Lewis (Cape).

"Animal Life," "The World of Books" column, *The Nation & The Athenaeum* 41 (16 July 1927): 515. Review essay on *Moses My Otter* by Frances Pitt (Arrowsmith); *Tropical Aquarium Fishes, How to Breed and Rear Them* by Mr. A. E. Hodge, President of the British Aquarists' Association (Witherby); *Bird Life at Home and Abroad* by Mr. T. A. Coward (Warne); *How Birds Live* by Mr. E. M. Nicholson (Williams & Norgate); and *Social Life in the Animal World* by Fr. Alverdes (Kegan Paul).

"The Number of the Beast," "The World of Books" column, *The Nation & The Athenaeum* 41 (23 July 1923): 549. Review of *The Mind and Face of Bolshevism* by Herr Rene Fueloep-Miller (Putnam).

"The Decline and Fall of Monarchy," "The World of Books" column, *The Nation & The Athenaeum* 41 (30 July 1927): 580. Review essay on *The Memoirs of Catherine the Great of Russia* by Katherine Anthony (Knopf) and *Franz Joseph as Revealed by His Letters*, edited by Otto Ernst, translated by Agnes Blake (Methuen).

"The Big Drummers," "The World of Books" column, *The Nation & The Athenaeum* 41 (6 August 1927): 609. Review essay on *Struggles and Triumphs or The Life of P. T. Barnum Written by Himself*, 2 vols., edited by George S. Bryan (Knopf); *Trumpets of Jubilee* [biography of Lyman Beecher, his children Harriet Beecher Stowe and Henry Ward Beecher, and of the journalist Horace Greeley] by Constance Mayfield Rourke (Cape).

"A Filthy Little Atheist," "The World of Books" column, *The Nation & The Athenaeum* 41 (13 August 1927): 638. Review of *Thomas Paine, Prophet and Martyr of Democracy* by Mary Agnes Best (Allen & Unwin).

"The Revolt Against Europe," "The World of Books" column, *The Nation & The Athenaeum* 41 (20 August 1927): 666. Review of *Survey of International Affairs, 1925*, Vol. I : *The Islamic World Since the Peace Settlement* by Arnold J. Toynbee (Oxford University Press and Milford).

"From Socrates to Sacco," "The World of Books" column, *The Nation & The Athenaeum* 41 (27 August 1927): 695. Review of *Historical Trials* by Sir John Macdonell , edited by R. W. Lee (Clarendon Press).

"The Heart and Not the Brain," "The World of Books" column, *The Nation & The Athenaeum* 41 (3 September 1927): 722. Review essay on *A Victorian American, Henry Wadsworth Longfellow* by Herbert S. Gorman (Cassell) and *The Golden Day: A Study in American Experience and Culture* by Lewis Mumford (Oxford University Press and Milford).

"Rhapsody or Dusty Answer?" "The World of Books" column, *The Nation & The Athenaeum* 41 (10 September 1927): 749. Review essay on *Dusty*

Answer by Rosamond Lehmann (Chatto & Windus); *Rhapsody* by Dorothy Edwards (Wishart); and *Faint Amorist* by Elizabeth Sprigge (Knopf).

"**Montaigne**," "The World of Books" column, *The Nation & The Athenaeum* 41 (17 September 1927): 778. Review of *The Essays of Montaigne*, 2 vols., translated by E. J. Trechmann, with an introduction by J. M. Robertson (Oxford University Press and Milford).

"**The Two Journalists**," "The World of Books" column, *The Nation & The Athenaeum* 41 (24 September 1927): 806. Review essay on *Life, Journalism, and Politics* by J. A. Spender (Cassell) and *Lord Northcliffe, A Study* by R. Macnair Wilson (Benn).

"**Tolstoy's Diary**," "The World of Books" column, *The Nation & The Athenaeum* 41 (1 October 1927): 840. Review of *The Private Diary of Leo Tolstoy, 1853–1857*, translated by Mr. and Mrs. Aylmer Maude (Heinemann).

"**The Autumn Crop**," "The World of Books" column, *The Nation & The Athenaeum* 42 (8 October 1927): 22. List of recently published books:

BIOGRAPHY, MEMOIRS, AND LETTERS: *Bismarck* by Emil Ludwig (Allen & Unwin); *The Letters of Gertrude Bell* (Benn); *Shelley: His Life and Works* by Walter E. Peck; *Anatole France Abroad* by Jean Jacques Brousson (Thornton Butterworth); *Genius and Character* by Emil Ludwig (Cape); *Fifty Years in a Changing World* by Sir Valentine Chirol (Cape); *Life, Journalism, and Politics* by J. A. Spender (Cassell); *Impressions and Memories* by Lord Ribbesdale (Cassell); *All Alone: The Life and Private History of Emily Bronte* by Romer Wilson (Chatto & Windus); *The Bronte Sisters* by Ernest Dimnet (Cape); *Memoirs of Prince Max of Baden* (Constable); *Journal of Katherine Mansfield* (Constable); *Some People* by Harold Nicolson (Constable); *The Life and Letters of Joseph Conrad* by G. Jean Aubrey (Heinemann); *The Private Diary of Leo Tolstoy, 1853–1857*, translated by Mr. and Mrs. Aylmer Maude (Heinemann); *The Life and Letters of Woodrow Wilson: Preliminary Years* by Ray Stannard Baker (Heinemann); *R. L. Stevenson* by G. K. Chesterton (Hodder & Stoughton); *Disraeli* by Andre Maurois (Lane); *King Edward VII*, Vol. II: *The Reign of King Edward VII*, by Sir Sidney Lee (Macmillan); *Marcel Proust* by Leon Pierre-Quint (Knopf); *The Letters of Queen Victoria* (Second Series; Extra Volume), edited by G. E. Buckle (Murray); *Sir John Hawkins* by J. A. Williamson (Oxford University Press); *The Correspondence of Henry Crabb Robinson with the Wordsworth Circle* (Oxford University Press); *A Life of Francois Villon* by D. B. Wyndham Lewis (Peter Davies); *A Diary of Thomas De Quincey* (Noel Douglas); *Fateful Years* by S. Sazonov (Cape); *The Cleghorn Papers* (Black); *Field-Marshal Lord Napier of Magdala* by Colonel H. D. Napier (Arnold); *Viscount Leverhulme* by his son (Allen & Unwin); *The Life of William Blake* by Mona Wilson (Nonesuch Press); and *More English Diaries* and *Scottish and Irish Diaries* by Arthur Ponsonby (Methuen).

NOVELS: *Meanwhile* by H. G. Wells (Benn); *Pretty Creatures* by William Gerhardi (Benn); *But Gentlemen Marry Brunettes* by Anita Loos (Brentano); *Dancing Mad* by W. H. Davies (Cape); *Red Sky at Morning* by Margaret Kennedy (Heinemann); *The Midnight Folk* by John Masefield (Heinemann); *Gallion's Reach* by H. M. Tomlinson (Heinemann); *I Speak of Africa* by William Plomer (Hogarth Press); *The Ugly Duchess* by Lion Feuchtwanger (Secker); *New Wine* by Geoffrey Moss (Hutchinson); *The Fifth Pestilence* by Alexei Remizov (Wishart); *The Fairy Goose* by Liam O'Flaherty (Faber & Gwyer); *Oberland* by Dorothy Richardson (Duckworth); *Count Stephan* by A. E. Coppard (Golden Cockerel Press); *The Blessing of Pan* by Lord Dunsany (Putnam); *These Men, thy Friends* by Edward Thompson (Knopf); *Mr. Balcony* by C. H. B. Kitchin (Hogarth Press); *Greenlow* by Romer Wilson (Collins); *Demophon* by Forrest Reid (Collins); *Helen and Felicia* by E. B. C. Jones (Chatto & Windus); *Mr. Weston's Good Wine* by T. A. Powys (Chatto & Windus); *Our Mr. Dormer* by R. H. Mottram (Chatto & Windus); *Right Off the Map* by C. E. Montagu (Chatto & Windus; *A Girl Adoring* by Viola Meynell (Arnold); *The Unburied Dead* by Stephen McKenna (Thornton Butterworth); *Jeremy at Crale* by Hugh Walpole (Cassell); *Vestal Fire* by Compton Mackenzie (Cassell); and *The Secret of Father Brown* by G. K. Chesterton (Cassell).

UNUSUAL AND INTERESTING BOOKS: Three books in the Eumorfopoulos Collection: *Catalogue of Chinese, Korean, and Persian Pottery*, Vol. V, by Mr. R. L. Hobson, and *Chinese Frescoes* and *Chinese Paintings* by Laurence Binyon (Benn). *German Baroque Art* by Sacheverell Sitwell (Duckworth); *Cezanne and His Circle* by Julius Meier-Graeffe (Benn); *Cezanne* by Roger Fry (Hogarth Press); and *Art and the Reformation* by G. G. Coulton (Blackwell). Criticism, Literature, and Essays: *Nine Essays* by Arthur Platt (Cambridge University Press); *Proper Studies* by Aldous Huxley (Chatto & Windus); *The Road to Xanadu* by J. L. Lowes (Constable); *A Survey of Modernist Poetry* by Laura Riding and Robert Graves (Heinemann); and *Leaves and Fruit* by Sir Edmund Gosse (Heinemann).

HISTORY: *Five Centuries of Religion*, Vol. II, by G. G. Coulton (Cambridge University Press); *A History of the English People, 1830–1841* by Elie Halevy (Benn); *The Correspondence of King George III* (Macmillan); *The Transition from Aristocracy, 1832–1867* by O. F. Christie (Seeley & Service); and *The House of Lords in the Eighteenth Century* by A. S. Turberville (Oxford University Press).

SOCIOLOGY AND POLITICS: *A Short History of the British Working Class Movement*, Vol. III, by G. D. H. Cole (Labour Publishing Co.); *Speeches* by the Earl of Oxford and Asquith (Hutchinson); *Olives of Endless Age* by Henry Noel Brailsford (Harper); *Sovereignty* by Paul Ward (Routledge); *Political Pluralism, a Study in Modern Political Theory* by K. C. Hsiao (Kegan

Paul); *Fathers or Sons? A Study in Social Psychology* by Prynce Hopkins (Kegan Paul); *Kenya from Within* by W. McGregor Ross (Allen & Unwin); *Lord Grey and the World War* by Hermann Lutz (Allen & Unwin); *India and the West* by F. S. Marvin (Longmans); and *Nigeria Under British Rule* by Sir William Geary (Methuen).

"Landor," "The World of Books" column, *The Nation & The Athenaeum* 42 (15 October 1927): 86. Review of the *Complete Works of Walter Savage Landor*, Vols. 1 and 2, edited by Earle Welby (Chapman & Hall). The complete set will be at least 16 volumes. Woolf also discusses the different editions of Landor's works.

"To See the Kings Go Riding By," "The World of Books" column, *The Nation & The Athenaeum* 42 (22 October 1927): 118. Review essay on *King Edward VII, a Biography*, Vol. II, by Sir Sidney Lee (Macmillan); *Queen Mary, a Life and Intimate Study* by Kathleen Woodward (Hutchinson); and *Speeches by H. R. H. the Prince of Wales, 1912-1926* (Hodder & Stoughton).

"Noble Lords," "The World of Books" column, *The Nation & The Athenaeum* 42 (29 October 1927): 155. Review essay on *The House of Lords in the Eighteenth Century* by A. S. Turberville (Clarendon Press) and *The Transition from Aristocracy, 1832-1867* by O. F. Christie (Seeley & Service).

"Two Professionals and an Amateur," "The World of Books" column, *The Nation & The Athenaeum* 42 (5 November 1927): 187. Review essay on *Bismarck* by Emil Ludwig (Allen & Unwin); *Disraeli, Picture of the Victorian Age* by Andre Maurois, translated by Hamish Miles (Bodley Head); and *Talleyrand, 1754-1838* by Anna Bowman Dodd (Putnam).

"The Greville Scandal," "The World of Books" column, *The Nation & The Athenaeum* 42 (12 November 1927): 224. Review of *The Greville Diary* [Charles Greville], 2 vols., edited by Philip Whitwell Wilson (Heinemann).

"Mrs. Bartlett and Some Others," "The World of Books" column, *The Nation & The Athenaeum* 42 (19 November 1927): 279. Review essay on *Trial of Adelaide Bartlett*, edited by Sir John Hall, Notable British Trials series (Hodge); *Judicial Dramas* by Horace Wyndham (Fisher Unwin); *Passion, Murder, and Mystery* by Bruce Graeme (Hutchinson); *Outlaws of Modern Days* by Mr. H. Ashton-Wolfe (Cassell); and *Criminology and Penology* by Professor John Lewis Gillin (Cape).

"The Art of Reviewing Books," "The World of Books" column, *The Nation & The Athenaeum* 42 (26 November 1927): 320. Review of *Book Reviewing* by Wayne Gard, Instructor in Journalism, Grinnell College (Knopf).

"The Novel of To-Day," "The World of Books" column, *The Nation & The Athenaeum* 42 (3 December 1927): 356. Review essay on *Beauty and the Beast* by Joseph Gordon Macleod (Chatto & Windus); *The English Novel* by

Mr. Priestly, Sixpenny Library (Benn); and *Scheherazade or the Future of the English Novel* by John Carruthers (Kegan Paul).

"East and West," "The World of Books" column, *The Nation & The Athenaeum* 42 (10 December 1927): 396. Review of *The Pedigree of Fascism, a Popular Essay on the Western Philosophy of Politics* by Aline Lion (Sheed & Ward); *Defence of the West* by Henri Massis, translated F. S. Flint, with a preface by G. K. Chesterton (Faber & Gwyer); *Lenin and Gandhi* by Rene Fueloep-Miller (Putnam); and *Materialism and Empirio-Criticism* by Vladimir Lenin (Lawrence).

"John Webster," "The World of Books" column, *The Nation & The Athenaeum* 42 (17 December 1927): 454. Review of *The Complete Works of John Webster*, 4 vols., edited by Mr. F. L. Lucas (Chatto & Windus).

"Short Stories," "The World of Books" column, *The Nation & The Athenaeum* 42 (24 December 1927): 487. Review essay on *Great Stories of All Nations*, collected and edited by Maxim Lieber and Blanche C. Williams (Harrap); *Great Short Novels of the World*, collected and edited by Barrett H. Clark (Heinemann); and *Select Tales of Tchehov*, translated from Russian by Constance Garnett (Chatto & Windus).

"Politics in Horsham," "The World of Books" column, *The Nation & The Athenaeum* 42 (31 December 1927): 515. Review of *A Parliamentary History of Horsham, 1295–1885* by William Albery, with an introduction by Hilaire Belloc (Longmans).

"The Imperialist," "The World of Books" column, *The Nation & The Athenaeum* 42 (7 January 1928): 541. Review of *Rhodes: a Life* by J. G. McDonald (Allan).

"Fools Contest," "The World of Books" column, *The Nation & The Athenaeum* 42 (14 January 1928): 569. Review essay on *The Development of Political Ideas* by Professor Hearnshaw, Sixpenny Library series (Benn); *Archon, or the Future of Government* by Hamilton Fyfe, To-day and Tomorrow Series (Kegan Paul).

"Thomas Hardy," *The Nation & The Athenaeum* 42 (21 January 1928): 597–98. Critical essay on Thomas Hardy's works.

"Queen Victoria and the Liberal Party," "The World of Books" column, *The Nation & The Athenaeum* 42 (21 January 1928): 617. Review of *Letters of Queen Victoria, 1879–1885*, Vol. 3, edited by Mr. Buckle (Murray).

"The Education of an American," "The World of Books" column, *The Nation & The Athenaeum* 42 (28 January 1928): 652. Review of *The Education of Henry Adams* by Henry Adams (Constable).

"The Nineteenth-Century Mind," "The World of Books" column, *The Nation & The Athenaeum* 42 (4 February 1928): 687. Review of *Politicians and Moralists of the Nineteenth Century* [*Politiques et moralists du 19e siecle*, Vol.

3, by Emile Faguet, translated by Dorothy Galton], edited by [Harold?] Laski, Library of European Thought series (Benn).

"The Other Side," "The World of Books" column, *The Nation & The Athenaeum* 42 (11 February 1928): 718. Review of *The Great Problem, and the Evidence of its Solution* by George Lindsay Johnson, M. A., M. D., B. S., F. R. C. S., with a foreword by Sir Arthur Conan Doyle (Hutchinson).

"Who Are the Criminals?" "The World of Books" column, *The Nation & The Athenaeum* 42 (18 February 1928): 751. Review essay on *Trial of the Duchess of Kingston* [Elizabeth Chudleigh], edited by Lewis Melville, Notable British Trials series (Hodge), and the following volumes in The Famous Trials Series, edited by George Dilnot: *The Thaw Case* [Harry Thaw] by F. A. Mackenzie; *The Pelzer Case* [Leon Pelzer] by Gerard Harry; *The Trial of Patrick Mahon*, with an introduction by Edgar Wallace; and *The Trial of Professor Webster* by George Dilnot (Geoffrey Bles).

"Trial by Whitehall," "The World of Books" column, *The Nation & The Athenaeum* 42 (25 February 1928): 782. Review of *Justice and Adminstrative Law* by William A. Robson (Macmillan).

"Phantasmagoric Life," "The World of Books" column, *The Nation & The Athenaeum* 42 (3 March 1928): 815. Review of *The Pilgrimage of Henry James* by Van Wyck Brooks (Cape).

"The Promise of Spring," "The World of Books" column, *The Nation & The Athenaeum* 42 (10 March 1928): 849. List of recently published books:

BIOGRAPHIES, DIARIES, MEMOIRS, AND LETTERS: *Further Correspondence of Samuel Pepys*, edited by J. R. Tanner (Bell); *The Life of Lord Curzon* by the Earl of Ronaldshay (Benn); *The Intimate Papers of Colonel Edward M. House*, Vols. III and IV, edited by Professor Charles Seymour (Benn); *The Travel Diaries of William Beckford of Fonthill*, edited by Guy Chapman (Constable); *Letters of Joseph Conrad to Edward Garnett* (Nonesuch Press); *The Last Twelve Years of Joseph Conrad* by Mr. Curle [a close friend of Conrad] (Sampson Low); and *The Letters of Queen Victoria*, Vol. III: *1879–1885* (Murray).

FICTION: *The Eternal Moment and Other Stories* by E. M. Forster (Sidgwick & Jackson); *Winter Sonata* by Dorothy Edwards (Wishart); *Blue Trousers* by Lady Murasaki, translated from Japanese by Mr. Waley (Allen & Unwin); *Point Counter Point* by Aldous Huxley; and *The Woman Who Rode Away* by D. H. Lawrence (Seeker).

REPRINTS: *The Complete Works of Sir Thomas Browne*, Vol. I, edited by Geoffrey Keynes (Faber & Gwyer); *The Letter Book* by Samuel Richardson [probably "Familiar Letters" written for Mr. Osborne and Mr. Rivington], edited by Brian W. Downs (Routledge); *The Intelligent Woman's Guide to Socialism* by G. B. Shaw (Constable); and *The Formation of Philosophical Radicalism* by M. Elie Halevy, translated by Mary Morris (Faber & Gwyer).

ARCHAEOLOGY AND ART: *The Palace of Minos* by Sir Arthur Evans (Macmillan); *The Statues of London* by Nina Hamnett and Osbert Sitwell (Duckworth); and *London's Open-Air Statuary* by Lord Edward Gleichen (Longmans).

FORTHCOMING AND RECENTLY PUBLISHED BIOGRAPHIES, LETTERS: *Fouche, the Man Whom Napoleon Feared* [Joseph Fouche, Napoleon's Minister of Police] by Dr. Nils Forssell, translated by Anna Barwell (Allen & Unwin); *War Memoirs* by Dr. Eduard Benes [Czechoslovakian statesman] (Allen & Unwin); *Memoirs of Prince Max of Baden* (Constable); *Fateful Years, 1909–1916* by Serge Sazonov [former Russian Foreign Minister] (Cape); *Rossetti: The Last Born of Eve* by Evelyn Waugh (Duckworth); *Dante Gabriel Rossetti* by R. L. Megroz (Faber & Gwyer); *Life of Francois Villon* by Wyndham Lewis (Peter Davies); *All Alone: the Life and Private History of Emily Bronte* by Romer Wilson (Chatto & Windus); *Correspondence of Catherine the Great with Sir Charles Hanbury Williams and Count Poniatowski* (Butterworth); *Gladstone and Palmerston* by Philip Guedalla (Gollancz); *The Rise of the House of Rothschild*, Vol. I, by Count Corti, translated from German by Brian Lunn and Beatrix Lunn (Gollancz); *L. E. L.: A Mystery of the Thirties* [the life of the poetess Letitia Landon] by D. E. Enfield (Hogarth Press); *Dr. Arnold of Rugby* by Arnold Whitridge (Constable); *Goethe* by Dr. Emil Ludwig (Putnam); *Dostoevsky: the Man and His Work* by Julius Meier-Graefe (Routledge); *George Eliot: Her Family Life and Letters* by Arthur Paterson (Selwyn & Blount); and *Charles Baudelaire* by F. Porche (Wishart).

CRITICISM, LITERATURE, AND ESSAYS: *English Prose-Style* by Herbert Read (Bell); *A Pamphlet Against Anthologies* by Laura Riding and Robert Graves (Cape); *The Last Sheaf* by Edward Thomas (Cape); *The Savour of Life* by Arnold Bennett (Cassell); *The Book of Catherine Wells*, edited by H. G. Wells (Chatto & Windus); *Dialogues and Monologues* by Humbert Wolfe (Gollancz); Hogarth Lectures on Literature: *A Lecture on Lectures* by Sir A. Quiller-Couch ("Q"); *Tragedy* by F. L. Lucas; *Studies in Shakespeare* by Professor Allardyce Nicoll; *The Development of English Biography* by Harold Nicholson (Hogarth Press); and *Selected Addresses and Essays* by Viscount Haldane (Murray).

HISTORY: *Life in the Middle Ages* by G. G. Coulton (Cambridge Press); *A Study of the Fuggers and Their Connections* by Richard Ehrenberg (Cape); *A Short History of the World, 1918–1928* by C. Delisle Burns (Gollancz); *A History of Lloyd's* by Charles Wright and C. Ernest Fayle (Macmillan); and *The Correspondence of King George III*, Vols. III and IV (Macmillan).

REPRINTS: *A Story without a Tail* by William Maginn, well-known, 19th century, Irish journalist and writer (Elkin Mathews); and *Memoirs of Letitia Pilkington*, edited by Iris Barry (Routledge).

"Napoleon at St. Helena," "The World of Books" column, *The Nation & The Athenaeum* 42 (17 March 1928): 907. Review of *Napoleon in Captivity* [reports of the French Commissioner, the Marquis de Montchenu, on life on St. Helena], translated by Julian Park (Allen & Unwin).

"Nathaniel Hawthorne," "The World of Books" column, *The Nation & The Athenaeum* 42 (24 March 1928): 939. Review essay on *The Rebellious Puritan: Portrait of Mr. Hawthorne* by Lloyd Morris (Constable) and Hawthorne's works.

"Sir Thomas Browne," "The World of Books" column, *The Nation & The Athenaeum* 42 (31 March 1928): 971. Review essay on *The Complete Works of Sir Thomas Browne*, Vol. I, edited by Geoffrey Keynes, set of six volumes (Faber & Gwyer).

"Sir Robert Peel," "The World of Books" column, *The Nation & The Athenaeum* 43 (21 April 1928): 79. Review of *Sir Robert Peel* by Miss A. A. W. Ramsay, Makers of the Nineteenth Century series (Constable).

"Geld ist der Mann," "The World of Books" column, *The Nation & The Athenaeum* 43 (28 April 1928): 110. Review of *The Rise of the House of Rothschild*, Vol. I, by Count Corti, translated from German by Brian Lunn and Beatrix Lunn (Gollancz).

"The Anatomy of Nations," "The World of Books" column, *The Nation & The Athenaeum* 43 (5 May 1928): 143. Review of *Englishmen, Frenchmen, Spaniards* by Salvador de Madariaga (Oxford University Press and Milford).

"Emily Bronte," "The World of Books" column, *The Nation & The Athenaeum* 43 (12 May 1928): 178. Review essay on *The Bronte Sisters* by Ernest Dimnet (Cape); *Haworth Parsonage, a Picture of the Bronte Family* by Isabel C. Clarke (Hutchinson); *All Alone, the Life and Private History of Emily Jane Bronte* by Romer Wilson (Chatto & Windus); and *Wuthering Heights* by Emily Bronte, with an introduction by Valentine Dobree (Knopf).

"'I Remember' and Other Motives," "The World of Books" column, *The Nation & The Athenaeum* 43 (19 May 1928): 210. Review essay on *My Life* by Isadora Duncan (Gollancz); *A Diplomat Off Duty* by Sir Francis Lindley (Benn); *Diplomacy and Foreign Courts* by Meriel Buchanan (Hutchinson); *James the Second* by Hilaire Belloc (Faber & Gwyer); *Letizia Bonaparte (Madame Mere)* by Clement Shaw (Howe); and *Charles Baudelaire* by Francois Porche (Wishart).

"So this is History," "The World of Books" column, *The Nation & The Athenaeum* 43 (26 May 1928): 255. Review of *The Diaries of Sylvester Douglas (Lord Glenbervie)*, 2 vols., edited by Francis Bickley (Constable).

"Who Goes Home?" "The World of Books" column, *The Nation & The Athenaeum* 43 (2 June 1928): 299. Review of *How Animals Find Their Way About* by Professor Etienne Rabaud, University of Paris, translated by I. H. Myers, International Library of Psychology, etc., series (Routledge)

"Civilization," "The World of Books" column, *The Nation & The Athenaeum* 43 (9 June 1928): 331. Review essay on *Civilization* by Clive Bell (Chatto & Windus) and *The Case of Jean Calas* [1761] by Mr. F. H. Maugham, K. C. (Heinemann).

"Women in the Eighteenth Century," "The World of Books" column, *The Nation & The Athenaeum* 43 (16 June 1928): 363. Review of *The Woman of the Eighteenth Century* by Edmond de Goncourt and Jules de Goncourt, translated by Jacques le Clerq and Ralph Roeder (Allen & Unwin).

"English Prose," "The World of Books" column, *The Nation & The Athenaeum* 43 (23 June 1928): 395. Review of *English Prose Style* by Herbert Read (Bell).

"Is Shakespeare a Great Poet?" "The World of Books" column, *The Nation & The Athenaeum* 43 (30 June 1928): 427. Review essay on *A Question of Taste* by John Bailey (Oxford University Press and Milford).

"Granville Sharp," "The World of Books" column, *The Nation & The Athenaeum* 43 (7 July 1928): 463. Review of *Granville Sharp* by E. C. P. Lascelles (Oxford University Press and Milford). Sharp was an activist in the Anti-Slavery Movement.

"Lives of the Saints," "The World of Books" column, *The Nation & The Athenaeum* 43 (14 July 1928): 498. Review essay on *Saints and Leaders* by Rev. H. F. B. Mackay, Vicar of All Saints, Margaret Street (Philip Allen and the Society of SS. Peter and Paul, Ltd.); *St. Martin of Tours* [Sulpicius Severus], translated from French by Mary Caroline Watt (Sands & Co.); and *St. Basil: The Letters*, Vol. 2, with an English translation by Roy J. Deffari, Loeb Classical Library series (Heinemann).

"Barrow's 'Celebrated Trials,'" "The World of Books" column, *The Nation & The Athenaeum* 43 (21 July 1928): 531. Review of *Celebrated Trials*, 2 vols., originally compiled and edited by George Barrow in 1825, revised and edited by Edward Hale Bierstadt (Cape)

"Why We Laugh," "The World of Books" column, *The Nation & The Athenaeum* 43 (28 July 1928): 563. Review of *The Springs of Laughter* by Mr. C. W. Kimmins (Methuen)

"The Well of Loneliness," "The World of Books" column, *The Nation & The Athenaeum* 43 (4 August 1928): 593. Review of *The Well of Loneliness* by Radclyffe Hall, with a foreword by Havelock Ellis (Cape).

"The Stuarts," "The World of Books" column, *The Nation & The Athenaeum* 43 (11 August 1928): 623. Review of *English Constitutional Conflicts of the Seventeenth Century, 1603–1689* by Dr. J. R. Tanner (Cambridge University Press).

"Ruskin's Literary Criticism," "The World of Books" column, *The Nation & The Athenaeum* 43 (18 August 1928): 650. Review of *Ruskin as Literary Critic*, edited by A. H. R. Ball (Cambridge University Press).

"Making of English," "The World of Books" column, *The Nation & The Athenaeum* 43 (25 August 1928): 679. Review of *Shakespeare's English* by Professor George Gordon, S. P. E. Tract No. XXIX (Clarendon Press)

"The Antibabelists," "The World of Books" column, *The Nation & The Athenaeum* 43 (1 September 1928): 706. Review of *An International Language* by Professor Otto Jespersen, University of Copenhagen (Allen & Unwin).

"The Young Swinburne," "The World of Books" column, *The Nation & The Athenaeum* 43 (8 September 1928): 734. Review essay on *Swinburne's Hyperion and Other Poems, with an Essay on Swinburne and Keats* by Georges Lafourcade (Faber & Gwyer) and *La Jeunesse de Swinburne (1837–1867)*, 2 vols., by Georges Lafourcade (England; Humphrey Milford).

"Admiral Byng," "The World of Books" column, *The Nation & The Athenaeum* 43 (15 September 1928): 726. Review of *Admiral Byng and the Loss of Minorca* by Brian Tunstall, Lecturer at the Royal Naval College, Greenwich (Philip Allan).

"Truth and Fiction," "The World of Books" column, *The Nation & The Athenaeum* 43 (22 September 1928): 794. Review essay on *This Side of Idolatry* a novel by Ephesian (C. E. Bechhofer Roberts) (Mills & Boon). The book is actually a biography of Charles Dickens. Woolf also addresses another biography, *Charles Dickens* by Ralph Straus (Gollancz).

"Through German Eyes," "The World of Books" column, *The Nation & The Athenaeum* 43 (29 September 1928): 823. Review essay on *The Tragedy of Edward VII: A Psychological Study* by Dr. W. H. Edwards, translated from German (Gollancz) and *The Memoirs of Prince Max of Baden* [former German Chancellor], 2 vols., translated from German (Constable).

"Dorothy Osborne," "The World of Books" column, *The Nation & The Athenaeum* 44 (6 October 1928): 18. Review of *The Letters of Dorothy Osborne to William Temple*, edited by Mr. G. C. Moore Smith (Clarendon Press).

"The New Crop," "The World of Books" column, *The Nation & The Athenaeum* 44 (13 October 1928): 50. List of recently published books:

BIOGRAPHY: *The Life of Lord Cruzon*, Vol. III, by the Earl of Ronaldshay (Benn); *Elizabeth and Essex* by Lytton Strachey (Chatto & Windus); *Letters of Katherine Mansfield*, edited by J. Middleton Murry (Constable); *Gladstone and Palmerston* by Philip Guedalla (Gollancz); *After Thirty Years* by Lord Gladstone (Macmillan); *Early Life of Thomas Hardy* by Mrs. Hardy (Macmillan); *The Life of Charles M. Doughty* by D. G. Hogarth (Oxford University Press); and *Memories and Reflections, 1852–1927* by the Earl of Oxford and Asquith (Cassell).

NOVELS: *Mr. Blettsworthy on Rampole Island* by H. G. Wells (Benn); *Point Counter Point* by Aldous Huxley (Chatto & Windus); and *In the Beginning* by Norman Douglas (Chatto & Windus).

POLITICS, HISTORY, PHILOSOPHY, ETC.: *The Structure of Politics at the Accession of George III*, 2 vols., by L. B. Namier (Macmillan); *The World Crisis: The Aftermath* by Winston Churchill (Thornton Butterworth); *Sceptical Essays* by Bertrand Russell (Allen & Unwin); *The Centenary Edition of Tolstoy's Works*, edited by Mr. Aylmer Maude (Oxford Press); and *Winter Words* by Thomas Hardy (Macmillan).

ART AND CRITICISM: *The Leverhulme Art Monographs* (Batsford); *A Literary History of Persia* by E. G. Browne (Cambridge Press); *Cross Currents in English Literature of the Seventeenth Century* by H. J. C. Grierson (Chatto & Windus); *Swinburne's Hyperion and Other Poems, with an Essay on Swinburne and Keats* by Georges Lafourcade (Faber & Gwyer); *Proust* by Clive Bell (Hogarth Press); *Reading for Pleasure, and Other Essays* by R. Ellis Roberts (Methuen); and *The Making of Literature* by R. A. Scott James (Secker).

ECONOMICS, EDUCATION, AND HISTORY: *The Economics of Rail Transport in Great Britain* by C. E. R. Sherrington (Allen & Unwin); *The Money Game* by Norman Angell (Dent); *A History of European Diplomacy, 1451–1789* by R. B. Mowat (Arnold); *Life in the Middle Ages*, Vol. II, by G. G. Coulton (Cambridge Press); *Why the Reformation Happened* by Hilaire Belloc (Cape); and *The History of British Civilization* by E. Wingfield Stratford (Routledge).

NEW EDITIONS: *The Poetical and Dramatic Works of Sir Charles Sedley* (Constable); *Complete Works of Beddoes*, edited by Sir Edmund Gosse (Fanfrolico Press); *The Complete Poetry and Selected Prose of John Donne* (Nonesuch Press): and *The Works of Izaak Walton* (Nonesuch Press).

POETRY: *The Collected Poems of W. H. Davies* (Cape); *Midsummer Night* by John Masefield (Heinemann); *Collected Poems of D. H. Lawrence* (Secker); and *Five Poems* by Edith Sitwell (Duckworth).

SOCIOLOGY AND POLITICS: *The Origin, Structure, and Working of the League of Nations* by C. Howard-Ellis (Allen & Unwin); *Europe* by Count Keyserling (Cape); *A Handbook on Hanging* by Charles Duff (Cayme Press); *The Growth of Philosophic Radicalism* by E. Halvey (Faber & Gwyer); *More Famous Trials* by the Earl of Birkenhead (Hutchinson); *The History of the Privy Council* by Sir Almeric Fitzroy (Murray); and *A New Way with Crime* by A. Fenner Brockway (Williams & Norgate).

TRAVEL: *On Mediterranean Shores* by Emil Ludwig (Allen & Unwin); *The Star Spangled Manner* by Beverley Nichols (Cape); and *Twelve Days* by Vita Sackville-West (Hogarth Press).

FICTION: *The Love Nest* by Ring Lardner (Philip Allan); *The Children* by Edith Wharton (Appleton); *But Soft, We Are Observed!* by Hilaire Belloc (Arrowsmith); *Swan Song* by John Galsworthy (Heinemann); *The Captain's Daughter* by Alexander Pushkin (Dent); a new novel by Rebecca West (Hutchinson); *The Silver Thorn* by Hugh Walpole (Macmillan); and *Winter Sonata* by Dorothy Edwards (Wishart).

BIOGRAPHY: *Undertones of War* by Edmund Blunden (Cobden-Sanderson); *Charles James Fox* by John Drinkwater (Benn); *Heine, the Strange Guest* by Henry Baerlein (Bles); *The Tragedy of John Ruskin* by Amabel Williams-Ellis (Cape); *Memoirs of Prince Max of Baden* (Constable); *Memoirs of My Father* by Sir Henry F. Dickens (Gollancz); *Wellington* by Oliver Brett (Heinemann); *The Last Twelve Years of Conrad's Life* by Richard Curle (Sampson Low); *Charles Darwin* by Henshaw Ward (Murray); *Montrose* by John Buchan (Nelson); *Last Changes, Last Chances* by H. W. Nevinson (Nisbet); and *Goethe* by Emil Ludwig (Putnam).

"From Moses to Wellington," "The World of Books" column, *The Nation & The Athenaeum* 44 (20 October 1928): 110. Review essay on *Charles James Fox* by John Drinkwater (Benn); *Wellington* by Oliver Brett (Heinemann); *Mary Queen of Scots* by Margarete Kurlbaum-Siebert, translated from German by Mary Agnes Hamilton (Cape); *John Law, a Fantastic Financier, 1671–1729* by George Oudard, translated from French by G. C. E. Masse (Cape); and *The Life of Moses* by Edmond Fleg, translated from French by Stephen Haden Guest (Gollancz).

"Slapdashdom," "The World of Books" column, *The Nation & The Athenaeum* 44 (27 October 1928): 144. Review of *The Victorian Illusion* by E. H. Dance (Heinemann).

"Memories of the War," "The World of Books" column, *The Nation & The Athenaeum* 44 (3 November 1928): 178. Review essay on *My War Memoirs* by Dr. Eduard Benes [Czechoslovakian Foreign Minister] (Allen & Unwin); *The Intimate Papers of Colonel Edward M. House*, Vols. III and IV, edited by Professor Charles Seymour (Benn); and *Versailles* by Karl Friederich Nowak (Gollancz). Woolf mentions the *Memoirs of Prince Max of Baden* (Constable).

"The Life of the Artist," "The World of Books" column, *The Nation & The Athenaeum* 44 (10 November 1928): 211. Review essay on *Dante Gabriel Rossetti* by R. L. Megroz (Faber & Gwyer) and *The Life of Charles M. Doughty* by D. G. Hogarth (Oxford University Press).

"The Freedom of the Press," "The World of Books" column, *The Nation & The Athenaeum* 44 (17 November 1928): 258. Review essay on *The Struggle for the Freedom of the Press, 1819–1832* by William H. Wickwar (Allen & Unwin).

"A Fly Is Struggling in the Web," "The World of Books" column, *The Nation & The Athenaeum* 44 (24 November 1928): 294. Review essay on *The Diary* of *Tolstoy's Wife, 1860–1891* [Countess Sophie Andreevna Tolstoy], translated by Alexander Werth (Gollancz) and *The Diary of Dostoyevsky's Wife* [Anna Grigorevna], translated from German by Madge Pemberton (Gollancz).

"Crime and Criminals," "The World of Books" column, *The Nation & The Athenaeum* 44 (1 December 1928): 326. Review essay on *More Famous Trials* by the Earl of Birkenhead (Hutchinson); *Landru* by F. A. Mackenzie, The Famous Trials Series (Bles); *Trial of Charles the First* by J. G. Muddiman, Notable British Trials series (Hodge); *The Case of Constance Kent* by John Rhode, The Famous Trials Series (Bles); and *A Handbook on Hanging* by Charles Duff (Cayme Press).

"Healy and O'Brien," "The World of Books" column, *The Nation & The Athenaeum* 44 (8 December 1928): 359. Review essay on *Letters and Leaders of My Day* by Tim Healy (Thornton Butterworth) and *The Life of William O'Brien* by Michael MacDonagh (Benn).

"What We May Be Coming To," "The World of Books" column, *The Nation & The Athenaeum* 44 (15 December 1928): 415. Review of *Anthony Comstock* by Heywood Broun and Margaret Leech (Wishart).

"Youth Among the Ruins," "The World of Books" column, *The Nation & The Athenaeum* 44 (22 December 1928): 446. Review essay on *Alma Mater or the Future of Oxford and Cambridge* by Julian Hall, To-day and To-morrow Series (Kegan Paul) and *The New Universities, an External Examination* by H. G. Herklots (Benn).

"Just for the Riband to Stick to Their Coats," "The World of Books" column, *The Nation & The Athenaeum* 44 (29 December 1928): 468. Review of *The Great Betrayal* by Julien Benda, translated from French by Mr. Aldington (Routledge).

"Novels and Decency," "Letters to the Editor" column, *The Nation & The Athenaeum* 44 (5 January 1929): 488. Woolf's response to a letter to the Editor by F. E. Pollard on the treatment of sex in novels.

"Butterflies," "The World of Books" column, *The Nation & The Athenaeum* 44 (5 January 1929): 495. Review essay on *Collected Works of Ronald Firbank*, 5 vols., with an introduction by Arthur Waley and a memoir by Osbert Sitwell (Duckworth) and *The Dreadful Dragon of Hay Hill* by Max Beerbohm (Heinemann).

"The First Radicals," "The World of Books" column, *The Nation & The Athenaeum* 44 (12 January 1929): 526. Review of *The Growth of Philosophic Radicalism* by Elie Halevy, translated by Mary Morris (Faber & Gwyer).

"'Whigs' and 'Tories,'" "The World of Books" column, *The Nation & The Athenaeum* 44 (19 January 1929): 555. Review of *The Structure of Politics at the Accession of George III*, 2 vols., by L. B. Namier (Macmillan).

"1778–1878," "The World of Books" column, *The Nation & The Athenaeum* 44 (26 January 1929): 585. Review essay on *Barnard Letters*, edited by Anthony Powell (Duckworth); *The Farington Diary*, Vol. VIII, by Joseph Farington, R. A., edited by James Greig (Hutchinson); and *The Paris Embassy During the Second Empire*, edited by Colonel, the Hon. F. A. Wellesley (Butterworth).

"The Popularity of Dean Inge," "The World of Books" column, *The Nation & The Athenaeum* 44 (2 February 1929): 619. Review of *Assessments and Anticipations* by William Ralph Inge, C. V. O., D. D., F. B. A., Dean of St. Paul's (Cassell).

"Russian Novelists," "The World of Books" column, *The Nation & The Athenaeum* 44 (9 February 1929): 654. Review essay on the *Centenary Edition of Tolstoy's Works*, Vol. 3: *Childhood, Boyhood, and Youth* and Vol. 19: *Resurrection*, 21 volumes in the set (Oxford University Press and Milford). H. G. Wells wrote an introduction to Vol. 19: *Resurrection*.

"Force Is No Remedy," "The World of Books" column, *The Nation & The Athenaeum* 44 (16 February 1929): 689. Woolf's response to a letter to the editor, published 9 February 1929, written by Edwyn Bevan criticizing Woolf's review of *Assessments and Anticipations* by William Ralph Inge. See "The Popularity of Dean Inge" (2 February 1929): 619 above.

"Spengler," "The World of Books" column, *The Nation & The Athenaeum* 44 (23 February 1929): 722. Review of *The Decline of the West*, Vol. 2: *Perspectives of World-History* by Oswald Spengler, translated by Charles Francis Atkinson (Allen & Unwin).

"The Pilgrim's Progress," "The World of Books" column, *The Nation & The Athenaeum* 44 (2 March 1929): 753. Review of *The Pilgrim's Progress* by John Bunyan, edited by James Blanton Wharey (Clarendon Press).

"The Spring Lists," "The World of Books" column, *The Nation & The Athenaeum* 44 (9 March 1929): 786. List of recently published books:

BIOGRAPHIES AND AUTOBIOGRAPHIES: *My Memoirs* by T. P. O'Connor (Benn); *Alice Meynell* by her daughter Viola Meynell (Cape); and *The Autobiography of Lord Haldane* (Hodder & Stoughton).

ECONOMICS: *A Treatise on Money* by John Maynard Keynes (Macmillan). Fiction: *No Love* by David Garnett (Chatto & Windus); *The King Who Was a King* by [H. G.?] Wells (Benn); and *Accident* by [Arnold?] Bennett.

NEW EDITIONS: *Vathek and the Episodes of Vathek* by William Beckford, edited by Guy Chapman (Constable); and *The Works of Shakespeare*, text of the First Folio, edited by Herbert Farjeon (Nonesuch Press).

Reprints: *Harriette Wilson's Memoirs of Herself and Others*, with a preface by James Laver (Peter Davies).

RELIGION AND POLITICS: *An Interpretation of Genesis* by Mr. T. F. Powys (Chatto & Windus); and *Power and the People* by the Lord Chief Justice (Benn).

ARCHAEOLOGY, ART, AND ARCHITECTURE: *On Alexander's Track to the Indus* by Sir Aurel Stein (Macmillan); *Bindings in Cambridge Libraries* and *English Binding before 1500* by G. D. Hobson (Cambridge Press); *Tattershall Castle: Its Fabric and Its Owners* by Lord Curzon (Cape); *Undying Faces* [a collection of death masks] by Ernst Benkard (Hogarth Press); and *Prefaces on Art, a Selection of Prefaces by Eminent Writers to Catalogues of Exhibitions Held at the Leicester Galleries*, with a preface on the prefaces by Hugh Walpole (Macmillan).

BIOGRAPHIES AND AUTOBIOGRAPHIES: *Sykes of Sledmere* by J. J. Fairfax-Blakeborough (Allan); *William the First* by Paul Wiegler, translated from German by Constance Vesey (Allen & Unwin); *A Fatalist at War* by Rudolf G. Binding (Allen & Unwin); *Further Correspondence of Samuel Pepys*, edited by J. R. Tanner (Bell); *Peel and the Conservative Party* by G. K. Clark (Bell); *Richelieu* by Hilaire Belloc (Benn); *The Life of Peter the Great* by Stephen Graham (Benn); *George III* by Romney Sedgwick (Benn); *Life of Sir Charles Hanbury-Williams* by the Earl of Ilchester and Mrs. Langford-Brooke (Butterworth); *The Life of Sir Walter Scott* by Stephen Gwynn (Butterworth); *Shades of Eton* by Percy Lubbock (Cape); *John Knox* by Edwin Muir (Cape); *The Life of the First Earl of Halsbury* by Mrs. A. Wilson-Fox (Chapman & Hall); *C. E. Montague* by Oliver Elton (Chatto & Windus); *The Life of Lady Byron* by Ethel Colburn Mayne (Constable); *Life of William Congreve* by J. Isaacs (Peter Davies); *Frederick the Great* by Margaret Goldsmith (Gollancz); *The Countess Tolstoy's Later Diary* (Gollancz); *Life's Ebb and Flow* [memoirs of Frances, Countess of Warwick] (Hutchinson); *La Duchesse de Maine* by Francis Birrell (Howe); *The Life of Annie Besant* by Geoffrey West (Howe); *The Letters of the Tsar to the Tsaritsa* (Lane); *Letters of Tolstoy and His Cousin, Countess Alexandra Tolstoy 1857–1903*, translated by Leo Islavin (Methuen); *Sir Thomas Mallory* by E. Vinaver (Oxford Press); *The Politics of Laurence Sterne* by L. P. Curtis (Oxford Press); *Carlyle to Threescore and Ten* by David Alec Wilson (Kegan Paul); *War Diaries* by Major-General Hoffmann (Secker); and *Life of Eleonora Duse* by E. A. Rheinhardt (Secker).

CRITICISM AND LITERATURE: *Studies in Literature, III* by Sir A. Quiller-Couch (Cambridge Press); *Paleface* by Wyndham Lewis (Chatto & Windus); *Cross Currents in English Literature of the Seventeenth Century* by Professor Grierson (Chatto & Windus); and *Walter de la Mare* by Forrest Reid (Faber & Gwyer).

ECONOMICS: *The Economics of Inheritance* by Josiah Wedgewood (Routledge).

NOVELS: *Diana* by Emil Ludwig (Allen & Unwin); *Oblomov* by Ivan Goncharov (Allen & Unwin); *Dodsworth* by Sinclair Lewis (Cape); *The Mountain Tavern* by Liam O'Flaherty (Cape); *Barbarian Stories* by Naomi Mitchison (Cape); *The True Heart* by Sylvia Townsend Warner (Chatto & Windus); *The Squire's Daughter* by F. M. Mayor (Constable); *Hucca's Moor* by Ruth Manning-Sanders (Faber & Gwyer); *The Good Companions* by J. B. Priestly (Heinemann); *Night Falls on Siva's Hill* by Edward Thompson (Heinemann); *Paper Houses* by William Plomer (Hogarth Press); a new novel by Rebecca West (Hutchinson); *Swords and Roses* by Joseph Hergesheimer (Knopf); and *Farthing Hall* by Hugh Walpole and J. B. Priestly (Macmillan).

HISTORY AND POLITICS: The Decline of the West, Vol. 2: *Perspectives of World-History* by Oswald Spengler, translated by Charles Francis Atkinson (Allen & Unwin); *The Age of Grey and Peel* by H. W. Carless Davis (Oxford Press); *French Liberal Thought in the Eighteenth Century* by Kingsley Martin, Library of European Thought series, edited by Harold Laski (Benn); *Life in the Middle Ages*, edited by G. G. Coulton (Cambridge Press); *The World Crisis: the Aftermath* by Winston Churchill (Butterworth); *The Ascent of Society* by Gerald Heard (Cape); *Conservative Policy* by Sir R. M. Bankes (Chapman & Hall); *Liberal Policy* by Hubert Phillips (Chapman & Hall); and *Labour Policy* by Arthur Greenwood (Chapman & Hall).

"Life and Lives," "The World of Books" column, *The Nation & The Athenaeum* 44 (16 March 1929): 842. Review essay on *The Tempestuous Prince* [German Prince Hermann Ludwig Heinrich Pueckler-Muskau] by Miss E. M. Butler (Longmans); *Life of Sir Charles Hanbury-Williams* [an adviser of Catherine the Great] by the Earl of Ilchester and Mrs. Langford-Brooke (Butterworth); and *The Letters of the Tsar to the Tsaritsa, 1914–1917*, translated by A. L. Hynes, with an introduction by Dr. Hagberg Wright (Bodley Head).

"The Science and Art of Biography," "The World of Books" column, *The Nation & The Athenaeum* 44 (23 March 1929): 882. Review essay on *Aspects of Biography* by Andre Maurois [Clark Lectures delivered at Trinity College, Cambridge University by Andre Maurois], translated from French by S. C. Roberts (Cambridge University Press) and *Alexander the Great* by E. Iliff Robson (Cape).

"Obscenity in Literature," "Letters to the Editor" column, *The Nation & The Athenaeum* 44 (30 March 1929): 908. Woolf responds to a letter written by Professor Gilbert Murray on obscenity that was published in the 23 March 1929 issue, p. 876. In the 13 April 1929 issue (p. 40), Professor Murray responded to L. Woolf's letter that was published on 30 March.

"The Romance of Journalism," "The World of Books" column, *The Nation & The Athenaeum* 44 (30 March 1929): 914. Review essay on *The Autobiography of a Journalist* by an anonymous journalist and writer, with an introduction by Michael Joseph (Hutchinson); *Secrets of Your Daily Paper: The Veil Off Fleet Street* by Frederick W. Carter, an English journalist (Cassell); and *The Truth Behind the News, 1918-1928* by George Seldes, an American journalist (Faber & Gwyer).

"Reticence," "The World of Books" column, *The Nation & The Athenaeum* 45 (6 April 1929): 17. Review essay on *Centenary Edition of Tolstoy's Works*, Vol. I: *The Life of Tolstoy: First Fifty Years* by Aylmer Maude and Vol. 18: *What Is Art? and Essays on Art*, 21 volumes in the set (Oxford University Press and Milford); *Letters of Tolstoy and His Cousin, Countess Alexandra Tolstoy 1857-1903*, translated by Leo Islavin (Methuen); and *The Autobiography of Lord Alfred Douglas* (Secker).

"The Drama," "The World of Books" column, *The Nation & The Athenaeum* 45 (13 April 1929): 45. Review essay on *Great Modern British Plays* [playwrites Coward, Milne, Sutro, etc.], selected by J. W. Marriott (Harrap); *Oil Islands* and *Warren Hastings* by Leon Feuchtwanger, translated by Willa and Edwin Muir (Secker); and Strindberg's plays in translation, Vol. I: *Easter and Other Plays*, by Johan August Strindberg, with an introduction by Dr. Robertson (Cape).

"Obscenity and the Censor," "The World of Books" column, *The Nation & The Athenaeum* 45 (20 April 1929): 77. Review essay on *To the Pure...* by Morris L. Ernst and William Seagle (Cape) and the issue of obscenity—a topic of discussion in *The Nation & The Athenaeum* from time to time.

"The Tory Mind," "The World of Books" column, *The Nation & The Athenaeum* 45 (27 April 1929): 111. Review essay on *Peel and the Conservative Party* by George Kitson Clark (Bell); *Toryism and the People, 1832-1846* by Richard Hill (Constable); *Seven Nineteenth-Century Statesmen* by Mr. G. R. Stirling Taylor (Cape); and *Daniel O'Connell and the History of Catholic Emancipation* by Michael Macdonagh (Burns, Oates & Washbourne).

"Through French Eyes," "The World of Books" column, *The Nation & The Athenaeum* 45 (4 May 1929): 162. Review of *A History of the English People; Epilogue*, Vol. I: *1895-1905* by Elie Halevy (Benn).

"Judge Jeffreys in the West Country," "The World of Books" column, *The Nation & The Athenaeum* 45 (11 May 1929): 204. Review of *The Bloody Assize* by His Honour Sir Edward Parry (Benn).

"Obscenity in Literature," "Letters to the Editor" column, *The Nation & The Athenaeum* 45 (18 May 1929): 235. L. Woolf comments on a point that Professor Gilbert Murray made on obscenity in literature in a letter to the Editor (published on 23 March 1929, p. 876) as well as an observation that David Cecil made on the subject in a letter to the Editor published on 11 May 1929, p. 198.

"Kings and Queens," "The World of Books" column, *The Nation & The Athenaeum* 45 (18 May 1929): 240. Review essay on *Louis XI* by Pierre Champion, translated and adapted by Winifred Stephens Whale (Cassell); *Queen Louise of Prussia* by Gertrude Aretz, translated from German by Ruth Putnam (Putnam); *William the First* by Paul Wiegler, translated from German by Constance Vesey (Allen & Unwin); *Ludwig II of Bavaria* by Guy de Portales, translated from French (Butterworth); *Napoleon III* by Edmund B. D'Auvergne (Nash & Grayson); and *The English King* by Michael Macdonagh (Benn).

"Another Son of Hilkiah," "The World of Books" column, *The Nation & The Athenaeum* 45 (25 May 1929): 275. Review of *Paleface: The Philosophy of the Melting Pot* by Wyndham Lewis (Chatto & Windus).

"Jack the Ripper and Others," "The World of Books" column, *The Nation & The Athenaeum* 45 (1 June 1929): 307. Review essay on *The Mystery of Jack the Ripper* by Leonard Matters (Hutchinson); *The Trial of T. H. Allaway*, edited by W. Lloyd Woodland, Famous Trials Series (Bles); *Trial of John Donald Merrett*, edited by William Roughead, Notable British Trials Series (Hodge); *Guilty or Not Guilty* by Guy B. H. Logan (Stanley Paul); and *Curious Trials and Criminal Cases* by Edward Hale Bierstadt (Hutchinson).

"The Victorian Woman," "The World of Books" column, *The Nation & The Athenaeum* 45 (8 June 1929): 338. Review of *Victorian Working Women* by Wanda Fraiken Neff (Allen & Unwin).

"The Founders of Liberalism," "The World of Books" column, *The Nation & The Athenaeum* 45 (29 June 1929): 434. Review of *French Liberal Thought in the Eighteenth Century* by Kingsley Martin, Library of European Thought series, edited by Harold Laski (Benn).

"Lady Byron," "The World of Books" column, *The Nation & The Athenaeum* 45 (6 July 1929): 478. Review of *The Life of Lady Byron* by Ethel Colburn Mayne (Constable).

"Harriet Wilson," "The World of Books" column, *The Nation & The Athenaeum* 45 (13 July 1929): 509. Review of *Harriette Wilson's Memoirs of Herself and Others*, with a preface by James Laver (reprint; Peter Davies).

"How Not to Read Poetry," "The World of Books" column, *The Nation & The Athenaeum* 45 (20 July 1929): 538. Review of *Practical Criticism: A Study of Literary Judgment* by I. A. Richards (Kegan Paul).

"From Mozart to Miss Stein," "The World of Books" column, *The Nation & The Athenaeum* 45 (27 July 1929): 566. Review essay on *Memoirs of Lorenzo da Ponte*, translated by L. A. Sheppard, Broadway Diaries, Memoirs, and Letters series, edited by Eileen Power and Elizabeth Drew (Routledge); *The Diary of the Revd. William Jones, 1777–1821*, edited with an introduction by his great-grandson O. F. Christie (Brentano); *Pomp and Circumstance* by

E. de Gramont, ex-Duchesse de Clermont Tonnerre (Cape); *Relations and Complications* by H. H. the Dayang Muda of Sarawak [nee Miss Palmer] (Bodley Head); and *Harlequinade* by Constance Collier (Bodley Head).

"Modern Art," "The World of Books" column, *The Nation & The Athenaeum* 45 (3 August 1929): 597. Review of *The New Interior Decoration* by Dorothy Todd and Raymond Mortimer (Batsford).

"Count Hermann Keyserling," "The World of Books" column, *The Nation & The Athenaeum* 45 (10 August 1929): 626. Review of *Creative Understanding* and *The Recovery of Truth* by Count Hermann Keyserling (Cape).

"The Old Fox," "The World of Books" column, *The Nation & The Athenaeum* 45 (17 August 1929): 654. Review of *Henry VIII* by Francis Hackett (Putnam).

"The Art of Thought," "The World of Books" column, *The Nation & The Athenaeum* 45 (24 August 1929): 682. Review of *The Art of Thinking* by M. Ernest Dimnet (Cape).

"Varieties of Crime," "The World of Books" column, *The Nation & The Athenaeum* 45 (31 August 1929): 709. Review essay on *The Trial of Jean Pierre Vaquier*, edited by R. H. Blundell and R. E. Seaton, Notable British Trials series (Hodge); *The Trial of Norman Thorne* by Helena Normanton, Famous Trials series (Bles); *The Milligan Case*, edited by Samuel Klaus, American Trials series (Routledge); and *Indian Village Crimes* by Sir Cecil Walsh (Benn).

"International Thought," "The World of Books" column, *The Nation & The Athenaeum* 45 (7 September 1929): 737. Review of *The Growth of International Thought* by F. Melian Stawell, Home University Library series (Butterworth)

"The Compleat Walton," "The World of Books" column, *The Nation & The Athenaeum* 45 (14 September 1929): 765. Review of *The Compleat Walton*, edited by Geoffrey Keynes (Nonesuch Press).

"Born Writers," "The World of Books" column, *The Nation & The Athenaeum* 45 (21 September 1929): 798. Review essay on *Alice Meynell, A Memoir* by Viola Meynell (Cape) and *A Book About Myself* by Theodore Dreiser (Constable).

"Ad Astra?" "The World of Books" column, *The Nation & The Athenaeum* 45 (28 September 1929): 829. Review essay on *The Ascent of Humanity* by Gerald Heard (Cape) and *The Universe Around Us* by Sir James Jeans (Cambridge University Press).

"The Letters of Disraeli," "The World of Books" column, *The Nation & The Athenaeum* 46 (5 October 1929): 17. Review of *The Letters of Disraeli to Lady Bradford and Lady Chesterfield*, 2 vols., edited by the Marquis of Zetland (Benn).

"Autumn Books," "The World of Books" column, *The Nation & The Athenaeum* 46 (12 October 1929): 51. List of recently published books:
BIOGRAPHIES, MEMOIRS, AND LETTERS: *The Letters of Disraeli to Lady Bradford and Lady Chesterfield*, 2 vols., edited by the Marquis of Zetland (Benn); *Up to Yesterday* [autobiography] by Robert Graves (Cape); *The Countess Tolstoy's Later Diary* (Gollancz); *The Letters of James Elroy Flecker* (Heinemann); *Memories of My Life* by Professor Westermarck (Allen & Unwin); *Peter the Great* by Stephen Graham (Benn); *Livingstone* by Rev. R. J. Campbell (Benn); *George III* by Romney Sedgwick (Benn); *Crusaders Coast* by Edward Thompson (Benn); *The Life of Victor Hugo* by Raymond Escholier (Butterworth); *The Letters of Sir Joshua Reynolds* (Oxford University Press); *King George V* by Sir George Arthur (Cape); *The Life and Letters of Sir Harry Johnston* by his brother Alex Johnston (Cape); *Alice Meynell, A Memoir* by Viola Meynell (Cape); *History of the Sackville Family* by Charles J. Phillips (Cassell); *The Life of Viscount Cowdray* by J. A. Spender (Cassell); *The Life of the First Earl of Halsbury* by Mrs. A. Wilson-Fox (Chapman & Hall); *The Letters and Friendships of Sir Cecil Spring-Rice* by Stephen Gwynn (Constable); *The Hardman Papers; a Further Selection* (Constable); *A Book About Myself* by Theodore Dreiser (Constable); *The Life of Napoleon* by Dimitri Merezhkovsky (Dent); *New Light on the Youth of Dante* by Gertrude Leigh (Faber & Faber); *The Life of Sir Edward Marshall* by Edward Marjoribanks (Gollancz); *Isadora Duncan's End* by Mary Desti (Gollancz); *My War Diary* by Crown Prince Rupprecht of Bavaria (Heinemann); *H. R. H. the Duke of Connaught* by Sir George Ashton (Harrap); *The Life of the Prince of Wales* by Hector Bolitho (Heinemann); *La Duchesse de Maine* by Francis Birrell (Howe); *The Diary and Papers of Lord Cowley* (Hutchinson); *James Ramsay MacDonald* by H. Hessell Tiltman (Jarrolds); *Nelson* by C. S. Forester (Lane); *Chicago May, Her Story by Herself* (Sampson Low); *The Life of the Marquis of Lansdowne* by Lord Newton (Macmillan); *Marlow and His Circle* by F. S. Boas (Oxford University Press); *The Life and Work of Mrs. Piper* by Alla Piper (Kegan Paul); *Mrs. Eddy* by Edwin Franden Dakin (Scribners); *The Memoirs of General Wrangel* (Williams & Norgate); *Lord Fisher, Admiral of the Fleet* by Admiral Sir Reginald H. Bacon (Hodder & Stoughton); *The Memoirs of Philip Scheidemann* (Hodder & Stoughton); *Elizabeth Barrett Browning, Letters to Her Sister* (Murray); *About Myself* by Ben Turner (Richards & Toulmin); *La Fayette* by Brand Whitlock (Appleton); and *C. E. Montague* by Oliver Elton (Chatto & Windus).
FICTION: *A High Wind in Jamaica* by Richard Hughes (Chatto & Windus); *Adolphe, 1920* by John Rodke (Aquila Press); *The Near and the Far* by L. H. Myer (Cape); *The Emperor's Tigers* by Valentine Dobree (Faber & Faber); *The Hawbucks* by John Masefield (Heinemann); *The Man Who Loved Islands*

by D. H. Lawrence (Heinemann); *The Hoax* by Italo Svevo (Hogarth Press); *Conscience of Zeno* by Italo Svevo (Putnam); *Harriet Hume* by Rebecca West (Hutchinson); *Hans Frost* by Hugh Walpole (Macmillan); *Death of a Hero* by Richard Aldington (Chatto & Windus); and *Seven Tales and Alexander* by H. E. Bates (Scholartis).

ARCHAEOLOGY AND ART: *The Place Names of Sussex* by A. Mawer and F. M. Stenton (Cambridge University Press); *Auguste Renoir* [selection of facsimiles, etc.] (Batsford); and *From Toulouse-Lautrec to Rodin* by Arthur Symons (Lane).

CRITICISM AND LITERATURE: *Second Journal to Eliza* by Laurence Sterne (Bell); *The Sense of Glory* by Herbert Read (Faber & Faber); *Belphegor* by Julien Benda (Faber & Faber); *Notes on English Verse Satire* by Humbert Wolfe (Hogarth Press); *English Humour* by J. B. Priestly (Longmans); and *The Diabolical Principe* by Wyndham Lewis (Chatto & Windus).

ECONOMICS: *The Post-War Unemployment Problem* by Henry Clay (Macmillan) and *A History of Financial Speculation* by R. H. Mottram (Chatto & Windus).

EDUCATION: *The English Public School* by Bernard Darwin (Longmans).

HISTORY: *A History of the British People* by D. C. Somervell (Bell); *The Hittite Empire* by John Garstang (Constable); and *German Diplomatic Documents, 1871–1914* (Methuen).

POETRY: *Near and Far* by Edmund Blunden (Cobden-Sanderson); *King's Daughter* by Vita Sackville-West (Hogarth Press); and *The Testament of Beauty* by Robert Bridges (Oxford University Press).

SOCIOLOGY, ETC.: *Marriage and Morals* by Bertrand Russell (Allen & Unwin); *The New Despotism* by Lord Hewart of Bury (Benn); and *Studies in the English Social and Political Thinkers of the Nineteenth Century* by R. H. Murray (Heffer).

"A Great Man," "The World of Books" column, *The Nation & The Athenaeum* 46 (19 October 1929): 109. Review of *Lord Fisher, Admiral of the Fleet* by Admiral Sir Reginald H. Bacon (Hodder & Stoughton).

"Passionate Pilgrims," "The World of Books" column, *The Nation & The Athenaeum* 46 (26 October 1929): 141. Review essay on *Diaries of William Johnston Temple, 1780–1796*, edited by Lewis Bettany who also writes a memoir (Clarendon Press); *Livingstone* by Rev. R. J. Campbell (Benn); *The Life and Letters of Sir Harry Johnston* by his brother Alex Johnston (Cape); *Mrs. Eddy* by Edwin Franden Dakin (Scribners); *Isadora Duncan's End* by Mary Desti (Gollancz); and *The Career of Sir Basil Zaharoff* by Richard Lewinsohn (Gollancz).

"The Gramophone," "The World of Books" column, *The Nation & The Athenaeum* 46 (2 November 1929): 173. Review of Modern *Gramophones and*

Electrical Producers by P. Wilson and G. W. Webb, with a foreword by Compton Mackenzie (Cassell).

"The Holy Strife of Disputatious Men," "The World of Books" column, *The Nation & The Athenaeum* 46 (9 November 1929): 205. Review of *A History of Freethought in the Nineteenth Century*, 2 vols., by J. M. Robertson (Watts).

"The German Tribes," "The World of Books" column, *The Nation & The Athenaeum* 46 (16 November 1929): 254. Review essay on *Lord D'Abernon's Diary*, Vol. 2: *The Years of Crisis* [June 1922–December 1923—Lord D'Abernon served as British ambassador to Germany] (Hodder & Stoughton); *Walter Rathenau, His Life and Work* [former German Foreign Minister] by Count Harry Kessler (Howe); *July, 1914* by Emil Ludwig (Putnam); and *War Diaries and Other Papers* of Major-General Max Hoffman (Secker).

"Puritans and Impuritans," "The World of Books" column, *The Nation & The Athenaeum* 46 (23 November 1929): 286. Review essay on *After Puritanism* by Hugh Kingsmill (Duckworth) and *The Impuritans* by Harvey Wickham (Allen & Unwin).

"Russian Literature," "The World of Books" column, *The Nation & The Athenaeum* 46 (30 November 1929): 318. Review essay on *The Countess Tolstoy's Later Diary* (Gollancz); *New Dostoevsky Letters*, translated by S. S. Koteliansky (Mandrake Press); and *Oblomov* by Ivan Goncharov, translated by Natalie Duddington (Allen & Unwin).

"The East Goes West," "The World of Books" column, *The Nation & The Athenaeum* 46 (7 December 1929): 351. Review of *A History of Nationalism in the East* by Hans Kohn, translated from German by Miss M. M. Green (Routledge).

"The Bolshies on Parnassus," "The World of Books" column, *The Nation & The Athenaeum* 46 (14 December 1929): 402. Review of *Tradition and Experiment in Present-Day Literature* [lectures or essays by Mr. Mottram, Mr. Blunden, Mr. A. I. A. Symons, Ashley Dukes, Rebecca West, Mr. Beresford, Miss Sitwell, Mr. Burdett, Mr. C. K. Munro, and Mr. Eliot] (Oxford University Press and Milford).

"Montaigne," "The World of Books" column, *The Nation & The Athenaeum* 46 (21 December 1929): 434. Review essay on Montaigne and *Montaigne, an Essay in Two Parts* by Andre Gide (Blackamore Press).

"On the Bench and in the Dock," "The World of Books" column, *The Nation & The Athenaeum* 46 (28 December 1929): 460. Review essay on *The Young Person's Complete Guide to Crime* by Mr. C. G. L. du Cann (Richards & Toulmin); *Chief Justice Coke, His Family and Descendants at Holkham* by Charles Warburton James (Country Life); and *The Bloody Assizes*, edited by J. G. Muddiman, Notable Trials Series (Hodge).

"**Mr. Chesterton and Mr. Belloc,**" "The World of Books" column, *The Nation & The Athenaeum* **46** (4 January 1930): **486**. Review essay on *A Companion to Mr. Wells's "Outline of History"* by Hilaire Belloc (Sheed & Ward); *The Thing* by G. K. Chesterton (Sheed & Ward); *G. K. C. as M. C.* [collection of thirty-seven introductions by G. K. Chesterton], edited by J. P. de Fonseka (Methuen); and *The Philosophy of St. Thomas Aquinas* by Etienne Gilson, translated by Edward Bullough, edited by Rev. G. A. Elrington (2nd ed.; Heffer).

"**The Natural History of a Political Animal,**" "The World of Books" column, *The Nation & The Athenaeum* **46** (11 January 1930): **512**. Review essay on *Democracy, Its Defects and Advantages* by Delisle Burns (Allen & Unwin); *Studies in the English Social and Political Thinkers of the Nineteenth Century*, 2 vols., by R. H. Murray (Heffer); and *Edmund Burke and the Revolt Against the Eighteenth Century* by Alfred Cobban (Allen & Unwin).

"**A Premium on Safe Driving,**" *The Nation & The Athenaeum* **46** (18 January 1930): **533-34**. A column on the dangers posed by reckless drivers with a number of proposals to encourage the average driver to drive responsibly.

"**Browsing in the Past,**" "The World of Books" column, *The Nation & The Athenaeum* **46** (18 January 1930): **542**. Review essay on *The Hardman Papers* [Sir William Hardman], edited by S. M. Ellis (Constable); *The Diary of a Country Parson, The Reverend James Woodforde*, Vol. IV [1793-1796], edited by John Beresford (Oxford University Press and Milford); *The Life of Napoleon* by Dimitri Merezhkovsky (Dent); and *The Autobiography of Calvin Coolidge* (Chatto & Windus).

"**Meditations on Religion,**" "The World of Books" column, *The Nation & The Athenaeum* **46** (25 January 1930): **578**. Review of *The Past and Future of Religion* by Mr. C. E. M. Joad (Benn).

"**Motoring and Insurance,**" "Letters to the Editor" column, *The Nation & The Athenaeum* **46** (1 February 1930): **604**. L. Woolf's reply to critics' letters published on 25 January 1930 about the article "A Premium on Safe Driving" 18 January 1930. See above.

"**The Count of Monte Cristo,**" "The World of Books" column, *The Nation & The Athenaeum* **46** (1 February 1930): **610**. Review of *Dumas, the Incredible Marquis* [Alexandre Dumas] by Herbert S. Gorman (Gollancz).

"**A Censorship at Work,**" "The World of Books" column, *The Nation & The Athenaeum* **46** (8 February 1930): **642**. Review essay on *Cato, or the Future of Censorship* by William Seagle, To-day and To-morrow series (Kegan Paul) and *Index of Prohibited Books* [translation of *Indice dei Libri Proibiti, riveduto e pubblicato per ordine di Sua Santita Pio Papa XI*] (Burns, Oates & Washbourne).

"The Ideals of Journalism," "The World of Books" column, *The Nation & The Athenaeum* 46 (15 February 1930): 674. Review essay on *The Newspaper of To-morrow* by Harold Herd (Allen & Unwin) and *Deucalion* [on the future of literary criticism] by Geoffrey West, To-day and To-morrow series. (Routledge).

"England and the World, *The Nation & The Athenaeum* 46 (8 March 1930): 770, 772. Reviews of *England* by Wilhelm Dibelius, translated from German by Mary Agnes Hamilton (Cape) and *England's Voice of Freedom. An Anthology of Liberty*, pieces selected by Henry W. Nevinson who also wrote the introduction (Gollancz).

"Dibelius's *England*," "Letters to the Editor" column, *The Nation & The Athenaeum* 46 (22 March 1930): 858. Woolf's response to Charles Wright's letter published on 15 March 1930 about the Dibelius review of 8 March 1930. See above.

"Voltaire and Casanova," *The Nation & The Athenaeum* 46 (29 March 1930): 896–97. Reviews of *Voltaire, reconte par ceux qui l'ont vu*, edited by J. G. Prod'homme (Stock) and *Casanova: His Life and Memoirs*, 2 vols., translated from French by Arthur Machen. Selected and edited with connecting links by G. D. Gribble (Routledge).

"Dibelius," "Letters to the Editor" column, *The Nation & The Athenaeum* 47 (5 April 1930): 12. Woolf's response to Charles Wright's letter published on 29 March 1930 about the Dibelius review of 8 March 1930. See above.

"Tiger or Tom-Cat?" "Reviews" section, *The Nation & The Athenaeum* 47 (19 April 1930): 85–86. Review of *Grandeur and Misery* by Georges Clemenceau (Harrap).

"The Female at Home and Abroad," *The Nation & The Athenaeum* 47 (10 May 1930): 178, 180. Reviews of *Mary Gladstone (Mrs. Drew); Diary and Letters*, edited by Lucy Masterman (Methuen) and *The Letters of Gertrude Bell*, edited by Lady Bell (new edition; Benn).

"Tolstoy Again," "Reviews" section, *The Nation & The Athenaeum* 47 (17 May 1930): 219–20. Reviews of *The Life of Tolstoy; Later Years*, Vol. II, by Aylmer Maude, Tolstoy Centenary Edition (Oxford University Press and Milford); *Childhood, Boyhood, and Youth* by Leo Tolstoy and *What is Art? and Essays on Art* by Leo Tolstoy, translated by Aylmer Maude, The World's Classics series (Oxford University Press).

"The Problem of Africa," *The Nation & The Athenaeum* 47 (24 May 1930): 254. Reviews of *Africa and Some World Problems* by General J. C. Smuts (Clarendon Press) and *White and Black in Africa. A Critical Examination of the Rhodes Lectures of General Smuts* by J. H. Oldham (Longmans).

"A European Sensation," *The Nation & The Athenaeum* 47 (7 June 1930): 322–23. Review of *A Cultural History of the Moderna Age, from the Black*

Death to the World War, Vol. I: *Introduction: Renaissance and Reformation*, by Egon Friedell, translated from German by Charles Francis Atkinson (Knopf).

"The Scholar's Life," *The Nation & The Athenaeum* 47 (21 June 1930): 381. Review of *My Recollections, 1848–1914* by Professor Ulrich von Wilamowitz-Moellendorff, translated by G. C. Richards (Chatto & Windus).

"Marriage and the Family," *The Nation & The Athenaeum* 47 (28 June 1930): 412. Reviews of *Marriage, Past, Present, and Future* by Ralph de Pomerai (Constable) and *Chronos or the Future of the Family* by Eden Paul, M. D. (Kegan Paul).

"A Revolutionary," "Reviews" section, *The Nation & The Athenaeum* 47 (12 July 1930): 474. Review of *My Life* by Leon Trotsky (Butterworth).

"A Traveller in the East," *The Nation & The Athenaeum* 47 (26 July 1930): 535. Reviews of *Oriental Memories of a German Diplomatist* by Friedrich Rosen (Methuen) and *The Quatrains of Omar Khayyam*, new translation by Friedrich Rosen who also wrote the introduction (Methuen).

"An Irritable and Erratic Ego," *The Nation & The Athenaeum* 47 (2 August 1930): 569. Review essay on *Bengal Lancer* by Major F. Yeats-Brown (Gollancz); *Misfit* by Captain J. R. White (Cape); and *Some Personal Experiences* by Sir Bampfylde Fuller (Murray) [autobiographies of colonial administrators].

"States and Churches," "Reviews" section, *The Nation & The Athenaeum* 47 (23 August 1930): 651. Review of *State, Church, and Study* [collection of essays and papers by the author] by Ernest Barker (Methuen).

"Dreams and Realities," "Reviews" section, *The Nation & The Athenaeum* 47 (13 September 1930): 735. Review of *The Problem of the Twentieth Century* by David Davies (Benn).

"Modern Witchcraft," "Reviews" section, *The Nation & The Athenaeum* 47 (27 September 1930): 795. Review essay on *The Story of Psychic Science (Psychical Research)* by Hereward Carrington (Rider); *Rudi Schneider: A Scientific Examination of His Mediumship* by Harry Price (Methuen); and *Some Modern Mediums* by Theodore Besterman (Methuen).

"Lord D'Abernon and Locarno," "Reviews" section, *The Nation & The Athenaeum* 48 (4 October 1930): 18. Review of *An Ambassador of Peace: Lord D'Abernon's Diary*, Vol. III: *The Years of Recovery, January, 1924–October, 1925* [British diplomat] (Hodder & Stoughton).

"Soviet Foreign Policy," *The Nation & The Athenaeum* 48 (18 October 1930): 109. Review of *The Soviets in World Affairs*, 2 vols., by Louis Fischer (Cape).

"Three Sides of a Picture," *The Nation & The Athenaeum* 48 (25 October 1930): 139. Reviews of *The Age of the Chartists, 1832–1854. A Study of Discontent* by J. L. Hammond and Barbara Hammond (Longmans); *Lord John*

Russell by A. Wyatt Tilby (Cassell); and *British Colonial Policy in the Age of Peel and Russell* by W. P. Morrell (Clarendon Press).

"The Late Lord Montagu of Beaulieu," *The Nation & The Athenaeum* 48 (29 November 1930): 293. Letter to the Editor. Woolf comments on remarks about the subject of death made by a close friend of Lord Montagu in a letter published on 22 November 1930.

"Cobbett," "Reviews" section, *The Nation & The Athenaeum* 48 (29 November 1930): 298. Review of *Cobbett's Rural Rides*, 3 vols., edited by G. D. H. Cole and Margaret Cole (Peter Davies).

"The Antediluvians," "Reviews" section, *The Nation & The Athenaeum* 48 (13 December 1930): 379. Review of *The Diaries of John Bright*, edited by Mr. R. A. J. Walling, with a foreword by Philip Bright (Cassell).

"Much Ado About Nothing," "Reviews" section, *The Nation & The Athenaeum* 48 (3 January 1931): 461–62. Review of *In Defence of Sensuality* by John Cowper Powys (Gollancz).

"John Bright," *The Nation & The Athenaeum* 48 (10 January 1931): 479. Letter to the Editor. Woolf responds to Mr. F. E. Pollard's letter published on 3 January 1931 about the review of *The Diaries of John Bright* 13 December 1930. See above.

"The Adams Family," *The Nation & The Athenaeum* 48 (17 January 1931): 514, 516. Review essay on *The Adams Family* by James Truslow Adams (Oxford University Press and Milford) and *Letters of Henry Adams (1858–1891)*, edited by Worthington Chauncey Ford (Constable).

"John Bright," *The Nation & The Athenaeum* 48 (31 January 1931): 569. Letter to the Editor. Woolf responds to Dr. Paul Bernard Roth's letter published on 24 January 1931 about the review of *The Diaries of John Bright* 13 December 1930. Roger Clark also entered this discussion with a letter published on 7 February 1931. See above.

"The Law," "Reviews" section, *The Nation & The Athenaeum* 48 (31 January 1931): 575–76. Review essay on *Essays in Jurisprudence and the Common Law* by Arthur L. Goodhart (Cambridge University Press) and *In Quest of Justice* by Claud Mullins (Murray).

"The World," "Reviews" section, *The Nation & The Athenaeum* 48 (7 February 1931): 604. Review essay on *Survey of International Affairs, 1929* by Arnold J. Toynbee, assisted by V. M. Boulter (Oxford University Press) and *Documents on International Affairs, 1929*, edited by John W. Wheeler-Bennett, with an introduction by Lieutenant-General Sir George Macdonogh (Oxford University Press and Milford).

"Economic Equality," "Reviews" section, *The Nation & The Athenaeum* 48 (21 February 1931): 669. *Equality* by R. H. Tawney (Allen & Unwin).

3.4. THE NEW STATESMAN

The New Statesman was created as a Fabian Society organ under the auspices of Sidney and Beatrice Webb and George Bernard Shaw in 1912–13. Clifford Sharp served as editor from 1913 to 1931.

Letter to the Editor, *The New Statesman* I, No. 9 (7 June 1913): 270. Response to a review of a book on Scientific Management that deals with Mr. Taylor's theories.

"Two Characters," *The New Statesman* I, No. 25 (27 September 1913): 787–88. A critical account of two fictional characters, Lady Matilda Jones and Dorothea, who live non-descript, timid lives.

"The Road Home," *The New Statesman* II, No. 46 (21 February 1914): 626–28. Essay about a fictional fifty-six year-old solicitor who learns that he must make changes in his life due to his age.

"The Diplomatic Service," *The New Statesman* IV, No. 93 (16 January 1915): 359–60. Comment on the Royal Commission on the Civil Service's work from April 29 and July 16 on recruitment for diplomatic service and the Commission's Blue Book of findings and recommendations.

"The Cautious Co-operator," *The New Statesman* V, No. 113 (5 June 1915): 198–99. Comment on the Co-operative Congress meeting of late May in Leicester with an analysis of the mission and goals of the Cooperative Movement.

"Working Women and the War," *The New Statesman* V, No. 116 (26 June 1915): 275–76. Comments on wartime policies discussed at the recent Congress of the Women's Co-operative Guild in Liverpool.

"Suggestions for the Prevention of War," *The New Statesman Special Supplement* V, No. 118 (10 July 1915): 1–24. Memorandum prepared by L. Woolf for the International Agreements Committee of the Fabian Research Department. In the *New Statesman Special Supplement* V, No. 119 (17 July 1915): 1–8, the Committee published articles on the prevention of war to be considered for adoption by an international conference.

"Perpetual Peace," "Miscellany" column, *The New Statesman* V, No. 121 (31 July 1915): 398–99. L.W. on Kant and war debts. Woolf is critical of war debts.

"Crowds and Their Leaders," *The New Statesman* VI, No. 147 (29 January 1916): 398–99. Observations on the relationship between crowds and their leaders drawn in part from *The Executive and His Control of Men* by E. B. Gowin, *The Psychology of Leadership* by Abdul Majid, and *The Crowd in Peace and War* by Sir Martin Conway.

"Study of International Relations," "Correspondence" column, *The New Statesman* VI, No. 154 (18 March 1916): 567–68. Letter to the Editor with a response by the Editor. L. Woolf responds to a recent article on the balance of power and gives his own views on the subject.

"Study of International Relations," "Correspondence" column, *The New Statesman* VI, No. 155 (25 March 1916): 592. Letter to the Editor. L. Woolf and Editor continue their discussion on the balance of power started with Woolf's letter published on 18 March 1916.

"The Inhuman Herd," *The New Statesman* (8 July 1916): 327-28. Essay on rational and irrational tendencies in man with observations on the *Instincts of the Herd in Peace and War* by W. Trotter. Woolf ends by emphasizing the importance of environment.

"The Gentleness of Nature," "Miscellany" column, *The New Statesman* (6 January 1917): 326-27. The title is ironic because the essay is about how cruel and capricious nature can be. Woolf draws on his experiences in Ceylon, especially dealing with the rinderpest epidemic.

"The Character of Herbert Spencer," "Miscellany" column, *The New Statesman* (10 March 1917): 541-42. A character sketch of Herbert Spencer.

"The Two Kings of Jerusalem," "Miscellany" column, *The New Statesman* 9 (28 April 1917): 85-87. Essay on diplomatic etiquette and language with reference to Sir Ernest Satow's *A Guide to Diplomatic Practice* (Longmans).

"Tchehov," "Miscellany" column, *The New Statesman* 9 (11 August 1917): 446-48. Review of Tchehov's short stories which have been translated by Mrs. Garnett. (Constance Garnett?)

"Hazlitt," "Miscellany" column, *The New Statesman* 10 (15 December 1917): 257-58. Essay on the life and works of William Hazlitt, literary critic and essayist. *Hazlitt; Selected Essays*, edited by George Sampson (Cambridge University Press) is mentioned.

"Winged and Unwinged Words," "Miscellany" column, *The New Statesman* 11 (6 July 1918): 72-73. Review essay of *Public Speaking and Debate* by George Jacob Holyoake. References to politicians, especially Gladstone.

"The Dutch Convoy," "Correspondence" column, *The New Statesman* 11 (20 July 1918): 310. Letter to the Editor. Woolf challenges the assertion on the part of a writer who accused the Foreign Office of abandoning the right of search under international laws of naval warfare.

"Imperial Capitalism," "Correspondence" column, *The New Statesman* 13 (8 May 1919): 117. Letter to the Editor. Woolf challenges the statement, in a recent article, that 10 % of the nation's income came from foreign investments. He argues that wealth generated from colonial possessions is much greater and that imperialism exploits colonial peoples.

"The New Slave Policy in East Africa," "Correspondence" column, *The New Statesman* (2 October 1920): 700. Letter to the Editor. Woolf explains the economic reasons for compulsory labor in East Africa. (See 21 February and 10 April for Woolf's articles on the subject.)

3.5. THE NEW STATESMAN AND NATION

John Maynard Keynes merged *The New Statesman* and *The Nation* in 1931 primarily for financial reasons. [See Edward Hyams, *The New Statesman: The History of the First Fifty Years, 1913–1963* (London and Southhampton: The Camelot Press Ltd., 1963), 119–21.] Kingsley Martin served as editor from 1931 to 1960.

"**Russia and the Russians,**" "Current Literature" column, *The New Statesman and Nation* 1 (28 February 1931): 22, 24. Review of *Russia: A Social History* by D. S. Mirsky, Vol. 1, Cresset Historical Series, edited by Professor C. G. Seligman (Cresset Press).

"**The Tragic Comedian,**" *The New Statesman and Nation* 1 (6 June 1931): 547–48. Review of *Lassalle* [Ferdinand Lassalle, a founder of the German Social-Democratic Party] by Arno Shirokauer, translated from German by Eden Paul and Cedar Paul (Allen & Unwin).

"**Gramophone Records,**" "Correspondence" column, *The New Statesman and Nation* 2 (18 July 1931): 76. Woolf's response to a letter by Mr. Alec Robertson of 11 July 1931.

"**British Justice and the Rouse Case,**" *The New Statesman and Nation* 2 (1 August 1931): 143. Review of *Trial of Alfred Rouse*, edited by Helena Normanton (Hodge).

"**Educating the Listener-In,**" *The New Statesman and Nation* 2 (5 September 1931): 274–75. This piece is unsigned, but Leonard Woolf is listed as the author in the index. The piece is a notice of the *This Changing World* series of talks to be broadcast by the BBC from October to March. The subjects of the talks will be: Industry and Trade; Literature and Art; Science; the Modern State; Education and Leisure; and the Modern Dilemma—"how men and women are to adjust their minds and lives in a situation which is so continuously in process of change." About 20 different speakers will be featured in the talks.

"**French Political Thought,**" *The New Statesman and Nation* 2 (7 November 1931): 580, 582. Review of *French Political Thought in the Nineteenth Century* by Roger Soltau (Benn).

"**Rosebery,**" *The New Statesman and Nation* 2 (21 November 1931): 645–46. Review of *Lord Rosebery* [former prime minister], 2 vols., by the Marquess of Crewe [Lord Rosebery's son-in-law] (Murray).

"**Keynessandra,**" *The New Statesman and Nation* 2 (19 December 1931): 788. Review of *Essays in Persuasion* by J. M. Keynes (Macmillan).

"**An Angel of Peace,**" *The New Statesman and Nation* 3 (9 January 1932): 43. Review of *The Unseen Assassins* by Sir Norman Angell (Hamilton).

"**Lytton Strachey,**" "Miscellany" column, *The New Statesman and Nation* 3 (30 January 1932): 118–19. Eulogy for Lytton Strachey.

"**Lytton Strachey and Gordon,**" "Correspondence" column," *The New Statesman and Nation* 3 (13? February 1932): 196. Woolf responds to Henry W. Nevinson's letter of 6 February 1932, p. 163, on Woolf's eulogy for Lytton Strachey of 30 January 1932. See above.

"**Mr. Wells's Works and Days,**" *The New Statesman and Nation* 3 (27 February 1932): 266. Review of *The Work, Wealth and Happiness* of Mankind by H. G. Wells (Heinemann). See Leonard Woolf, *Beginning Again: An Autobiography of the Years 1911–1918* (1964; Hogarth Press, 1972), pp. 194–97, for a discussion of Wells' reaction to the review.

"**Behind the Bars,**" *The New Statesman and Nation* 4 (9 July 1932): 44. Review of *Twenty Thousand Years in Sing Sing* by Warden Lewis E. Lawes (Constable).

"**Lord Oxford,**" *The New Statesman and Nation* 4 (22 October 1932): 485–86. Review of *The Life of Lord Oxford and Asquith* [Liberal Party leader], 2 vols., by J. A. Spender and Cyril Asquith (Hutchinson).

"**General Gordon,**" *The New Statesman and Nation* 5 (28 January 1933): 105. Review essay on *Gordon: An Intimate Portrait* by H. E. Wortham (Harrap) and *Gordon: The Sudan and Slavery* by Pierre Crabites (Routledge).

"**Intellectual Crime,**"*The New Statesman and Nation* 5 (25 February 1933): 227–28. Review essay on *Intellectual Crime* by Janet Chance (Noel Douglas) and *Is Christianity True?* A discussion between Arnold Lunn and C. E. M. Joad (Eyre & Spottiswoode).

"**Etherial Problems,**"*The New Statesman and Nation* 6 (22 July 1933): 99–100. An article on the mission and programs of the BBC with a couple of references to books: *Shall I Listen* by Filson Young (Constable) and *Wireless for Over 30 Years* by R. N. Vyvyan (Routledge).

"**Socialism in Our Time,**" *The New Statesman and Nation* 6 (9 September 1933): 302, 304. Review of *Problems of a Socialist Government* by Sir Stafford Cripps and others (Gollancz).

"**Biography 'In Extremis,'**" *The New Statesman and Nation* 6 (7 October 1933): 418. Review of *The Post Victorians* [collection of forty biographies written by forty different people], with an introduction by the Very Reverend W. R. Inge (Nicholson and Watson).

"**We Prefer Cathay,**" *The New Statesman and Nation* 6 (14 October 1933): 448. Review of *Fifty Years in Europe. A Study in Pre-War Documents* by J. A. Spender (Cassell).

"**Mr. Monkhouse and Moscow,**" *The New Statesman and Nation* 6 (14 November 1933): 606. Review of *Moscow,1911–1933* by Allan Monkhouse [autobiographical account of Monkhouse's experiences] (Gollancz).

"Quack, Quack! Or Having It Both Ways," *The New Statesman and Nation* 6 (2 December 1933): 702, 704. Review of *Counter Attack from the East, the Philosophy of Radhakrishnan* by C. E. M. Joad (Allen & Unwin).

"How We Won the War," *The New Statesman and Nation* 7 (3 February 1934):157-58. Review of *Four and a Half Years*, Vol. I, by the Rt. Hon. Christopher Addison (Hutchinson).

"British in India," *The New Statesman and Nation* 7 (30 June 1934): 997-98. Review of *The Rise and Fulfilment of British Rule in India* by Edward Thompson and G. T. Garrat (Macmillan).

"Civilisations," *The New Statesman and Nation* 8 (18 August 1934): 213-14. Review of *A Study of History*, Vols. I-III, by Arnold J. Toynbee (Oxford University Press).

"To True to Be Good," *The New Statesman and Nation* 8 (8 September 1934): 298. Review of *Prefaces* by Bernard Shaw (Constable).

"How We Have Done It," *The New Statesman and Nation* 9 (12 January 1935): 49-50. Review of *Our Own Times*, Vol. I, by Stephen King-Hall (Nicholson and Watson).

"A History of Europe," *The New Statesman and Nation* 9 (2 March 1935): 285-86. Review of *A History of Europe*, Vol. I: *Ancient and Mediaeval*, by the Rt. Hon. H. A. L. Fisher (Eyre and Spottiswood).

"The Modern Tory," *The New Statesman and Nation* 9 (9 March 1935): 330, 332. Review of *Frederick Edwin Earl of Birkenhead; The Last Phase* by his son, Lord Birkenhead, with a foreword by the Rt. Hon. D. Lloyd George and an appreciation by the Rt. Hon. Sir Austen Chamberlain (Thornton Butterworth).

"If I Were Dictator," *The New Statesman and Nation* 9 (30 March 1935): 457. Review essay on *If I Were Dictator* by James Maxton (Methuen) and *If I Were Dictator* by H. R. L. Sheppard (Methuen).

"Up and Up Or Down and Down," *The New Statesman and Nation* 9 (29 June 1935): 957-58. A piece on the political situation in Europe based on the author's observations and travels to Italy, the Netherlands, and Germany in 1933 and in May 1935. The piece is signed "A. C.," but the index lists Leonard Woolf as the author. Leonard and Virginia visited France and Italy in May 1933 and again in May 1935 when they visited Germany and the Netherlands, too.

"What Is Called A Liberal," *The New Statesman and Nation* 10 (6 July 1935): 24-25. Review of *Condorcet and the Rise of Liberalism* by J. Salwyn Schapiro (Harcourt Brace).

"The Failure of Fascism," *The New Statesman and Nation* 10 (27 July 1935): 130-31. Review essay on *Mussolini's Italy* by Dr. Herman Finer (Gollancz) and *Mussolini Red and Black* by Armando Borghi (Wishart).

"At Europe's Bedside," *The New Statesman and Nation* 10 (10 August 1935): 198. Review of *Europe's Crisis* by Andre Siegfried (Cape).

"Bad Consciences," *The New Statesman and Nation* 10 (12 October 1935): 498. Review of *The Eve of 1914* by Theodor Wolff (Gollancz).

"The Great Divide," *The New Statesman and Nation* 10 (23 November 1935): 778–79. Review of Armand Charpentier's *The Dreyfus Case*, translated by J. Lewis May (Bles).

"Robespierre," *The New Statesman and Nation* 11 (4 January 1936): 19. Review of *Robespierre*, 2 vols., by J. M. Thompson (Blackwell).

"Mr. Belloc on the Holy Land," *The New Statesman and Nation* 11 (22 February 1936): 276, 278. Review of *The Battle Ground* by Hilaire Belloc (Cassell).

"Hitler," *The New Statesman and Nation* 11 (20 June 1936): 984, 86. Review of *Hitler the Pawn* by Rudolf Olden (Gollancz).

"Meditations on Life and Death," *The New Statesman and Nation* 12 (15 August 1936): 230–31. Review of *Euthanasia and Other Aspects of Life and Death* by Harry Roberts (Constable).

"One Damn Thing After Another," *The New Statesman and Nation* 12 (19 September 1936): 400. Review of J. A. Spender's *Great Britain, Empire and Commonwealth, 1886–1935* (Cassell).

"Shining Armour," *The New Statesman and Nation* 12 (24 October 1936): 634, 636. Review of *The Kaiser and English Relations* by E. F. Benson (Longmans).

"Goetterdaemmerung," *The New Statesman and Nation* 12 (14 November 1936): 784, 786. Review of *Arthur James Balfour, First Earl of Balfour, K. G., O. M., F. R. S.*, Vol. II [1906–1930], by his niece Blanche E. C. Dugdale (Hutchinson).

"A London Diary," *The New Statesman and Nation* 12 (26 December 1936): 1054–55. A broad-ranging discussion of the psychology of the British people after King Edward VIII's abdication on December 11. Within this context, Woolf also discusses a number of essays and books, including *The Witchcraft Trial in Moscow* by Friedrich Adler (Labour Publications Department).

"A London Diary," *The New Statesman and Nation* 13 (2 January 1937): 6–7. Woolf shares observations about events during the holidays, including Hitler's Christmas Eve address which was delivered by Hitler's deputy, Rudolf Hess.

"Talleyrand," *The New Statesman and Nation* 13 (13 March 1937): 420, 422. Review essay on *Talleyrand* by Comte de Saint-Aulaire, translated from French by George Frederic Lees and Frederick J. Stephens (Macmillan) and *The Lives of Talleyrand* by Crane Brinton (Allen & Unwin).

"Napoleon," *The New Statesman and Nation* 13 (15 May 1937): 817. Review of *Bonaparte* by Eugene Tarle, translated from Russian by John Cournos (Secker and Warburg).

"The Future of the Co-operative Movement," *The New Statesman and Nation* 13 (26 June 1937): 1068, 1070. Review of *England Cradle of Co-operation* by Sydney R. Elliott (Faber).

"The Defeat of Pacifism," *The New Statesman and Nation* 14 (18 September 1937): 410, 412. Review of *Collective Insecurity* by H. M. Swanwick (Cape).

"Portrait of a Great Man," *The New Statesman and Nation* 14 (16 October 1937): 616. Review of *Great Contemporaries* by Winston S. Churchill (Thornton Butterworth).

"Unheard-Of Adventures," *The New Statesman and Nation* 14 (4 December 1937): 971–72. Review essay on *Michael Bakunin* by E. H. Carr (Macmillan) and *History of Anarchism in Russia* by E. Yaroslavsky (Lawrence and Wishart).

"Anatomy of Empire," *The New Statesman and Nation* 15 (12 March 1938): 444. Review of *Trials in Burma* by Maurice Collis (Faber & Faber).

"The Religion of the Stake," *The New Statesman and Nation* 15 (9 April 1938): 624. Review of *Inquisition and Liberty* by G. G. Coulton (Heinemann).

"Words and Things," *The New Statesman and Nation* 15 (7 May 1938): 778, 780. Review of *The Tyranny of Words* by Stuart Chase (Methuen).

"The Prophet," *The New Statesman and Nation* 16 (3 September 1838): 352–53. Review of *Mohammad* by Essad Bey, translated by Helmut L. Ripperger (Cobden-Sanderson).

"Modern History," *The New Statesman and Nation* 16 (1 October 1938): 502. Review essay on *The Modern Historian* by C. H. Williams (Nelson) and *Aspects of History* by E. E. Kellett (Cape).

"Whiteley," *The New Statesman and Nation* 16 (22 October 1938): 624, 626. Review of The Universal Provider: *A Study of William Whiteley and the Rise of the London Department Store* by Richard S. Lambert (Harrap).

"The Constitution Under Strain," *The New Statesman and Nation* 16 (12 November 1938): 782, 784. Review essay on *The British Constitution* by H. R. G. Greaves (Allen & Unwin) and *Parliamentary Government in England* by Harold J. Laski (Allen & Unwin).

"Canonization of North," *The New Statesman and Nation* 16 (10 December 1938): 1014, 1016. Review of *Lord North* by W. Baring Pemberton (Longmans).

"Chatham," *The New Statesman and Nation* 17 (18 February 1939): 256. Review of *William Pitt, Earl of Chatham* by Brian Tunstall (Hodder and Stoughton).

"The Defeat of Democracy," *The New Statesman and Nation* 17 (11 March 1939): 392. Review of *The Pursuit of Happiness. The Story of American Democracy* by Herbert Agar (Eyre and Spottiswoode).

"Democracies, Unite!" *The New Statesman and Nation* 17 (18 March 1939): 434, 436. Review of *Union Now* by Clarence Street (Cape).

"The Perfect American," *The New Statesman and Nation* 17 (1 April 1939): 510. Review of *Benjamin Franklin* by Carl Van Doren (Putnam).

"Lord Brougham," *The New Statesman and Nation* 17 (6 May 1939): 702, 704. Review of *Lord Brougham and the Whig Party* by Arthur Aspinall (Manchester University Press).

"Moribund Civilisations," *The New Statesman and Nation* 18 (23 September 1939): 433–34. Review of *A Study of History*, Vols. IV, V, and VI, by Arnold J. Toynbee (Oxford Press).

"European Civilisation," *The New Statesman and Nation* 18 (21 October 1939): 586, 588. Review of *The Rise of European Civilisation* by Professor Charles Seignobos, translated from French by Catherine Alison Philips (Cape).

"Two Revolutionaries," *The New Statesman and Nation* 18 (11 November 1939): 686. Review essay on *Lafayette* by W. E. Woodward (Cresset Press) and *Saint Just* by J. B. Morton (Longmans.

"Richelieu," *The New Statesman and Nation* 19 (13 April 1940): 508. Review of *Richelieu, His Rise to Power* by Carl J. Burckhardt, translated and abridged by Edwin Muir and Willa Muir (Allen and Unwin).

"The National Assembly," *The New Statesman and Nation* 19 (18 May 1940): 646–47. Review of *The Beginning of the Third Republic in France. A History of the National Assembly (February to September 1871)* by Rev. F. H. Brabant, Canon of Winchester (Macmillan).

"Jews and Their Future," *The New Statesman and Nation* 19 (1 June 1940): 706–07. Review of *The Jewish Fate and Future* by Professor Arthur Ruppin (Macmillan).

"Principia Sociologica," *The New Statesman and Nation* 19 (29 June 1940): 807. Review of *Man and Society in an Age of Reconstruction* by Karl Mannheim (Kegan Paul).

"The Politician and the Intellectual," *The New Statesman and Nation* 20 (20 July 1940): 56–57. A commentary on the relationship between politicians and intellectuals. Woolf observes that British governments could examine a much fuller range of policies if intellectuals served as cabinet ministers.

"A Golden Branch Amid the Shadows," *The New Statesman and Nation* 20 (3 August 1940): 120, 122. Review of *James George Frazer* [biography of an influential anthropologist] by R. Angus Downie (Watts).

"Sahibs or Socialists?" *The New Statesman and Nation* 20 (17 August 1940): 164. Review of T. C. Worsley's *Barbarians and Philistines: Democracy and the Public Schools* (Hale).

"**Renascent Democracy,**" *The New Statesman and Nation* 21 (4 January 1941): 16, 18. Review of *Marxism and Democracy* by Lucien Laurat (Gollancz).

"**The Future of Imperialism,**" *The New Statesman and Nation* 21 (25 January 1941): 76–77. Opinion piece on the role of the British Empire in the postwar world. Woolf recommends that all empires be dissolved and that the international community establish an international trading system in which all nations, including former colonies, participate. He refers to the *Survey of British Commonwealth Affairs*, Vol. II: *Problems of Economic Policy, 1918–1939*, Part I, by W. K. Hancock (Oxford Press, Milford, and Royal Institute of International Affairs).

"**Inquest on Geneva,**" *The New Statesman and Nation* 21 (15 February 1941): 162–64. Review essay on *A Great Experiment: An Autobiography* by Viscount Robert Cecil [former Undersecretary for Foreign Affairs] (Cape).

"**Cultural Chaos,**" *The New Statesman and Nation* 21 (8 March 1941): 253–54. Review essay on *The Culture of Cities* by Lewis Mumford, Cheap edition (Secker and Warburg).

"**English Socialism,**" *The New Statesman and Nation* 21 (22 March 1941): 304–05. Review essay on *British Working Class Politics, 1832–1914* by G. D. H. Cole (Routledge).

"**What Is History?**" *The New Statesman and Nation* 21 (12 April 1941): 390, 392. Review of *History as the Story of Liberty* by Benedetto Croce (Allen and Unwin).

"**The Tradition of Liberty,**" *The New Statesman and Nation* 21 (24 May 1941): 536. Review of *Political Liberty: A History of the Conception in the Middle Ages and Modern Times* by A. J. Carlyle (Oxford University Press).

"**Back to Samuel Smiles,**" *The New Statesman and Nation* 22 (26 July 1941): 86. Review of *The Recovery of the West* by Michael Roberts (Faber).

"**Lenin Turns the Key,**" *The New Statesman and Nation* 22 (6 September 1941): 234. Review of *To the Finland Station* by Edmund Wilson (Secker and Warburg).

"**The Indian Riddle,**" *The New Statesman and Nation* 22 (4 October 1941): 333. Review essay on *Modern India and the West; A Study of the Interactions of Their Civilisations*, edited by L. S. S. O'Malley (Oxford Press and Royal Institute of International Affairs); *India and Democracy* by Sir George Schuster and Guy Wint (Macmillan); and *The Choice Before India* by J. Chinna Durai (Cape).

"**The Second Risorgimento,**" *The New Statesman and Nation* 22 (8 November 1941): 413. Review of *The Remaking of Italy* by Pentad [five anonymous authors] (Penguin).

"**Dodging Reality,**" *The New Statesman and Nation* 22 (27 December 1941): 528–29. Review of *The Pool of Memory* [autobiography] by E. Phillips Oppenheim (Hodder & Stoughton).

"The Way They Have in the Army," *The New Statesman and Nation* 23 (31 January 1942): 80. Review essay on *Khaki and Gown. An Autobiography* by Field-Marshal Lord Birdwood (Ward Lock); *The Life of General Sir Charles Warren* by Watkin Williams (Blackwell); and *Tinned Soldier* by Alec Dixon (Right Book Club).

"The Tangle in Palestine," *The New Statesman and Nation* 23 (18 April 1942): 260–61. Review of *Palestine: A Policy* by Albert M. Hyamson, with a foreword by Sir Ronald Storrs (Methuen).

"The Candid Friend," *The New Statesman and Nation* 24 (11 July 1942): 29. Review of *And Hell Followed* by Odette Keun (Constable).

"The Economic Determination of Jane Austin," *The New Statesman and Nation* 24 (18 July 1942): 39–41. A commentary on Jane Austin's works.

"U. S. S. R.," *The New Statesman and Nation* 24 (29 August 1942): 148. Review of *Russia and Her Western Neighbours* by George W. Keeton and Dr. Rudolf Schlesinger (Cape).

"Hitler Speaks," *The New Statesman and Nation* 24 (26 September 1942): 208–09. Review essay on *Hitler's Speeches, 1922–1939*, 2 vols., English translation of representative passages, edited by Norman Baynes (Oxford Press and Royal Institute of International Affairs).

"Bernard Shaw," *The New Statesman and Nation* 24 (5 December 1942): 375–76. Review essay on *Bernard Shaw: His Life and Personality* by Hesketh Pearson (Collins).

"Back to Mumbo-Jumbo," *The New Statesman and Nation* 25 (9 January 1943): 28–29. Review of *Man the Master* by Gerald Heard (Faber).

"Playing with Figures," *The New Statesman and Nation* 25 (23 January 1943): 64–65. Review of *A Short History of Labour Conditions Under Industrial Capitalism*, Vol. I: *Great Britain and the Empire, 1750 to the Present Day* by Jurgen Kuczynski (Muller).

"Lord Olivier," *The New Statesman and Nation* 25 (27 February 1943): 138–39. Eulogy for Sydney Olivier, who was a high-ranking member of the Colonial Office, a Fabian Socialist, and Labour Party member.

"Hippy and Hitler," *The New Statesman and Nation* 25 (1 May 1943): 294. Review of *Hippy. In Memoriam. The Story of a Dog* by Sir Nevile Henderson [former British ambassador to Germany] (Hodder).

"Asia After the War," *The New Statesman and Nation* 26 (31 July 1943): 78–79. Review of *The Future of South-East Asia* by K. M. Panikkar (Allen and Unwin).

"Babel," *The New Statesman and Nation* 27 (26 February 1944): 144. Review essay on *The Loom of Language* by Frederick Bodmer, edited and arranged by Lancelot Hogben (Allen and Unwin) and *Interglossa* by Lancelot Hogben (Penguin Books).

"A Liberal," *The New Statesman and Nation* 27 (8 April 1944): 246. Review of *Ramsay Muir. An Autobiography and some essays* [Liberal Party member], edited by Stuart Hodgson (Humphries).

"Books in General," *The New Statesman and Nation* 27 (29 April 1944): 291. Commentary on the autobiography as a genre. *Tolstoy, His Life and Work* by Derrick Leon (Routledge?) is used as an example.

"Chimpanzee," *The New Statesman and Nation* 27 (27 May 1944): 358. Review of *Chimpanzees: A Laboratory Colony* by Professor Robert M. Yerkes, Yale University (Oxford Press).

"The Trouble about Kenya," *The New Statesman and Nation* 27 (3 June 1944): 372. Review essay on *Race and Politics in Kenya*. A correspondence between Elspeth Huxley and Margery Perham, with and introduction by Lord Frederick Lugard (Faber) and *Soviet Light on the Colonies* by Leonard Barnes (Penguin). Both books examine British colonial policies.

"G. B. S.," *The New Statesman and Nation* 28 (16 September 1944): 188. Review essay on *Everybody's Political What's What* by George Bernard Shaw (Constable).

"Twice Removed from Doughty," *The New Statesman and Nation* 28 (23 December 1944): 425. Review of *The Golden Carpet* by Somerset de Chair (Faber).

"An English Knight Errant," *The New Statesman and Nation* 29 (10 February 1945): 96–97. Review of *Visions and Memories* by H. W. Nevinson (Oxford Press).

"Nationalism and Self-Determination," *The New Statesman and Nation* 29 (14 April 1945): 243–44. Review essay on *National Self-Determination* by Alfred Cobban (Oxford Press and Institute of International Affairs) and *Nationalism and After* by Edward Hallett Carr (Macmillan).

"Disillusion," *The New Statesman and Nation* 29 (19 May 1945): 324 Review of *The Yogi and the Commissar* [collection of essays] by Arthur Koestler (Cape).

"The Virtues of Democracy," *The New Statesman and Nation* 29 (26 May 1945): 340–41. Review of *The Free State* [modeled on the British and American experience] by Professor D. W. Brogan (Hamilton).

"The Centenary of the Co-op," *The New Statesman and Nation* 30 (4 August 1945): 81–82. Review of *A Century of Co-operation* by G. D. H. Cole (Co-operative Union).

"Truth and Public Opinion," *The New Statesman and Nation* 30 (3 November 1945): 303–04. Review of *Truth and the Public* by Kingsley Martin [Kingsley Martin's Conway Memorial Lecture] (Watts).

"Paths to Peace," *The New Statesman and Nation* 31 (5 January 1946): 12–13. Review essay on *Patterns of Peacemaking* by David Thomson, E. Meyer, and

A. Briggs (Kegal Paul) and *The Path to Peace*. A Debate [collection of essays], edited by George W. Keeton (Pitman).

"**The Unrepentant Liberal,**" *The New Statesman and Nation* 31 (30 March 1946): 234–35. Review of *Victors Beware* by Salvador de Madariaga (Cape).

"**Eminent Respectability,**" *The New Statesman and Nation* 31 (11 May 1946): 344–45. Review of *J. A. Spender* [influential Liberal Party member and journalist] by Wilson Harris (Cassell).

"**The Repetitions of History,**" *The New Statesman and Nation* 32 (27 July 1946): 68. Review of *The Congress of Vienna: A Study in Allied Unity, 1812–1822* by Harold Nicolson (Constable).

"**Two Ambassadors,**" *The New Statesman and Nation* 32 (31 August 1946): 156. Review essay on *Ambassador on Special Mission* by Sir Samuel Hoare (Viscount Templewood) [former British special ambassador to Spain] (Collins) and An *Ambassador in Bonds* by Sir Lancelot Oliphant [former British ambassador to Turkey, Persia, and Belgium] (Putman).

"**Blum,**" *The New Statesman and Nation* 32 (12 October 1946): 270. Review of *For All Mankind* by Leon Blum [Socialist Party member, former French premier], translated from French by W. Pickles (Gollancz).

"**Books in General,**" *The New Statesman and Nation* 32 (19 October 1946): 285–86. Commentary on the book trade with some discussion of *The Truth about Publishing* by Sir Stanley Unwin (4th edition; Allen & Unwin).

"**Hitler at Work,**" *The New Statesman and Nation* 32 (7 December 1946): 425. Review of *The Nuremberg Documents: Some Aspects of German War Policy, 1939–45* by Peter de Mendelssohn (Allen and Unwin).

"**Pattern in History,**" *The New Statesman and Nation* 32 (14 December 1946): 446. Review of *History Has Tongues* by Wilfred Wolfendale, with a foreword by W. L. Cuttle (Gollancz).

"**British Foreign Policy,**" *The New Statesman and Nation* 33 (8 March 1947): 158–59. Review of *Documents on British Foreign Policy, 1919–1939*, Second Series Vol. I, edited by E. L. Woodward and Rohan Butler (H. M. Stationary Office).

"**I Know Everything,**" *The New Statesman and Nation* 33 (5 April 1947): 339. Review of *Secretary of Europe, The Life of Friedrich Gentz* [German publicist and statesman] by Golo Mann, translated by W. H. Woglom (Yale and Oxford Press).

"**Too Much Knowledge,**" *The New Statesman and Nation* 33 (14 June 1947): 439–40. Review of *Machiavelli* by J. H. Whitfield (Blackwell).

"**Sense or Sensibility in Politics,**" *The New Statesman and Nation* 34 (18 October 1947): 314. Review essay on *Reason and Unreason in Society* by Morris Ginsberg (Longmans) and *The Comforts of Unreason* by Rupert Crayshaw-Williams (Kegan Paul).

"The Concert of Europe," *The New Statesman and Nation* 35 (17 January 1948): 55–56. Review of *The Aftermath of the Napoleonic Wars* by H. G. Schenk (Kegan Paul).

"History and Mr. Brainballa," *The New Statesman and Nation* 35 (10 April 1948): 300–01. Review of *Documents on British Foreign Policy, 1919–1939*, First Series Vol. I: *1919*; and Second Series Vol. II: *1931*, edited by E. L. Woodward and Rohan Butler (H. M. Stationary Office).

"The French Revolution," *The New Statesman and Nation* 35 (24 April 1948): 339. Review of *The Coming of the French Revolution* by Georges Lefebvre, translated by R. R. Palmer (Oxford University Press).

"Mr. Reed's Nightmares," *The New Statesman and Nation* 36 (24 July 1948): 80–81. Review of *From Smoke to Smother* by Douglas Reed (Cape).

"The Danger of Words," *The New Statesman and Nation* 36 (23 October 1948): 355–56. Review of *The Pattern of Imperialism* by E. M. Winslow (Columbia University Press).

"Society," *The New Statesman and Nation* 37 (26 February 1949): 213–14. Review of *The State and the Citizen: An Introduction to Political Philosophy* by J. D. Mabbottt (Hutchinson).

"The Habsburgs," *The New Statesman and Nation* 37 (5 March 1949): 235–36. Review of *The Habsburg Monarchy 1809–1918* by A. J. P. Taylor (Hamish Hamilton).

"Between Two Worlds," *The New Statesman and Nation* 37 (14 May 1949): 510. Review of *Edwardian Heritage. A Study in British History, 1901–1906* by William Scovell Adams (Muller).

"A Life of Tolstoy," *The New Statesman and Nation* 37 (21 May 1949): 534–35. *Leo Tolstoy* by Ernest J. Simmons (Lehmann).

"The Stalin Mystery," *The New Statesman and Nation* 38 (9 July 1949): 46. Review of *Stalin* by J. Deutscher (Oxford).

"The Promised Land," *The New Statesman and Nation* 38 (29 October 1949): 490, 492. Review of *Promise and Fulfilment: Palestine, 1917–1949* by Arthur Koestler (Macmillan).

"The Utopians," *The New Statesman and Nation* 38 (26 November 1949): 624. Review of *Paths to Utopia* by Martin Buber, translated by R. F. C. Hull (Routledge).

"The Modern Scholasticism," *The New Statesman and Nation* 39 (25 March 1950): 345. Review of *Marx, His Time and Ours* by Rudolf Schlesinger (Routledge).

"The Brighter Side of History," *The New Statesman and Nation* 39 (3 June 1950): 636, 638. Review of *From Napoleon to Stalin: Comments on History and Politics* by A. J. P. Taylor (Hamish Hamilton).

"Life with Tolstoy," *The New Statesman and Nation* 40 (16 November 1950): 462. Review of *The Tolstoy Home: The Diaries of Tatiana Sukhotin-Tolstoy*, translated by Alec Brown (Harvell Press).

"The Nature of Politics," *The New Statesman and Nation* 42 (6 October 1951): 384, 386. Review essay on *Dominations and Powers* by George Santayana (Constable) and *Civitas Dei* by Lionel Curtis (Allen & Unwin).

"Politics of a Mathematician," *The New Statesman and Nation* 42 (10 November 1951): 540. Review of *New Hopes for a Changing World* by Bertrand Russell (Allen & Unwin).

"Splendours and Miseries of Reason," *The New Statesman and Nation* 42 (15 December 1951): 712. Review of *After All*. The Autobiography of Norman Angell (Hamish Hamilton).

"The League of Nations," *The New Statesman and Nation* 43 (29 March 1952): 377. Review of *A History of the League of Nations*, 2 vols., by F. P. Walters (Oxford).

"Father Worship," *The New Statesman and Nation* 44 (20 December 1952): 761–62. Review of *Jan Christian Smuts* by his son, J. C. Smuts (Cassell).

"The Genius of Hitler," *The New Statesman and Nation* 45 (16 May 1953): 586, 588. Review of *Hitler's Table Talk, 1941–1944*, with an introductory essay H. R. Trevor-Roper (Weidenfeld & Nicolson).

"Lucus a non Lucendo," *The New Statesman and Nation* 46 (8 August 1953): 160–61. Review essay on *Malenkov* [Georgi Malenkov, Soviet statesman] by Martin Ebon (Weidenfeld & Nicolson) and *Russia after Stalin* by Isaac Deutscher (Hamish Hamilton).

"Words and Politics," *The New Statesman and Nation* 46 (26 September 1953): 352. Review of *The Vocabulary of Politics* by T. W. Weldon (Penguin Books).

"Kot," *The New Statesman and Nation* 49 (5 February 1955): 170, 172. Eulogy for S. S. Koteliansky who worked in collaboration with Leonard Woolf, Virginia Woolf, D. H. Lawrence and Katherine Mansfield to translate books by Tolstoy, Dostoevsky, Tchekhov, Gorky, and Bunin.

"Thou Shalt Not Kill," *The New Statesman and Nation* 50 (12 November 1955): 608, 610. Review essay on the pamphlet, *Capital Punishment, the Heart of the Matter* by Victor Gollancz. Woolf places the pamphlet within the context of the "National Campaign against capital punishment."

"The Prehistoric 'N. S. & N,'" *The New Statesman and Nation* 51 (12 May 1956): 528, 530. Commentary on the establishment and culture of *The New Statesman* in 1913 and its marriage with *The Nation* in 1931. This issue is the "Silver Wedding Number."

3.6. THE NEW STATESMAN

The New Stateman and Nation became simply *The New Statesman* in July 1957. (See http://www.newstatesman.com/about-new-statesman.)

"Nemesis of Being too Late," *The New Statesman* 55 (4 January 1958): 4–6. An opinion piece on the international arms race. Woolf makes specific recommendations, including nuclear test ban and disarmament agreements.

"Not So Utopian," *The New Statesman* 55 (24 May 1958); 670. Review of *World Peace Through World Law* by Grenville Clark and Louis B. Sohn (Oxford: Harvard).

"Shakespeare on Records," *The New Statesman* 56 (2 August 1958): 143. Review of complete and uncut versions of Shakespeare's plays, *Othello*, *Troilus and Cressida*, and *As You Like It*, performed by members of the Cambridge Society and recorded by the Argo Record Company. The British Council, The Cambridge University Press, The Marlowe Society of Cambridge, and Mr. George Rylands have made possible the production of these plays. They also intend to have all of Shakespeare's plays produced in this way.

"All Our Woe?" *The New Statesman* 56 (13 September 1958): 358. Review of *Soviet-American Relations, 1917–1920*, Vol. 2: *The Decision to Intervene* by George Kennan [U. S. diplomat] (Faber).

"After Fifty Years," *The New Statesman* 59 (23 April 1960): 579–80, 582. Retrospective article on how Ceylon has changed between 1904, when Woolf first moved there as a British colonial civil servant, and February 1960 when he returned for a visit as guest of the Ceylon government.

"History and Common Sense," *The New Statesman* 59 (28 May 1960): 798. Review essay on *The New Cambridge Modern History*, Vol. XII: *The Era of Violence, 1898–1945*, edited by David Thomson (Cambridge) and *The First World War* by Cyril Falls (Longmans).

"Dulwich Made Me," *The New Statesman* 68 (25 September 1964): 458. Review of *The Voyage Home* by Richard Church [autobiography of a former civil servant in the Ministry of Labour] (Heinemann).

"Radicals Comment on the Anniversary," Feature column: "Labour's First Year: A Review of the Government's Record," *The New Statesman* 70 (15 October 1965): 557. Woolf's responses to questions on the Labour Government's record that were posed by the Editor to everyone who was featured in the article. Woolf explains some of his responses in the second paragraph.

"A Civilised Woman," *The New Statesman* 73 (10 March 1967): 332. Review of *In a World I Never Made* by Barbara Wootton [autobiography of a woman who had many high profile careers which included becoming Deputy Speaker of the House of Lords] (Allen & Unwin).

"**Dying of Love,**" *The New Statesman* 74 (6 October 1967): 438. Review of *Lytton Strachey*, Vol. I: *The Unknown Years 1880–1910*, by Michael Holroyd (Heinemann).

"**Aunt Bo,**" *The New Statesman* 74 (19 November 1967): 642. Review of *Beatrice Webb, A Life 1858–1943* by Kitty Muggeridge and Ruth Adam (Secker & Warburg).

"**Menage a Cinq,**" *The New Statesman* 75 (23 February 1968): 241. Review of *Lytton Strachey: A Critical Biography*, Vol. II: *The Years of Achievement (1910–1932)*, by Michael Holroyd (Heinemann).

"**Thugs and Beetles,**" *The New Statesman* 75 (31 May 1968): 728–29. Review of *Bloomsbury* by Quentin Bell, The Pageant of History series (Weidenfeld & Nicolson).

3.7. THE POLITICAL QUARTERLY

Leonard S. Woolf and William A. Robson founded *The Political Quarterly* in 1930. William A. Robson and Kingsley Martin were the first editors. But when Martin became editor of *The New Statesman* in 1931, Woolf joined Robson as co-editor of *The Political Quarterly*. Woolf served as an editor until 1959 and stayed on as literary editor until 1962. (See *Down Hill All the Way*, 206–07.)

"***From Serajevo to Geneva,*** *The Political Quarterly* 1 (1930): 186–206.** Analysis of the strengths and weaknesses of the alliance system in place when the Serbian crisis brought about World War I and of the international system created through the League of Nations at Geneva.

"**The Future of British Broadcasting,**" *The Political Quarterly* 2 (1931): 172–85. Commentary on and analysis of the history and mission of the BBC.

Book Review section, *The Political Quarterly* 2 (1931): 288–92. Review of *England in the Age of the American Revolution*, Vol. I, by L. B. Namier (Macmillan).

Book Review section, *The Political Quarterly* 2 (1931): 440–44. Review essay on *Democracy on Trial* by the Rt. Hon. the Lord Eustace Percy (Lane) and *A Realist Looks at Democracy* by Alderton Pink (Benn).

Book Review section, *The Political Quarterly* 3 (1932): 136–38. Review of *Politics and the Younger Generation* by A. L. Rouse (Faber & Faber).

Book Review section, *The Political Quarterly* 3 (1932): 143–44. Review of *A Political Biography: Stresemann* by Antonina Vallentin, translated by Eric Sutton (Constable).

Book Review section, *The Political Quarterly* 3 (1932): 298–300. Review of *England in Palestine* by Norman Bentwich, O. B. E., M. C. (Kegan Paul).

Book Review section, *The Political Quarterly* 3 (1932): 443–44. Review of *Studies in Law and Politics* by Harold J. Laski (Allen & Unwin).

"From Geneva to the Next War," *The Political Quarterly* 4 (1933): 30–43. Analysis of the international system of cooperation and the breakdown of the postwar peace.

Book Review section, *The Political Quarterly* 4 (1933): 130–32. Review of *The Life of Joseph Chamberlain*, Vol. I: *1836–1885*, by J. L. Garvin (Macmillan).

Book Review section, *The Political Quarterly* 4 (1933): 145–47. Review of *Faith and Society* by Maurice B. Reckitt (Longmans, Green).

Book Review section, *The Political Quarterly* 4 (1933): 298–300. Review essay on *Survey of International Affairs, 1931* by Arnold J. Toynbee, assisted by V. M. Boulter (Oxford University Press & Milford); *Documents on International Affairs, 1931*, edited by J. W. Wheeler-Bennett (Oxford University Press & Milford); *Denmark's Right to Greenland* by Knud Berlin (Oxford University Press & Milford); *Essays on the Manchurian Problem* by Shuhsi Hsu (China Council Institute of Pacific Relations); *The League on Trial* by Max Beer, translated by W. H. Johnston (Allen & Unwin); *The League of Nations in Theory and Practice* by C. K. Webster, with some chapters on International Co-operation by Sydney Herbert (Allen & Unwin); and *The Religious Foundations of Internationalism* by Norman Bentwich (Allen & Unwin).

Book Review section, *The Political Quarterly* 4 (1933): 452–55. Review of *The Life of Joseph Chamberlain*, Vol. II: *1885–1895*, by J. L. Garvin (Macmillan).

"Labour's Foreign Policy," *The Political Quarterly* 4 (1933): 504–24. Analysis of Labour Party foreign policy and the pamphlet *Labour's Foreign Policy* by Labour Party Secretary Arthur Henderson (Labour Party).

Book Review section, *The Political Quarterly* 4 (1933): 607–09. Review essay on *The Bloody Traffic* by A. Fenner Brockway (Gollancz); *Air Power and War Rights* by J. M. Spaight, 2nd ed. (Longmans); and *War, Sadism and Pacifism* by Edward Glover (Allen and Unwin).

Book Review section, *The Political Quarterly* 5 (1934): 300–02. Review of *Government in Transition* by Lord Eustace Percy (Methuen).

Book Review section, *The Political Quarterly* 5 (1934): 430–32. Review of *Curzon: The Last Phase, 1919–1925* by Harold Nicolson (Constable).

Book Review section, *The Political Quarterly* 5 (1934): 595–97. Review essay on *A History of National Socialism* by Conrad Heiden (Methuen); *Germany Unmasked* by Robert Dell (Hopkinson); *Fascism and Social Revolution* by R. Palme Dutt (Lawrence); *Hitler's Official Program* by Gottfried Feder (Allen & Unwin).

Book Review section, *The Political Quarterly* 6 (1935):137–39. Review essay on *Survey of International Relations, 1933* by Arnold Toynbee assisted by V. M. Boulter (Oxford University Press and Milford); *A Short History of International Affairs, 1920–1934* by G. M. Gathhorne-Hardy (Oxford University Press and Milford); *Peace with Honour* by A. A. Milne (Methuen); *Labour and*

War by Bjarne Braatoy with a preface by Harold J. Laski (Allen & Unwin); *A Better League of Nations* by F. N. Keen (Allen & Unwin); *Nationality and the Peace Treaties* by W. O'Sullivan Molony (Allen & Unwin); *International Narcotics Control* by L. E. S. Eisenlohr (Allen & Unwin); and *The Saar and the Franco-German Problem* by B. T. Reynolds (Arnold). [Woolf identified as the author by Leila Luedeking in *Leonard Woolf: A Bibliography*, by Leila Luedeking and Michael Edmonds (New Castle: Oak Knoll Books, 1992).]

Book Review section, *The Political Quarterly* 6 (1935): 139–42. Review essay on *The Life of Joseph Chamberlain*, Vol. III: *1895–1900*, by J. L. Garvin (Macmillan); *The Life of Lord Carson*, Vol. II, by Ian Colvin (Gollancz); *The Rise of Gladstone to the Leadership of the Liberal Party, 1859–1868* by W. E. Williams (Cambridge University Press); *Mr. Gladstone at the Board of Trade* by Francis E. Hyde, with a foreword by F. W. Hirst (Cobden-Sanderson); *George Tierney* by H. K. Olphin (Allen & Unwin); and *Fox* by Christopher Hobhouse (Constable).

Book Review section, *The Political Quarterly* 6 (1935): 290–93. Review of *The State in Theory and Practice* by Harold J. Laski (Allen & Unwin).

Book Review section, *The Political Quarterly* 6 (1935): 302–03. Review of *Political Power* by Charles E. Merriam (McGraw-Hill Publishing Co.).

Book Review section, *The Political Quarterly* 6 (1935): 450–51. Review essay on *The History of The Times. "The Thunderer" in the Making, 1785–1841* (Printing House Square); *The Press in England* by Kurt von Stutterheim (Allen & Unwin); and *Newspaper Headlines* by Heinrich Straumann (Allen & Unwin).

Book Review section, *The Political Quarterly* 6 (1935): 605–06. Review of *The Defence of Freedom* by M. Alderton Pink (Macmillan).

"Mediation on Abyssinia," *The Political Quarterly* 7 (1936): 16–32. Analysis of the Abyssinian crisis and the British response to it.

Book Review section, *The Political Quarterly* 7 (1936): 137–39. Review essay on *Dwight Morrow* by Harold Nicolson (Constable); *Gustav Stresemann; His Diaries, Letters and Papers*, Vol. I, edited and translated by Eric Sutton (Macmillan); and *The Eve of 1914* by Theodor Wolff (Gollancz).

Book Review section, *The Political Quarterly* 7 (1936): 288–91. Review essay on *Survey of International Affairs, 1934* by Arnold J. Toynbee, assisted by V. M. Boulter (Oxford University Press & Milford); *The League of Nations and the Rule of Law* by Alfred Zimmern (Macmillan); *International Law*, Vol. II: *Disputes, War and Neutrality*, by L. Oppenheim, 5th ed., edited by H. Lauterpacht (Longmans); and *The Anti-Drug Campaign* by S. H. Bailey (King).

"The Ideal of the League Remains," *The Political Quarterly* 7 (1936): 330–45. Analysis of the prospects for an effective collective security system and of British policy regarding the League.

Book Review section, *The Political Quarterly* **7 (1936): 455–56.** Review of *The Rise of European Liberalism* by Harold J. Laski (Allen & Unwin).

Book Review section, *The Political Quarterly* **7 (1936): 588–97.** Review essay on *The Dangers of Being Human* by Edward Glover (Allen & Unwin) and *The Retreat from Reason* by Lancelot Hogben (Watts).

"Arms and Peace," *The Political Quarterly* **8 (1937): 21–35.** Analysis of British arms policies.

Book Review section, *The Political Quarterly* **8 (1937): 300–01.** Review of *Survey of International Affairs, 1935*, Vols. I–II, by Arnold J. Toynbee, assisted by V. M. Boulter (Oxford Press & Milford).

"The Resurrection of the League," *The Political Quarterly* **8 (1937): 337–52.** Analysis of international affairs with the recommendation that Britain, France, and Russia confront Germany and Italy through the League.

Book Review section, *The Political Quarterly* **9 (1938): 123–24.** Review essay on *The House that Hitler Built* by Stephen H. Roberts (Methuen); *The Spirit and Structure of German Fascism* by Robert A Brady (Gollancz); *Government in the Third Reich*, rev. ed., by Morstein Marx (Mcgraw-Hill); and *What Next, O Duce?* by Beatrice Baskerville (Longmans).

Book Review section, *The Political Quarterly* **9 (1938): 295–97.** Review of *Gustav Stresemann: His Diaries, Letters and Papers*, Vol. II, edited and translated by Eric Sutton (Macmillan).

Book Review section, *The Political Quarterly* **9 (1938): 444–45.** Review of *Victorian Critics of Democracy* by B. E. Lippincott (University of Minnesota Press).

Book Review section, *The Political Quarterly* **10 (1939): 147–49.** Review essay on *Gladstone* by Erich Eyck, translated by Bernard Miall (Allen & Unwin).

Book Review section, *The Political Quarterly* **10 (1939): 453–56.** Review essay on *Fascism: Who Benefits?* by Max Ascoli and Arthur Feiler (Allen & Unwin); *When There Is No Peace* by Hamilton Fish Armstrong (Macmillan); *Men Must Act* by Lewis Mumford (Seeker & Warburg); and *Security: Can We Retrieve It?* by Sir Arthur Salter, M. P. (Macmillan).

"De Profundis," *The Political Quarterly* **10 (1939): 463–76.** Analysis of factors that contribute to a postwar peace. Woolf argues that Britain should define its "peace aims" and secure a victory that ensures peace.

Book Review section, *The Political Quarterly* **10 (1939): 617–18.** Review of *Capital Investment in Africa; Its Course and Effects* by S. Herbert Frankel (Oxford Press & Milford).

Book Review section, *The Political Quarterly* **11 (1940): 120–23.** Review essay on *The Smaller Democracies* by Sir E. D. Simon (Gollancz); *Democracy Up-to-Date* by Sir Stafford Cripps (Allen & Unwin); *The Defence of Democracy* by

John Middleton Murry (Cape); *Democracy and Socialism* by A. Rosenberg (Bell); and *Personality in Politics* by David Thomson (Nelson).

"Utopia and Reality," *The Political Quarterly* **11 (1940): 167–82.** Wide-ranging examination of conflict and cooperation in international relations that takes into account E. H. Carr's *The Twenty Years Crisis, 1919–1939* (Macmillan).

Book Review section, *The Political Quarterly* **11 (1940): 271–73.** Review of *The Politics of Democratic Socialism* by E. F. M. Durbin (Routledge).

Book Review section, *The Political Quarterly* **11 (1940): 301–03.** Review of *Men and Ideas: Essays by Graham Wallas*, edited by Wallas' daughter, with an introduction by Gilbert Murray (Allen & Unwin).

"Editorial Note," *The Political Quarterly* **11 (1940): 313.** Notices of changes in staffing, in the journal format, and in submissions policies due to the war.

"Democracy at Bay," *The Political Quarterly* **11 (1940): 335–40.** Analysis of the French surrender to Germany on June 16, 1940 and its implications for democratic governments.

Book Review section, *The Political Quarterly* **11 (1940): 419–21.** Review essay on *Recent Revelations of European Diplomacy* by G. P. Gooch, 4th ed. (Longmans); *The War Crisis in Berlin, July-August 1914* by Sir Horace Rumbold (Constable); *Life and Letters of the Rt. Hon. Sir Austin Chamberlain, K. G., P. C., M. P.*, Vol. II, by Sir Charles Petrie, Bart. (Cassell); *Gustav Stresemann; His Diaries, Letters, and Papers*, Vol. III, edited and translated by Eric Sutton (Macmillan); and *The Causes of the War* by A. Berriedale Keith (Nelson).

Book Review section, *The Political Quarterly* **12 (1941): 108–11.** Review essay on *Stalin's Russia and the Crisis in Socialism* by Max Eastman (Allen & Unwin).

Book Review section, *The Political Quarterly* **12 (1941): 118–19.** Reviews of *A History of Gambia* by J. M. Gray (Cambridge Press); *Portrait of a Colony* by Alan Hattersley (Cambridge Press); and *A History of South Africa* by Eric A. Walker 2nd ed. (Longmans).

Book Review section, *The Political Quarterly* **12 (1941): 229–30.** Review of *The Cambridge History of the British Empire*, Vol. II: *The New Empire, 1783–1870* (Cambridge Press).

Book Review section, *The Political Quarterly* **12 (1941): 350–51.** Review of *The British Constitution* by W. Ivor Jennings (Cambridge Press).

Book Review section, *The Political Quarterly* **12 (1941): 351–52.** Review of *Ideas and Ideals of the British Empire* by Ernest Barker (Cambridge Press).

"How to Make the Peace," *The Political Quarterly* **12 (1941): 367–79.** Analytical essay on the main points of the Atlantic Charter of August 1941.

Book Review section, *The Political Quarterly* **12 (1941): 457–59.** Review essay on *The Roots of National Socialism, 1783–1933* by Rohan D'O. Butler (Faber and Faber); *Thus Spake Germany*, edited by W. W. Coole and M. F. Potter, with an introduction by Lord Vansittart (Longmans); *German versus Hun* by Carl Brinitzer and Berthe Grossbard, with a forward by Duff Cooper (Allen & Unwin); and *What to Do with Germany* by Colonel T. H. Minshall (Allen & Unwin).

Book Review section, *The Political Quarterly* **13 (1942): 115–16.** Review of *Survey of International Relations, 1938*, Vol. I, by Arnold J. Toynbee, assisted by V. M. Boulter (Oxford Press and Royal Institute of International Affairs).

Book Review section, *The Political Quarterly* **13 (1942): 219–21.** Review essay on *Treitschke's Origins of Prussianism*, translated by Eden Paul and Cedar Paul (Allen & Unwin) and *The Prussian Spirit: A Survey of German Literature and Politics, 1914–1940* by S. D. Stirk (Faber).

Book Review section, *The Political Quarterly* **13 (1942): 223–25.** Review essay on *The Lost Peace* by Harold Butler (Faber) and *The Impulse to Dominate* by D. W. Harding (Faber).

Book Review section, *The Political Quarterly* **13 (1942): 328–32.** Reviews of *Conditions of Peace* by E. H. Carr (Macmillan); *The New Freedom of the Seas* by W. Arnold-Forster (Methuen); and *Versailles Twenty Years After* by Paul Birdsall (Allen & Unwin).

Book Review section, *The Political Quarterly* **13 (1942): 341–43.** Review of *The Life and Times of Sir Robert Peel* by Sir Tresham Lever (Allen & Unwin).

"Hitler's Psychology," *The Political Quarterly* **13 (1942): 373–83.** Analysis of Hitler's personality and psychology and how they related to Hitler's political goals. Throughout the essay, Woolf draws on *The Speeches of Adolf Hitler, April, 1922--August, 1939*, 2 volumes. English translation of representative passages of the speeches edited by Norman H. Baynes (Oxford Press and Institute of International Relations).

Book Review section, *The Political Quarterly* **14 (1943): 113–14.** Review of *Diary of a Diplomatic Correspondent* by George Bilainkin (Allen & Unwin). Mr. Bailainkin served as a diplomatic correspondent of Allied Newspapers in 1940.

Book Review section, *The Political Quarterly* **14 (1943): 202.** Review of *Science and Ethics* by C. H. Waddington and others (Allen & Unwin).

Book Review section, *The Political Quarterly* **14 (1943): 205–06.** Review essay on *The Russian Peasant and Other Studies* by Sir John Maynard (Gollancz) and *Soviet Planning and Labour in Peace and War. Four Studies.* by Maurice Dobb (Routledge).

"The Future of the Small State," *The Political Quarterly* **14 (1943): 209–24.** Historical analysis of problems faced by small states such as Abyssinia,

Austria, Czechoslovakia, and Poland. Woolf concludes that the establishment of an international government can ensure the freedom of small states.

Book Review section, *The Political Quarterly* 14 (1943): 289-90. Review of *The Spanish Labyrinth; An Account of the Social and Political Background of the Civil War* by Gerald Brenan (Cambridge Press).

Book Review section, *The Political Quarterly* 15 (1944): 90-92. Review essay on *Constructive Democracy* by John Macmurray (Faber) and *Business as a System of Power* by Robert A. Brady (Columbia University Press, Oxford Press, and Milford).

Book Review section, *The Political Quarterly* 15 (1944): 176-77. Review of *Great Britain, France and the German Problem, 1918-1959* by W. M. Jordan (Oxford Press).

Book Review section, *The Political Quarterly* 15 (1944): 183-84. Review essay on *The Transition from War to Peace. Report of the Delegation on Economic Depressions*, Part I: *League of Nations* (Allen and Unwin); *The Displacement of Population in Europe* by Eugene M. Kulischer (International Labour Office & King); and *The United States in the World Economy*, Department of Commerce, U. S. A. (H. M. Stationary Office).

Book Review section, *The Political Quarterly* 15 (1944): 268-69. Review essay on *How It Can Be Done* by Sir Richard Acland, with a preface by J. B. Priestly (Macdonald) and *The New Age* by Edward Hulton (Allen & Unwin).

"The United Nations," *The Political Quarterly* 16 (1945): 12-20. Analysis of the United Nations Charter.

Book Review section, *The Political Quarterly* 16 (1945): 177-78. Reviews of *The Peace Conference of 1919. Organization and Procedure* by F. S. Marston (Oxford Press and Royal Institute of International Affairs) and *Public Opinion and the Last Peace* by R. B. McCallum (Oxford Press).

"Britain in the Atomic Age," *The Political Quarterly* 17 (1946): 12-24. Commentary on atomic power and on policies Britain ought to adopt to control the peaceful and military use of atomic power.

Book Review section, *The Political Quarterly* 17 (1946): 275, 277. Review of *Winston Churchill, 1874-1945* by Lewis Broad (Hutchinson).

Book Review section, *The Political Quarterly* 17 (1946): 359-60. Review essay on *Our Threatened Values* by Victor Gollancz (Gollancz) and *For All Mankind* by Leon Blum (Gollancz), an English translation of *A L'Eshelle Humaine* by Leon Blum (Gallimard).

"The Man of Munich," *The Political Quarterly* 18 (1947): 199-205. Review of *The Life of Neville Chamberlain* by Keith Feiling (Macmillan).

Book Review section, *The Political Quarterly* 18 (1947): 264-66. Review essay on *The Anatomy of Peace* by Emery Reves (Allen & Unwin); *War, Sadism & Pacifism* by Edward Glover (Allen & Unwin); and *Peace & The Public: A*

Study in Mass-Observation, a report prepared for The New Commonwealth (Longmans).

Book Review section, *The Political Quarterly* **18 (1947): 270-71.** Review of *The Last Days of Hitler* by H. R. Trevor-Roper (Macmillan).

Book Review section, *The Political Quarterly* **18 (1947): 367.** Review of *Palestine Mission* by Richard Crossman, M. P. (Hamilton).

Book Review section, *The Political Quarterly* **19 (1948): 77-78.** Review essay on *Philosophy and Politics* by Bertrand Russell (National Book League and Cambridge University Press) and *Ethical and Political Thinking* by E. F. Carritt (Oxford University Press).

Book Review section, *The Political Quarterly* **19 (1948): 78.** Review *Personality in Politics. Studies of Contemporary Statesmen* by Sir Arthur Salter (Faber & Faber).

The Political Quarterly **19 (1948): 184.** Review of *The History of The Times,* Vol. III: *The Twentieth Century, 1884-1912* (The Times).

The Political Quarterly **19 (1948): 192.** Review of *India Called Them* by Lord Beveridge (Allen & Unwin). Biography of Lord Beveridge's parents, Henry Beveridge and Annette Susannah Akroyd who were colonial civil servants in India.

Book Review section, *The Political Quarterly* **19 (1948): 277-78.** Review of *Our Partnership* by Beatrice Webb, edited by Barbara Drake and Margaret I. Cole (Longmans).

Book Review section, *The Political Quarterly* **19 (1948): 376-77.** Review essay on *Sydney Olivier: Letters and Selected Writings,* edited by Margaret Olivier (Olivier's wife), with some impressions by Bernard Shaw (Allen and Unwin) and *Charles Roden Buxton. A Memoir* by Victoria de Bunsen (Buxton's sister) (Allen and Unwin).

Book Review section, *The Political Quarterly* **20 (1949): 182-83.** Review essay on *The White House Papers of Harry L. Hopkins. An Intimate History,* Vol. I: *September 1939-January 1942,* by Robert E. Sherwood (Eyre & Spottiswoods) and *Ciano's Diplomatic Papers,* edited by Malcolm Muggeridge (Odhams).

"Music in Moscow," *The Political Quarterly* **20 (1949): 210-18.** Review essay on *Musical Uproar in Moscow* by Alexander Werth (Turnstile Press) and *Realist Music* by Rena Moisenko (Meridian Books).

Book Review section, *The Political Quarterly* **20 (1949): 284-85.** Review essay on *Trial and Error. The Autobiography of Chaim Weizmann* (Hamilton); *Mahatma Gandhi* by H. S. L. Polak, H. N. Brailsford, and Lord Pethick-Lawrence (Odhams); and *The Story of My Experiments with Truth* by M. K. Gandhi (Phoenix).

The Political Quarterly 20 (1949): 388. Reviews of *Economic Survey of Europe in 1948* (United Nations & H. M. Stationary Office) and *Yearbook on Human Rights for 1947* (United Nations & H. M. Stationary Office).

Book Review section, *The Political Quarterly* 21 (1950): 96–97. Review essay on *Socialism: A Short History* by Norman MacKenzie (Hutchinson): *The Socialist Tragedy* by Ivor Thomas, M. P. (Latimer); *Fifty Years' March. The Rise of the Labour Party* by Francis Williams (Odhams); *Can Parliament Survive?* by Christopher Hollis, M. P. (Hollis); *Parliamentary Government in Britain. A Symposium* (Hansard Society); *Marxism and Contemporary Science* by Jack Lindsay (Dobson); and *Dialectical Materialism and Science* by M. Cornforth (Lawrence and Wishart).

The Political Quarterly 22 (1951): 108, 110. Review of *The State of Europe* by Howard K. Smith, foreign correspondent for the Columbia Broadcasting System (Cresset).

Book Review section, *The Political Quarterly* 22 (1951): 205–06. Review of *Testament for Social Service: An Essay in the Application of Scientific Method to Human Problems* by Barbara Wootton (Allen and Unwin).

Book Review section, *The Political Quarterly* 22 (1951): 209–10. Review of *The History of Soviet Russia*, Vol. I: *The Bolshevik Revolution, 1917–1923* by Edward Hallet Carr (Macmillan).

"A **Political Quarterly,**" a prospectus for *The Political Quarterly* signed by Leonard Woolf and others **in "Bernard Shaw and** *The Political Quarterly*," by William A. Robson, *The Political Quarterly* 22 (1951): 221–25. The article is a tribute to Bernard Shaw and the role that he played in founding *The Political Quarterly*.

Book Review section, *The Political Quarterly* 22 (1951): 302–04. Review essay on *Freedom and Catholic Power* by Paul Blanshard (Secker and Warburg) and *Roman Catholicism* by Thomas Corbishley, S. J. (Hutchinson).

Book Review section, *The Political Quarterly* 22 (1951): 396–97. Reviews of *The Life of Joseph Chamberlain*. Vol. IV: *1901–1903* by Julian Amery (Macmillan) and *With Milner in South Africa* by Lionel Curtis (Blackwell).

Book Review section, *The Political Quarterly* 23 (1952): 99–101. Review essay on *The Inhuman Land* by Joseph Czapski, translated by Gerard Hopkins (Chatto and Windus); *It Happens in Russia* by Vladimir Petrov (Eyre and Spottiswoode); *Russian Purge and the Extraction of Confession* by F. Beck and W. Godin (Hurst and Blackett); *The Katyn Wood Murders* by Joseph Mackiewicz (Hollis and Carter); and *Stalin's Slave Camps* by the International Confederation of Free Trade Unions (International Confederation of Free Trade Unions).

Book Review section, *The Political Quarterly* 23 (1952): 102, 104. Review essay on *Freedom, Power and Democratic Planning* by Karl Mannheim

(Routledge) and *The Logic of Liberty: Reflections and Rejoinders* by M. Polanyi (Routledge).

Book Review section, *The Political Quarterly* **23 (1952): 196–97.** Review of *Leslie Stephen. His Thought and Character in Relation to His Time* by Noel Gilroy Annan (MacGibbon & Kee).

"Something New Out of Africa," *The Political Quarterly* **23 (1952): 322–31.** Analysis of a proposal in the House of Commons to create a Central African Federation of British territories in southern Africa, Southern Rhodesia, Northern Rhodesia, and Nyasaland. Woolf argues against the proposal for a number of reasons.

Book Review section, *The Political Quarterly* **24 (1953): 116–17.** Review essay on *Hitler: A Study in Tyranny* by Alan Bullock (Odhams); *Ernest Bevin: Portrait of a Great Englishman* by Francis Williams, with a foreword by the Rt. Hon. Clement Attlee (Hutchinson); and *The Forsaken Idea: A Study of Viscount Milner* by Edward Crankshaw (Longmans).

Book Review section, *The Political Quarterly* **24 (1953): 210–12.** Review essay on *Harold Laski* by Kingsley Martin (Gollancz); *The Dilemma of Our Times* by Harold Laski (Allen & Unwin); and *The Attack* by R. H. Tawney (Allen & Unwin).

Book Review section, *The Political Quarterly* **24 (1953): 325.** Review of *Socialist Thought*, Vol. I: *The Forerunners, 1789–1850* by G. D. H. Cole (Macmillan).

Book Review section, *The Political Quarterly* **25 (1954): 179–80.** Review essay on *The Prophet Armed*, Vol. I: *Trotsky: 1879–1921* by Isaac Deutscher (Oxford Press).

Book Review section, *The Political Quarterly* **25 (1954): 191.** Review essay on *Report on the Atom. What You Should Know about Atomic Energy* by Gordon Dean, former chairman of the Atomic Energy Commission (Eyre and Spottiswoods).

Book Review section, *The Political Quarterly* **25 (1954): 280–82.** Review essay on *Pio Nono: A Study in European Politics and Religion in the XIX Century* by E. E. Y. Hales (Eyre and Spottiswoods); *The Quaker Approach to Contemporary Problems* edited by John Kavanagh (Allen and Unwin); and *Communism and Christ* by Charles W. Lowry (Eyre and Spottiswoods).

Book Review section, *The Political Quarterly* **25 (1954): 400–02.** Review essay on *German Marxism and Russian Communism* by John Plamenatz (Longmans), *Socialist Thought*, Vol. II: *Marxism and Anarchism. 1850–1890* by G. D. H. Cole (Macmillan), and *The Challenge of Socialism* edited by Henry Pelling (Black).

Book Review section, *The Political Quarterly* **26 (1955): 85–86.** Review essay on *Gladstone: A Biography* by Philip Magnus (Murray) and *Tempestuous*

Journey: Lloyd George, His Life and Times by Frank Owen (Hutchinson) with an analysis of major Liberty Party figures.

Book Review section, *The Political Quarterly* **26 (1955): 93–94.** Review of *The Spy Web: A Study in Communist Espionage* by Francis Noel-Baker (Batchworth).

"What is History?" *The Political Quarterly* **26 (1955): 220–28.** Commentary on how historians have interpreted history from ancient to modern times. Woolf discusses the different philosophical approaches used by Thucydides, Herodotus, Isaiah Berlin, Arnold Toynbee, and others.

Book Review section, *The Political Quarterly* **26 (1955): 297–98.** Review essay on *The Origin of the Communist Autocracy. Political Opposition in the Soviet State. First Phase: 1917–1922* by Leonard Schapiro (London School of Economics and Bell); *The Russian Revolution 1917. A Personal Record* by N. N. Sukhanov, translated and edited by Joel Carmichael (Oxford); *The Illusion of an Epoch. Marxism-Leninism as a Philosophical Creed* by H. B. Acton (Cohen and West); and *Heretics and Renegades* by Isaac Deutscher (Hamilton).

Book Review section, *The Political Quarterly* **27 (1956): 120–21.** Review of *The Unknown Prime Minister: The Life and Times of Andrew Bonar Law, 1858–1923* by Robert Blake (Eyre & Spottiswoods).

"Espionage, Security, and Liberty," *The Political Quarterly* **27 (1956): 152–62.** Analysis of high-profile espionage cases such as Dr. J. Robert Oppenheimer, Vladimar Mikhailovich Petrov, and others and how these cases affect national security and civil liberties.

Book Review section, *The Political Quarterly* **27 (1956): 342–43.** Review of *Beatrice Webb's Diaries, 1924–1932*, edited with an introduction by Margaret Cole (Longmans).

Book Review section, *The Political Quarterly* **28 (1957): 81–82.** Review of *Governments of Greater European Powers: A Comparative Study of the Governments and Political Culture of Great Britain, France, Germany, and the Soviet Union* by Herman Finer (Methuen).

Book Review section, *The Political Quarterly* **28 (1957): 98–99.** Review of *Men and Power, 1917–18* by Lord Beaverbrook (Hutchinson).

Book Review section, *The Political Quarterly* **28 (1957): 190–92.** Review essay on *Essays in Sociology and Social Philosophy*, Vol. I: *On the Diversity of Morals* and Vol. II: *Reason and Unreason in Society* by Morris Ginsberg (Heinemann) and *German Sociology* by Raymond Aron (Heinemann).

Book Review section, *The Political Quarterly* **28 (1957): 405–06.** Review of *The Opium of the Intellectuals* by Raymond Aron, translated by Terence Kilmartin (Secker).

Book Review section, *The Political Quarterly* **29 (1958): 186–87.** Review of *Sovereignty: An Inquiry into the Political Good* by Bertand De Jouvenel. Translated by J. F. Huntington (Cambridge University Press).

Book Review section, *The Political Quarterly* **29 (1958): 301–02.** Review essay on *Defence in the Nuclear Age* by Commander Sir Stephen King-Hall (Gollancz); *Defence and the English-Speaking Role* by Sir Norman Angell (Pall Mall); *Russia, the Atom, and the West* by George F. Kennan (Oxford University Press); *Will the Atom Unite the World?* by Angelos Angelopoulos (The Bodley Head); and *World Peace Through World Law* by Grenville Clark and Louis B. Sohn (Harvard and Oxford University Press).

Book Review section, *The Political Quarterly* **29 (1958): 399.** Review of *The Arms Race* by Philip Noel-Baker (Stevens).

Book Review section, *The Political Quarterly* **30 (1959): 90–91.** Review of *Conviction*, edited by Norman Mackenzie (MacGibbon & Kee). "The book is a symposium of twelve disappointed socialists," according to Woolf. He maintains that it is useful for its diagnosis of the problems faced by socialism and the Labour Party rather than for providing solutions to the problems.

Book Review section, *The Political Quarterly* **30 (1959): 197–98.** Review essay on *The Charm of Politics* by R. H. S. Crossman, M. P. (Hamilton) and *Distinguished for Talent* by Woodrow Wyatt (Hutchinson). Both books are a collection of essays about prominent politicians.

Book Review section, *The Political Quarterly* **30 (1959): 309–11.** Review of *Seat of Pilate; An Account of the Palestine Mandate* by John Marlowe (Cresset Press).

Book Review section, *The Political Quarterly* **30 (1959): 430.** Review of *The Dictionary of National Biography, 1941–1950* edited by L. G. Wickham-Legg and E. T. Williams (Clarendon Press: Oxford University Press). This is the fifth decennial supplement to *The Dictionary of National Biography* that was edited by Sir Leslie Stephen and Sir Sidney Lee.

Book Review section, *The Political Quarterly* **30 (1959): 430–31.** Review of *Primitive Rebels* by E. J. Hobsbawm (Manchester University Press).

Book Review section, *The Political Quarterly* **31 (1960): 89–90.** Review essay on *Trotsky's Diary in Exile 1935*, translated from Russian by Elena Zarudnaya (Faber) and *The Prophet Unarmed*, Vol. II: *Trotsky: 1921–1929* by Isaac Deutscher (Oxford University Press). Volume I of Isaac Deutscher's biography of Trotsky was published four years earlier and was reviewed by Leonard Woolf in *The Political Quarterly* in 1954.

Book Review section, *The Political Quarterly* **31 (1960): 204–06.** Review essay on *Common Sense About Africa* by Anthony Sampson (Gollancz) and *African Nationalism* by Ndabaningi Sithole (Oxford University Press).

Book Review section, *The Political Quarterly* **31 (1960): 226–27.** Review of *Journey to America* by Alexis de Tocqueville, translated by George Lawrence, edited by J. P. Mayer (Faber).

Book Review section, *The Political Quarterly* **31 (1960): 394–95.** Review essay on *The Observer and J. L. Garvin, 1908–1914* by Alfred M. Gollin (Oxford University Press).

Book Review section, *The Political Quarterly* **31 (1960): 403–04.** Review of *Dr. Goebbels; His Life and Death* by Roger Manvell and Heinrich Fraenkel (Heinemann).

Book Review section, *The Political Quarterly* **31 (1960): 511.** Review of *Neither War nor Peace; The Struggle for Power in the Post-War World* by Hugh Seton-Watson (Methuen).

Book Review section, *The Political Quarterly* **32 (1961): 296–99.** Review essay on *Jomo Kenyatta* by George Delf (Gollancz). Note: The page numbers for this essay are incorrectly cited as 196–99 in *Leonard Woolf: A Bibliography*, by Leila Luedeking and Michael Edmonds (New Castle: Oak Knoll Books, 1992), p. 266.

Book Review section, *The Political Quarterly* **32 (1961): 401–02.** Review of *Administrators in Action. British Case Studies*, Vol. I by F. M. G. Willson (Allen and Unwin). The book is sponsored by the Royal Institute of Public Administration.

Book Review section, *The Political Quarterly* **33 (1962): 228–29.** Review of *The Story of Fabian Socialism* by Margaret Cole (Heinemann).

Book Review section, *The Political Quarterly* **33 (1962): 93–94.** Review essay on *Hanged by the Neck* by Arthur Koestler and C. H. Rolph (Penguin) and *Hanged in Error* by Leslie Hale, M. P. (Penguin).

Book Review section, *The Political Quarterly* **34 (1963): 110–11.** Review of *John Anderson, Viscount Waverly* by John W. Wheeler-Bennett (Macmillan).

Book Review section, *The Political Quarterly* **35 (1964): 116–17.** Review of *Ernest Simon of Manchester* by Mary Stocks (Manchester).

Book Review section, *The Political Quarterly* **36 (1965): 106–07.** Review of *The Eichmann Trial* by Peter Papadatos (Stevens). Professor Papadatos of the University of Athens served as an observer of the International Commission of Jurists at the trial.

Book Review section, *The Political Quarterly* **37 (1966): 96–97.** Review essay on *Plough My Own Furrow; The Story of Lord Allen of Hurtwood as Told Through His Writings and Correspondence* by Martin Gilbert (Longmans). Biography of Clifford Allen.

Book Review section, *The Political Quarterly* **38 (1967): 96–97.** Review essay on *Winds of Change, 1914–1939* by Harold Macmillan (Macmillan) and

The Middle Way by Harold Macmillan (1938; reprint Macmillan). *Winds of Change* is the first volume of Macmillan's autobiography.

Book Review section, *The Political Quarterly* 38 (1967): 315–16. Review of *The Autobiography of Bertrand Russell*, Vol I: *1872–1914* (Allen & Unwin).

Book Review section, *The Political Quarterly* 39 (1968): 343, 347. Review of *The Autobiography of Bertrand Russell*, Vol. II: *1914–1944* (Allen & Unwin).

"Kingsley Martin," *The Political Quarterly* 40 (1969): 241–45. Eulogy for Kingsley Martin who helped establish *The Political Quarterly* in 1930 and served as editor of *The New Statesman* from 1931 to 1960.

PART 2

UNSIGNED PUBLISHED WRITINGS
BY LEONARD S. WOOLF IN *THE NATION*,
THE NEW STATESMAN, *THE ATHENAEUM*,
THE NATION & THE ATHENAEUM, AND
THE POLITICAL QUARTERLY

Works cited in Part Two are arranged in the following sequence:

1. Articles
1.1. *The Nation* (3 Aug. 1912–4 Jun. 1921)
1.2. *The New Statesman* (21 June 1913–18 Dec. 1920)
1.3. *The Athenaeum* (4 Apr. 1919–24 Oct. 1919)
1.4. *The Nation & The Athenaeum* (13 Jan. 1923–23 Aug. 1930)
1.5. *The Political Quarterly* (1934–1960)

For helpful definition of "marked files" and a visual instance of one in *The Athenaeum*, see "Related Collections and Resources": "About the Athenaeum (City University of London)," page 275 below. See also Appendix A, 254–57.

For context and additional reading on the unsigned journalism, see Appendix B, pages 258–62 below: "Collaborative Reviewing by Leonard and Virginia Woolf" by Wayne K. Chapman, from *Women in the Milieu of Leonard and Virginia Woolf*.

Leonard Woolf's and Virginia Woolf's authorship of many of the pieces in sections 1.2 and 1.4 has been confirmed by Brownlee J. Kirkpatrick (hereafter B.J.K.) through her correspondence of 1991–1996 with Wayne K. Chapman. Her contributions are noted below. B. J. Kirkpatrick's *Bibliography of Virginia Woolf*, 3rd ed. (Oxford: Clarendon Press, 1980) is, of course, an indispensable tool for Virginia Woolf scholars.

1. Articles

1.1. THE NATION

The Nation was established in 1907 by the Rowntree family whose members belonged to the Liberal party. Henry William Massingham, a Liberal who drifted into the Labour party by 1922, served as editor from 1907–1923. Leonard S. Woolf became the acting political editor in 1920 and then took over that position in 1922.

"An Essay in 'Scientific Management,'" *The Nation* (3 August 1912): 652–54.
[ILL slip identifies author as L. Woolf.] On the time management system for workers established by Mr. Taylor.

"A Parliament of Women," "Social Types" column, *The Nation* (21 June 1913), 456–57. [marginal note identifies L.W. as the author.] On Women's Co-operative Guild Congress in June 1913.

"Guild and Trade Union," *The Nation* (16 August 1913): 757. [attached note states that V.W. saved the clipping]. Review of M. Fothergill Robinson's *The Spirit of Association: Being Some Account of the Guilds, Friendly Societies, Co-operative Movement, and Trade Unions of Great Britain* (Murray).

"War and International Law," *The Nation* (4 September 1915): 742, 744. [V.W. saved the clipping]. Review of Coleman Phillipson's *International Law and the Great War* (Fisher Unwin).

"The Problem of Empire," *The Nation* (19 August 1916): 638, 640. [V.W. saved the clipping]. Review of *The Commonwealth of Nations* Part I, edited by L. Curtis (Macmillan).

"The History of the Entente," *The Nation* (16 September 1916), 766. [V.W. saved the clipping]. Review of *Histoire de l'Entente Cordiale Franco-Anglaise: Les Relations de la France et de l'Angleterre depuis le XVI.e siecle jusqu'a nos Jours* by J.-L. De Lanessan (Felix Alcan).

"Society and the Guilds," *The Nation* (15 May 1920): 212. [marginal note attributing piece to L. Woolf]. Review of G. D. H. Cole's *Social Theory* (Methuen).

[L. Woolf served as the acting political editor of *The Nation* from July to October 1920. He wrote the "Politics and Affairs" column.]

"Politics and Affairs" column, *The Nation* (July 31, 1920), 544–47. "The Irish Republic." Woolf takes the position that Ireland is a nation. Other pieces in the column, "Peace in the Balance" and "The New German Economic Conference," are on developments after the Spa Conference and the German Economic Conference.

"Politics and Affairs" column, *The Nation*, (21 August 1920), 628–31. Pieces in the column are "The New Veto on War" (on recent government action related to the European problems associated with the Versailles Treaty), "The Isolation of France" (on French foreign policies in Europe), and "The Irish War" (on deteriorating situation in Ireland which is described as a state of war).

"Politics and Affairs" column, *The Nation* (4 September 1920), 684–87. Pieces in the column are "The End of our Government in Ireland" (on the lack of an effective English occupation government in Ireland), "The Miners and the Nation" (on working conditions in the coal mines and government mining policy) and "The Near East" (on political problems in the region associated with the 1919 Versailles Treaty).

"Politics and Affairs" column, *The Nation* (9 October 1920), 32–36. Pieces in the column are "The Proposal of the Irish Settlement" (outlines recommendations for the settlement) and "The League of M. Leygues" (current problems before the League and French policies—French President Leygues).

"The Turbid East," *The Nation* (4 June 1921): 368. Review of *China, Japan, and Korea* by J. O. P. Bland (Heinemann). Leila Luedeking identifies L. Woolf as the author in *Leonard Woolf: A Bibliography*, by Leila Luedeking and Michael Edmonds (New Castle: Oak Knoll Books, 1992).

1.2. THE NEW STATESMAN

The New Statesman was created as a Fabian Society organ under the auspices of Sidney and Beatrice Webb and George Bernard Shaw in 1912–13. Clifford Sharp served as editor from 1913 to 1931.

"A Democracy of Working Women," *The New Statesman* I, No. 11 (21 June 1913): 328–29. Cited in Duncan Wilson, *Leonard Woolf: A Political Biography* (1978), p. 53; B.J.K. also identifies L. W. as the author. Comments on the Women's Co-operative Guild Congress in June 1913 and analysis of WCG policies.

"A Syndicalist on Scientific Management," *The New Statesman* III, No. 57 (9 May 1914): 153. Review of *L'Organisation du Surmenage* (Le Systeme Taylor) by Emile Pouget (Marcel Riviere et Cic.). Confirmed by B.J.K.

"The Daily Round," *The New Statesman* III, No. 63 (20 June 1914): 344–45. Review of *The Psychopathology of Everyday Life* by Professor Dr. Sigmund Freud, LL.D., authorized English edition, with an introduction by A. A. Brill, Ph. B., M. D. (Unwin). Confirmed by B.J.K.

"The Modern State," *The New Statesman* III, No. 64 (27 June 1914): 375–76. Review of *The Great Society* by Graham Wallas (Macmillan). Confirmed by B.J.K.

"Work and Wealth," *The New Statesman* III, No. 69 (1 August 1914): 536–37. Review of *Work and Wealth: A Human Valuation* by J. A. Hobson (Macmillan). Confirmed by B.J.K.

"Socialism and the War," *The New Statesman* V, No. 115 (19 June 1915): 259. Review of *The Socialists and the War* by W. E. Walling (Henry Holt & Co.). Confirmed by B.J.K.

"What is Wrong with Germany," *The New Statesman* V, No. 116 (26 June 1915): 283–84. Review essay on *The World in the Crucible* by Sir Gilbert Parker, M. P. (Murray); *Changing Germany* by Charles Tower (Fisher Unwin); and *America and the German Peril* by Howard Pitcher Okie (Heinemann). Confirmed by B.J.K.

"Nationality and Conflict," *The New Statesman* V, No. 118 (10 July 1915): 332. Review essay on *Nationality on the War* by Arnold J. Toynbee (Dent) and *The Interpretation of History* by L. Cecil Jane (Dent). Confirmed by B.J.K.

"**Do Ut Des,**" *The New Statesman* V, No. 119 (17 July 1915): 343–44. Comment on "The Monsoon and the War Loan," London *Times*, and Indian economic problems. Confirmed by B.J.K.

"**Roumania,**" *The New Statesman* V, No. 119 (17 July 1915): 356. Review of *Roumania and the Great War* by R. W. Seton-Watson, D. Litt. (Constable). Confirmed by B.J.K.

"**The Prevention of War,**" *The New Statesman* V, No. 120 (24 July 1915): 379–80. Review of *Towards International Government* by J. A. Hobson (George Allen & Unwin). Confirmed by B.J.K.

"**J'Accuse,**" *The New Statesman* V, No. 122 (7 August 1915): 428–29. Review of *J'Accuse* by a German, translated by Alexander Gray (Hodder & Stoughton). Confirmed by B.J.K.

"**Philosophical Neutrality,**" *The New Statesman* V, No. 123 (14 August 1915): 451. Review essay on *The International Crisis in its Ethical and Psychological Aspects*. Lectures by Eleanor M. Sidgwick, Gilbert Murray, A. C. Bradley, L. P. Jacks, G. F. Stout, and B. Bosanquet. (Milford); *Evolution and the War* by P. Chalmers Mitchell (Murray); and *Reflections of a Non-Combatant* by M. D. Petre (Longmans). Confirmed by B.J.K.

"**The War and International Law,**" *The New Statesman* V, No. 124 (21 August 1915): 474. Review of *International Law and the Great War* by Coleman Philippson, LL. D., Litt. D., with an introduction by Sir John MacDonell, K. C. B., LL. D. (Fisher Unwin) . Confirmed by B.J.K.

"**Rival Kulturs,**" *The New Statesman* V, No. 125 (28 August 1915): 499. Review essay on *The Soul of Europe* by Joseph M'Cabe (Fisher Unwin); *L'Esprit Europeen* (Nouvelle edition) by L. Dumont-Wilden (Eugene Figuiere); *Serbia* by W. M. Petrovitch (Harrap); *The Spirit of the Allied Nations*, edited with an introductory essay by Sidney Low (A. & C. Black); and *Why Europe is at War* by F. R. Coudert, F. W. Whitridge, E. von Mach, Toyokichi Iyenaga, and F. V. Greene (Putnam). Confirmed by B.J.K.

"**Annals of the Parish,**" *The New Statesman* V, No. 125 (28 August 1915): 501. Reviews of *Liverpool Vestry Books, 1681–1834*, Vol. I: 1681–1799 and Vol. II: 1800–1834, edited by Henry Peet, (Constable) and *A History of the Parishes of Minchinhampton and Avening* by Arthur Twisden Playne (Bellows). Confirmed by B.J.K.

"**Shorter Notices,**" *The New Statesman* V, No. 125 (28 August 1915): 501. Reviews of *Palestine Exploration Fund, 1914: The Wilderness of Zin* (Archaeological Report) by C. Leonard Woolley and T. E. Lawrence, with a chapter on the Greek inscriptions by M. N. Tod (Palestine Exploration Fund); *The History of Twelve Days, July 24 to August 4, 1914* by J. W. Headlam (Fisher Unwin); and *Documents Relating to the Great War*, selected and arranged by

G. A. Andriulli, with an introduction by Professor G. Ferrero, translated by T. Okey (Fisher Unwin). Confirmed by B.J.K.

"The Harvest of War Books," *The New Statesman* V, No.126 (4 September 1915): 523-24. Review essay on *The Meaning of the War* by Henri Bergson (Fisher Unwin); *The War and After* by Sir Oliver Lodge (Methuen); *The German Peril* by Frederic Harrison (Fisher Unwin); *Some Aspects of the War* by S. Perez Triana (Fisher Unwin); *The Holy War—"Made in Germany"* by Dr. Snouck Hurgronje (Putnam); *War Thoughts of an Optimist* by B. A. Gould (Dent). Confirmed by B.J.K.

"The Southern Slavs and Italy," *The New Statesman* V. No 127 (11 September 1915): 534-36. Analysis of political problems in the Balkans and a pamphlet, *The Balkans, Italy, and the Adriatic*, by R. W. Seton-Watson D. Litt. (Nisbet). Confirmed by B.J.K.

"Nationalism and the Balkan Wars," *The New Statesman* V, No. 127 (11 September 1915): 547. Review of *Nationalism and War in the Near East* by a Diplomatist, edited by Lord Courtney of Penwith (Clarendon Press). Confirmed by B.J.K.

"The Realities of War," *The New Statesman* V, No. 128 (18 September 1915): 571-72. Reviews of *A Journal of Impressions in Belgium* by May Sinclair (Hutchinson & Co.); *France in War Time, 1914-1915* by Maud F. Sutton-Pickhard (Methuen); and *The Irish Nuns at Ypres* [no author given] (Smith, Elder). Confirmed by B.J.K.

"Men as Machines," *The New Statesman* V, No. 129 (25 September 1915): 583-84. Commentary on industrial working conditions, especially long hours. Confirmed by B.J.K.

"The Riddle of Austria," *The New Statesman* V, No. 129 (25 September 1915): 595. Review of *Modern Austria: Her Racial and Social Problems* by Virginio Gayda (Fisher Unwin). Confirmed by B.J.K.

"Martial Law in Ceylon," *The New Statesman* V, No. 130 (2 October 1915): 610-11. Analysis of the political situation in Ceylon after the colonial governor declared martial law in response to disturbances in late May. Woolf criticizes government policies and argues that they are counter productive. Confirmed by B.J.K.

"Man and the Mountains," *The New Statesman* V, No. 130 (2 October 1915): 624-25. Reviews of *Geographical Aspects of Balkan Problems, in Relation to the Great European War* by Marion I. Newbegin, D.Sc. (Constable) and *Arms and the Map* by Ian C. Hannah (Fisher Unwin). Confimed by B.J.K.

"Constantinople," *The New Statesman* VI, No. 132 (16 October 1915): 43-44. Review essay on *Forty Years in Constantinople* by Sir Edwin Pears (Jenkins) and *Journal d'un Habitant de Constantinople (1914-15)* by Emile Edwards (Plon-Nourrit). Confirmed by B.J.K.

"Treaties of Guarantee," *The New Statesman* VI, No. 133 (23 October 1915): 67. Review of England's Guarantee to Belgium and Luxemburg by C. P. Sanger and H. T. J. Norton (Allen & Unwin). Confirmed by B.J.K.

"The Pentecost of Calamity," *The New Statesman* VI, No. 135 (6 November 1915): 114. Review essay on *The Pentecost of Calamity* by Owen Wister (Macmillan); *The German Mole* by Jules Claes, with a preface by J. Holland Rose, Litt. D. (Bell); *The War of Freedom and the Unity of Christendom* by W. Felce (Griffiths); and *Civilisation in the Melting Pot* by George A. Greenwood, with a preface by Arthur Ponsonby, M. P. (Headley Bros.). Confirmed by B.J.K.

"The German Socialists," *The New Statesman* VI, No. 138 (27 November 1915): 187. Review essay on *The Socialist Party in the Reichstag and the Declaration of War* by P. G. La Chesnais (Fisher Unwin) and *German Socialists and Belgium* by Emile Royer, Member of the Belgian Parliament, with a preface by E. Vandervelde, Minister of State (Allen & Unwin). Confirmed by B.J.K.

"Women's Wages," *The New Statesman* VI, No. 139 (4 December 1915): 199–201. Commentary on trade unions wage policies based on gender. Woolf argues for the Women's Co-operative Guide policy of "equal pay for equal work." Confirmed by B.J.K.

"Atrocities and Humanities," *The New Statesman* VI, No. 139 (4 December 1915): 211–12. Review essay on *Germany's Violations of the Laws of War, 1914–15*, compiled under the auspices of the French Ministry for Foreign Affairs, translated by J. O. P. Bland (Heinemann); *Belgium and Germany* [texts and documents], with a foreword by Henri Davignon (Nelson); *The Prisoners of War Information Bureau in London* by R. F. Roxburgh, with an introduction by L. Oppenheim, LL.D. (Longmans); and *The Work of the War Refugees Committee*: an Address by Lady Lugard (Bell). Confirmed by B.J.K.

"Views of the War," *The New Statesman* VI, No. 141 (18 December 1915): 260–61. Review essay on *My Year of the War* by Frederick Palmer (Murray); *A Frenchman's Thoughts on the War* by Paul Sabatier (Fisher Unwin); *France at Bay* by Charles Dawbarn (Mills & Boon); and *In the Hands of the Enemy* by B. G. O'Rorke (Longmans). Confirmed by B.J.K.

"The Factory in Peace and War," *The New Statesman, Blue Book Supplement* VI, No. 141 (18 December 1915): 2–3. Review essay on the *Report of the Chief Inspector of Factories and Workshops for 1914* (Cd. 8051); *Report of the Clerical and Commercial Employments Committee* (Cd. 8110); and *Report of the "Shops Committee"* (Cd. 8113). Confirmed by B.J.K.

"Hospital Accommodation," *The New Statesman, Blue Book Supplement* VI, No. 141 (18 December 1915): 10. Review of *Return as to Hospital Accommodation in England and Wales*, prepared by the Local Government Board. This report is a periodic report on hospitals (number and type, beds available, etc.) for England and Wales. Confirmed by B.J.K.

"**Royal Patriotic Fund,**" *The New Statesman, Blue Book Supplement* **VI, No. 141 (18 December 1915): 10.** Review of the *Royal Patriotic Fund Corporation: 11th Report*, for the year 1914 (Cd. 8026). Woolf explains that these funds are raised through public contributions and are then distributed to the families (usually widows and children) of military personnel (soldiers and sailors) who have lost their lives in service to their country. Confirmed by B.J.K.

"**The New Japan,**" *The New Statesman* **VI, No. 143 (1 January 1916): 308–09.** Reviews of *Japan, the New World Power* by Robert P. Porter (Humphrey Milford) and *Japan (Madame Chrysantheme)* by Pierre Lott, translated by Laura Ensor (Werner Laurie). Confirmed by B.J.K.

"**The Workers' Money Box,**" *The New Statesman* **VI, No. 143 (1 January 1916): 395–96.** Opinion piece. Woolf addresses the Chancellor of the Exchequer's policies of encouraging individual savings with the recommendation that the Chancellor cooperate with the Co-operative Societies to advance these policies. Woolf explains that the Co-operative Movement has established banks, the Retail Societies bank and the Co-operative Wholesale Society's Bank, where workers maintain savings accounts and secure loans. Confirmed by B.J.K.

"**The Chinese Revolution,**" *The New Statesman* **VI, No. 146 (22 January 1916): 379–80.** Review of *Through the Chinese Revolution* by Fernand Farjenel, translated by Dr. Margaret Vivian (Duckworth). Confirmed by B.J.K.

"**Hospitals and Heroism,**" *The New Statesman* **VI, No. 147 (29 January 1916): 403–04.** Reviews of *Letters from a Field Hospital* by Mabel Dearmer, with a Memoir of the Author by Stephen Gwynn (Macmillan) and *Fighting France: From Dunkerque to Belfort* by Edith Wharton (Macmillan). Confirmed by B.J.K.

"**England v. Germany,**" *The New Statesman* **VI, No. 149 (12 February 1916): 453.** Review of *War and Civilisation* by the Rt. Hon. J. M. Robertson, M. P. (Allen & Unwin). Confirmed by B.J.K.

"**The Nemesis of Democracy,**" *The New Statesman* **VI, No. 151 (26 February 1916): 499.** *Political Parties* by Robert Michels, translated from Italian by Eden Paul and Cedar Paul (Jarrold). Confirmed by B.J.K.

"**The Civilisation of States,**" *The New Statesman* **VI, No. 152 (4 March 1916): 524.** Review essay on *The Morality of Nations* by C. Delisle Burns (University of London Press); *The Unity of Western Civilisation*, edited by F. S. Marvin (Humphrey Milford); and *What Is Diplomacy?* by C. W. Hayward (Grant Richards). Confirmed by B.J.K.

"**Contraband of War,**" *The New Statesman* **VI, No. 153 (11 March 1916): 551.** Review of *The Law of Contraband of War* by H. Reason Pyke, LL.B. (Humphrey Milford). Confirmed by B.J.K.

"**The Riots in Ceylon**," *The New Statesman, Blue Book Supplement* VI, No. 153 (11 March 1916): 6–7. Review of *Ceylon. Correspondence relating to Disturbances in Ceylon.* (Cd. 8163). Woolf observes that the account of the riots (May 29 to June 5) given through letters from the colonial governor to the Secretary of State for the Colonies is sketchy. Nevertheless, Woolf notes that evidence provided in the Blue Book indicates that the riots were caused by religious tensions. He criticizes the way the governor handled the situation. Confirmed by B.J.K.

"**The Need for the Discussion of Peace Terms**," *The New Statesman* VII, 173 (26 August 1916), 486. The introduction to this series is attributed to Leonard Woolf by Edward S. Hyams. *The New Statesman…1913–1963*, pp. 59–60. (Focuses on European issues, especially the peace settlement as shaped by the belligerents.)

"**Bolshevik Russia**," *The New Statesman* 13 *(*12 July 1919): 373. Review of *Six Weeks in Russia in 1919* by Arthur Ransom (Allen & Unwin). Identified by Wayne K. Chapman.

"**The Empire and the African**," *The New Statesman* 14 (21 February 1920): 575–77. Woolf explains the history of colonial policies on compulsory labor in British East Africa and why African people resist the resumption of compulsory labor. Identified by Wayne K. Chapman.

"**A Jewish Novelist**," *The New Statesman* 14 (13 March 1920): 682–83. Review of *Jewish Children* from the Yiddish of Shalom Aleichem (Heinemann). Confirmed by B.J.K.

"**Native Labour in Africa**," *The New Statesman* 15 (10 April 1920): 7–8. This is a response to critics of Woolf's piece, "The Empire and the African," (21 February 1920) and to Major Dudgeon's letter to the Editor, 27 March, on the essay. Woolf defends his argument against the use of compulsory labor and addresses Major Dudgeon's criticism. Identified by Wayne K. Chapman.

"**Article XXII**," *The New Statesman* 15 (1 May 1920): 94–95. Woolf explains the importance of Article XXII of the League of Nations Covenant on the Mandate System, particularly how it will be applied to the Middle East. He recommends that the European governments be sensitive to complex political realities and the aspirations of Middle Eastern peoples. Identified by Wayne K. Chapman.

"**The Bolshevik Contra Mundum**," *The New Statesman* 16 (18 December 1920): 342–44. Review essay on *The Practice and Theory of Bolshevism* by Bertrand Russell (Allen & Unwin) and *Terrorism and Communism* by Karl Kautsky, translated by W. H. Kerridge (Allen & Unwin). Identified by Wayne K. Chapman.

1.3. THE ATHENAEUM

The Athenaeum was established in 1828. Liberal M. P. Arnold Rowntree acquired it after World War I. Due to declining circulation, *The Athenaeum* was joined with *The Nation* in 1921. (See www.newstatesman.com/nsabout.htm.)

"Education and Social Movements," *The Athenaeum* **(4 April 1919), 138–39.** L. Woolf reviewed *Education and Social Movements, 1700–1850* by A. E. Dobbs (Longmans).

"The Infancy of Socialism," *The Athenaeum* **(23 May 1910): 362–63.** L. Woolf reviewed *A History of British Socialism*, vol. I, by M. Beer. Introduction by R. H. Tawney (Bell & Sons).

"Is This Poetry?" *The Athenaeum* **(20 June 1919): 491.** L. Woolf reviewed The *Critic in Judgment* by J. M. Murry (Hogarth Press) and *Poems* by T. S. Elliot (Hogarth Press).

"India's Past To-Day," *The Athenaeum* **(1 August 1919): 684–85.** L. Woolf reviewed *Ceylon and the Hollanders, 1658–1796* by P. E. Pieris (American Ceylon Mission Press); *India's Nation Builders* by D. N. Bannerjea (Headley); and *The Future Government of India* by Ernest Barker (Methuen).

"Women's Wages," *The Athenaeum* **(1 August 1919): 688.** L. Woolf reviewed *The Wages of Men and Women: Should They Be Equal?* By Mrs. Sidney Webb (Fabian Society and Allen & Unwin).

"Samuel Butler" "Reviews" section, *The Athenaeum* **(29 August 1919): 808–09.** L. Woolf review essay on *The Note-Books of Samuel Butler*, edited by Henry Festing Jones (Fifield).

"The Bolshevist Revolution," *The Athenaeum* **(19 September 1919): 914.** L. Woolf reviewed *Ten Days That Shook the World* by John Reed (Boni & Liveright).

"What Is Bolshevism?" *The Athenaeum* **(24 October 1919): 1061.** Review of *Bolshevism: The Enemy of Political and Industrial Democracy* by John Spargo (Murry).

1.4. THE NATION & THE ATHENAEUM

By 1923. John Maynard Keynes bought a controlling interest in *The Nation* from the Rowntree Trust. (According to Leonard S. Woolf, The Rowntrees, who were Liberals, decided to sell *The Nation* because of Henry William Massingham's Labourite editorial policies. See *Down Hill All the Way*, 92, 96–97.) The journal appeared as *The Nation & The Athenaeum* under Keynes' management. Woolf served as the literary editor from 1923 to 1930. Hubert Henderson replaced Massingham as editor and held the post until 1930.

"What Should Britain Do?" "Politics and Affairs" column, *The Nation & The Athenaeum* (13 January 1923), 570–71. Cited in Duncan Wilson, *Leonard Woolf: A Political Biography* (1978), p. 142. (on British and French policies on German reparations).

"The Next Great War Begins," "Politics and Affairs" column, *The Nation & The Athenaeum* (20 January 1923), 602–03. Cited in Duncan Wilson, *Leonard Woolf: A Political Biography* (1978), p. 142. (analysis of the policies of the major powers regarding the French invasion of the Ruhr).

"Stop the New War," "Politics and Affairs" column, *The Nation & The Athenaeum* (27 January 1923), 636–37. Cited in Duncan Wilson, *Leonard Woolf: A Political Biography* (1978), p. 142. (more comment on the Ruhr crisis).

"The Dangers of Neutrality," "Politics and Affairs" column, *The Nation & The Athenaeum* (3 February 1923), 676–77. Cited in Duncan Wilson, *Leonard Woolf: A Political Biography* (1978), p. 142. (opposes British neutrality during the Ruhr crisis).

"France's Case for Herself," "Politics and Affairs" column, *The Nation & The Athenaeum* (17 February 1923), 742–43. Cited in Duncan Wilson, *Leonard Woolf: A Political Biography* (1978), p. 142. (the Ruhr crisis).

"Not Neutrality, But Opposition," "Politics and Affairs" column, *The Nation & The Athenaeum* (24 February 1923), 774–75. Cited in Duncan Wilson, *Leonard Woolf: A Political Biography* (1978), p. 142. (opposes British neutrality during the Ruhr crisis).

"A Secret Document," "Politics and Affairs" column, *The Nation & The Athenaeum* (3 March 1923), 810–11. Cited in Duncan Wilson, *Leonard Woolf: A Political Biography* (1978), p. 143. (on British policy during the Ruhr crisis).

"Once More in the Spider's Web," "Politics and Affairs" column, *The Nation & The Athenaeum* (10 March 1917), 848–49. Cited in Duncan Wilson, *Leonard Woolf: A Political Biography* (1978), p. 143. (attempts to form a new alliance system of the great powers).

"Why Perish?" "Politics and Affairs" column, *The Nation & The Athenaeum* (17 March 1923), 906–07. Cited in Duncan Wilson, *Leonard Woolf: A Political Biography* (1978), p. 143. (the price of World War I in money and lives).

"From Alpha to Omega" column, *The Nation & The Athenaeum* 35 (5 April 1924): 16. First paragraph Review of Mr. Sutro's play, "Far Above Rubies" and paragraph entitled "Things to see and hear in the coming week:—" (list of plays and films: "Polly Preferred," "Merchant of Venice," "Yolanda," and "Cosmopolitan." And a list of musical recitals and concerts.) Both paragraphs were written by L. Woolf. (Woolf's name is next to "Omicron"in marked copy). Second paragraph from the top in "From Alpha to Omega" beginning with "I was given the opportunity to see a demonstration…" were written by Mrs. Woolf.

"Books in Brief" column, *The Nation & The Athenaeum* 35 (5 April 1924): 26. L. Woolf wrote reviews of *Far Eastern Jaunts* by Gilbert Collins (Methuen) and *Misadventures with a Donkey in Spain* by Jan Gordon and Cora J. Gordon (Blackwood), [Other reviews in this column are by other writers].

"From Alpha to Omega" column, *The Nation & The Athenaeum* 35 (12 April 1924): 50. Paragraph entitled "Things to see and hear in the coming week:—" (list of musical recitals and concerts. And a list of plays and performances: "Measure for Measure," "The Mikado," and Yiddish Theatre) written by L. Woolf.

"Books in Brief" column, *The Nation & The Athenaeum* 35 (12 April 1924): 62. L. Woolf wrote reviews for the following: *The French Revolution in English History* by Philip Anthony Brown (Allen & Unwin); *A Short History of the French Revolution* by I. Hutchinson Humphreys (Sidgwick & Jackson); Benham's Book of Quotations by W. Gurney Benham (Ward & Lock); and *Debretts House of Commons and Judicial Bench 1924* (Dean).

"Books in Brief" column, *The Nation & The Athenaeum* 35 (26 April 1924): 126. L. Woolf wrote reviews for the following: *Time Measurement* by L. Bolton (Bell); *A Song to David and Other Poems* by Edmund Blunden (Cobden-Sanderson); *A Short History of Birbeck College* by C. Delisle (University of London Press); *Prohibition Inside Out* by Roy A. Haynes (Fisher Unwin); *A Social History of the American Negro* by Benjamin Brawley (Macmillan); "The Studio" Yearbook of Decorative Art, 1924 ("The Studio"); *Ernest Gimson: His Life and Work* [no author given] (Blackwell); and *English Homes:Period II*, Vol. I: *Early Tudor, 1485–1558* by H. Avray Tipping ("County Life").

"Books in Brief" column, *The Nation & The Athenaeum* 35 (10 May 1924): 186. L. Woolf wrote reviews for the following: *Social Aspects of Psycho-Analysis*, edited by Ernest Jones (Williams & Norgate); *An Anthology of English Verse* by John Drinkwater (Collins); *How to be Healthy* by A. Physician (Palmer); and *North Wales* (originally compiled by M. J. B. Baddeley and C. S. Ward) (10th ed., Ward & Lock).

"Novels in Brief" column, *The Nation & The Athenaeum* 35 (24 May 1924): 261. "Things to see or hear in the coming week:—" (List of musical recitals, and the following plays and performances: "Wife to a Famous Man;" "La Megere Apprivoisee;" and Elena Gerhardt and Fritz Reiner. And a lecture by John Galsworthy on "Expression.") written by L. Woolf.

"The Russian Riddle," "Reviews" section, *The Nation & The Athenaeum* 35 (24 May 1924): 268. L. Woolf wrote reviews for the following: *The Russian Soviet Republic* by Edward A Ross (Allen & Unwin); *The Bolshevik Persecution of Christianity* by Captain Francis McCullagh (Murray); and *Impressions of Soviet Russia* by Charles Sarolea (Nash & Grayson).

"Books in Brief" column, *The Nation & The Athenaeum* 35 (24 May 1924): 270. L. Woolf wrote reviews for the following: *Genesis: Twelve Woodcuts* by Paul Nash (Nonesuch Press); *A Handbook of Garden Irises* by W. R. Dykes (Hopkinson); and *The Education Authorities Directory, 1924-25* (School Government Publishing Co.).

"From Alpha to Omega" column, *The Nation & The Athenaeum* 35 (7 June 1924): 321. L. Woolf wrote first paragraph (review of "The Nibelungs"—Sigfried Saga) and "Things to see or hear in the coming week:—" (List of plays: "Henry IV" and the season of "Old Vic"; and list of musical recitals and concerts).

"India and Indian Politics,""Reviews" section, *The Nation & The Athenaeum* 35 (7 June 1924): 326-27. L. Woolf wrote reviews for the following: *Indian Politics* by J. T. Gwynn (Nisbet); *India: A Bird's-eye View* by Lord Ronaldshay (Constable); *Mahatma Gandhi* by Romain Rolland (English translation, Swarthmore Press); and *Mahatma Gandhi* by Romain Rolland (French edition, Paris: Stock.)

"Books in Brief" column, *The Nation & The Athenaeum* 35 (7 June 1924): 332. Woolf [no first initial] reviewed both books in column: *Memories* by Katherine Tynan; and *Marie Elizabeth Towneley: A Memoir*. B.J.K. maintains that V. Woolf reviewed Towneley's book.

"From Alpha to Omega" column, *The Nation & The Athenaeum* 35 (14 June 1924): 353. L. Woolf wrote "Things to see or hear in the coming week:—" (List of musical recitals and matinee, "Tiger-Cats").

"From Alpha to Omega" column, *The Nation & The Athenaeum* 35 (21 June 1924): 380. Woolf [no first initial] wrote first paragraph (review of "Tannhaeuser"), and L. Woolf wrote "Things to see or hear in the coming week:—" (List of musical performances and recitals. And a list of plays: "Hamlet"; "The Street Singer; and a matinee, "The Trojan Women."

"Books in Brief" column, *The Nation & The Athenaeum* 35 (21 June 1924): 392. L. Woolf wrote reviews on *The Children's Bible* (Cambridge University Press); *The Little Children's Bible* (Cambridge University Press); *Robert Smith Surtees (Creator of "Jorrocks"), 1803-1864* by Robert Smith Surtees and E.D. Cuming (Blackwood), and *Statesman's Yearbook 1924*, edited by Sir John Scott Keltie and M. Epstein (Macmillan). Mrs. Woolf wrote first two pieces [on *Unwritten History* and *The Life and Last Words of Wilfrid Ewart*]. B.J.K.

"The Empire," "Reviews" section, *The Nation & The Athenaeum* 35 (28 June 1924): 418. L. Woolf wrote reviews for the following, which are part of *A British Empire Survey*, twelve volumes to be published by Collins: *The Story of the British Empire* by Sir Charles Lucas; *The Resources of the Empire* by Evans Lewin; and *Health Problems of the Empire* by Andrew Balfour and Henry H. Scott.

"Books in Brief" column, *The Nation & The Athenaeum* 35 (28 June 1924): 420. L. Woolf wrote reviews of the following: *Cambridge Readings in the Literature of Science*, arranged by W. C. Dampier Whetham and M. Dampier Whetham (Cambridge University Press); *The Soul of a Criminal* by John C. Goodwin (Hutchinson); and *Illustrated Guide to London and the British Empire Exhibition* (45th edition, revised, Ward & Lock).

"Books in Brief" column, *The Nation & The Athenaeum* 35 (5 July 1924): 454. L. Woolf reviewed *Days That are Gone* by Colonel B. De Sales La Terriere (Hutchinson).

"From Alpha to Omega" column, *The Nation & The Athenaeum* 35 (12 July 1924): 476. "-olf" [Woolf? most of name cut off] reviewed the play, "In the Snare," produced by Mr. Lion and Mr. Walls. The play is an adaptation of a play by Mr. Sabatini.

"Books in Brief" column, *The Nation & The Athenaeum* 35 (12 July 1924): 490. L. Woolf reviewed *These Things Considered* by Margaret A. Pollock (Parsons) and *John T. W. Mitchell* [leader of the Co-operative Movement] by Percy Redfern (Fisher Unwin).

"Big Game and the Camera," "Reviews" section, *The Nation & The Athenaeum* 35 (26 July 1924): 539–40. L. Woolf reviewed *Stalking Big Game with a Camera in Equatorial Africa* by Marius Maxwell (Medici Society).

"Books in Brief" column, *The Nation & The Athenaeum* 35 (2 August 1924): 572, 574. "L. Woolf" reviewed *Unsolved Murder Mysteries* by Charles E. Pearce (Stanley Paul); and *A Dictionary of the Characters and Proper Names in the Works of Shakespeare* by Francis Griffin Stokes (Harrap). The initial for the first name of the reviewer is cut off for reviews of the following: *The London of Charles Dickens* by E. Beresford Chancellor (Grant Richards); and *A George Eliot Dictionary* by Isadore G. Mudge and M. E. Sears (Routledge). However, it looks as though the initial was an "L."; the last name is clearly "Woolf."

"Plants, Gardens, and Insects," "Reviews" section, *The Nation & The Athenaeum* 35 (16 August 1924): 626. L. Woolf reviewed the following: *The Biology of Flowering Plants* by MacGregor Skene (Sidgwick & Jackson); *The Practical Book of Outdoor Flowers* by Richardson Wright (Lippincott); and *Insect Pests* by E. T. Ellis (Allen & Unwin).

"Books in Brief" column, *The Nation & The Athenaeum* 35 (16 August 1924): 626. L. Woolf wrote the list of books by Robert Louis Stevenson in Heinemann's Tusitala Edition (*An Inland Voyage*; *Travels with a Donkey*; *The Merry Men and Other Tales*; *Virginibus Puerisque* and other Essays in Belles Lettres; *Catriona*; *Lay Morals* and other Ethical Papers; *Edinburgh: Picturesque Notes*; *Weir of Hermiston*; and some unfinished stories and plays); and a review of *Book Prices Current, 1923*. Vol. XXXVII (Elliot Stock).

"Books in Brief" column, *The Nation & The Athenaeum* 35 (23 August 1924): 650. L. Woolf reviewed *Foreign Politics of Soviet Russia* by Alfred L. P. Dennis (Dent).

"Books in Brief" column, *The Nation & The Athenaeum* 35 (6 September 1924): 700, 702. L. Woolf reviewed *Hannibal Crosses the Alps* by Cecil Torr (Cambridge University Press); *Etruria and Rome* by R. A. L. Fell (Cambridge University Press); and *Conscious Auto-Suggestion* by Emile Coue and J. Louis Orton (Fisher Unwin), and he probably reviewed *Plato: Euthyphro, Apology and Crito*, edited by John Burnet (Oxford University Press), as well. First initial cut off of author's name for review of *Plato*, but it looks like the "tail" of the "L," followed by the surname "Woolf." [only 2nd piece in this column not written by Woolf]

"Books in Brief" column, *The Nation & The Athenaeum* 35 (13 September 1924): 730. L. Woolf reviewed *Philip's Handy Gazetteer of the British Isles* (Philip); and *York* by Joseph E. Morris, the Little Guides series, (Methuen)

"From Alpha to Omega" column, *The Nation & The Athenaeum* 35 (20 September 1924): 749. L. Woolf wrote last two paragraphs: Description of courses of the University Extension Lectures program of the University of London: "The History of Science," "The Development of Modern English Literature," "Modern French Literature," "The Art of the Renaissance," "Modern Ethical Ideas," and "The History of Architecture." And "Things to see or hear in the coming week:—" (a musical recital; the following plays: "All's Well that Ends Well," "The Letter of the Law," and "The Devil's Disciple"; and an American film: "The Thief of Bagdad").

"Books in Brief" column, *The Nation & The Athenaeum* 35 (20 September 1924): 756. L. Woolf reviewed *My Fight for Irish Freedom* by Dan Breen (Talbot Press).

"From Alpha to Omega" column, *The Nation & The Athenaeum* 35 (27 September 1924): 777. L. Woolf wrote "Things to see or hear in the coming week:—" (List of a musical recital, a concert, a lecture on "The Winning of the Legislative Initiative by the Commons," and the following plays: "The Royal Visitor," "Much Ado About Nothing," and "The Looking-Glass;" and a matinee, "The Trojan Women"). Mrs. Woolf wrote the preceding paragraph [on motor cars].

"Our Own Times," "Reviews" section, *The Nation & The Athenaeum* 35 (27 September 1924): 784. L. Woolf reviewed *These Eventful Years: The Twentieth Century in the Making* (Encyclopedia Britannica).

"From Alpha to Omega" column, *The Nation & The Athenaeum* 37 (4 April 1925): 16. L. Woolf wrote review of "Persevering Pat," performed by the Irish Players at the Little Theatre.

"On the Editor's Table" column, *The Nation & The Athenaeum* 37 (4 April 1925): 24. L. Woolf' comments on recent books: *History of Irish State to 1014* by Alice Stopford Green (Macmillan); *The Political Debates between Abraham Lincoln and Stephen A. Douglas*, with introduction by George Haven Putnam (Putnam); *A King's Private Letters*, with preface by Admiral Mark Kerr (Nash & Grayson); *The Marxian Economic Handbook and Glossary* by W. H. Emmett (Allen & Unwin); *The Labour Revolution* by Karl Kautsky (Allen & Unwin); *Christian Social Duty* by John Lee (Student Christian Movement); *The Story of Woman* by W. L. George (Chapman & Hall); *St. Paul and the Church of Jerusalem* by Wilfred L. Knox (Cambridge University Press); Oxford Editions of Standard Authors series reprint of Southey's *The Life of Wesley*, 2 volumes (Oxford University Press); *Oliver Cromwell* by Andrew Dakers, The Roadmaker Series (Parsons); *Ballads*, edited by Frank Sidgwick (Sidgwick & Jackson); Prisoners of War by J. R. Ackerley (Chatto & Windus); *Principia Mathematica* of Whitehead and Russell, 2nd ed., volume 1 (Cambridge University Press); *The Handbook of Sierra Leone* by T. N. Goddard (Grant Richards); and *Bird Islands of Peru* by R. C. Murphy (Putnam).

"The Modern Naturalist," "Reviews" section, *The Nation & The Athenaeum* 37 (11 April 1925): 53. L. Woolf reviewed *Waterside Creatures* by Frances Pitt (Allen & Unwin) and *The Life of the Bat* by Charles Derennes (Thornton Butterworth).

"Books in Brief" column, *The Nation & The Athenaeum* 37 (11 April 1925): 54. L. Woolf reviewed *Palgrave's Dictionary of Political Economy*, first two volumes edited by Henry Higgs (Macmillan). V. Woolf reviewed *Guests and Memories: Annuals of a Seaside Villa* by Una Taylor (Cambridge University Press); and *Mainly Victorian* by Stuart M. Mills (Hutchinson). B.J.K. identified V.W. pieces here; first initial missing from review of Taylor book.

"From Alpha to Omega" column, *The Nation & The Athenaeum* 37 (18 April 1925): 75. L. Woolf wrote the paragraph on new fee policies at The Leeds' Civic Theatre and "Things to see or hear in the coming week:—" (List of musical recitals and performances such as "Ariadne," an exhibition of Max Beerbohm's Caricatures, lectures on "Western Civilization" and "Is the Play the Thing on the Players?"; and the following plays and performances: "Love Labour's Lost," "The Nature of the Evidence," "Beltane Night," "The Torchbearers," "Fallen Angels," and "Caesar and Cleopatra").

"From Alpha to Omega" column, *The Nation & The Athenaeum* 37 (25 April 1925): 105. L. Woolf wrote the review of the exhibition of Max Beerbohm's caricatures at the Leicester Galleries and "Things to see or hear in the coming week:—" (List of musical recitals and concerts, a water color exhibit, and the following plays or performances: "Magic Hours" and "On with the Dance").

Mrs. Woolf wrote the third paragraph, reviews of a Music Hall performance at the Coliseum and the ballet,"The Postman").

"On the Editor's Table" column, *The Nation & The Athenaeum* **37 (25 April 1925): 112, 114.** L. Woolf comments on recent books: *The Sea and the Jungle* by H. M. Tomlinson (Duckworth); two volumes in the Shrewsbury Edition of the complete works of Samuel Butler, *The Iliad of Homer* and *The Authoress of the Odyssey* (Cape); *English Masques*, introduction by Herbert Arthur Evans, Standard English Classics (Blackie & Son's); The *House of Madame Tellier* by Guy de Maupassant, translated by Marjorie Laurie, volume 4 in works of Maupassant (Werner Laurie); *The Last Years of Rodin* by Marcelle Tirel (Philpot); *Sex at Choice* by Mrs. Monteith Erskine (Christophers); *The Town Councillor* by C. R. Attlee and William A. Robson (Labour Publishing Company); *Agriculture and the Unemployed* by William Wright, M. P., and Arthur J. Penty (Labour Publishing Company); *The Shadowgraph* by Edward Shanks (Collins); *Pen and Ink* by Guy N. Pocock (Dent); *The Principles of Decoration* by R. G. Hatton (Chapman & Hall); *Elege de la Folie* by Jean Cassou (Emile-Paul); *La Nuit Kurde* by J. R. Bloch (Nouvelle Revue Francaise); *Levy* by J. R. Bloch (Nouvelle Revue Francaise); *Ronsard et Son Temps* by Pierre Champion (Champion); and *Cassandre, ou le Secret de Ronsard* by Roger Sorg (Payot).

"From Alpha to Omega column, *The Nation & The Athenaeum* **37 (2 May 1925): 135-36.** L. Woolf wrote the review of George B. Shaw's play "Ceasar and Cleopatra" and "Things to see or hear in the coming week:—" (List of musical concerts and recitals and the following plays, performances, and lectures: "Southernwood," "Forbidden Fluids," "The Signal," "Just a King," "Is Woman's Place in the Home?" "Central Europe, Rumania, and the Near East," and "Commercial Aviation").

"On the Editor's Table" column, *The Nation & The Athenaeum* **37 (2 May 1925): 146.** L. Woolf comments on recent books: *Axel* by Villiers de l'Isle-Adam, translated by H. P. R. Finberg, preface by [W. B.?] Yeats (Jarrolds); *Coach and Sedan*, Haslewood Book series (1636, reprint; Etchells & Macdonald); *Hull Down* by Sir Bertram Hayes (Cassell); *Constance Grande* by Julian Grande (Chapman & Hall); *A Traveller in News* by Sir William Beach Thomas (Chapman & Hall); *Recollections of a Happy Life* by Maurice Francis Egan (Duckworth); *The Country that I Love* by Marie, Queen of Rumania (Duckworth); *H.R.H. the Prince of Wales's Sport in India* by Bernard C. Ellison (Heinemann); *Wonderful Africa* by F. A. Donnithorne (Hutchinson); *Redburn* and *Israel Potter* by Herman Melville (reprints, Jarrolds); *Christmas Stories, Reprinted Pieces, & etc.*, and *Uncommercial Traveller* by Charles Dickens (reprints, Macmillan); *The Return of the Kings* by X .7 (Nash & Grayson);

The Neuroses of the Nations by C. E. Playne; and *The Cinema in Education*, edited by Sir James Marchant (Allen & Unwin).

"From Alpha to Omega" column, *The Nation & The Athenaeum* 37 (9 May 1925): 176. L. Woolf wrote the tribute to John Randall who worked as a proof-reader for *The Athenaeum* and *The Nation & The Athenaeum* for fifty years, and Woolf wrote "Things to see or hear in the coming week:—" (List of musical concerts and recitals, and the following plays, performances, and lectures: "The Trial of Jesus," Otway's "The Orphan," "By Right of Conquest," "Macbeth," "The Round Table," "Rain," "Does Golf Do More Harm than Good?" "From 'Henry V' to 'Hamlet,'" and an Exhibition of Posters of E. McK. Kauffer).

"Uneducated Poets," "Reviews" section, *The Nation & The Athenaeum* 37 (9 May 1925): 180–81. L. Woolf reviewed *The Lives and Works of the Uneducated Poets* by Robert Southey, edited by J. S. Childers (Milford).

"On the Editor's Table" column, *The Nation & The Athenaeum* 37 (9 May 1925): 182. L. Woolf comments on recent books: *The Physiology of Marriage* by Honore de Balzac, translated by Francis Macnamara (The Casanova Society); *Fragments of Auld Lang Syne* by Mrs. Frank Russell (Hutchinson); *The Two Pins Club*, two volumes, by Harry Furness (Murray); *Robert Moffat* by Edwin W. Smith (Student Christian Movement); *Britain and Egypt* by M. Travers Symons (Palmer); *Palestine and the Mandate* by W. Basil Worsfold (Fisher Unwin); *Selections from the Correspondence of Theodore Roosevelt and Henry Cabot Lodge, 1884–1918*, two volumes (Charles Scribner's Sons); *International Library of Psychology, Philosophy, and Scientific Method: The Psychology of Time* by Mary Sturt (Kegan Paul); *The Metaphysical Foundations of Modern Physical Science* by A. E. Burtt (Kegan Paul); *The Life after Death in Oceania and the Malay Archipelago* by Rosalind Moss (Clarendon Press); *The West Indies* by George Manington (Parsons); and *Sir John Soane*, Masters of Architecture series (Benn).

"Books in Brief" column, *The Nation & The Athenaeum* 37 (9 May 1925): 182–83. Column written entirely by both Woolfs. First review [on *The Tragic Life of Vincent Van Gogh*] is by V. Woolf. [The first initial of author's name is cut off for 2nd and 3rd pieces in the column, but the reviewer's surname is "Woolf." These pieces are: *H. R. H. the Prince of Wales's Sport in India* by Bernard C. Ellison, edited by Sir H. Perry Robinson, preface by the Earl of Cromer (Heinemann) and *The Elements of Chess* by J. Du Mont (Bell).] L. Woolf reviewed the 4th piece: *The History of the Fabian Society* by Edward R. Pease, second edition (Allen & Unwin). B.J.K. verified information here.

"From Alpha to Omega" column, *The Nation & The Athenaeum* 37 (16 May 1925): 206. L. Woolf wrote "Things to see or hear in the coming week:—" (List of musical concerts and performances; a play: "The Right Age to Marry;"

an exhibition of Russian posters and books; and the following lectures: "Did Boswell Make Johnson?" and "The Taungs Skull—Missing Links").

"On the Editor's Table," column *The Nation & The Athenaeum* 37 (16 May 1925): 214. L. Woolf comments on recent books: Reprint of Drayton's *Endimion and Phoebe*, edited by J. William Hebel (Blackwell); *The Civile Conversation* by M. Steeven Guazzo, edited by George Pettie and Barth. Young in the Tudor Translations series (Constable); *Cambridge and Charles Lamb*, edited by George Wherry (Cambridge University Press); *Arthur Symons: A Critical Study* by T. Earle Welby (Philpot); *The England of Dickens* by Walter Dexter (Palmer), third volume in *English Topography of Dickens*; The Shakespeare Canon, Part III by J. M. Robertson (Routeledge); *Glamour* by Stark Young (Scribner's); *William Purdie Treloar* by C.E. Lawrence (Murray); *A King in the Making* by Genevieve Parkhurst (Putnam); *The Socialist Movement*, 2 vols., by Dr. A. Shadwell (Philip Allan); *The State and its Ailments* by R. V. Wynne (Simpkin); *The Employment and Welfare of Juveniles* by O. Bolton King (Murray); *My Brother's Face* by Dhan Gopal Mukerji (Thornton Butterworth); *How Britain is Governed* by Kate Rosenberg (Labour Publishing Co.); *A Fellowship of Anglers* by Horace G. Hutchinson (Longmans); *Going Fishing: Letters to a Brother Angler* (Arrowsmith); and *The Week-End Book* (Nonesuch Press). B.J.K. verified information.

"Books in Brief," column *The Nation & The Athenaeum* 37 (16 May 1925): 214. L. Woolf reviewed *Nature at the Desert's Edge* by R. W. G. Hinston (Witherby). V. Woolf reviewed *Celebrities of Our Time* by Herman Bernstein (Hutchinson). B.J.K. verified information.

"From Alpha to Omega" column, *The Nation & The Athenaeum* 37 (23 May 1925): 237. L. Woolf wrote "Things to see or hear in the coming week:—" (List of musical concerts and recitals; plays and performances: "Hamlet," "The Cherry Orchard," and "Cleopatra;" and lectures: "Nationalism," and "Why Not Brighten London?").

"Books in Brief" column, *The Nation & The Athenaeum* 37 (23 May 1925): 246. L. Woolf reviewed *The Trial of Kate Webster*, edited by Elliot O'Donnell (Hodge); *The Gardener's Calendar* by T. Geoffrey W. Henslow (Dean); *Gladioli* by A. J. Macself (Thornton Butterworth); and Book Prices Current, 1924, Vol. 38 (Scott). [entire column except book on League]

"From Alpha to Omega" column, *The Nation & The Athenaeum* 37 (30 May 1925): 268. L. Woolf wrote review of Russian ballet "Narcisse" and "Things to see or hear in the coming week:—" (List of musical concerts, and performances or plays, lectures, and exhibitions: "The River;" "Parallel between Eastern and Western Art and Thought;" Exhibition of seventeenth century Italian art; and The London Group Exhibition).

"Reviews" section, *The Nation & The Athenaeum* 37 (30 May 1925): 271. L. Woolf reviewed *Modern Russian Literature* by Prince D. S. Mirsky (Oxford University Press).

"Books in Brief" column, *The Nation & The Athenaeum* 37 (30 May 1925): 274. L. Woolf reviewed *A Memoir of Lord Balfour of Burleigh* by Lady Frances Balfour (Hodder & Stoughton); *The Gentle Art of Cookery* by Mrs. C. F. Level and Miss Olga Hartley (Chatto & Windus); *Food and the Family* by Professor V. H. Mottram (Nisbet); and *Celebrated Crimes* by George Dilnot (Stanley Paul).

"From Alpha to Omega" column, *The Nation & The Athenaeum* 37 (6 June 1925): 295. L. Woolf reviewed Richard Wagner's opera "Die Walkuere" and the Epstein Hudson Memorial located in Hyde Park. Wrote an obituary notice for J. E. C. Bodley, a frequent contributor to *The Athenaeum* and *The Nation*. And "Things to see or hear in the coming week:—" (List of musical concerts, performances, plays, exhibitions, and lectures, including the following: "The Beaux' Stratagem;" The London Group Exhibition; Present-Day British Art Exhibit; "Hay Fever;" "Hiawatha" in operatic form; Hilaire Belloc and Bernard Shaw on "What Is Coming?;" "Pippa Passes;" and "The Scheming Lieutenant."

"Books in Brief" column, *The Nation & The Athenaeum* 37 (6 June 1925): 302, 304. L. Woolf reviewed *The Days I Knew* by Lillie Lantry (Hutchinson); *Portraits: Real and Imaginary* by Ernest Boyd (Cape); *Round About Sussex Downs* by Frederick F. Wood (Duckworth); and *The ABC of Stocks and Shares* by Hargreaves Parkinson (Longmans).

"On the Editor's Table" column, *The Nation & The Athenaeum* 37 (6 June 1925): 302. L. Woolf comments on recent books: *Mary Hamilton*, edited by Elizabeth G. Anson (Murray); *The Temple Memoirs* by Colonel J. A. Temple (Witherby); *Sixty Years Ago* by Alexander Hill Gray (Murray); *The Truth About Kitchener* by Victor Wallace Germains, "A Rifleman" (Lane); *Russia in Division* by Stephen Graham (Macmillan); *My Pilgrimages to Ajanta and Bagh* by Sri Mukul Chandra Dey, with an introduction by Laurence Binyon (Thornton Butterworth); *Wanderings in the Middle East* by A. Sloan (Hutchinson); *Land Travel and Seafaring* by H. R. McClure (Hutchinson); *Nigerian Days* by A. C. G. Hastings, with an introduction by Cunninghame Graham (Lane); *The Ao Naga Tribe of Assam* by W. C. Smith (Macmillan); and *The Heart of the Middle East* by Richard Coke (Thornton Butterworth). Four volumes of the Everyman's Library series published by J. M. Dent: Robert L. Stevenson's *Treasure Island* and *Kidnapped*; *The Master of Ballantrae* and *Black Arrow*; *An Inland Voyage* and *Travels with a Donkey*; and *Virginibus Puerisque* and *Familiar Studies*. The eighth volume of *The Dramatic Works of Gerhart Hauptmann* on poetic drama (Secker); *Shaw* [on George Bernard

Shaw] by J. S. Collis (Cape); and *The Dance* by Margaret Newell H'Doubler (Cape).

"**A New Kind of Atlas,**" "Reviews" section, *The Nation & The Athenaeum* 37 (13 June 1925): 328, 330. L. Woolf reviewed *The Chambers of Commerce Atlas*, edited by George Philip and T. Swinborne Smeldrake (Philip).

"**From Alpha to Omega**" column, *The Nation & The Athenaeum* 37 (20 June 1925): 369. L. Woolf reviewed Noel Coward's play, "Hay Fever" and Ashley Duke's play, "Man with a Load of Mischief."

"**On the Editor's Table**" column, *The Nation & The Athenaeum* 37 (20 June 1925): 378. L. Woolf comments on recent books: *A History of the Pharaohs*, Vol. I: *The First Eleven Dynasties* by Arthur Weigall (Thornton Butterworth); *Under the Italian Alps* by E. L. Broadbent (Methuen); *Through the Chilterns to the Fens* by Gordon Home (Dent); *The English Lake District Fisheries* by John Watson, revised edition (T. N. Foulis); *Religions of the Empire* [selected papers from a Conference on Some Living Religions within the Empire], edited by William Loftus Hare (Duckworth); and *The Gospel and the Modern Mind* by Walter Robert Matthews (Macmillan). *Education* [report presented to the Conference on Christian Politics, Economics, and Citizenship, Vol. II of the C.O.P.E.C. Commission Report] (Longmans); *An Introduction to Kant's Philosophy* by Norman Clark (Methuen); *Money and Mines* by Hugh Frederick Marriott (Benn); *Principles of British Constitutional Law* by Cecil S. Emden (Methuen); *Springs of Water and How to Discover Them by the Diving Rod* by B. Tompkins, 3rd edition (Hurst & Blackett); and *What Is Rhythm?* By E. A. Sonnenschein (Blackwell).

"**Books in Brief**" column, *The Nation & The Athenaeum* 37 (20 June 1925): 378. L. Woolf reviewed *The Statesman's Year-Book*, edited by Sir John Scott Keltie and M. Epstein (Macmillan).

"**From Alpha to Omega**" column, *The Nation & The Athenaeum* 37 (27 June 1925): 400. L. Woolf wrote "Things to see or hear in the coming week:—" (List musical concerts and recitals, and the following plays, performances, and lectures: "The Rehearsal;" "Rule a Wife and Have a Wife;" "The Golden Ballot;" "Zephyr and Flora;" "The Gorilla;" "The Show;" and "Italian Portraiture in the Fifteenth Century."

"**Golf Artist,**" "Reviews" section, *The Nation & The Athenaeum* 37 (27 June 1925): 405. L. Woolf reviewed *The Golf Courses of Great Britain* by Bernard Darwin, illustrated by Harry Rountree, revised edition (Cape).

"**On the Editor's Table**" column, *The Nation & The Athenaeum* 37 (27 June 1925): 406. L. Woolf comments on recent books: *Restoring Shakespeare* by Leon Kellner (Allen & Unwin); *Chief Pre-Shakespearian Dramas*, edited by J. Quincy Adams (Harrap); *Literature and Revolution* by Leon Trotsky (Allen & Unwin); *Beyond Life* by James Branch Cabell (Bodley Head); *The Olympian*

Catastrophe by Sir Arthur Gorges (Cayme Press); *Three Plays: "The Rat Trap," "The Vortex" and "Fallen Angels"* by Noel Coward (Benn); *The Opera Goers Complete Guide* by Leo Melitz (Dent); *The Co-operative Movement in Italy* by E. A. Lloyd (Allen & Unwin and the Fabian Society); *Rolling Around the World for Fun* by Stanton Hope (Hurst & Blackett); *Atlantis in America* by Lewis Spence (Benn); *The History of Materialism* by F. A. Lang, new edition in the International Library of Psychology, Philosophy, and Scientific Method series (Kegan Paul); *Critical Moments in British History* by Professor Robert S. Rait (Hodder & Stoughton); *A Short History of Mediaeval England* by A. Gordon Smith (Burns, Oates & Washbourne); and *A Sketch of the History of India, from 1858 to 1918* by H. Dodwell (Longmans).

"**From Alpha to Omega**" **column,** *The Nation & The Athenaeum* **37 (4 July 1925): 429.** L. Woolf reviewed the Russian ballet "Les Matelots" and wrote "Things to see or hear in the coming week:—" (List of musical concerts and recitals, and the following plays, performances, and exhibitions: "Paintings and Drawings by Paul Cezanne;" "Cartoons and Sketches of Sir F. Carruthers Gould;" "Prisoners of War;" "Charlot's Revue;" "Comfort;" "We Moderns;" and the Gramophone Congress at Central Hall.

"**On the Editor's Table**" **column,** *The Nation & The Athenaeum* **37 (4 July 1925): 438.** L. Woolf comments on recent books: *Kelvin the Man* by Agnes Gardner King (Hodder & Stoughton); *Lafcadio Hearn's American Days* by E. L. Tinker (Bodley Head); *By Car to India* by Major Forbes-Leith (Hutchinson); *Some German Spas* by S. L. Bensusan (Noel Douglas); *Speculations in Economics* by Ian Berry (Williams & Norgate); *Labour in Politics* by Keith Hutchinson (Labour Publishing Co.); *Childhood's Fears* by G. F. Morton (Duckworth); *Time, Taste, and Furniture* by John Gloag (Grant Richards); *The Hero* by Albert Beaumont (Routledge); *Les Fabliaux* by Joseph Bedier, revised edition (Champion); *La Ville Anonyme* by Andre Beucler (Nouvelle Revue Francaise); *Le Gouvernement de M. Thiers*, 2 vols., revised edition, by Gabriel Hanotaux (Plon); and *Etudes de l'Espagne*, Fourth Series, by A. Morel-Fato (Champion).

"**Books in Brief**" **column,** *The Nation & The Athenaeum* **37 (4 July 1925): 438, 440.** L. Woolf reviewed *Some Other Bees* by Herbert Mace (Hutchinson); *Illustrations of English Synonyms* by M. Alderton Pink (Routledge); *Webster's Royal Red Book*, 1925 (Webster); and probably *With Brush and Pencil* by P. G. Jacomb-Hood, M.V.O. (Murray).

"**From Alpha to Omega**" **column,** *The Nation & The Athenaeum* **37 (11 July 1925): 460.** L. Woolf reviewed the play, "The Rehearsal."

"**From Alpha to Omega**" **column,** *The Nation & The Athenaeum* **37 (18 July 1925): 488.** L. Woolf reviewed Lytton Strachey's play, "The Son of Heaven" and wrote "Things to see or hear in the coming week:—" (List of plays, performances, and a lecture: "The Wild Goose Chase;" "The Czarina;" "The Cuckoo in the Nest;" and Mr. C. Delisle Burns on "The Arts and Civilization."

"The Pruning of Fruit Trees," "Reviews" section, *The Nation & The Athenaeum* **37 (18 July 1925): 494.** L. Woolf reviewed *The Lorette System of Pruning* by Louis Lorette, translated by W. R. Dykes (Hopkinson).

"On the Editor's Table" column, *The Nation & The Athenaeum* **37 (18 July 1925): 494.** L. Woolf comments on recent books: *By Mail and Messenger* by Sir T. Comyn-Platt (Constable); *My Anecdotage* by W. G. Elliot (Philip Allen); *The Arts in Early England; Anglo-Saxon Architecture* by G. Baldwin Brown, revised edition (Murray); *Collectivist Economics* by James Haldane Smith (Routledge); *Evolution, Heredity, and Variation* by D. Ward Cutler (Christophers); *The Psychology of the Servant Problem* by Violet M. Firth (Daniel); *Isles of Illusion* by Bohun Lynch (Constable); *The Gay City* by Arthur Phillips (Palmer); and *The Writers of Greece* by Gilbert Norwood, The World's Manuals series (Oxford University Press). And two volumes in the Contemporary British Dramatists series: *Sons and Fathers* by Allan Monkhouse (Benn); and *Churchill* by H. F. Rubinstein and A. J. Talbot (Benn).

"Books in Brief" column, *The Nation & The Athenaeum,* **37 (18 July 1925): 494.** L. Woolf reviewed *Kelvin the Man* by Agnes Gardner King (Hodder & Stoughton) and *Trial of Jessie M'Lachlan*, edited by William Roughead (Hodge).

"From Alpha to Omega" column, *The Nation & The Athenaeum* **37 (25 July 1925): 515.** L. Woolf reviewed the Russian ballet, "House Party."

"On the Editor's Table" column, *The Nation & The Athenaeum* **37 (25 July 1925): 521.** L. Woolf comments on recent books: *Joyfull Newes Out of the Newe Founde Worlde*, 2 vols., by Nicholas Monardes, translated from Spanish by John Frampton, with an introduction by Stephen Gaselee, The Tudor Translations series (1577; Constable); *Old Inns of Kent* by D. C. Maynard (Philip Allen); *The Reformation in Northern England* by J. S. Fletcher (Allen & Unwin); *The Spirit of Jesus* by A. F. Winnington Ingram (Wells Gardner); *Smoke* by Julius B. Cohen and Arthur G. Ruston, 2nd edition (Arnold); *Phases of Modern Science* [articles by scientists who contributed to the Handbook to the Royal Society's exhibit at Wembley in 1924] (Denny); *The Anthocyanin Pigments of Plants* by Muriel Wheldale Onslow (Cambridge University Press); *International Commerce and Economic Theory* by R. G. Geale (King); *The Science of Prices* by John A. Todd (Oxford University Press); *Cricket* by Gilbert Jessop, Masters of Sports series (Harrap); *Athletics for Women and Girls* by S. C. Elliott-Lynn (Scott); and *The Appreciation of Music by Means of the "Pianola" and "Duo-Art"* by Percy A. Scholes (Oxford University Press).

"Books in Brief" column, *The Nation & The Athenaeum* **37 (25 July 1925): 522.** L. Woolf reviewed *Lady Susan* by Jane Austen (Clarendon Press); *The*

Unpublished and Uncollected Letters of William Cowper, edited by Thomas Wright (Farncombe); and *Greek Ethical Thought* by Hilda D. Oakeley (Dent).

"On the Editor's Table" column, *The Nation & The Athenaeum* 37 (1 August 1925): 550. L. Woolf comments on recent books: *Coleridge, Poetry, and Prose* [collection of Coleridge's writings and essays about Coleridge], with an introduction and notes by H. W. Garrod (Clarendon Press); *British Archives and the Sources for the History of the World War* by Hubert Hall (Oxford University Press); *The Lure of the Sea* [anthology of verse and prose], selected by F. H. Lee (Harrap); *The Lure of Happiness* by W. Charles Loosmore (Murray); *Pearls from the Pacific* by Florence S. H. Young (Marshall); *The Early Church and the World* by C. J. Cadoux (Clark); *Health in Childhood* [lectures delivered at the Institute of Hygiene] (Bell); *Concerning the Habits of Insects* by F. Balfour Browne (Cambridge University Press); and *The Writers of Greece and Rome* [Gilbert Norwood's *Writers of Greece* and Wight Duff's *Writers of Rome*] (Oxford University Press).

"International Facts," "Reviews" section, *The Nation & The Athenaeum* 37 (8 August 1925): 572–73. L. Woolf reviewed *The World After the Peace Conference* by A. Toynbee (Milford) and *Survey of International Affairs, 1920–1923* by A. Toynbee (Milford).

"On the Editor's Table" column, *The Nation & The Athenaeum* 37 (8 August 1925): 575. L. Woolf comments on recent books: *"The Show"* by Mr. [John?] Galsworthy (Duckworth); *At Prior Park, and Other Papers* and *A Paladin of Philanthropy, and Other Papers* by Austin Dobson, The World's Classics series (Oxford University Press); *Alaska, An Empire in the Making* by John J. Underwood (Lane); *Through Field and Woodland* by Alice Rich Northrop, edited by O. F. Medsger (Putnam); *British Light Infantry in the Eighteenth Century* by Colonel J. F. C. Fuller (Hutchinson); *Anglo-Saxon Unity and Other Essays* by C. A. Brooke-Cunningham (Selwyn & Blount); *The Tenure of Agricultural Land* by C. S. Orwin and W. R. Peel (Cambridge University Press); *English Rooms and Their Decorations at a Glance*, Vol. I, by Charles H. Hayward (Architectural Press); *The Fishes of the British Isles* by J. Travis Jenkins, Wayside and Woodland series (Harrap); and *The Religion of Tomorrow* [correspondence between H. H. Powers and William Archer] (Watts).

"On the Editor's Table" a column, *The Nation & The Athenaeum* 37 (15 August 1925): 604. L. Woolf comments on recent books: *The Quebec Act* by R. Coupland (Clarendon Press); *The British Empire* by Albert Demangeon, translated by Ernest F. Row (Harrap); *Rebuilding Empire* by Ruth Rouse (Student Christian Movement); *The International Year-Book of Child Care and Protection* (Longmans); *A Flying Visit to the Middle East* by Sir Samuel Hoare (Cambridge University Press); *The Mountains of Snowdonia*, edited by H. R. C. Carr and G. A. Lister (Bodley Head); *Leaving the Hermitage* by Rohan

Koda, translated from Japanese by Jiro Nagura (Allen & Unwin); *Diderot et l'Italie* by Manlio D. Busnelli (Champion); *La Mennais, La Dispute de 'L'Essai sur l'Indifference* by Christian Marechal (Champion): *Oeuvres de Moliere*, Vol. I (Payot); *Passions et Romans d'Autrefois* by Victor Giraud (Champion); *La Turque* by Eugene Montfort (Flammarion); and *Portraits d'Hier et d'Aujourd'hui* by W. D'Ormesson (Champion). Confirmed by B.J.K.

"Books in Brief" column, *The Nation & The Athenaeum* 37 (15 August 1925): 604. L. Woolf reviewed *The History of Mathematics* by J. W. N. Sullivan (Oxford University Press) and *Concerning the Habits of Insects* by F. Balfour-Browne (Cambridge University Press). V. Woolf reviewed *Time, Taste, and Furniture*. Confirmed by B.J.K.

The Nation & The Athenaeum 37 (22 August 1925): 613. L. Woolf wrote the long paragraph on "White Paper on 'Compulsory Labour for Government Purposes'" (Cmd. 2464). The White Paper deals with the practice of using compulsory labor in Kenya. [This piece stops at * * *.]

"From Alpha to Omega" column, *The Nation & The Athenaeum* 37 (22 August 1925): 622. L. Woolf wrote the first two paragraphs. The first is a review of summer band concerts in Brighton. The second paragraph is a notice for summer concerts in Salzburg, Austria, Venice, Italy, Bad Homburg, Germany, and Haslemere, England.

"The Problem of the State," "Reviews" section, *The Nation & The Athenaeum* 37 (22 August 1925): 625. L. Woolf reviewed Harold Laski's *The Grammar of Politics* (Allen & Unwin).

"Books in Brief" column, *The Nation & The Athenaeum* 37 (22 August 1925): 628. L. Woolf reviewed *The Co-operative Movement in Italy* by A. E. Lloyd (Fabian Society and Allen & Unwin).

"From Alpha to Omega" column, *The Nation & The Athenaeum* 37 (5 September 1925): 677. L. Woolf wrote "Things to see or hear in the coming week:—" (List of the following plays and performances: "Joan of Arc;" "Tess of the D'Urbervilles;" "You Never Can Tell;" and "The Emperor Jones."

"Books in Brief" column, *The Nation & The Athenaeum* 37 (12 September 1925): 712. L. Woolf reviewed *Epitaphs: Graveyard Humor and Eulogy*, compiled by W. H. Beable (Simpkin, Marshall) and *Co-operation at Home and Abroad* by C. R. Fay, 3rd ed. (King).

"From Alpha to Omega" column, *The Nation & The Athenaeum* 37 (19 September 1925) 733. L. Woolf wrote "Things to see or hear in the coming week:—" (List of musical recitals and concerts, and the following plays and lectures: "Two Gentlemen of Verona;" "Measure for Measure;" "The Moon and Sixpence;" and Mr. S. K. Ratclliffe on "Thirty Years of Fleet Street."

"The Indian Peasant," "Reviews" section, *The Nation & The Athenaeum* 37 (19 September 1925): 737–38. L. Woolf reviewed *The Punjab Peasant in*

Prosperity and Debt by Malcolm Lyall Darling, with a foreword by Sir Edward Maclagan (Milford).

The Nation & The Athenaeum 37 (26 September 1925): 753. L. Woolf wrote the paragraph [part of columns 1 & 2] on the Institute of Pacific Relations, The Institute dealt with problems of immigration, particularly the American Immigration Act.

"From Alpha to Omega" column, *The Nation & The Athenaeum* 37 (26 September 1925): 764. L. Woolf wrote "Things to see or hear in the coming week:—" (List of musical recitals, and the following plays, performances, and lectures: "Mrs. Warren's Profession;" "The Great Adventures;" "Coeurs en Folie;" "Fanny's First Play;" Mlle. Pavlova's season at Covent Garden; "Chauve-Souris" season at the Strand; and Mr. Delisle Burns on "What I Saw in Poland."

"Peace and War," "Reviews" section, *The Nation & The Athenaeum* 37 (26 September 1925): 767–68. L. Woolf reviewed *The Roots and Causes of the Wars (1914–1918)*, 2 vols., by John S. Eward (Hutchinson); *How the War Began: the Diary of the Russian Foreign Office*, translated by Major W. Cyprian Bridge, a forward by S. D. Sazonov (Allen & Unwin); *The Problem of International Sanctions* by D. Mitrany (Milford); and *Now is the Time* by Arthur Ponsonby (Parsons).

"Books in Brief" column, *The Nation & The Athenaeum* 37 (26 September 1925): 772. L. Woolf reviewed *British Flora* by Gaston Bonnier, translated by Ethel Mellor (Dent).

"Know Thyself," "Reviews" section, *The Nation & The Athenaeum* 38 (3 October 1925): 22, 24. L. Woolf reviewed *The Galton System of Mind Training* (Galton Institute, London).

"From Alpha to Omega" column, *The Nation & The Athenaeum* 38 (10 October 1925): 55. L. Woolf wrote last four items which are notices of up-coming events: plays produced by the Greek Play Society, including "Oedipus Tyrannus," "Oedipus at Colonus," and "The Frogs;" plays performed by the Incorporated Stage Society, including "Brand," "Exiles," "Ivanov," and "Le Cocu Magnifique;" Mr. Robert Mayer's Orchestral Concerts for Children; and a series of musical recitals performed at the new Chenil Galleries.

"From Alpha to Omega" column, *The Nation & The Athenaeum* 38 (17 October 1925): 116. L. Woolf wrote the notice for the modern International Exhibition on art which would held at the Royal Academ y in November and December. [2nd piece from the last in the column],

"On the Editor's Table" column, *The Nation & The Athenaeum* 38 (17 October 1925): 124. L. Woolf comments on recent books: *Norway* by G. Gathorne Hardy, The Modern World series (Benn); *History of England and the British Commonwealth* by Laurence M. Larson (Cape); *The Last Age of Roman Britain* by Edward Foord (Harrap); *The Making of India* by A. Yusuf Ali (Black); *The English Factories in India, 1665–1667* by Sir William Foster (Oxford University Press); *A Short History of the American People*, Vol. I: *1492–1860* by R. G. Caldwell (Putnam); *The History of Tattooing and Its Significance* by W. D. Hambly (Witherby); *Social Classes in Postwar Europe* by Lothrop Stoddard (Scribner); *Five Years of the Work of the League of Nations* by Maurice Fanshawe (Allen & Unwin); *Superstition or Rationality in Action for Peace: A Criticism of Jurisprudence* by A. V. Lundstedt (Longmans); *The Philosophy of Labour* by C. Delisle Burns (Allen & Unwin); *X-Rays* by Maurice de Broglie (Methuen); *Astronomical Physics* by F. J. M. Stratton (Methuen); *Science and Scientists in the Nineteenth Century* by Rev. R. H. Murray (Shelton Press); *The Ascent of Man by Means of Natural Selection* by Alfred Machin (Longmans); *An Introduction to Psychology* by Hugh A. Reyburn (Harrap); and *The Evolution of Anatomy* by Charles Singer (Kegan Paul).

"Books in Brief" column, *The Nation & The Athenaeum* 38 (17 October 1925): 126. Written by both Woolfs. L. Woolf reviewed *Shelley and Keats, as They Struck Their Contemporaries*, edited by Edmund Blunden, limited edition (Beaumont); *The Permanent International Court of International Justice* by Alexander P. Pachiel (Oxford University Press); *Garden Craftsmanship in Yew and Box* by Nathaniel Lloyd (Benn); *Introducing London* by E. V. Lucas (Methuen); *The Complete Jam Cupboard—Green Salads and Fruit Salads—Summer Drinks and Wine Cordials* by Mrs. C. F. Leyel (Routledge); and *The Second Book of the Gramophone Record* by Percy A. Scholes (Oxford University Press). V. Woolf reviewed *Twenty Years of My Life* by Louise Jopling-Rowe (The Bodley Head). Probably confirmed by B.J.K.

"On the Editor's Table" column, *The Nation & The Athenaeum* 38 (24 October 1925): 160. L. Woolf comments on recent books: *Treasure Island, Kidnapped, Catriona*, and *Familiar Studies of Men and Books* by Robert L. Stevenson, Lothian Edition (Eveleigh Nash & Grayson); *Ixion in Heaven* by Benjamin Disraeli (Cape); *Letters to Katie* by Sir Edward Burne-Jones (Macmillan); *An Ambassor's Memoirs*, Vol. 3, by Maurice Paleologue (Hutchinson); *The Wit and Wisdom of Queen Bess* by Frederick Chamberlin (Lane); *The Log of a Shellback* by H. F. Farmer (Witherby); *Warriors in Undress* by F. J. Hudleston (John Castle); *Wives* by Gamaliel Bradford (Harper); *The Diary of Thomas Turner of East Hoathly, Sussex (1754–1765)* by Thomas Turner (Lane); *By Airplane Towards the North Pole* by Walter Mittleholzer and others (Allen & Unwin); *Rahwedia* by C. Harold Smith (Appleton); *The Lost Sword of Shamyl* by Lewis Stanton Palen (Lane); *Luther and the Reformation*, Vol. I, by James Mackinon (Longmans); *The Sayings of Confucius*, translated by Leonard A. Lyall, 2nd edition (Longmans); *Instinct: A Study in Social Psychology* by L. L. Bernard (Allen & Unwin); *Foster's Modern Bridge Tactics* by

R. F. Foster (Lane); *Auction Bridge Play and Problems* by A. E. Manning Foster (Methuen); and *Hints on Auction Bridge* by Lt.-Col. E. H. Hingley (Bell).

"Books in Brief" column, *The Nation & The Athenaeum* 38 (24 October 1925): 160. L. Woolf reviewed *The Art of the Printer* by Stanley Morison (Benn).

"From Alpha to Omega" column, *The Nation & The Athenaeum* 38 (31 October 1925): 182. L. Woolf reviewed the first program of the Film Society, including: "Absolute Films;" "Waxworks;" and "Champion Charlie" [Charlie Chaplin].

"On the Editor's Table" column, *The Nation & The Athenaeum* 38 (31 October 1925): 192. L. Woolf comments on recent books: *Melodies and Memories* by Nellie Melba (Thornton Butterworth); *Old Q and Barrymore* by Mr. E. Beresford Chancellor, The Lives of Rakes series (Philip Allan); *Keir Hardie* by William Stewart, new edition (Independent Labour Party); *Occidental Gleanings*, 2 vols., [the sketches and essays of Lafcadio Hearn] collected by Albert Mordell (Heinemann); *One Act Plays of Today, Second Series* [J. M. Synge, Sir Arthur Conan Doyle, Lady Augusta Gregory, Houghton, and eight others] (Harrap); a volume of plays by Eugene O'Neill, including "All God's Chillum Got Wings," "Desire Under the Elms," and "Welded" (Cape); a selection of editions of Young's *A Tour in Ireland* [first published in 1781], edited by Constantia Maxwell (Cambridge University Press); *Foreign Policy and Our Daily Bread* and *Human Nature and the Peace Problem* by Norman Angell (Collins); *The Northern Tribes of Nigeria*, 2 vols. by C. K. Meek (Oxford University Press); *Game Pie* by Eric Parker (Philip Allan); *Science, Religion, and Reality*, [symposia], with an introduction by the Earl of Balfour, edited by Joseph Needham (Sheldon Press); and *A Manual of Rugby Football for Public Schools* by Robert M. Rayner (Melrose).

"On the Editor's Table" column, *The Nation & The Athenaeum* 38 (14 November 1925): 268. L. Woolf comments on recent books: *The Fourth Earl of Carnarvon*, 3 vols., by Sir Arthur Hardinge (Milford); *Coleridge at Highgate* by Lucy Eleanor Watson (Longmans); *Madame de Pompadour* by Marcelle Tinayre, translated by Ethel Colburn Mayne (Putnam); *Hearsay* by Lord Saye and Sele (Nisbet); *Looking Back* by L. A. Atherley-Jones, K. C. (Witherby); *To All and Singular* by Sir Nevile Wilkinson (Nisbet); Sir Edward Cooke's *The Life of Florence Nightingale*, abridged edition (Macmillan); *Ariel* by Andre Maurois, translated by Ella D'Arcy, illustrated edition (Bodley Head); *A Short Life of William Pitt* by J. Holland Rose (Bell); *The Pioneer Policewoman* by Commandant Mary S. Allen (Chatto & Windus); *My Polar Flight* by Roald Amundsen (Hutchinson); *Simen, Its Heights and Abysses* by Major J. C. Maydon (Witherby); *Unknown Sweden* by James W. Barnes Steveni (Hurst & Blackett); *A Wayfarer in Unfamiliar Japan* by Walter Weston (Methuen);

On the Diamond Trail in British Guiana by Gwen Richardson (Methuen); *A Chinese Mirror* by Florence Ayscough (Cape); and *Stage Lighting for 'Little' Theatres* by C. Harold Ridge (Heffer).

"Books in Brief" column, *The Nation & The Athenaeum* 38 (14 November 1925): 268. L. Woolf reviewed *The Unpublished Diary and Political Sketches of Princess Lieven*, edited by Harold Temperly (Cape) and *The Annals of Ennius*, edited by E. M. Steuart (Cambridge University Press).

"On the Editor's Table" column, *The Nation & The Athenaeum* 38 (21 November 1925): 300. L. Woolf comments on recent books: *Gleanings from Irish History* by W. F. T. Butler (Longmans); *The Golden Age of the Medici (Cosimo, Piero, Lorenzo de' Medici)* by Selwyn Brinton (Methuen); *The Approach to the Reformation* by Roger B. Lloyd (Parsons); *Lectures on Foreign Policy, 1494–1789* by J. M. Thompson (Blackwell); *The Rise and Progress of Assyriology* by Sir E. A. Wallis Budge (Hopkinson); *The Senate and the League of Nations* by Henry Cabot Lodge (Scribners); *The "Teddy" Expedition* by Kai R. Dahl, translated by Grace Isabel Colbron (Appleton); *Sunlight in New Granada* by William McFee (Heinemann); *Temple Bells and Silver Sails* by Elizabeth C. Enders (Appleton); *Story Lives of Nineteenth-Century Authors* by R. Brimley Johnson (Wells Gardner); *The Silver Treasury of English Lyrics*, edited by T. Earle Welby (Chapman & Hall); *Beethoven* by Paul Bekker, translated from German by M. M. Bozman, Dent's International Library of Books on Music series (Dent); *Fifty Favourite Operas* by Paul England (Harrap); and *Warfare* by Oliver Spaulding, Hoffman Nickerson, and John W. Wright (Harrap).

"Books in Brief" column, *The Nation & The Athenaeum* 38 (21 November 1925): 300. L. Woolf reviewed *Wynkyn de Worde and His Contemporaries from the Death of Caxton to 1535* by Henry R. Plomer (Grafton); *The Human Factor in Business* by B. Seebohm Rowntree (Longmans); *The Conduct of the Kitchen* by X. Marcel Boulestin (Heinemann).

"From Alpha to Omega" column, *The Nation & The Athenaeum* 38 (28 November 1925): 320–21. L. Woolf wrote the commentary on Jacob Epstein's sculpture "Rima," a memorial to W. H. Hudson, located on the north bank of the Serpentine, Hyde Park, London, and a review of Sean O'Casey's "Juno and the Paycock." ["Rima" had been defaced.]

"On the Editor's Table" column, *The Nation & The Athenaeum* 38 (12 December 1925): 412, 414. L. Woolf comments on recent books: *Napoleonic Anecdotes* by Louis Cohen (Holden); *Bernadotte, Prince and King, 1810–1844* by Sir Plunket Barton (Murray); *Mr. Secretary Walsingham and the Policy of Queen Elizabeth*, 3 vols., by Conyers Read (Clarendon); *Cobbett* by G. K. Chesterton (Hodder & Stoughton); *E. T. Busk, A Pioneer of Flight*, with a short memoir of H. A. Busk, by Mary Busk (Murray); *Some Records of the Wingfield Family* by Lt.-Col. John M. Wingfield, D. S. O. (Murray);

The Anonymous Romances of Mayfair (Stanley Paul); *China and the West, a Sketch of Their Intercourse* [six lectures by Professor W. E. Soothill, Oxford University] (Oxford University Press); *Women in Ancient India, Moral and Literary Studies* by Clarisse Bader, Trubner's Oriental Series (Kegan Paul); *Quaint Specimens* by "Evoe" [Mr. E. V. Knox] (Methuen); *Sacrifice in the Old Testament, Its Theory and Practice* by George Buchanan Gray (Clarendon Press); *A History of the Mediaeval Church, 590–1500* by Margaret Deanesly (Methuen); *According to Saint John* by Lord Charnwood (Hodder & Stoughton); *Wild Animals on the Films* by Joseph Delmont, translated from German (Methuen); *The House of Quiet* and *The Thread of Gold* by A. C. Benson, reprint (Murray); and *A Thought for Every Day*, selected works of A. C. Benson (Murray).

"Books in Brief" column, *The Nation & The Athenaeum* 38 (12 December 1925): 414. L. Woolf reviewed *Shakespeare's Sonnets Reconsidered—The Odyssey Rendered into English Verse—Brewhon Revisited—The Way of All Flesh*, Vols. 14–17 the Shrewsbury Edition of *Samuel Butler's Works*, by Samuel Butler (Cape); *Diplomatic Relations of Great Britain and the United States* by R. B. Mowat (Arnold); and *The Consumers' Co-operative Movement in Germany* by Dr. Theodor Cassau, translated by J. F. Mills (Fisher Unwin).

"On the Editor's Table" column, *The Nation & The Athenaeum* 38 (19 December 1925): 448. L. Woolf comments on recent books: *Ruysbroeck, the Admirable* by A. Wautier d'Aygalliers, translated by Fred Rothwell (Dent); *Henry VIII and His Wives* by Walter Jerrold (Hutchinson); *The Life of George Cadbury* by A. G. Gardiner (Cassell); *Grandmother Tyler's Book* by Mrs. Tyler (Putnam); *Letters to a Friend* by Alexandre Ribot (Hutchinson); *Palestine and Pamela* by Lady Buckmaster (Heffer); *Bedouin Justice* by Austin Kennett (Cambridge University Press); *Round the World with the Battle Cruisers* by Instructor-Lieutenant Benstead (Hurst & Blackett); *Unknown Norfolk* by Donald Maxwell (Bodley Head); *The Fen Country* by Christopher Marlowe (Palmer); *Meddlesome Matty* by Jane Taylor and Anne Taylor (Bodley Head); *The Fairyland Express* by Anthony Raine Barker (Bodley Head); *Portraits in the London Zoo* by Silvia Baker (Putnam); and *A Short History of the British Working Class Movement*, Vol. 1, by G. D. H. Cole (Labour Publishing Co.).

"Books in Brief" column, *The Nation & The Athenaeum* 38 (19 December 1925): 448. L. Woolf reviewed *The Aquarium Book* by E. G. Boulenger (Duckworth) and *Bulb Gardening* by A. J. Macself (Thornton Butterworth).

"On the Editor's Table" column, *The Nation & The Athenaeum* 38 (26 December 1925): 476. L. Woolf comments on recent books: *Mary Macarthur, A Biographical Sketch* by Mary Agnes Hamilton (Parsons); *Lord Grenfell's Memoirs* (Hodder & Stoughton); *Mathilda Wrede of Finland* by Lilian Stevenson (Allen & Unwin); *Famous Gentlemen Riders at Home and Abroad* by Charles

A. Voigt (Hutchinson); *Southward Ho!* by Ralph Deakin, with a preface by H. R. H. the Prince of Wales (Methuen); *Papua of To-day* by Sir Hubert Murray (King); *The Argentina of To-day* by L. E. Elliott (Hurst & Blackett); *Beyond the Moon Gate* by Welthy Honsinger (Gay & Hancock); *The Bookman Treasury of Living Poets*, edited by St. John Adcock (Hodder & Stoughton); *Rugby Football* by R. Cove Smith, with a foreword by W. W. Wakefield (Methuen); *A Comprehensive Treatise on Inorganic and Theoretical Chemistry*, Vol. VI, by J. W. Mellor (Longmans); *Some Lesser-Known Architecture of London* by James Burford and J. D. M. Harvey (Benn); *Dutch Architecture of the XXth Century* by J. P. Mieras and F. R. Yerbury (Benn); and *The Letters of Jane Austin*, [selected letters] with an introduction by R. Brimley Johnson (Bodley Head).

"Books in Brief" column, *The Nation & The Athenaeum* 38 (26 December 1925): 476. Reviews of last three books in the column have no reviewer's name beside them. "L. Woolf" is penned in at bottom of page; he may have reviewed the last book, *Minims* by Kapp (Faber & Gwyer). L. Woolf may have also reviewed *Co-operative Storekeeping* by Sydney R. Elliot, with an introduction by Margaret Llewelyn Davies (Labour Publishing Co) and *The Diary of a Young Lady of Fashion in the Year 1764–1765* (Thornton Butterworth). V. Woolf reviewed *From Hall-Boy to House Steward*.

"From Alpha to Omega," *The Nation & The Athenaeum* 38 (2 January 1926): 496. L. Woolf reviewed the "Publisher's Circular."

"Two Ambassadors," "Reviews" section, *The Nation & The Athenaeum* 38 (2 January 1926): 500. L. Woolf reviewed *The Life and Letters of Walter Hines Page*, Vol. III, by Burton Henrick (Heinemann) and *Social and Diplomatic Memories, 1902–1919* by Sir J. Rennell Rodd (Arnold).

"On the Editor's Table" column, *The Nation & The Athenaeum* 38 (2 January 1926): 504. L. Woolf comments on recent books: *The Mountains of Youth* by Arnold Lunn (Oxford University Press); *A Walk-about in Australia* by Philippa Bridges (Hodder & Stoughton); *Fuji from Hamstead Heath* by Gonnoske Komai (Collins); *The Fairies up to Date* (Thornton Butterworth); *The Cathedral Churches of England* by A. Hamilton Thompson (S. P. C. K.); *The Story of the 29th Division* by Captain Stair Gillon (Nelson); *The Scots Guards in the Great War, 1914–1918* by F. Loraine Petre, Wilfrid Ewart, and Major-General Sir Cecil Lowther (Murray); *Cinema* in *Les Cahiers du Mois* (Emile-Paul); *Notes sur la Technique Poetique* by Georges Duhamel and Charles Vildrac (Champion); *L'Homme couvert de Femmes* by Drieu La Rochelle (Nouvelle Revue Francaise); *La Fee aux Miettes*, essai sur le role du subconscient dans l'oeuvre de Charles Nodier by Jules Vodoz (Champion).

"Books in Brief" column, *The Nation & The Athenaeum* 38 (2 January 1926): 504. L. Woolf reviewed *Coleridge at Highgate* by Lucy E. Watson (Longmans); *The Wonderland of Big Game* by A. Radclyffe Dugmore (Arrowsmith); *The*

Bench and the Dock by Charles Kingston (Kegan Paul); *Madame de Pompadour* by Marcelle Tinayre translated by Ethel Colburn Mayne (Putnam); *Elizabethan Lyrics*, chosen and arranged by Norman Ault (Longmans); *Canine Distemper: A Practical Handbook* by Louis Sewell (Routledge); *English of To-Day* by Professor W. T. Webb (Routledge); and *A Key to Language* by Isabel Fry (Sidgwick & Jackson).

"A Chronological Shakespeare," "Reviews" section, *The Nation & The Athenaeum* 38 (9 January 1926): 530. L. Woolf reviewed *The Works of Shakespeare Chronologically Arranged*, 3 vols., with an introduction by Charles Whibley (Macmillan).

"Books in Brief" column, *The Nation & The Athenaeum* 38 (9 January 1926): 531–32. L. Woolf reviewed *Rapid Calculations* by A. H. Russell (Gregg Publishing Co.); *Beethoven* by Paul Bekker, translated by M. M. Bozman (Dent); and *Reminiscences* by Marie, Princess of Battenberg (Allen & Unwin).

"On the Editor's Table" column, *The Nation & The Athenaeum* 38 (16 January 1926): 564. L. Woolf comments on recent books: *The Mummy* by Sir E. A. Wallis Budge, 2nd ed. (1893; Cambridge University Press); *A State Trading Adventure* by Frank H. Coller (Oxford University Press); *Justice and the Poor in England* by F. C. G. Gurney-Champion (Routledge); *The Healing of Nations* by Archibald Chisholm (Student Christian Movement); *College Chemistry* by Lyman C. Newell (Harrap); *Wonder Tales of Alsace-Lorraine* by B. L. K. Henderson and C. Calvert (Philip Allan); *Five Indian Tales* by F. F. Shearwood (Student Christian Movement); *Kew Gardens Adventures; Fairy Tales for Grown-Ups* by M. A. Muegge (Daniel); *The Poetry of Nonsense* by Emile Cammaerts (Routledge); and *Love's Bitter-Sweet, Translations from the Irish Poets of the Sixteenth and Seventeenth Centuries* by Robin Flower (Cuala Press).

"Books in Brief" column, *The Nation & The Athenaeum* 38 (16 January 1926): 564. L. Woolf reviewed *Opium: an Account of the Traffic in Narcotic Drugs* by John Palmer Gavit (Routledge) and *Opium as an International Problem: the Geneva Conferences* by W. W. Willoughby (Johns Hopkins Press).

"On the Editor's Table" column, *The Nation & The Athenaeum* 38 (23 January 1926): 592. L. Woolf comments on recent books: *Our Mr. Willie* by W. Pett Ridge; *The Political Consequences of the Reformation* by R. H. Murray (Benn); *Four Centuries of Modern Iraq* by S. H. Longrigg (Oxford University Press); *The Foundations of Society and the Land* by J. W. Jeudwine, revised ed. (Williams & Norgate); *Roman London* by Gordon Home (Benn); *History in English Words* by Owen Barfield (Methuen); *A New Europe* by Dr. C. F. Heerfordt (Allen & Unwin); *Food, Its Use and Abuse* and *The Health of the Workers* by Sir Thomas Oliver, The Modern Health Books series (Faber & Gwyer); *On the Panel, General Practice as a Career* by A Panel Doctor (Faber

& Gwyer); *A Handbook on the Death Duties* by H. Arnold Woolley (Fisher Unwin); *An Englishman's Castle, or Every Householder's Manual* by J. E. H. Wartnaby and E. Holroyd Pearce (Methuen); *The Other London Galleries* by Margaret E. Tabor (Methuen); and *The Gospel of Evolution* by Professor J. Arthur Thomson (Newnes).

"Books in Brief" column, *The Nation & The Athenaeum* 38 (23 January 1926): 592. L. Woolf reviewed *London Nights* by Stephen Graham (Hurst & Blackett) and Joseph Conrad's *The Rover* (Dent).

"On the Editor's Table," a column *The Nation & The Athenaeum* 38 (30 January 1926): 624. L. Woolf comments on recent books: *George Wale, 1846–1925*, [collection of essays] with an introduction by Mr. E. S. P. Haynes (Cape); *Twenty-five: Being a Young Man's Candid Recollections of His Elders and Betters* by Beverley Nichols (Cape); *Through the Belgian Congo* by Diana Strickland (Hurst & Blackett); *The New Russia* by L. Haden Guest (Thornton Butterworth); *National Economics, for Britain's Day of Need* by Edward Batten (Pitman); *Karl Marx's Capital* by A. D. Lindsay, Master of Balliol, The World's Manuals series (Oxford University Press); and *Winged Defense* by William Mitchell, former Assistant Chief of the United States Air Force (Putnam). Confirmed by B.J.K.

"Books in Brief" column, *The Nation & The Athenaeum* 38 (30 January 1926): 624. L. Woolf reviewed *From Groves of Palm* by Bella Sidney Woolf (Heffer); *A Voyage in Space* by H. H. Turner (Sheldon Press); *The Argentina of To-day* by L. E. Elliot (Hurst & Blackett); and *The Great Abnormals* by Theo B. Hyslop. Mrs. Woolf reviewed *Mary Elizabeth Haldane, a Record of a Hundred Years*, edited by her daughter. Confirmed by B.J.K.

"From Alpha to Omega" column, *The Nation & The Athenaeum* 38 (6 February 1926): 646. L. Woolf probably wrote the notice for yearly concerts of "the Bach Cantata Club." [Marginal note beside Bach Club is: "L. Woolf?"] and the notice for the concerts of the Backhouse Quartet. Woolf did write "Things to see or hear in the coming week:—" (List of musical recitals and concerts and the following plays, performances, and exhibitions: The Ridley Art Club at Spring Garden Galleries; "Richard the Second;" "Julius Caesar;" "Marriage a la Mode;" and "Henry the Fourth, Part II." Lectures: "Family Endowment;" "Parody;" "The Youth of Milton;" "Modern View of Vitamins;" "Public Libraries and Reading;" and Professor Graham Wallas on "Social Leadership.")

"On the Editor's Table" column, *The Nation & The Athenaeum* 38 (6 February 1926): 654. L. Woolf comments on recent books: *An Amateur in Africa* by L. Lestock Reid (Fisher Unwin); *Whaling in the Frozen North* by A. J. Villiers (Hurst & Blackett); *My Crowded Solitude* by Jack McLaren (Fisher Unwin); *Issues of European Statesmanship* by B. G. de 'Montgomery (Routledge); *Germany's Industrial Revival* by Sir Philip Dawson, M. P. (Williams &

Norgate); *The Empire in Eclipse* by Richard Jebb (Chapman & Hall); *The History of Political Science from Plato to the Present* by R. H. Murray (Heffer); *The Art of Water Colour Printing* by E. Barnard Lintott, the Universal Art Series (Chapman & Hall); *The New Anecdotes of Painters and Printing* by Herbert Furst (Bodley Head); *A Literary History of the English People*, Vol. I, by J. J. Jusserand, revised ed. (Fisher Unwin); *Tennyson*, edited by S. S. Sopwith, The Campanion Poets series (Christophers); *The Marriage of Loti* by Pierrie Loti (Rarahu), translation of the work published by Werner Laurie; *The Savoy Operas* by W. S. Gilbert [text of Gilbert and Sullivan operas, 1875–1896] (Macmillan); *Burns and the Common People* by William Stewart (I. L. P.); and *Burns, from a New Point of View* by Sir James Crichton-Browne (Hodder and Stoughton). Confirmed by B.J.K.

"Books in Brief" column, *The Nation & The Athenaeum* 38 (6 February 1926): 654. L. Woolf reviewed *The Bible*, Vol. II (Nonesuch Press); *Southward Ho!* by Ralph Deakin (Methuen); and *Mystery Cities: Exploration and Adventure in Lubaantun* by Thomas Gann (Duckworth). Mrs. Woolf reviewed *Queen Alexandra the Well-Beloved* by E. Villiers. Confirmed by B.J.K.

"From Alpha to Omega" column, *The Nation & The Athenaeum* 38 (13 February 1926): 680–81. L. Woolf reviewed the opera, "The Student Prince."

"On the Editor's Table" column, *The Nation & The Athenaeum* 38 (13 February 1926): 688, 690. L. Woolf comments on recent books: *Wanderings in Arabia* by Charles M. Doughty (Duckworth) abridged edition of Doughty's *Travels in Arabia Deserta* (1908); *America and Belgium* by Thomas K. Gorman (Fisher Unwin); *The Rise of the Spanish Empire*, Vol. III: *The Emperor* by R. Bigelow Merriman (Macmillan); *History of Russia* by S. F. Platonov (Macmillan); *Prehistoric and Roman Wales* by R. E. M. Wheeler (Clarendon Press); *The Making of the English Constitution* by Albert Beede White, 2nd ed. (Putnam); *Builders of the Empire* by J. A. Williamson (Clarendon Press); *Jesus the Nazarene—Myth or History* by Maurice Goguel, translated by Frederick Stephens (Fisher Unwin); *The Origin of Islam and its Christian Environment* by Richard Bell (Macmillan); *Mystical Phenomena* by Mgr. Albert Farges, translated by S. P. Jacques (Burns, Oates & Washbourne); *Meditations on Various Aspects of Spiritual Life* by Sadhu Sundar Singh (Macmillan); *Arabian Medicine and Its Influence on the Middle Ages*, 2 vols., by Dr. Donald Cambell, Trubner's Oriental series (Kegan Paul); *The Underworld* by Ashton Wolfe (Hurst & Blackett); *Night Life—London and Paris—Past and Present* by Ralph Nevill (Cassell); *London's Lost Theatres of the Nineteenth Century* by Erroll Sherson (Bodley Head); and *The Happy Fisherman* by Walter M. Gallichan (Heath Cranton).

"Books in Brief" column, *The Nation & The Athenaeum* 38 (13 February 1926): 690. L. Woolf reviewed *Collected Essays*, Vols. I and II, by Samuel Butler [Vols. 18 and 19 in the 20 volume Shrewsbury Edition of Samuel

Butler's complete works] (Cape); *The Town Labourer, 1760–1832: The New Civilisation* by J. L. Hammond and Barbara Hammond, revised ed. (1917; Longmans); *Soils and Fertizers* by A. J. Macself (Thornton Butterworth); and *A German-English Dictionary* by Herman C. G. Brandt (Stechert).

"New Gramophone Records" column, *The Nation & The Athenaeum* 38 (13 February 1926): 692. L. Woolf reviewed Mozart. Symphony (No. 39) in E flat. Orchestra of the State Opera House, Berlin: Conductor, Dr. Weissman, three 12 inch records (Parlophone); Wagner. "Tristan and Isolde." Introductions to Acts I and III. Orchestra of the State Opera House, Berlin: Conductor, Ed. Moerike, two 12 inch records (Parlophone); Schubert. "Wiegenlied, Schlafe Schlafe." "Nacht und Traum." Sung by Emmy Bettendorf, with piano accompaniment, one double-sided 12 inch record (Parlophone); and Palestrina. "Confitebor Tibi." "Bonum Est." Sung by the Sistine-Vatican Choir: Conducted by Monsignore Casimiri, one double-sided 12 inch record (Parlophone).

"On the Editor's Table" column, *The Nation & The Athenaeum* 38 (20 February 1926): 722, 724. L. Woolf comments on recent books: *Proceedings of the British Academy, 1921–1923* (Milford); *Majorca* by Henry C. Shelley, with a preface by A. S. M. Hutchinson (Methuen); *A Tibetan on Tibet* by G. A. Combe (Fisher Unwin); *Spanish Towns and People* by Robert McBride (Fisher Unwin); *Highways and Byways in Leicestershire* by J. B. Firth (Macmillan); *English Monastic Finances in the Later Middle Ages* by R. H. Snape, The Cambridge Studies in Medieval Life and Thought series (Cambridge University Press); *Life and Work in Modern Europe* by G. Renard and G. Wenlersse (Kegan Paul); *In the Beginning* by Eva Erleigh (Heinemann); *Isabella Stewart Gardner and Fenway Court* by Morris Carter (Heinemann); *The Sunlit Hours: A Record of Sport and Life* by Theodore Andrea Cook (Nisbet); *A Diplomat Looks at Europe* by Richard Washburn Child, former American Ambassador to Italy (Fisher Unwin); *Interest Rates and Stock Speculation* by R. N. Owens and C. O. Hardy, The Institute of Economics Series (Allen & Unwin); and *Investments for All* by G. H. le Maistre (Murray).

"Books in Brief" column, *The Nation & The Athenaeum* 38 (20 February 1926): 724. L. Woolf reviewed *Whitaker's Cumulative Book List, 1925* (Whitaker).

"From Alpha to Omega" column, *The Nation & The Athenaeum* 38 (27 February 1926): 745. L. Woolf reviewed, the play, Chekhov's "Three Sisters" and wrote the notice for the James Forlong lectures at the School of Oriental Studies.

"On the Editor's Table" column, *The Nation & The Athenaeum* 38 (27 February 1926): 756. L. Woolf comments on recent books: Tavernier's *Travels in India*, translated by V. Ball, edited by William Cooke (Oxford University Press); *Sahara* by Angus Buchanan (Murray); *On the Roof of the Rockies* by Lewis R. Freeman (Heinemann); *Vanishing Trails, Ten Years of a Wanderer's Life* by Harrison Dale (Black); *Among the Bantu Nomads* by J. T. Brown

(Seeley, Service); *In Unknown New Guinea* by W. J. V. Saville (Seeley, Service); *The Bay of Naples* by Mrs. Steuart Erskins (A. & C. Black); *Lanfranc, A Study of His Life and Writing* by A. J. Macdonald (Oxford University Press); *Home Life Under the Stuarts* by Elizabeth Godfrey (Stanley Paul); *Beowulf*, translated into modern English rhyming verse by Archibald Strong, with a foreword by Professor R. W. Chambers (Constable); *Mrs. Delany at Court and Among the Wits*, edited by R. Brimley Johnson (Stanley Paul); *Life's Fitful Fever* by Margaret Wynne Nevinson (A. & C. Black); *Camp and Society* by Colonel Hugh M. Sinclair (Chapman & Hall); and *Manners and Tone of Good Society* by Hon. Mrs. Dowall (A. & C. Black).

"On the Editor's Table" column, *The Nation & The Athenaeum* 38 (6 March 1926): 784, 786. L. Woolf comments on recent books: *Essays of To-day and Yesterday* series, Vol. I, essays of Mr. Guedalla (Harrap); *Little Books on Great Masters* series, 5 vols.: Giorgione, Velasquez, Van Dyck, Frans Hals, and Leonardo da Vinci, by E. V. Lucas (Methuen); *Premier Architecte de Louis XV* [Ange-Jacques Gabriel], Masters of Architecture series (Benn); *The Quantum Theory of the Atom* by Mr. G. Birtwistle (Cambridge University Press); *Way Back in Papua* by J. H. Homes (Allen & Unwin); *A Tropical Tramp with the Tourists* by Harry L. Foster (Bodley Head); *Industrial Psychology in Great Britain* by Charles S. Myers (Cape); *Common Sense and Its Cultivation* by Dr. Hanbury Hankin (Kegan Paul); *Emotion and Insanity* by S. Thalbitzer, International Library of Psychology, Philosophy, and Scientific Method series (Kegan Paul); *Life and Work of the People of England* [fifteenth century] by Dorothy Hartley, People's Life and Work Series (Batsford); *Life and Work of the People of England* [sixteenth century] by Margaret M. Eliot, People's Life and Work Series (Batsford); and *Palgrave's Dictionary of Political Economy, N–Z*, Vol. 3 of the set, edited by Henry Higgs (Macmillan).

"Books in Brief" column, *The Nation & The Athenaeum* 38 (6 March 1926): 786. L. Woolf reviewed *The Augustan Books of Modern Poetry* series, 6 vols., *Frederick William Harvey, Sir Edmund Goss, A Religious Anthology, Walt Whitman, Andrew Lang*, and *Siegfried Sassoon* (Benn); *Karl Marx's "Capital"* by A. D. Lindsay (Oxford University Press); *Burke's Peerage, Baronetage and Knightage, 1926*, 84th ed. (Dean); and *Debrett's House of Commons and the Judicial Bench 1926* (Dean). V. Woolf reviewed *Paradise in Piccadilly* by Harry Furniss. Confirmed by B.J.K.

"Songs, Operatic, and Choirs," "New Gramophone Records" column, *The Nation & The Athenaeum* 38 (6 March 1926): 788. L. Woolf reviewed the following:

Song: Frederick Delius: "To Daffodils." H. & G. Bantoce: Serenade from "Six Jester Songs." Sung by Muriel Brunskill with piano. One 10 inch record (Columbia).

Operatic: Wagner: "Lohengrin." Finale of Act I. and King's Prayer (in English). Miriam Licette, Muriel Brunskill, Frank Mullings, Kingsley Lark, Thorpe Bates, and Grand Opera Chorus, with Orchestra conducted by Sir Hamilton Harty. One 12 inch record (Columbia); Puccini: "Vissi d'arte" from "Tosca" (in Italian), and "They Call Me Mimi" from "Boheme" (in German). Sung by Claire Dux, soprano. One 12 inch record (Polydor); Donizetti: "Vien Leonora" and "A Tanto Amor" from "La Favorita" (in Italian). Sung by Ricardo Stracciari, baritone, with orchestra. One 10 inch record (Columbia); Leoncavallo: "On With the Motley" and "No Pagliacci, No More," from "Pagliacci" (in English). Sung by William Haseltine, with orchestra. One 10 inch record (Columbia).

Choirs: The Sheffield Choir, conducted by Dr. Henry Cowen (sp.?) (unaccompanied). One side—R. Edwards: "I'm Going to My Lonely Bed;" W. Macfarren: "You Stole My Love." Other side—"The Bells of St. Michael," arranged by Sir R. P. Stewart. One 12 inch record (Columbia). Basilica Choir, "Gloria" from Bruckner's Mass in D (?) minor. One 12 inch record (Polydor).

Instrumental: Piano, Debussy: "Les Collines D'Ancapri (First Book of Preludes) and "Bruyeres" (Second Book of Preludes). Pianoforte solos by William Murdoch. One 10 inch record (Columbia). Violin, Paganini: Violin Concerto in D major. Parts I and II. Played by Vasa Prihoda. One 12 inch record (Polydor). Bazzini: "La Ronde des Lutins." H. Vieuxtempe: Polonaise, Op. 38. Violin solos by Mayer Gordon, with piano. One 12 inch record (Columbia). 'Cello, Granados: "Danse Espagnole." Kreisler: "Liebenfreud" (sp.?). Solo by Antoni Sala, with piano. One 10 inch record (Columbia). Octet, J. H. Squire Celeste Octet. Gavotte from A. Thomas' "Mignon" and Gabriel Marie's "La Cinquantaine." One 10 inch record (Columbia).

"On the Editor's Table" column, *The Nation & The Athenaeum* 38 (20 March 1926): 868, 870. L. Woolf comments on recent books: *Mary Dobson* by Una M. Saunders (A. & C. Black); *Regency Ladies* by Lewis Melville (Hutchinson); *Fight of the "Firecrest"* (Witherby); *Slaves and Ivory* by Major Henry Darley (Witherby); *Easter in Palestine* by Dame Millicent Fawcett (Fisher Unwin); *The Odes of Horace* [in English verse] by Hugh Macnaghten, Vice-Provost of Eton College (Cambridge University Press); *Greek Pottery* by Charles Dugas, translated from French by W. A. Thorpe (A. & C. Black); *Ovid and His Influence* by Edward Kennard Rand, Our Debt to Greece and Rome Series (Harrap); *The Charm of Indian Art* by W. E. Gladstone Soloman (Fisher Unwin); and *Syria* by Leonard Stein (Benn).

"Books in Brief" column, *The Nation & The Athenaeum* 38 (20 March 1926): 870. L. Woolf reviewed *Successful Advertising* by Philip Smith (Smith's Advertising Agency). Mrs. Woolf reviewed *Reminiscences of Mrs. Comys Carr* by Eve Adam; *The Days of Dickens* by Arthur Hayward; and *The Flurried Years* by Violet Hunt.

"Orchestral" and "Miscellaneous," "New Gramophone Records" column, *The Nation & The Athenaeum* 38 (20 March 1926): 872. L. Woolf reviewed the following: Orchestral: Berlioz: "Symphonie Fantastique." Op. 14. London Symphony Orchestra, conducted by Felix Weingartner. Six 12 inch records (Columbia). Rimsky-Korsakov: "Scheherazade." Parts I and II. Three 12 inch records (Polydor). Rossini: Overture to "Semiramide." B.B.C. Wireless Symphony Orchestra, conducted by Percy Pitt. One 12 inch record (Columbia). Sir Alexander Mackenzie: Britannia Overture. New Queen's Hall Light Orchestra, conducted by Sir Alexander Mackenzie. One 12 inch record (Columbia). Miscellaneous: Wembley Military Tattoo. "Tommy Atkins," "Onward Christian Soldiers," and "Tipperary." Two 12 inch records (Columbia).

"Alpha to Omega" column, *The Nation & The Athenaeum* 38 (27 March 1926): 894. Woolf [first initial missing] reviewed the play "Life Goes On."

"On the Editor's Table" column, *The Nation & The Athenaeum* 38 (27 March 1926): 906. L. Woolf comments on recent books: *A Study of the Oceans* by James Johnstone (Arnold); *Biological Memory* by Eugenio Rignano (Kegan Paul); *Certain Aspects of Biochemistry* by H. H. Dale, J. C. Drummond, L. J. Henderson, and A. V. Hill (University of London Press); *The Basis of Vital Activity* by Sir James Mackenzie (Faber & Gwyer); *The Principles of Physical Optics* by Ernst Mach (Methuen); *Seventy Years a Showman* by "Lord" George Sanger (Dent); *Last Memories of a Tenderfoot* by R. B. Townshend (Bodley Head); *Naphtali* by C. Lewis Hind, a well-known journalist (Bodley Head); *The Longs of Jamaica* by R. M. Howard (Simpkin); *The Mammoth* by Bassett Digby (Witherby); *A Primitive Arcadia* by Ellis Silas (Fisher Unwin); *We Tibetans* by Rin-Chen Lha-Mo (Mrs. Louis King) (Seeley, Service); *Beyond the Bosphorus* by Lady Dorothy Mills (Duckworth); *Behind the Third Gospel* by Vincent Taylor (Clarendon Press); *The Book of Life* by Benedict Williamson (Kegan Paul); *Religious Experience: Its Nature and Truth* by Kenneth Edward (T. & C. Clark); and *The Works of H. G. Wells; a Biography, Dictionary, and Subject-Index* by G. H. Wells (Routledge).

"Books in Brief" column, *The Nation & The Athenaeum* 38 (27 March 1926): 906, 908. L. Woolf reviewed *Trial of Abraham Thornton*, edited by Sir John Hall (Hodge). Mrs. Woolf reviewed *Steeple-Jacks and Steeplejacking* by William Larkins.

"Parlophone Records" and "Beltona Records," "New Gramophone Records" column, *The Nation & The Athenaeum* 38 (27 March 1926): 908. L. Woolf reviewed the following:

PARLOPHONE RECORDS: Beethoven: Violin and Piano Sonata, No. 5 Op. 24 in F major. Played by Edith Lorand and Michael Raucheisen. Three

12 inch records. Wagner: "Das Rheingold:" "Abendlich strahlt der Sonne Auge." "Tannhaeuser:" "Als du in kuehnem Sange." Sung by Robert Berg, baritone, with orchestra. One 12 inch record. Richard Strauss: "Ariadne in Naxos:" "Mit seinem Stab regiert er die Seelen" and "Ein Schoenes war." Sung by Emmy Bettendorf, soprano, with orchestra. One 12 inch record. Raff: Cavatina, and Gluck-Kreisler, Melody. Violin solo played by Tossy Spiwakowsky, with piano (E 10417, one record). Johann Strauss: "Poet's Love." Waltz. Played by Marek Weber and his famous orchestra (E 10418, one record).

BELTONA RECORDS: Mussorgsky's "Song of the Flea." Gounod's "Even Bravest Heart" from "Faust," sung by Hebden Foster, baritone (6039, one record). "Ye Banks and Braes" and "Angus Macdonald," sung by Catherine Stewart, a moderate contralto (6038, one record). "Down in the Forest" and "Love's a Merchant," sung by Jean Summers, soprano (6035, one record). "Arise O Sun" and "Soul of Mine, sung by Justine Griffiths, contralto (6037, one record). "Mountain Lovers" and "My Queen," sung by Herbert Thorpe (6036, one record). "Invictus," the famous poem by Henley, with music by Huhn, and "Blow, Blow, Thou Winter Wind," sung by Manuel Hemingway, bass (9390, one record). "The Banks of Allan Water" and "Braw, Braw Lads," sung by Minnie Mearns contralto. "The Rosary" and "In an Old Fashioned Town," cornet solo, played by Lieut. Harry M. Pell (936, one record). "Tam o' Shanter," a bagpipe solo.

"Books and The Public," *The Nation & The Athenaeum* **40 (26 February 1927): 714–15.** L. Woolf wrote this article as part of a series on the publishing industry. He mentioned the article in a signed piece entitled "On Advertising Books," *The Nation & The Athenaeum* 40 (19 March 1927): 848–49.

"Books in Brief" column, *The Nation & The Athenaeum* **43 (7 April 1928): 22.** L. Woolf reviewed Stephen Reynolds' *A Poor Man's House*, Travellers' Library (Cape). Mrs. Woolf reviewed L. C. Dunsterville's *Stalky's Reminiscences*. Confirmed by B.J.K.

"Events of the Week" column, *The Nation & The Athenaeum* **43 (21 April 1928): 65.** L. Woolf wrote the last item on the page beginning with "Most of the readers of *The Nation* will remember Miss Jane Harrison…."

"Foreign Affairs," "Reviews" section, *The Nation & The Athenaeum* **43 (21 April 1928): 84.** L. Woolf reviewed *Survey of International Affairs, 1925* by C. A. Macartney and others (Oxford University Press and Milford); *Survey of International Affairs, 1925. Supplement Chronology of Events and Treaties* (Oxford University Press and Milford); *Recent Revelations of European Diplomacy* by G. P. Gooch (3rd printing; Longmans); and *Lord Grey and the World War* by Hermann Lutz, translated by E. W. Dickes (Allen & Unwin).

"New Gramophone Records" column, *The Nation & The Athenaeum* 43 (21 April 1928): 86, 88. "Woolf" [first initial missing] reviewed the following:

H. M. V. RECORDS: Schubert: 7th Sympony in C major. "Song of the Volga Boatmen," sung by Chaliapine and "The Prophet," by Rimsky-Korsakov. One record. "Kol Nidrei" [ancient synagogue melody], arranged by Bruch, played by Madame Suggia. Dvorak's most popular Slavonic Dance, played by Erica Morini, violin. "When the Day is Done" [jazz], played by Paul Whiteman's Concert Orchestra. Mendelssohn: "Spring Song," the Loughborough War Memorial Carillon performance. "Chiqiulina" and "Orgullosa" [tangoes].

BRUNSWICK RECORDS: Mascagni: "Mascherae" Overture, played by the Berlin State Opera, conducted by Mascagni. "The Blind Ploughman" and "The Fairy Pipers," sung by Sigrid Onegin. "Farewell Blues" and "Sobbing Blues" [jazz], by King Oliver and his Dixie Syncopaters. "Call of Broadway" and "Without You Sweetheart," played by Vincent Lopez' Orchestra. "I Told Them All About You" and "Go Home and Tell Your Mother," sung by Alice Morley.

COLUMBIA RECORDS: Schubert: 7th Sympony in C major. Schubert: Sonatina in D major, played by Albert Sammons and William Murdoch. Brahms: Pianoforte Quintet in F minor, Op. 34 played by the Lener Quartet and Mrs. Oscar Loeser-Lebert. Five 12 inch records. Bach: two Chorale Preludes played by Harriet Cohen, piano. One 10 inch record. Glazounov's "Melodie Arabe" and Saint Saens' "Le Cygne" played by Gaspar Cassado, 'cello. One 10 inch record. J. C. Bach: Sinfonia played by Mengelberg and the Concertgebouw Orchestra. One 12 inch record. Schubert: "Lilac Time" played by the London Theatre Orchestra. One 12 inch record. The Afghanistan National Athem played by the Royal Air Force Band on one side of this record and "La Marseillaise" played by the Garde Republicaine Band on the other side. Vocal records: "Sou geloso del zeffiro" from Bellini's "La Somnambula," sung by Marie gentile and Enzo de Muro Lomarto. One 10 inch record. "In Springtime" and "At Love's Beginning," sung by Dora Labbette and Norman Allin. One 10 inch record.

"Events of the Week" column, *The Nation & The Athenaeum* 43 (28 April 1928): 95–96. "Woolf" [first initial missing] wrote the last paragraph on page 95 that continues on to page 96. The paragraph starts "The American proposals for outlawing war and…" This is a brief account of the status of the "Briand-Kellogg" negotiations between France and the U. S.

"On the Editor's Table" column, *The Nation & The Athenaeum* 43 (28 April 1928): 120. "Woolf" [first initial missing but tail of what appears to be an "L" remains] comments on recent books: *Russia in Resurrection* by an English Europasian (Routledge); *Life and Times of C. R. Das* by P. C. Ray, former editor of Bengalee (Oxford University Press); *Twelve Bad Men* by Sidney Dark (Hodder & Stoughton); *The Women Lincoln Loved* by William E. Barton (Melrose); *Diplomacy and Foreign Courts* by Meriel Buchanan (Hutchinson); *Stephen Langton* [The Ford Lecture, 1927] by F. M. Powicke (Clarendon Press); *Caricature* by C. R. Ashbee, Universal Art Series (Chapman & Hall); Bentham's *A Comment on the Commentaries, a Criticism of William Blackstone's Commentaries on the Laws of England*, edited by Mr. C. W. Everett (Clarendon Press); and *The Evolution of Charles Darwin* by George A. Dorsey (Allen & Unwin).

"Books in Brief" column, *The Nation & The Athenaeum* 43 (28 April 1928): 120. L. Woolf reviewed *The Story of the Hive* by Canning Williams (Black). Mrs. Woolf reviewed *Behind the Scenes with Cyril Maude* by Himself. Confirmed by B.J.K.

"Books in Brief" column, *The Nation & The Athenaeum* 43 (5 May 1928): 152, 154. L. Woolf reviewed *A Select Bibliography of the Principal Modern Presses, Public and Private, in Great Britain and Ireland* by G. S. Tomkinson (First Edition Club), and according to B.J.K., possibly *Auction Bridge* by Taylor and Hervey (Putnam). Mrs. Woolf reviewed *Behind the Brass Plate* by Dr. A. T. Schofield (Sampson Low) and is credited with reviewing *Auction Bridge* by Taylor and Hervey (Putnam). B.J.K.'s input noted above.

"On the Editor's Table" column, *The Nation & The Athenaeum* 43 (12 May 1928): 186. L. Woolf comments on recent books: *The Diaries of Sylvester Douglas (Lord Glenbervie)*, 2 vols., edited by Francis Bickley (Constable); *Charles XII of Sweden: A Study in Kingship* by Hon. Eveline Godley (Collins); *Oude in 1857* by Colonel John Bonham (Williams & Norgate); *The Diary of John Young, S. T. P.* [Dean of Winchester], edited by Florence Remington Goodman (S. P. C. K.); *Antarctica* by J. Gordon Hayes (Richards); *Vertical Land* by le Comte de Janze (Duckworth); *Alpine Valleys of Italy* by Ellinor L. Broadbent (Methuen); *The Familiar Guide to Paris* by John N. Ware (Methuen); *Songs and Lyrics from the Plays of Beaumont and Fletcher*, with contemporary musical settings, edited by E. H. Fellowes, Haslewood Book series (Etchells & Macdonald); and *Hibernia or the Future of Ireland* by Bolton C. Waller (Routledge).

"Books in Brief" column, *The Nation & The Athenaeum* 43 (12 May 1928): 186. L. Woolf reviewed *Human Migration and the Future* by J. W. Gregory (Seeley & Service).

"On the Editor's Table" column, *The Nation & The Athenaeum* 43 (19 May 1928): 218. L. Woolf comments on recent books: *The Son of Man* by Emil Ludwig (Benn); *Richelieu* by Karl Federn, translated from German (Allen & Unwin); *The Correspondence of Spinoza* by Professor A. Wolf [in translation] (Allen & Unwin); *The Amazing Career of Edward Gibbon Wakefield* by A. J.

Harrop (Allen & Unwin); *The India We Served* by Sir Walter R. Lawrence (Cassell); *Women's Work in Modern England* by Vera Brittain (Noel Douglas); *The Invasion of Europe by the Barbarians* [the Cambridge lectures of Professor J. B. Bury] (Macmillan); *The Tragedy of Greece* by S. P. P. Cosmetatos, with an introduction by Cyril Hughes Hartmann (Kegan Paul); *Anarchism is not Enough* by Laura Riding (Cape); and *Tennis* by Helen Wills (Scribners).

"Books in Brief" column, *The Nation & The Athenaeum* **43 (19 May 1928): 218, 220.** L. Woolf reviewed *The Public Schools Yearbook, 1928* (Deane) and *The Short Stories of Thomas Hardy* (Macmillan).

"H. M. V. Records" and "Columbia Records," "New Gramophone Records" column, *The Nation & The Athenaeum* **43 (19 May 1928): 220.** L. Woolf reviewed the following:

H. M. V. RECORDS: Schubert: Quartet in D Minor, "Death and the Maiden," played by the Budapest String Quartet. Five 12 inch records. Schubert songs sung by Elisabeth Schumann: "In Abenroth," "Die Voegel," "Die Post," and "Wohin?" (D1441, one record). Schubert songs sung by John McCormack: "Die Liebe hat gelogen" and "Who is Sylvia?" One 10 inch record. Cesar Franck: Symphony in D minor played by the Philadelphia Symphony Orchestra conducted by Leopold Stokowski. Five 12 inch records. Chopin: Twelve Studies, Op. 10, played on piano by Wilhelm Backhaus. Three 12 inch records. Waltz in E flat, Op. 16 and Berceuse, Op. 57 played on piano by Wilhelm Backhaus. (DB 1131, one record).

COLUMBIA RECORDS: Haydn: "Clock Symphony," played by the Halle Orchestra conducted by Hamilton Harty. Four 12 inch records. Delius: "On Hearing the First Cuckoo in Spring," played by the Royal Philharmonic Orchestra conducted by Sir Thomas Beecham. One 12 inch record. "Song of the Rhine Daughters" from "Gotterdaemmerung" and "The Ride of the Valkyries," played by Sir Henry Wood and the New Queen's Hall Orchestra. (L1993-4, two records). Strauss: "Till Eulenspiegel," played by the Brussels Royal Conservatoire conducted by D. Defauw. Two 12 inch records. Schubert: Sonata in G major, Op. 78, played on piano by M. Leff Pouishnoff. Five 12 inch records. Dvorak: Quartet in F, the "Nigger" quartet, played by the London String Quartet. Three 12 inch records.

"The Corpse Factory," "Reviews" section, *The Nation & The Athenaeum* **43 (26 May 1928): 259-60.** L. Woolf reviewed Arthur Ponsonby's *Falsehood in Wartime* (Allen & Unwin).

"On the Editor's Table" column, *The Nation & The Athenaeum* **43 (26 May 1928): 260.** L. Woolf comments on recent books: Four books in Cassell's Pocket Library: *Riceyman Steps* by Arnold Bennett; *Tidemarks* by H. M. Tomlinson; *Jeremy* by Hugh Walpole; and *Memoirs of Vidocq. The Birth of Romance* and *Some Little Tales*, edited by R. Brimley Johnson, The Novel series, The English Literature Library (Bodley Head). Biography: *Christopher Columbus* by Marius Andre, translated from French by E. Parkhurst-Huguenin (Knopf); *Albert Schweitzer: Some Biographical Notes*, compiled by C. T. Campion (Black); *Minstrel Memories* by Harry Reynolds (Alston Rivers); and *Studies of Yesterday by a Privy Councillor* (Allan). Essays and Criticism: *Reconsiderations* by E. E. Kellett (Cambridge University Press); *The Collected Papers of Henry Bradley*, with a memoir by Robert Bridges (Clarendon Press); and *Anarchism Is Not Enough* by Laura Riding (Cape).

"Plays and Pictures," *The Nation & The Athenaeum* 43 (2 June 1928): 297. Last review in the column: L. Woolf reviewed Isadora Duncan's *My Life*.

"On the Editor's Table" column, *The Nation & The Athenaeum* 43 (2 June 1928): 306. L. Woolf comments on recent books: *Understanding Human Nature* by Alfred Adler, translated by W. Brian Wolfe (Allen & Unwin); *Standing Room Only* by Edward Alsworth Ross (Chapman & Hall); *A Study of Modern Drama* by Barrett H. Clark (Appleton); *The Artists of the 1890's* by John Rothenstein (Routledge); *The Diaries of Mary, Countess of Meath*, edited by Lord Meath (Hutchinson); *Memories of Land and Sky* by Gertrude Bacon, daughter of Rev. John Bacon (Methuen); *Tigers, Gold, and Witch-Doctors* by Bassett Digby (Bodley Head); *Round About Andorra* by Bernard Newman (Allen & Unwin); *Peaks and Frescoes, A Study of the Dolomites* by Arthur McDowell (Milford and Oxford University Press); and *The Modern Malay* by L. Richmond Wheeler (Allen & Unwin).

"Books in Brief" column, *The Nation & The Athenaeum* 43 (2 June 1928): 306. L. Woolf reviewed *Tales of Hearsay and Last Essays* by Joseph Conrad (Dent) and *Libraries, Museums, and Art Galleries of the British Isles. Year Book, 1928-9* (The Librarian and Simpkin, Marshall).

"H. M. V. Records," "New Gramophone Records" column, *The Nation & The Athenaeum* 43 (2 June 1928): 308. L. Woolf reviewed the following: Bach: Toccata and Fugue in D minor, played by the Philadelphia Symphony Orchestra conducted by Leopold Stokowski. One 12 inch record. Delius: "On Hearing the First Cuckoo in Spring," played by the London Symphony Orchestra conducted by Geoffrey Toye. One 10 inch record. "Chi mi frena?" from "Lucia di Lammermoor" and "Bella figlia dell' amore" from "Rigoletto" sung by Galli-Curci, Homer, Gigli, de Luca, Pinza, and Bada (DQ102, one record). "Enzo Grimaldo" from "La Gioconda" and "Del Templo al limitar" from Bizet's "Pescatore di Perle" sung by Gigli and de Luca. One 12 inch record. Wagner: "Elsa's Dream" from "Lohengrin" and "Elisabeth's Greeting" from "Tannhaeuser" sung by Elisabeth Rethberg, soprano (D1420, one record). Schubert: "Hark! Hark! the Lark!" and "Who is Sylvia?" sung by Master Lough. One 10 inch record. Sonatina in G minor for violin and piano, Op.137, No. 3, played by Isolde Menges and Arthur de Greef. Two 12 inch records. "I Hear You Calling" and "Mother Machree" sung by Mr. [John?] McCormack. One 10 inch record.

"Naboth's Vineyard" [Native Reserves in Kenya], *The Nation & The Athenaeum* **43 (9 June 1928): 319–20.** Leonard Woolf analyzes the politics of the Governor of Kenya, Sir Edward Grigg, and his bill, the Native Lands Trust Ordinance, 1928. The bill is ostensibly crafted to protect the interests of native peoples, but Woolf finds much to criticize.

"On the Editor's Table" column, *The Nation & The Athenaeum* **43 (9 June 1928): 338.** L. Woolf comments on recent books: William Harvey's *De Motu Cordis* and *De Circulatione Sanguinis*, edited by Geoffrey Keynes (Nonesuch Press); *The British Empire* by Basil Williams, Home University Library (Thornton Butterworth); *A History of England* by J. R. M. Butler, Home University Library (Thornton Butterworth); *Arthur Lionel Smith, Master of Balliol, 1916–1924*, by Mrs. Arthur Lionel Smith (Murray); *Tramps of a Scamp* by Edward Michael in collaboration with J. B. Booth (Werner Laurie); *Spies* by Joseph Gollomb (Hutchinson); *The Celtic Song Book* by Mr. A. P. Graves, a song writer (Benn); *Thomas Hardy* by Samuel C. Chew (Knopf); The Legacy of Bunyan by W. Y. Fullerton (Benn); and *Realism* by S. Z. Hasan (Cambridge University Press).

"Books in Brief" column, *The Nation & The Athenaeum* **43 (9 June 1928): 338.** L. Woolf reviewed *The Statesman's Year-Book, 1928*, edited by M. Epstein (Macmillan).

"Some Books on Music," "Reviews" section, *The Nation & The Athenaeum* **43 (16 June 1928): 368.** L. Woolf reviewed *William Byrd* by Frank Howes (Kegan Paul); *Henry Purcell* by Dennis Arundell (Oxford University Press and Milford); *Tchaikovsky, Orchestral Works* by Eric Blom (Oxford University Press and Milford); *Schumann's Pianoforte Works* by J. A. Fuller-Maitland (Oxford University Press and Milford); and *Musical Meanderings* by W. J. Turner (Methuen).

"On the Editor's Table" column, *The Nation & The Athenaeum* **43 (16 June 1928): 370.** L. Woolf comments on recent books: *Mussolini, the Man of Destiny* by Vittorio E. de Fiori (Dent); *David Livingstone* by Charles J. Finger (Allen & Unwin); *Day In, Day Out* [reminiscences of Colonel Fred Burnaby, Mrs. Le Blond's first husband] by Mrs. Aubrey Le Blond (Bodley Head); *Undiscovered France* by Emile F. Williams (Harrap); *The Road to France* by Gordon S. Maxwell (Methuen); *The Station* by Robert Byron (Duckworth); *Journal d'un Poete* by Alfred de Vigny (revised edition; Scholartis Press); *Orion* by R. H. Horne, with an introduction by Eric Partridge (1843; reprint Scholartis Press); *Cancer, the Surgeon and the Researcher* by J. Ellis Barker, with an introduction by Sir W. Arbuthnot Lane (Murray); and *Engines* [based on lectures at the Royal Institution] by E. N. da C. Andrade (Bell).

"Education by Gramophone," "New Gramophone Records" column, *The Nation & The Athenaeum* 43 (16 June 1928): 372. L. Woolf reviewed the following: A series of nine lectures produced by the International Educational Society and issued through Columbia Company on 12 inch, double-sided records:
- LECTURE I—"Specimen Passages from Latin Authors," by Professor R. S. Conway. One record.
- LECTURE II—"Introduction to Virgil," by Professor R. S. Conway. Two records.
- LECTURE III—"The New Russia," by Rt. Hon. H. A. L. Fisher. Two records.
- LECTURE IV—"The Shakespearean Recital," by Sir J. Forbes-Robertson. Two records.
- LECTURE V—"What is History?" by Sir C. Oman. Two records.
- LECTURE VI—"What History Means to Man," by Sir C. Oman. Two records.
- LECTURE VII—"Man's Outlook on History," by Sir C. Oman. Two records.
- LECTURE VIII—"Good Speech," by W. Ripman. Two records.
- LECTURE IX—"Some Aspects of Eighteenth-Century England," by Professor G. M. Trevelyan. Two records.

"On the Editor's Table" column, *The Nation & The Athenaeum* 43 (23 June 1928): 402. L. Woolf comments on recent books: *The Unconscious in Action; Its Influence upon Education* by Barbara Low (University of London Press); *The Mixed School, a Study of Co-education* by B. A. Howard (University of London Press); *The Silver Tassie* by Sean O'Casey (Macmillan); *Lenin* by Valeriu Marcu, translated by E. W. Dickes (Gollancz); *Bench and Bar in the Saddle* by C. P. Hawkins (Nash & Grayson); *Granville Sharp and the Freedom of Slaves in England* by E. C. P. Lascelles (Oxford University Press and Milford); *Saints and Leaders* by Rev. H. F. B. Mackay (Allan); *The Gentleman's Recreation* by Nicholas Cox (1674; reprint Cresset Press); *The Story of Picture Printing in England during the Nineteenth Century* by C. T. Courtney Lewis (Sampson Low); and *Iona and Some Satellites* by Thomas Hannan (Chambers).

"Books in Brief" column, *The Nation & The Athenaeum* 43 (30 June 1928): 436, 438. L. Woolf reviewed *The Oxford Book of Medieval Verse*, selected by Stephen Gaselee (Clarendon Press). Mrs. Woolf reviewed *On the Stage: An Autobiography* by G. Arliss. Confirmed by B.J.K.

"On the Editor's Table" column, *The Nation & The Athenaeum* 43 (30 June 1928): 438. L. Woolf comments on recent books: *Queen Elizabeth and Some Foreigners* by Victor von Klarwill, translated by Professor T. H. Nash (Bodley

Head); *J. S. Bach* by Professor Charles Stanford Terry, Aberdeen University (Oxford University Press and Milford); *Aspects of Dr. Johnson* by E. S. Roscoe (Cambridge University Press); *Prophets True and False* by Oswald Garrison Villard, Editor of the New York *Nation* (Knopf); *Marie Ebner* by Eileen O'Connor (Palmer); *The Prose of To-day* (Longmans); *A Treasury of English Prose* by Pearsall Smith, Miscellany Series (reprint; Constable); *Ideas and Ideals* by Dean Hastings Rashdall (Blackwell); and *The Bunyan Country* by Charles G. Harper (Palmer).

"**H. M. V. Records" and "Columbia Records," "New Gramophone Records" column,** *The Nation & The Athenaeum* **43 (30 June 1928): 438, 440.** L. Woolf reviews the following:

H. M. V. RECORDS: Cesar Franck: Quintet in F minor, played by Corlot and the International String Quartet. Four 12 inch records. Haydn: Quartet in D minor, Op. 76, No. 2, the Elman String Quartet; Mischa Elman, first violin. Two 12 inch records. Respighi: "Fountains of Rome," played by the London Symphony Orchestra conducted by Alfred Coates. Two 12 inch records. Lane Wilson's "Carmena" and Marsden's "My Mother" sung by Dusolina Giannini, soprano. One 10 inch record.

COLUMBIA RECORDS: Schubert: Octet in F major, Op. 166, played by the Lener Quartet; C. Hobday, double bass; C. Draper, clarinet; E. W. Hinchcliff, bassoon; and Aubrey Brain, French horn. Six 12 inch records. Quintet in A major ("The Trout"); John Pennington, violin; H. Waldo-Warner, viola; C. Warwick-Evans, 'cello; Robert Cherwin, double-bass; and Ethel Hobday, piano. On the last side of the fifth record, the London String Quartet play "Andante Cantabile" from Tschaikowsky's Quartet in D. (L2098–2102, five records.) Schubert: Trio, No. 1 in B flat, Op. 99, played by Jelly d'Aranyl, violin; Felix Salmond, 'cello; and Myra Hess, piano. Four 12 inch records. Strauss: "Don Juan," played by the Royal Philharmonic Orchestra conducted by Bruno Walter. Two 12 inch records. "The Dance of the Sylphes" and the Rakoczy March from Berlioz's "Faust," played by the Halle Orchestra. (L2069, one record.) de Falla: "Love, the Magician," played by Pedro Morales' Symphony Orchestra. Three 12 inch records. Confirmed by B.J.K.

"**Before and After the Deluge," "Reviews" section,** *The Nation & The Athenaeum* **43 (7 July 1928): 472.** L. Woolf reviewed *The Memoirs of Raymond Poincare*, Vol. II: *January 1913–August 1914*, translated by Sir George Arthur (Heinemann); *The Tragedy of Trianon: Hungary's Appeal to Humanity* by Sir Robert Donald, with an introduction by Viscount Rothermere (Butterworth); *Justice for Hungary: Review and Criticism of the Effects of the Treaty of Trianon* by Count Albert Apponyi and others (Longmans); *The Law of Nations: An Introduction to the International Law of Peace* by J. L. Brierly (Clarendon Press); *Learning and Leadership* by Alfred Zimmern (Oxford

University Press and Milford); *The League of Nations* by John Spencer Bassett (Longmans); and *The New Democratic Constitutions of Europe* by Agnes Headlam-Morley (Oxford University Press and Milford).

"Music and Civilization," "Reviews" section, *The Nation & The Athenaeum* 43 (7 July 1928): 474. L. Woolf reviewed The History of Music by Cecil Gray (Kegan Paul).

"On the Editor's Table" column, *The Nation & The Athenaeum* 43 (7 July 1928): 474. L. Woolf comments on recent books: *The Transplanting* [narrative from the letters of Marie Balascheff, a Russian refugee from France] (Macmillan); *Reminiscences of an Old Civil Servant* by Sir John Arrow Kempe [Kempe served in the Treasury in the 1860s.] (Murray); *Six British Soldiers* by the Hon. Sir John Fortescue (Williams & Norgate); *Condemned to Devil's Island* by Mrs. Blair Niles [the first woman to visit the penal colony] (Cape); *Selected Letters of Byron*, edited by V. H. Collins (Clarendon Press); *A Selection from Thackeray's The Roundabout Papers*, edited by W. H. Williams (Alston Williams); *The Heroycall Epistles* of Ovid, translation by George-Turberville (1567; reprint; Cresset Press); *In the Beginning, the Origin of Civilization* by Professor Elliot Smith, The Beginning of Things series (Gerald Howe); *Epigrams* [anthology], edited by G. R. Hamilton (Heinemann); *Inspiration* [anthology of comments by creative artists about the creative process], collected by Jack Lindsay (Fanfrolico Press); and *A Pamphlet Against Anthologies* by Laura Riding and Robert Graves (Cape).

"On the Editor's Table" column, *The Nation & The Athenaeum* 43 (14 July 1928): 506. L. Woolf comments on recent books: *Correspondence of Catherine the Great*, translated and edited by the Earl of Ilchester and Mrs. Langford-Brooke (Butterworth); *Heading for the Abyss* by Prince Lichnowsky, former Ambassador to England (Constable); *The Case for Modern Socialism* by A. W. Humphrey (Allen & Unwin); *Great Britain; Essays in Regional Geography*, edited by A. G. Ogilvie, with an introduction by Sir E. J. Russell (Cambridge University Press); *Cheiron's Cave* [inspired by Mr. and Mrs. Faithfull's work in a Nature School in Norfolk] by Dorothy Revel (Heinemann); and *An International Language* by Professor Otto Jespersen (Allen & Unwin). Confirmed by B.J.K.

"Books in Brief" column, *The Nation & The Athenaeum* 43 (14 July 1928): 506. L. Woolf reviewed *Buying a Car? The Car Buyer's Annual, 1928* by Leonard Henslowe (Hutchinson) and *The Gardener's Year Book, 1928*, edited by D. H. Moutray Read (Allan). Mrs. Woolf reviewed *Clara Butt: Her Life Story* by Winifred Ponder (Harrap). Confirmed by B.J.K.

"On the Editor's Table" column, *The Nation & The Athenaeum* 43 (21 July 1928): 538. L. Woolf comments on recent books: Corrections noted regarding citation for *Epigrams* by George Rostrevor Hamilton (Heinemann). Mr.

Hamilton wrote all the epigrams. See column for 7 July 1928, p. 474. PLAYS: *Full Circle* by Storm Jameson (Basil Blackwell); *A Penny for the Guy* by Margaret Macnamara (Basil Blackwell); and *Gather Ye Rosebuds* by Blair (Basil Blackwell).

The Living Bible, edited from the King James version by Bolton Hall (Knopf); *Asoka* [on the career of Asoka, Buddhist emperor of India, c. 274–232 B. C.] by Radhakumud Mookerii (Macmillan); *The Future of an Illusion* by Sigmund Freud (Hogarth Press); *The Development of International Law* by Sir Geoffrey Butler and Simon Maccoby (Longmans); and *The Thirsty Earth* [on irrigation in various countries] by E. H. Carter (Christophers).

"H. M. V. Records" and "Columbia Records," "Gramophone Records" column, *The Nation & The Athenaeum* 43 (21 July 1928): 538. L. Woolf reviews the following:

H. M. V. RECORDS: Mozart: Symphony in G minor, played by the Royal Opera Orchestra conducted by Dr. Malcolm Sargent. Three 12 inch records. Handel's "Xerxes" Largo and Dvorak's Slavonic Dance in G minor, played by the Chicago Symphony Orchestra conducted by Frederick Stock. (D1432, one record.) "La Traviata," "Dite alla giovine," and "Imponete," sung by Galli-Curci, soprano, and De Luca, baritone. (DB1165, one record.) Waltz song from Gounod's "Romeo et Juliette" and "Caro nome" from "Rigoletto," sung by Evelyn Scotney, soprano. (D1435, one record). Two songs from Wagner's "Lohengrin," sung by Pertile, tenor, and the Scala Chorus. (DB1107, one record.) Mendelssohn: Sonata in B flat major, No. 4, Allegro con brio and Adagio, played by Marcel Dupre, organ. (D1433, one record.)

COLUMBIA RECORDS: Tschaikowsky: Trio No. 2, Op. 50, dedicated "To the Memory of the Great Artist," Nicholas Rubinstein, played by Mr. Catterall violin; Mr. Squire, 'cello; and Mr. Murdoch, piano. Six 12 inch records. Schubert: Sonata in A major, Op. 120, played by Myra Hess, pianoforte. Music from "Rosamunde" is also played in this set. Three 12 inch records.

"Books in Brief" column, *The Nation & The Athenaeum* 43 (28 July 1928): 570. "L. Woolf" appears under the last item in this column. He probably reviewed all of the following: *A Wayfarer in French Vineyards* by E. I. Robson (Methuen); *Printing of To-day* by Oliver Simon and Julius Rodenberg, with an introduction by Aldous Huxley (Peter Davies); and *The Advertiser's A. B. C.*, 1928 (T. B. Browne, Ltd.).

"On the Editor's Table" column, *The Nation & The Athenaeum* 43 (28 July 1928): 570. L. Woolf comments on recent books: *Holland* by Marjorie Bowen, Kitbag Travel Books series (Harrap); *The People of the Twilight* [two years with the Eskimos of the Coronation Gulf region] by Diamond Jenness (Macmillan); *Palestine, Old and New* by Albert M. Hyamson (Methuen); *Pleasant Days in Spain* by Nancy Cox McCormack (Williams & Norgate); *Through* *the Moon Door* [experiences of an American living in Peking] by Dorothy Graham (Williams & Norgate); *China, Where it is To-day—and Why!* by Thomas F. Millard (Williams & Norgate); *Lord Haig* by Sir George Arthur (Heinemann); *Those Quarrelsome Bonapartes* by Robert Gordon Anderson (Williams & Norgate); *Great Britain in Egypt* by Major E. W. Polson Newman (Cassell); *Soviet Union Year Book, 1928* (Allen & Unwin); and *Random Gleanings from Nature's Fields* [based on the author's essays in the *Illustrated London News*] by W. P. Pycraft (Methuen).

"Educational Records" and "Columbia Records," "New Gramophone Records" column, *The Nation & The Athenaeum* **43 (28 July 1928): 570.** L. Woolf reviewed the following:

EDUCATIONAL RECORDS: A second series of records produced by the International Educational Society and issued through the COLUMBIA COMPANY:

- Mr. Drinkwater on "The Speaking of Verse." (D40018–9, two records)
- Professor Barcroft's "Chemical Messages." (D40028–9, two records)
- Professor H. H. Turner's "The Stars—Spring" and "The Stars—Summer." (D40024–7, four records)
- Sir Edmund Gosse's "Thomas Hardy." (D40020–1, two records)
- Professor R. S. Conway's "Latin Pronunciation." (D40022–3, two records)

COLUMBIA RECORDS: Strauss: "Blue Danube" waltz, played by the Royal Philharmonic Orchestra conducted by Weingartner. (L2086, one record.) "The Emigrant" and "The Nightingale," sung by Dora Labette, soprano. (9243, one record.) Meditation from "Thais" and Massenet's "Elegie," violin solos played by Mr. Sammons. (9415, one record.) Three records of Northumbrian smallpipes, Irish Ulilean pipes, and Highland bagpipes. (4879–81.)

"Exporting Democracy," *The Nation & The Athenaeum* **43 (11 August 1928): 612–13.** L. Woolf critiques the Ceylonese governmental system, a democratic government modeled on the British parliamentary system. He refers to Lord Donoughmore's Commission Report on this issue.

"H. M. V. Records," "New Gramophone Records" column, *The Nation & The Athenaeum* **43 (11 August 1928): 629.** L. Woolf reviewed the following: Rimsky-Korsakov: "Scheherazade," played by the Philadelphia Symphony Orchestra conducted by Leopold Stokowski. Five 12 inch records. Donizetti: "La Figlia del Regimento," sung by Toti dal Monte, soprano. (DB1152, one record.) "Drink to Me Only with Thine Eyes" and "Believe Me if All Those Enduring Young Charms," sung by Lawrence Tibbett, baritone. (DA886, one record.) Schubert: "Nacht und Traum" and "Du bist die Ruh," sung by Georg A. Walter, tenor. (B2772, one record.) "Marche Militaire Viennoise" and "Syncopation," played by "the great violinist" Fritz Kreisler and Hugo Kreisler, 'cello. (DA961, one record.) Delius: "Brigg Fair," played by the London

Symphony Orchestra conducted by Mr. Toye. Two 12 inch records. The Ballet Music from "Samson and Delilah," played by the Berlin State Opera Orchestra conducted by Dr. Blech. (D1444, one record.) A selection from "Faust," played by Marek Weber's Orchestra. (C1511, one record.) Chopin: Barcarolle in F sharp major, played by Arthur Rubinstein. (DB1161, one record.) Cesar Franck's Andantino in G minor and Wesley's "Choral Song," played by Dr. Darke, organ. (B2730, one record.) "Su Dunque!" and "Rivedrai le foreste," from Verdi's "Aida," sung by Granforte, baritone, and Monti, soprano. (DB1153, one record.) Chopin's "The Betrothal" and a song of Gordigiani, sung by Florence Austral, soprano. (E506, one record.) Borodin: Nocture from Quartet in D major, played by the Budapest Quartet. (D1441, one record.)

"Columbia Records" and "Light Music Records," "New Gramophone Records" column, *The Nation & The Athenaeum* **43 (18 August 1928): 656.** L. Woolf reviewed the following:

COLUMBIA RECORDS: Grieg: Pianoforte Concerto in A minor, played by Ignaz Friedman. Four 12 inch records. Delius: "The Walk to the Paradise Garden" from "A Village Romeo and Juliet," played by the Royal Philharmonic Orchestra conducted by Sir Thomas Beecham. (L2087, one record.) "Un bel di vedremo" from "Madame Butterfly" and "Si me chiamano Mimi" from "La Boheme," sung by Rosetta Pampanini, soprano. (L2116, one record.) Handel's Largo and "Humoresque," played by Mr. Squire, 'cello. (L2128, one record.)

LIGHT MUSIC RECORDS: H. M. V. RECORDS: "Down de Lovers' Lane" and "Seem Lak to Me," sung by Paul Robeson. (B2777, one record.) "Sinner Please Doan' Let dis Harves' Pass" and "Scandalize My Name," sung by Paul Robeson. (B2771, one record.) Brunswick Dance Records: "When" and "Wings," foxtrots, played by the Kenn Sisson Orchestra. (3781, one record.) "Borneo" and "Speedy Boy," foxtrots, played by the Ben Bernie Orchestra. (3775, one record.) "Ah! Sweet mystery of life" and "Ramona," waltzes, played by the Brunswick House Orchestra. (3773, one record.) "Auf Wiedersehen" and "Ianasy [sp?]," waltzes, played by the Regent Club Orchestra. (3777, one record.)

"Jonah in Diplomacy," "Reviews" section, *The Nation & The Athenaeum* **43 (25 August 1928): 683.** L. Woolf reviewed *Heading for the Abyss* by Prince Lichnowsky, former German Ambassor to Britain (Constable).

"Beltona Records," "New Gramophone Records" column, *The Nation & The Athenaeum* **43 (1 September 1928): 712.** No author's name given. The following items reviewed: "A Song of Cove" and "I wish I were Single Again," sung by Harry Gordon, baritone. (1370, one record.) "The Wild Hills of Clare" and "The Gentle Maiden," sung by Nora Finn and P. J. O'Toole respectively. (1358, one record.) "Ol' Man River" and "Swing Low, Sweet Chariot," sung by John Roberts, baritone. (1382, one record.) "So Do All My Pals" and "Together," sung by George Campbell, baritone. (1383, one record.) "Charge of the Light Brigade" and "Ben Hur Chariot Race," played by the Scots Guards Band. (1381, one record.) "One More Night" and "Miss Annabelle Lee," foxtrots, played by the Sunny South Orchestra and the Holywood Dance Orchestra. (1386, one record.) "Together," waltz, and "I'm Going Back Again to Old Nebraska," foxtrot, played by the Bell Toners and Avenue Dance Band respectively. (1385, one record.)

"A Life of Bach," "Reviews" section, *The Nation & The Athenaeum* 43 (8 September 1928): 738. L. Woolf reviewed *J. S. Bach: A Biography* by Charles Sanford Terry (Oxford University Press and Milford).

"Columbia Records," "New Gramophone Records" column, *The Nation & The Athenaeum* 43 (15 September 1928): 772. L. Woolf reviewed the following: COLUMBIA RECORDS: Mozart: Symphony No. 39 in E flat, played by the Royal Philharmonic Orchestra conducted by Weingartner. Three 12 inch records. Schubert: "Rosamund," "Alphonso and Estrella" Overture, the three "Entr'actes, and the Ballet music played by the Halle Orchestra conducted by Sir Hamilton Harty. Four 12 inch records. Grieg: Sonata in A minor for 'cello and piano, played by Felix Salmond and Simeon Rumschisky. Four 12 inch records. Raff's "Cavatina" and Brahms' "Hungarian Dance" in D minor, played by Mr. Catterall, violin. One 12 inch record. "Dove sono...?" from "Figaro," sung by Miriam Licette in English. One 12 inch record. Schubert: "Erlkonig" and "Auf dem Wasser," sung by Frank Titterton in English. (9431, one record.) "Am Meer" and "Ave Maria," sung by Roy Henderson in English. (9432, one record.) "Tartarus" and "Der Wegweiser," sung by Roy Henderson in English. (9433, one record.) "Three Folk Songs" and an example of Russian church music, "Kolj Savenj," sung by the Don Cossacks Choir. (9438, one record.)

"The Law and Practice of Nations," *The Nation & The Athenaeum* 43 (29 September 1928): 830, 832. L. Woolf reviewed *British Documents on the Origins of the War, 1898–1914*, edited by G. P. Gooch and Harold Temperly (H. M. Stationary Office); *The Development of International Law* by Sir Geoffrey Butler and Simon Maccoby (Longmans); *The British Year Book of International Law, 1928* (Milford and Oxford University Press); and *Studies in International Law and Relations* by A. Pearce Higgins (Cambridge University Press).

"H. M. V. Records" and "Educational Records," "New Gramophone Records" column, *The Nation & The Athenaeum* 43 (29 September 1928): 832. L. Woolf reviewed the following:

H. M. V. RECORDS: Mozart: Quartet No. 8, in D major, played by the Flonzaley Quartet. Three 10 inch records. Debussy: Nocturne, No. 2—Fetes, played by the Philadelphia Symphony Orchestra conducted by Leopold Stokowski. One 10 inch record. Strauss: "Roses of the South" and "Wine, Women, and Song," waltzes, played by the Chicago Symphony Orchestra conducted by Frederick Stock. (D1452, one record.) "Traviata" Selection, played by Creatore's Band. (C1530, one record.) "O patria mia" and "Ritorna vincitor" from Verdi's "Aida," sung by Elisabeth Rethberg, soprano. (D1451, one record.) "Era la notte" and "Credo in un Dio crudel" from Verdi's "Otello," sung by Benvenuto Franco, baritone, accompanied by the La Scala Orchestra. (DB1154, one record.)

EDUCATIONAL RECORDS: A third series of records produced by the International Educational Society and issued through the COLUMBIA COMPANY:

- Professor Elliot-Smith on "Man and Civilization" (D40032–3)
- Professor F. G. Parsons on "The Englishman Through the Ages" (D40046–7)
- Professor Julian Huxley on "Ants and Their Habits" (D40052–3)
- Professor H. H. Turner on "The Stars" (D400-30-1)
- Professor Oliver Lodge on "Introduction to Physics" [two lectures] (D40042–5)
- Dr. Percy Buck on "How to Listen to Music" (D40050–1)
- Professor Fraser Harris on [William Harvey] and the "Circulation of the Blood" (D40040–1)
- Professor R. S. Conway on "Introduction to Vergil" (D40036–7)
- Professor R. S. Conway on "Introduction to Livy" (D40038–9)
- Professor R. S. Conway on "The Value of a Classical Training in Modern Life" (D40034–5)
- Professor Denis Saurat on "Victor Hugo" (D40048–9)

"**The Canonization of General Dyer,**" "Reviews" section, *The Nation & The Athenaeum* 45 (6 April 1929): 21. L. Woolf reviewed *General Dyer* by Ian Colvin (Blackwood).

"**The Text of Shakespeare,**" *The Nation & The Athenaeum* 45 (6 April 1929): 22. [Woolf's name appears at the bottom of this piece.] ~~Roger Fry~~ L. Woolf reviewed *The Works of Shakespeare*, Vol. I, edited by Herbert Farjeon (Nonesuch Press). *Anthony and Cleopatra*; *Julius Caesar*; *As You Like It*; and *The Winter's Tale*. Four separate volumes. Facsimiles of the First Folio text, with an introduction by J. Dover Wilson (Faber & Gwyer).

"**H. M. V. Records**" and "**Columbia Records,**" "New Gramophone Records" column, *The Nation & The Athenaeum* 45 (13 April 1929): 56. L. Woolf reviewed the following:

H. M. V. RECORDS: "Madre, pietosa vergine" from Verdi's "La Forza del Destino," sung by Dusolina Giannini, soprano. One 12 inch record. "Dei miei bollenti spiriti" from "La Traviata" and "Tombe degl' avi miei" from "Lucia di Lammermor," sung by Gigli, tenor. One 12 inch record. Massenet's "Meditation" and Kreisler's "Tambourin Chinois," Op. 3, played by [Fritz?] Kreisler. One 12 inch record. Bach's Organ Prelude and Fugue in A minor arranged by Liszt, played by Mischa Levitzi, piano. One 12 inch record. Ravel: "Pavane pour une Infante Defunte" and "L'Enfant et les Sortileges," played by a Symphony Orchestra conducted by Coppola. One 12 inch record. "Soldiers Changing the Guard" and "March of the Smugglers" from "Carmen," played by the Philadelphia Symphony Orchestra conducted by Leopold Stokowski. One 12 inch record. A recording of Easter services at St. Margaret's, Westminster featuring bells, organ, and choir. (B2970, one record.)

COLUMBIA RECORDS: Bach: Preludes and Fugues, Nos. 1–9 from the "Well-tempered Clavier," played by Harriet Cohen, piano. Six 12 inch records. Beethoven: "Harp" quartet in E flat major, played by the Capet String Quartet. Four 12 inch records. The Overture to "Der Freischuetz" and Schubert's "Rosamunde" Entr'acte No. 2, played by the Basle Symphony Orchestra conducted by Weingartner. Two 12 inch records. Ravel's "La Valse" and Debussy's "Nocturnes," played by the Orchestra of the Parisian "Societe des Concerts du Conservatoire." (L2245–6 and 9656–7, four records.) Lighter orchestral recordings: Arbos' "Noche de Arabia." (9583, one record.) The Overture to Offenbach's "Orpheus." (9646, one record.) Messager's "The Two Pigions." Two 12 inch records. "Judgment of Paris," Menuett, and "Music Box of the Little Nana," played by Ignaz Friedmann, piano. One 10 inch record. Tschaikowsky's "Chant sans Parole" and Rubinstein's Melody in F, played by Mr. Tertis, viola. (5230, one record.) Liszt's "Waldenrauschen" and "Liebestraum," played by Mr. Howard-Jones. One 12 inch record. A Scarlatti "Tempo di Ballo," played by the Madami Mandoline and Guitar Quartet. (5232, one record.) Haydn: Quartet, Op. 3, No. , played by the Lener Quartet. Two 12 inch records.

"On the Editor's Table" column, *The Nation & The Athenaeum* 45 (20 April 1929): 86. L. Woolf comments on recent books: *Field Marshal Earl Haig* by Brigadier-General John Charteris (Cassell); *William Wordsworth*, 2 vols., by G. McLean Harper, revised edition (Murray); The Life and Writings of Alexandre Dumas by H. A. Spurr, revised edition (1902; Dent); *Umbala, the Autobiography of Captain Harry Dean* (Harrap); *Enrico Cecchetti* by Cyril W. Beaumont (Beaumont); *The House of Memories* by Barbara Wilson (Heinemann); *All Sorts of People* by Gladys Storey (Metheun); *Saints and Scholars* by Stephen Gwynn (Butterworth); *The New Countries* [collection of stories by Dominion writers], edited by Hector Bolitho (Cape); *The Latin Portrait* [anthology of translations from Latin along with the original text], edited by G. Rostrevor Hamilton (Nonesuch Press) and; Paul Valery's *Leonardo da Vinci*, translated by Mr. T. McGreevy (Rodker).

"Self and Society Booklets" published by Benn: *The Nation and its Food* by the Rt. Hon. C. Addison; *The Wilderness of American Prosperity* by Le Roy E. Bowman; *Everyman's Statistics* by J. W. F. Rowe; *Twenty Faces the World* by Percy Redfern; *The Making of an Educationist* by Albert Manbridge; and *Parliament and the Consumer* by A. V. Alexander, M. P.

"On the Editor's Table" column, *The Nation & The Athenaeum* 45 (27 April 1929): 122. L. Woolf comments on recent books: *The Intelligent Woman's Guide to Socialism and Capitalism* by George Bernard Shaw (Constable); *Gallipoli Campaign*, Vol. I: *Inception of the Campaign to May, 1915*, 2 vols., by Brigadier-General C. F. Aspinall-Oglander, *Official History of the War* series (Heinemann); *The Holy Kabbalah* by A. E. Waite, *Secret Traditional Knowledge of the Hebrews* series (Williams & Norgate); *Elizabeth Barrett Browning* by Isabel C. Clarke (Hutchinson); *Foch Talks* [conversations between Marshal Ferdinand Foch and his Aide-de-Camp] by Commandant Bugnet (Gollancz); *Later Letters of Lady Augusta Stanley, 1864–1876*, edited by the Dean of Winsor and Hector Bolitho (Cape); *King of the Highland Hearts* [Prince Charlie's career after Culloden] by Winifred Duke (Chambers); *Tiberius Caesar* by G. P. Baker (Nash & Grayson); *First Word on Contract Bridge for All* by Mr. Manning-Foster (Benn); and *The Book of the Zoo* by F. Martin Duncan and Lucy T. Duncan (Nelson).

"On the Editor's Table" column, *The Nation & The Athenaeum* 45 (4 May 1929): 172, 174. L. Woolf comments on recent books: *The Wisdom of G. K. Chesterton* by Patrick Braybrooks (Palmer); *Thoughts from Rabindranath Tagore* [excerpts from Tagore] (Macmillan); *Tamerlane, the Earth Shaker* by Harold Lamb (Butterworth); *Bryan* [W. J. Bryan, former U. S. Secretary of State] by M. R. Werner (Cape); *Cameos from My Life* by April Day (Jenkins); *Ludwig II of Bavaria* by Guy de Pourtales (Butterworth); and *Trial of John Donald Merrett*, edited by William Roughead, *Notable British Trials* series (Hodges).

New books in the Six Penny Library published by Benn: *A History of Ireland* by Sir James O'Connor; *Scouting and Youth Movements* by Sir R. Baden-Powell; *Mediaeval European History, A. D. 455–1453* by Claude Jenkins; *The Meaning of Mathematics* by S. Brodetsky; *Logic and Reasoning* by S. V. Keeling; and *Napoleon* by J. Holland Rose.

The Voyage of the Annie Marble by C. S. Forester (Bodley Head); and *Coming of Age in Samoa* by Margaret Mead (Cape).

"Books in Brief" column, *The Nation & The Athenaeum* 45 (4 May 1929): 174. L. Woolf reviewed *The Gardener's Year-Book, 1929*, edited by D. H.

Moutray Read (Allan); *The Wild Garden* by W. Robinson (Murray); and *The Subject Index to Periodicals, 1927* (Library Association).

"On the Editor's Table" column, *The Nation & The Athenaeum* 45 (11 May 1929): 214. L. Woolf comments on recent books: *A History of British Socialism*, 2 vols., by Mr. Beers (Bell & Sons); *Melancholike Humours, in Verses of Diverse Nature set downe by Nich: Breton, Gent*, with an essay on Elizabethan melancholy by Mr. G. B. Harrison, reprint (1600; Scholartis Press); *The Autobiography of Pel. Verjuice* by Charles Reece Pemberton (Scholartis Press); *Queen Louise of Prussia* [wife of Frederick William III], translated from German of Gertrude Aretz (Putnam); *Gilbert and Sullivan* by Isaac Goldberg (Murray); Leaves from My Life, 2 vols., by H. Osborne O'Hagan (Bodley Head); *Auld Acquaintance* [reminiscences of the Marquis of Huntly] (Hutchinson); *Schools of To-day* by Bolton King, former Director of Education for Warwickshire (Dent); and *The Rising Tide, an Epic in Education* by J. G. Legge (Blackwell).

"H. M. V. Records," "New Gramophone Records" column, *The Nation & The Athenaeum* 45 (11 May 1929): 216. L. Woolf reviewed the following: Chopin: Chopin Studies, Nos. 7, 9, and 10 of Op. 25, played by Mr. Backhaus, piano. One 12 inch record. Liszt: "Venezia e [?] Napoli Tarantella," played by Mr. Lamond, piano. One 12 inch record. Mendelssohn: the Overture and Scherzo of "Midsummer Night's Dream," played by the San Francisco Orchestra conducted by Alfred Hertz. Two 12 inch records. The Overture of Verdi's "La Forza del Destino," played by Creatore's Band. One 12 inch record. Strauss: Act III of "Rosenkavalier," played at the Unter den Linden Opera House, Berlin, Germany. One 12 inch record. Leoncavallo's "Mattinata" and Tosti's "Non t'amo piu," sung by Pertile, tenor, accompanied by the La Scala Orchestra. One 10 inch record. Beethoven: chamber music, trio, B flat major, Op. 97, played by Thibaud, Casals, and Cortot. Five 12 inch records. "Me voici dans son boudoir" and "Connais-tu le pays?" from "Mignon," sung by Lucrezia Bori, soprano. One 10 inch record. "Carmen," Prelude to Act I and Entr'acte, Act 4, played by the Philadelphia Symphony Orchestra. One 10 inch record.

"Books on Music," "Reviews" section, *The Nation & The Athenaeum* 45 (18 May 1929): 244. L. Woolf reviewed *The Oxford History of Music* [introductory volume], edited by Percy C. Buck, Vol. I: *The Polyphonic Period*. Part I: *Method of Musical Art* by H. E. Wooldridge (Oxford University Press and Milford); *The Theories of Claude Debussy* by Leon Vallas, translated from French by Maire O'Brien (Oxford University Press and Milford); *Beethoven the Creator* by Romain Rolland (Gollancz); and *Moussorgsky* by Oskar von Riesemann, translated from German by Paul England (Knopf).

"On the Editor's Table" column, *The Nation & The Athenaeum* 45 (18 May 1929): 250. L. Woolf comments on recent books: *Survivals and New Arrivals* by Hilaire Belloc (Sheed & Ward); *Joan of Arc* by Hilaire Belloc (Cassell); *Leonid Krassin* by [his wife] Lubov Krassin (Skeffington); *Lord Chief Baron Pollock* by his grandson (Murray); *Five Men of Frankfort* [story of the Rothschilds] by M. E. Ravage (Harrap); *The Diaries of Mary, Countess of Meath*, Vol. II: *1900–1918* (Hutchinson); *The Life of Buddha* by A. Ferdinand Herold, translated from French by Paul C. Blum (Butterworth); *Joseph Estlin Carpender* [memorial volume], edited by Professor Herford (Clarendon Press); *My Philosophy of Industry* by Henry Ford (Harrap); *Fixation of Wages in Australia* by George Anderson (Macmillan); *Stones, Hilltops, and the Sea* by Ruth Alexander (Alston Rivers); and *Combing the Caribbees* by Harry L. Foster (Bodley Head).

"Columbia Records," "New Gramophone Records" column, *The Nation & The Athenaeum* 45 (18 May 1929): 252. L. Woolf reviewed the following: Verdi's "La Traviata," performed by the Milan Chorus and Orchestra, the libretto translated by Mr. Compton Mackenzie; key parts sung by Mercedes Capsir, Alfredo of Lionello Cecil, and Germont. Fifteen 12 inch records. Mozart: Clarinet Quintet in A major, played by the Lener Quartet and Mr. Draper. Four 12 inch records. Quartet in B flat major ["The Hunting Quartet"], played by the Budapest String Quartet. Three 12 inch records. Haydn: Quartet in D major, Op. 76, No. 5, played by the Lener Quartet. Three 12 inch records.

Stainer's "Crucifixion," played in the Central Hall with Francis Russell, Robert Easton, and the B. B. C. Choir. Six 12 inch records. Gershwin: Piano Concerto in F, played by Paul Whiteman and his Orchestra. Three 12 inch records. Beethoven: Quartet in A minor, Op. 132, played by the Capet String Quartet. Five 12 inch records. Quartet in C sharp minor, Op. 131, played by the Capet String Quartet. Five 12 inch records.

Stravinsky: "Firebird," played by the Orchestre Symphonique of Paris conducted by Stravinsky. Four 12 inch records. Falla's "Three-Cornered Hat" [Russian ballet] and Weber's "Invitation to Waltz" [Russian ballet], played by the Basle Symphony Orchestra conducted by Weingartner. Two 12 inch records. Brahms: Concerto in D for violin and orchestra, played by Joseph Szigeti and the Halle Orchestra. Five 12 inch records.

Weber: Clarinet Concerto, played by the Garde Republicaine of France. One 12 inch record. "Fantasia" [?] [medley of 17th century airs], played by the Grenadier Guards Band. One 12 inch record. Turina: "La Procesion del Rocio [?]," played by the Madrid Symphony Orchestra. One 12 inch record. The French Opera Comiquie, "Marouf" by Rabaud [?], two songs sung by Georges Th [?], tenor. (L2289, one record.) The French Opera Comiquie,

"Marouf" by Rabaud [?], [ballet music], played by the Orchestre Symphonique. (9702–3, two records.)

"Internationalism and Nationalism," "Reviews" section, *The Nation & The Athenaeum* 45 (25 May 1929): 280. L. Woolf reviewed *The Memoirs of Raymond Poincare*, Vol. III, translated by Sir George Arthur (Heinemann); *The Origins of the World War*, 2 vols., by Sidney Bradshaw Fay (Macmillan); *Survey of American Foreign Relations, 1928* by Charles P. Howland (Oxford University Press and Milford); *War as an Instrument of National Policy* by James T. Shotwell, with an introduction by Gilbert Murray (Constable); and *The International Community and the Right of War* by Don Luigi Sturzo (Allen & Unwin).

"Books in Brief" column, *The Nation & The Athenaeum* 45 (25 May 1929): 282, 284. L. Woolf reviewed Trial of James Blomfield Rush, edited by W. Teigmouth Shore (Hodge) and Remembered Yesterdays by Maha Mudaliyar Sir Solomon Dias Bandaranaike (Murray).

"On the Editor's Table" column, *The Nation & The Athenaeum* 45 (1 June 1929): 314. L. Woolf comments on recent books: *Nationality* by Bernard Joseph, a prominent lawyer, with a forward by Dr. Gooch (Allen & Unwin); *Stephen Hales, D. D., F. R. S.* [18th century devine and scientist] by Dr. Clark-Kennedy (Cambridge University Press); *Edward Gibbon Wakefield* by Irma O'Connor (Selwyn & Blount); *Life in Letters of William Dean Howells*, 2 vols., [influential American journalist] edited by Mildred Howells (Heinemann); *The Splendid Adventure* by Mr. W. M. Hughes, former Prime Minister of Australia (Benn); *In the Days of Queen Anne* by Lewis Melville (Hutchinson); *Scotland Yard and the Metropolitan Police* by J. F.Moylan, Whitehall Series (Putnam); *The Penn Country and the Chilterns* by Ralph M. Robinson (Bodley Head); and *Me—The Handicap* by Mr. Tilden, "the great lawn tennis player" (Methuen).

"H. M. V. Records" and "Columbia Records," "New Gramophone Records" column, *The Nation & The Athenaeum* 45 (1 June 1929): 314. L. Woolf reviewed the following:

H. M. V. RECORDS: Chopin: Prelude in D flat major and Prelude in A flat major, Op. 28, Nos. 15 and 17, played by Mr. M. Paderewski, pianoforte. One 12 inch record. Minuet from Mozart's "Don Giovanni," Rameau's "Le Tambourin," and Daquin's "Le Coucou," played by Wanda Landowska, harpsichord, accompanied by an orchestra. One 10 inch record. Liszt: "Le Preludes," played by the London Symphony Orchestra conducted by Albert Coates. Two 12 inch records. Ravel: the Introduction and Allegro for harp and strings and woodwind, played by the Vituoso String Quartet and J. Cockeril, R. Murchy, and C. Draper. Two 12 inch records. Rosa Ponselle, soprano, sings two songs from Verdi's "La Forza del Destino" and "Ernani," from the first "Pace, pace mio Dio" and from the second "Ernani! Ernani! Involami!" One 12 inch record.

COLUMBIA RECORDS: Wagner: "Lohengrin," narrative of the Grail and Farewell to the Swan, sung in French by J. Rogatchewsky, tenor. One 12 inch record. "Lohengrin," "O Re del Ciel," sung in Italian by Tancredi Pasero, bass, and "Grazie Signore," sung in Italian by Armando Borgio [?], baritone. One 10 inch record. "Si morir ella de" sung by Tancredi Pasero, bass, and "Cielo e [?] Mar," sung by Alessandro Granda, tenor, from Poncielli's "La Gioconda." One 12 inch record. The Shadow Song from Meyerbeer's "Dinorah" and "Fors e lui" from "Traviata," sung by Gertrude Johnson, soprano. (9700 [?], one record.)

"When Daisies Pied and Violets Blue" and Spohr's "Rose Softly Blooming," sung by Dora Labbette. One 12 inch record. "Ships that Pass in the Night" and "Vale," sung by Clara Serena, contralto. (5316, one record.) "Here in the Quiet Hills" and "O That It Were So," sung by Mr. A. R. Poole, baritone. (5318, one record.) Max Bruch: "Kol Nidrei," played by Felix Salmond, 'cello. (L2271, one record.) Drigox' "Les Millions d'Arlequin" and Schubert's "Ave Maria," played by Efrem Zimbalist, violin. (9674, one record.)

Verdi's "Aida," performed by the Milan Symphony Orchestra conducted by Cav. L. Molajoli; key parts sung by Maria Capuana, Giannina Arangi-Lombardi, Signor Gorgioli, and Aroldo Lindi [?] Eighteen 12 inch records.

"The Hours Press," "Reviews" section, *The Nation & The Athenaeum* 45 (8 June 1929): 344. L. Woolf reviewed *La Chasse au Snark* by Aragon (The Hours Press); *St. George at Silene* by Alvaro Guevara (The Hours Press); and *The Eaten Heart* by Richard Aldington (The Hours Press).

"Books in Brief" column, *The Nation & The Athenaeum* 45 (8 June 1928): 346. L. Woolf reviewed *The Truth about Publishing* by Stanley Unwin (3rd edition; Allen & Unwin) and *Etchings Today*, edited by C. Geoffrey Holme (Studio).

"Columbia Records" and "Educational Records," "New Gramophone Records" column, *The Nation & The Athenaeum* 45 (8 June 1929): 348. L. Woolf reviewed the following:

COLUMBIA RECORDS: Cesar Franck: Quartet in D major, played by the London String Quartet. Six 12 inch records. Respighi: "Pines of Rome," played by the Milan Symphony Orchestra conducted by Cav. Molajoli. Three 10 inch records. Sibelius: "Finlandia," played by the Queen's Hall Orchestra conducted by Sir Henry Wood. (9655, one record.) Debussy's "Golliwog's Cake Walk" and Rimsky-Korsakov's "Dance of the Tumblers," played by the B. B. C. Military Band. (9744, one record.) "Bella figlia dell' amore," "E l'ami," and "La donna e mobile" from "Rigoletto," sung by Maria Gentile, Stignani, Galeffi, and Alessandro Granda. (L2310, one record.) Wagner: the

Steersman's song and Eric's song from "Flying Dutchman," sung in English by Francis Russell. (9746, one record.) Gounod: choruses from "Faust," sung by the chorus of the Theatre National de l'Opera. (9747, one record.) "Abide with Me" and "Nearer, My God, to Thee," sung by Rex Palmer. (9714, one record.) Hubay's "The Zephyr" and Drigo's Valse "Bluette," played by Efrem Zimbalist, violin.

EDUCATIONAL RECORDS: New records produced by the International Educational Society and issued through the COLUMBIA COMPANY:
- Dr. George Dyson on keyboard music, variations, dances, and descriptive pieces. (D40137-9)
- Winifred Holtby on Fourteenth Century England (D40146)
- John Drinkwater reads his own poems (D40140-1)
- Walter Ripman reads Passages of Standard Prose from Charles [?] Lamb (D40131)
- Walter Ripman reads from John Ruskin (D40132)
- Walter Ripman reads from Washington Irving, Richard Blackmore, and William Hazlitt (D40148)
- Professor Barcroft on Smells (D40144-5)
- Dr. Fraser-Harris on Nerves and Nervousness (D40135-6)

"H. M. V. Records," "New Gramophone Records" column, *The Nation & The Athenaeum* 45 (22 June 1929): 410. L. Woolf reviewed the following: Spanish dances by Granados and Popper, played by Casals, 'cello. One 10 inch record. "Mira, O Norma" from Bellini's "Norma," sung by Rosa Ponselle, soprano, and Marion Telva. One 12 inch record. "Un bel di vedremo" from "Madame Butterfly" and "In quelle trine morbide" from "Manon Lescaut," sung by Dusolina Giannini, soprano. One 12 inch record. "Or son sei mesi" and "Ch' ella mi creda libero" from Puccini's "Fanciulla del West," sung by Alessandro Valente, tenor. (B3015, one record.) Tschaikowsky: pieces from "Capriccio Italien," played by the Berlin State Opera Orchestra. (D1593, one record.) Donizetti: "Daughter of the Regiment," played by the La Scala Orchestra. (C1654, one record.)

"More Documents," "Reviews" section, *The Nation & The Athenaeum* 45 (29 June 1929): 440. L. Woolf reviewed *British Documents on the Origins of World War I, 1898–1914*, Vol. IV, edited by G. P. Gooch and Harold Temperley (H. M. Stationary Office).

"On the Editor's Table" column, *The Nation & The Athenaeum* 45 (6 July 1929): 486. L. Woolf comments on recent books: *Pomp and Circumstance* by E. de Gramont, ex-Duchesse de Clermont Tonnere (Cape); *Relations and Complications* by H. H. the Dayang Muda of Sarawak (Bodley Head); *General Louis Botha* by Dr. F. V. Engelenburg (Harrap); and *English Comedy* by Professor Ashley H. Thorndike, Columbia University (Macmillan).

Volumes in Faber & Faber's new Criterion Miscellany series: *Two Masters* by A. W. Wheen and *Cote d'Or* by H. M. Tomlinson.

Concerning the Eccentricities of Cardinal Pirelli by Ronald Firbank (Duckworth); Baedeker's *Austria* [guide book] (12th edition; Allen & Unwin); and *Muirhead's Belgium*, Blue Guides series (Macmillan).

New volumes in Routledge's Introductions to Modern Knowledge series: *Music for All* by Cyril Winn; *What Darwin Really Said*, with an introduction by Julian Huxley; *The Will to Work* by G. H. Miles; and *The English* by H. W. Nevinson.

The Law of the Amateur Stage [legal handbook] by D. S. Page (Pitman).

"Books in Brief" column, *The Nation & The Athenaeum* 45 (13 July 1929): 514. L. Woolf reviewed *The Annual Register, 1928*, edited by M. Epstein, New Series (Longmans) and *The Book of the Tulip* by Sir A. Daniel Hall (Hopkinson).

"H. M. V. Records" and "Columbia Records," "New Gramophone Records" column, *The Nation & The Athenaeum* 45 (20 July 1929): 543. L. Woolf reviewed the following:

H. M. V. RECORDS: "Casta Diva" from Bellini's "Norma," sung by Rosa Ponselle, soprano. One 12 inch record. The Toreador song from "Carmen" and the Mirror song from "Tales of Hoffmann," sung by Rudolf Bockelmann, German baritone. One 12 inch record. Byrd's music from "Exsurge Domine" and Child's "O Bone Jesu," sung by the Westminster Choir. One 12 inch record. Grieg: sonata for piano and violin in C minor, played by Rachmaninoff and Kreisler. Three 12 inch records. Beethoven: Seventh Symphony, A major, Op. 92, played by the Philadelphia Symphony Orchestra conducted by Leopold Stokowski. Five 12 inch records. Bach's "Erbarme Dich, Mein Gott" from "St. Matthew Passion" and Handel's "Dank sei Dir Herr," sung by Rosette Anday, contralto. One 12 inch record.

COLUMBIA RECORDS: Rimsky-Korsakov: "Capriccio Espagnole," played by the Halle Orchestra conducted Sir Hamilton Harty. Two 12 inch records. Trio of Masks from Puccini's "Turandot," sung by Nessi, Baracchi, and Venturini. One 10 inch record. Arensky's "Silhouettes," played by the Eastbourne Municipal Orchestra or Band. (9749, one record.) Toselli's Second Serenata and Saint-Saens' Tarantelle for flute and clarinet. (9750, one record.) "Gaiety Echoes," played by Herman Finck's Orchestra. (9718, one record.) Songs from the musical comedy "New Moon," sung by Evelyn Laye, Howett Worster, and chorus. (9751, 9752, two records.) Beethoven: Quartet in A major, Op. 18, No. 5, played by the Capet String Quartet.

"French in the Original and in Translation," "Reviews" section, *The Nation & The Athenaeum* 45 (27 July 1929): 569. L. Woolf reviewed *Introduction to the Method of Leonardo da Vinci* by Paul Valery, translated by Thomas

McGreevy (Rodker); *Adolphe* by Benjamin Constant (Payot); and *Oeuvres de Moliere*, Vol. 5, with notes by B. Guegan (Payot).

"Novels in Brief" column, *The Nation & The Athenaeum* **45 (27 July 1929): 574.** L. Woolf reviewed *The Listener's History of Music*, Vols. II and III, by Percy A. Scholes (Oxford University Press and Milford); *The Works of Sir Thomas Browne*, Vol. IV, edited by Geoffrey Keynes, 6 vol. set (Faber & Faber); and *Survey of International Affairs, 1927* by Arnold J. Toynbee (Oxford University Press and Milford).

"Columbia Records," "Educational Records," and "The Summer Season," "New Gramophone Records" column, *The Nation & The Athenaeum* **45 (27 July 1929): 576.** L. Woolf reviewed the following:

COLUMBIA RECORDS: Handel: songs from "Judas Maccabaeus," sung by the Sheffield Choir. One 12 inch record. Simonetti's Madrigale and Mehul's Gavotte, played by Mr. Squire, 'cello. One 10 inch record. Vivaldi's Giga and Scarlatti's Andante Mosso, played by the Madami Guitar Quartet. One 10 inch record. J. Strauss: Overture to "Fledermaus," played by the Berlin State Orchestra conducted by Bruno Walter. One 12 inch record. Saint-Saens: "Le Rouet d'Omphale," played by a French Orchestra. (9719, one record.) Sullivan: selections from "Ivanhoe," played by the Grenadier Guards, and English band. (9721, one record.) Prelude to Act 3 of "La Tosca," played by the Italian Orchestra of Milan. (5394, one record.)

EDUCATIONAL RECORDS: New records produced by the International Educational Society and issued through the Columbia Company:
- Mr. Plunket on "The Art of Singing" (D40149–50)
- Dr. Ashby on "The Origin and the Growth of Rome" (D40153–4)
- Sir George MacDonald on "The Romans in Britain" (D40155–6)
- Professor F. G. Parsons on "The Englishman Through the Ages" (D40151–2)

THE SUMMER SEASON: H. M. V. RECORDS: Elgar: "Wand of Youth" Suite (overture, serenade, minuet, and sun dance), played by the London Symphony Orchestra conducted by Elgar. (D1636, one record.) Solveig's song from Grieg's "Peer Gynt" suite and "Lo! Here the Gentle Lark," sung by Amelita Galli-Curci. One 12 inch record. Weiniawski's "Caprice in E flat major" and Rachmaninoff's "Vocalise," played by Mischa Elman, violin. One 10 inch record. "Juba Dance" and "From the Canebrake," played by The New Light Symphony Orchestra. (B3043, one record.) Columbia Records: Vivaldi: Concerto Grosso in D minor, played by the Zurich Tonhalle Orchestra. (9823, one record.) Weber's "Oberon" Overture, played by the Concertgebouw Orchestra conducted by Mengelberg and Dvorak's Slavonic Dance in G minor, played by the New Queen's Hall Orchestra. Two 12 inch records.

Beethoven's "Rondino" and Gluck's "Melodie," played by Yelli d'Aranyi, violin. (5427, one record.) Haydn's Quartet in C and a Mendelssohn Quartet played by the Poltronieri String Quartet. (9824, one record.) Two duets from Verdi's "Otello," sung in English by Harold Williams and Francis Russell. (9827, one record.) "The Merry Brothers" and "The Echoes of the Valley," played by Bournemouth Municipal Orchestra conducted by Sir Dan Godfrey. (9821, one record.) "Four Ways" Suite, played by the Regal Cinema Orchestra. Two 12 inch records.

"Books in Brief" column, *The Nation & The Athenaeum* 45 (24 August 1929): 688. L. Woolf reviewed *A Greek-English Lexicon*, part 4, compiled by Henry George Liddell and Robert Scott (Clarendon Press).

"Decca Records," "New Gramophone Records" column, *The Nation & The Athenaeum* 45 (24 August 1929): 688. L. Woolf reviewed the following: DECCA RECORDS: Delius: "Sea Drift," sung by Roy Henderson, baritone, and the New English Symphony Choir and accompanied by the New English Symphony. Three 12 inch records. Parry's Choral Prelude on Old 104 and Chorale Prelude on Martyrdom with an organ solo by Arnold Goldsbrough. One 10 inch record. Coleridge Taylor's Dream Dances, 1, 2, and 3, played by the Hastings Municipal Orchestra. Two 10 inch records. "None Shall Sleep Tonight" from Puccini's "Turandot" and "Let Her Believe" from his "Girl of the Golden West." (M48, one record.) Elgar's "The Fate's Discourtesy" and "The Sweepers" from "Fringes of the Fleet," sung by Mr. Dale Smith, baritone. (M46, one record.)

Two Yiddish songs, sung by Solomon Stramer, tenor. (M7, one record.) "Back to Those Pre-war Days" and "The Rhyme of the Radio Comedian," sung by Stainless Stephen. (M47, one record.) "Mean to Me" and "Susiana," sung by Barrie Oliver, a "rhyme singer." (M50, one record.) "Am I Blue" and "Lady Divine," played by Herbert Jaeger and his Orchestra. (M51, one record.) "Lucky Boy" and "Florida by the Sea" from "The Cocoanuts." (M52, one record.) Rutolda's "Russian Romance and Dance" and Durand's "Waltz No. 1," played by Vladescu on the Cim'balon[?]. (F1505, one record.) "Cohen Owes Me 27 Dollars" and "Becky from Babylon," sung by Estelle Ross. (E1506, one record.)

"Books in Brief" column, *The Nation & The Athenaeum* 45 (31 August 1929): 714. L. Woolf reviewed *The Ponsonby Family* by Major-General Sir John Ponsonby (Medici Society).

"New Gramophone Records" column, *The Nation & The Athenaeum* 45 (31 August 1929): 714, 716. L. Woolf reviewed the following: Mozart: Andante for Flute and Orchestra and the Gavotte from "Idomeneo," played by the Zurich Tonhalle Orchestra. (Columbia, one 12 inch record.) Brahms: Hungarian Dances, Nos. 5 and 6, played by the Halle Orchestra conducted by Sir

Hamilton Harty. (Columbia, one 10 inch record.) Strauss: "Dorfschwalben" Waltz, played by the Vienna Philharmonic Orchestra.

Barcarole from "Tales of Hoffmann," sung by Osobelle Baillie and Nellie Walker, and "Give Me Your Darling Hands" from "Madame Butterfly," sung by Osobelle Baillie and Francis Russell. (Columbia, one 12 inch record.) "Carnations" and "Malaguena," sung in Spanish by Lucrezia Bori. (H. M. V., one 10 inch record.) "A Spring Morning" and "Blackbird Song," sung by Elsie Suddaby. (H. M. V., B3076, one record.) "Serenade Napolitaine" and "Serenata, sung in Italian by Giuseppe Danise, baritone. (Brunswick, 10278, one record.) The choral music for the Thanksgiving Service for the King performed in St. George's Chapel, Winsor Castle and Elgar's Coronation Offertorium. (Columbia, one 12 inch record.) Scarlatti's sonata in A major and Beethoven's Ecossaise, played by Mischa Levitzki, piano. (H. M. V., one 10 inch record.) Handel's Largo, played by Beatrice Harrison, piano, accompanied by another musican on the 'cello, and Kreisler's "Viennese Melody." (H. M. V., one 12 inch record.) Scriabine's Etude, Op. 2, and Chasins' Prelude in D major and "Rush Hour in Hongkong," piano solos. (Brunswick, one 10 inch record.)

COLUMBIA RECORDS: Military and Naval Marches (5471, one record), and Scottish and Anglo-American Marches (5472, one record), played by the Grenadier Guards Band.

BRUNSWICK RECORDS: "Wake Up, Cill'un, Wake Up!" and "I Get the Blues When It Rains," sung by Cotton and Morpheus. (5010, one record.) "Underneath the Russian Moon" and "My Sin," sung by Belle Baker. (5008, one record.) "Lover Come Back to Me" and "Vagabond King Waltz," sung by Jessica Dragonette. (5002, one record.) Sousa: "High School Cadets" and "Washington Post March," played by the United States Military Academy Band. (5003, one record.) Faure's "The Palms" and "The Holy City," played by Lew White, organ. (5005, one record.) Dance Music: "Breakaway" and "City Blues," fox trot, by Arnold Johnson. (5022, one record.) "Sing a Little Song" and "Hittin' the Ceiling," by King Solomon and His Miners. (5020, one record.) "That's What I Call Heaven" and "The Things That Were Made for Love," by Hal Kemp. (5011, one record.) "She's Got Great Ideas" and "O Baby, What a Night," foxtrots, and "Six Jumping Jaxs." (5017, one record.) "Dream Boat," waltz, and "Fioretta," foxtrot, by Bob Haring. (5013, one record.)

"Books in Brief" column, *The Nation & The Athenaeum* 45 (14 September 1929): 774. L. Woolf reviewed *A Guide to the Best Historical Novels and Tales* by Jonathan Nield (Elkin Mathews).

"Empires and Imperialisms," "Reviews" section, *The Nation & The Athenaeum* 45 (21 September 1929): 800, 802. L. Woolf reviewed *History of French Colonial Policy, 1870–1925*, 2 vols., by Stephen Roberts (King); *Empire to Commonwealth* by Walter Phelps Hall (Cape); *British Colonial Policy and the South*

African Republics, 1848-1872 by C. W. De Kiewiet (Longmans); *Bantu, Boer, and Briton, the Making of the South African Native Problem* by W. M. Macmillan (Faber & Gwyer); *The History of Nigeria* by A. C. Burns (Allen & Unwin); *East Africa in Transition; Being an Examination of the Principles of the Hilton Young Commission* (Student Christian Movement); The Future of the Negro by Sir Gordon Guggisberg and A. G. Frasier (Student Christian Movement); and *Black Democracy: the Story of Haiti* by H. P. Davis (Allen & Unwin).

"H. M. V. Records" and "Beltona Records," "New Gramophone Records" column, *The Nation & The Athenaeum* 45 (21 September 1929): 808. L. Woolf reviewed the following:

H. M. V. RECORDS: Two movements from Haydn's "Clock" Symphony and Mendelssohn's Scherzo from "Midsummer Night's Dream," played by the Philharmonic Symphony Orchestra of New York conducted by Toscanini. Four 12 inch records. Gershwin: "American in Paris," played by the New Light Symphony Orchestra conducted by Gershwin. Two 12 inch records. Chopin: The Revolutionary and Black Key Studies, played by Ignace Paderewski, piano. (DA1647, one record.) Bach: D minor Taccata and Fugue, played by Mark Hambourg, piano. (C1704, one record.) Vocal recordings of "What Ought We to Do, Gentle Sisters, Say?", "How Beautifully Blue the Sky," "Tis Mabel," and "Poor Wand'ring One" from Gilbert and Sullivan's "Pirates of Penzance." (D1681, one record.) "Comme une pale fleur" and "O vin, dissipe la tristesse" from Thomas' "Hamlet," sung by John Brownlee, baritone. (D1654, one record.)

BELTONA RECORDS: "Only a Sinner" and "Will the Circle Be Unbroken?", sung by John Roberts, baritone, accompanied by organ. (1453, one record.) "Down in the Forest" and "By the Waters of Minnetonka," sung by Agnes O'Kelly, accompanied by piano, violin, and 'cello. (1455, one record.) "The Inversnecky Fireman" and "The Bells of Inversnecky," sung by Harry Gordon, comedian. (1440, one record.) "Marquis of Huntly's Farewell," "Perthshire Volunteers," "Lochnagar," etc., played by Alec Sim, violin. "Barley Bree" and "The Blue Grampians," played by John Henry, accordean, accompanied by banjo. (1443, one record.)

"International Law," "Reviews" section, *The Nation & The Athenaeum* 45 (28 September 1929): 836. L. Woolf reviewed *Annual Digest of Public International Law Cases, Years 1925 and 1926*, edited by Arnold D. McNair and H. Lauterpacht. (Longmans).

"Columbia Records" and "Twelve Famous Authors," "New Gramophone Records" column, *The Nation & The Athenaeum* 45 (28 September 1929): 840. L. Woolf reviewed the following:

COLUMBIA RECORDS: John Ireland: Sonata for 'cello and piano, played by John Ireland and Antoni Sala, and "April," a piano solo. Four 12 inch records. Fantasies for two viols by Th. Morley and R. Dering's Fantasy for six viols, played by the Dolmetsch family. (9837, one record.) Repighi: "Fountains of Rome," played by the Milan Symphony Orchestra. Two 12 inch records. Tschaikowsky's Casse-Noisette Suite, played by the Royal Philharmonic Orchestra conducted by Oscar Fried. (L2318, one record.)

"I Heard the Voice of Jesus Say" and "The Wonderful Story," sung by William MacEwan, tenor, accompanied by organ and violin. (5488, one record.) Some of the "Songs of the Hebrides," sung by Patuffa Kennedy-Frasier. (9838, one record.) "Drink to Me Only with Thine Eyes" and "How Beautiful Are the Feet" from Handel's "Messiah," sung by John Gwilym Griffith, boy soprano. (5489, one record.) "Hear Ye, Israel" from Mendelssohn's "Elijah," sung by Isobel Baillie, soprano. (5487, one record.) A Cossack's Cradle Song and Tschaikowsky's "In the Church," sung by the Don Cossacks Choir. (9839, one record.)

TWELVE FAMOUS AUTHORS: A Twelve Record Album produced by DOMINION GRAMOPHONE RECORDS, LTD. Each of the following authors reads from his or her own works: Ian Hay, "My People." W. W. Jacobs, "Short Cruises." Sheila Kaye-Smith, "The George and the Crown." Rose Macaulay, "The Beleaguered City," "The Lovers," "The Alien," and "The Thief." Compton Mackenzie, "Rogues and Vagabonds." A. E. W. Mason, "No Other Tiger." A. A. Milne, "Winnie-the-Pooh." Alfred Noyes, "The Highwayman." H. de Vere Stacpoole, "The Drums of War." E. Temple Thurston, "The Patchwork Papers." Hugh Walpole, "Wintersmoon." Rebecca West, "Harriet Hume." Twelve 10 inch records.

"Books in Brief" column *The Nation & The Athenaeum* **47 (3 May 1930): 150.** L. Woolf reviewed *Herbs, Salads, and Seasonings* by X. M. Boulestin and Jason Hill (Heinemann).

"The Word of Elijah," *The Nation & The Athenaeum* **47 (5 July 1930): 431–32.** L. Woolf refers to his earlier article, "Naboth's Vineyard" [Native Reserves in Kenya], *The Nation & The Athenaeum* 43 (9 June 1928): 319–20, and then fills his readers in on recent developments, especially White Papers [the word of Elijah] written by Lord Passfield, Sidney Webb. The White Papers are A Memorandum on Native Policy in East Africa and the Statement of the Conclusions of His Majesty's Government in the United Kingdom as regards Closer Union in East Africa.

"Sir Edward Grigg," "From a Correspondent" [L. Woolf on marked copy], *The Nation & The Athenaeum* **47 (23 August 1930): 641–42.** Woolf refers to the White Papers discussed in "The Word of Elijah," *The Nation & The Athenaeum* 47 (5 July 1930): 431–32, in his criticism of Sir Edward Grigg, the colonial governor of Kenya. Woolf maintains that Grigg favors the interests of the white settlers at the expense of native Kenyans.

1.5. THE POLITICAL QUARTERLY

Leonard S. Woolf and William A. Robson founded *The Political Quarterly* in 1930. William A. Robson and Kingsley Martin were the first editors. But when Martin became editor of *The New Statesman* in 1931, Woolf joined Robson as co-editor of *The Political Quarterly*. Woolf served as an editor until 1959 and stayed on as literary editor until 1962. (See *Down Hill All the Way*, 206–07.)

Works indicated by an asterisk (*) in Part 1.5 are attributed to Leonard Woolf by Leila Luedeking and Michael Edmonds (New Castle: Oak Knoll Books, 1992).

Book Review section,* *The Political Quarterly* **5 (1934): 454–57.** Reviews of *Germany's Third Empire* by Moeller van der Bruck (Allen & Unwin); *The Hour of Decision* by Oswald Spengler (Allen & Unwin); *The Bloodless Pogrom* by Dr. Fritz Seidler (Golancz); *Socialism's New Start* (Allen & Unwin); *Democracy* by J. A. Hobson (Bodley Head); and *Democracy and Dictatorship* by Hugh Sellon (Lovat Dickson).

"The B. B. C. and Music," by A Listener, *The Political Quarterly* **6 (1935): 519–29.** Woolf comments on B. B. C. programming policies. See William Robson, "The Problems of the 1930s," *The Political Quarterly* 41 (1970): 32, regarding Woolf's authorship of the essay.

"Editorial Note," * *The Political Quarterly* **11 (1940): 313.** Information on changes in format and in submissions policies due to wartime conditions.

"An Announcement," * *The Political Quarterly* **12 (1941): half title page.** An explanation of the mission of *The Political Quarterly* in wartime.

"The Future of the International Labour Organisation," by An Observer,* *The Political Quarterly* **15 (1944): 66–76.** Woolf argues that the United Nations should support and strengthen the International Labour Organisation (I. L. O.) to ensure workers' rights, protect their interests, and thereby promote social justice and world peace. He recommends that I. L. O. activities be coordinated with those of other national and international agencies, departments, organizations, etc.

Notes and Comments column,* *The Political Quarterly* **21 (1950): 1–8.** Editorial on the Cold War in Europe.

Book Review section,* *The Political Quarterly* **21 (1950): 108.** Review of *Political Thought in France from the Revolution to the Fourth Republic* by J. P. Mayer (Routledge).

Notes and Comments column,* *The Political Quarterly* **21 (1950): 109–13.** Editorial introduction to a special issue on nationalization of key industries and related policies.

Notes and Comments column,* *The Political Quarterly* **21 (1950): 233–38.** gEditorial on the United Nations Organization (U. N. O.) and the creation of the Western European Union and the North Atlantic Union (North Atlantic Treaty Organization—N. A. T. O.).

Notes and Comments column,* *The Political Quarterly* **21 (1950): 333–37.** Critique of the pamphlet, *Labour and the New Society*, published by the authority of the National Executive Committee of the Labour Party. According to Woolf, the pamphlet would be used at the annual Labour Party conference to shape the party's political program for the next election.

Notes and Comments column,* *The Political Quarterly* **22 (1951): 1–6.** Editorial introduction to a special issue on the Cold War.

Notes and Comments column,* *The Political Quarterly* **22 (1951): 117–20.** Editorial on the B. B. C. Committee Report produced by Lord Beveridge and fellow committee members.

Notes and Comments column,* *The Political Quarterly* **22 (1951): 217–20.** Editorial on the dismissal of General Douglas MacArthur.

"Labour and Secondary Education," Notes and Comments column,* *The Political Quarterly* **22 (1951): 317–22.** Editorial on the Labour Party pamphlet *A Policy for Secondary Education* which served as the basis for Labour Party policy. See also "Secondary Education Again," Notes and Comments column,* *The Political Quarterly* 23 (1952): 121, for a note on reader response to the editorial.

Notes and Comments column,* *The Political Quarterly* **23 (1952): 1–4.** Editorial introduction to a special issue on the Soviet Union.

"Reflections on the Middle East," Notes and Comments column,* *The Political Quarterly* **23 (1952): 117–21.** Editorial on critical issues facing the Middle East, especially the problems of reconciling traditional values with modernism. Woolf also addresses specific political, economic, and legal issues such British interests in the Iranian oil fields and in the Suez Canal.

"Broadcasting," Notes and Comments column,* *The Political Quarterly* **23 (1952): 217–21.** Editorial on renewal of the B. B. C.'s charter, the controversy over the station's mission, and the lessons that Britain's experience with that "great journalistic engine" *The Times* provide.

Book Review section, Shorter Notices,* *The Political Quarterly* **23 (1952): 315.** Review of *Noel Buxton. A Life* by Mosa Anderson, with a foreword by G. P. Gooch (Allen and Unwin).

Notes and Comments column,* *The Political Quarterly* **24 (1953): 1–4.** Editorial introduction to a special issue on the Labour Party.

Notes and Comments column,* *The Political Quarterly* **24 (1953): 125–28.** Editorial introduction to a special issue on the Conservative Party.

Notes and Comments column,* *The Political Quarterly* **24 (1953): 233–35.** Editorial on the opportunities for more conciliatory U. S.-Soviet relations after the death of Joseph Stalin and the end of the Korean War. McCarthyism mentioned near the end of the piece.

Notes and Comments column,* *The Political Quarterly* 24 (1953): 333–37. Editorial introduction to a special issue on the future of television. The issue is a response to the Memorandum on the Report of the Broadcasting Committee, 1949 (published in May 1953) that provided for the introduction of commercial television in addition to the B. B. C.

"The Colonial Empire," Notes and Comments column,* *The Political Quarterly* 25 (1954): 1–4. Editorial on political crises in Africa, including British Guiana, Kenya, Northern Rhodesia and Nyasaland.

"The Berlin Conference and After," Notes and Comments column,* *The Political Quarterly* 25 (1954): 101–04. Editorial on the Berlin Conference of 1954 where Britain, France, the Soviet Union, and the United States attempted to resolve differences over the reunification of Germany and policies regarding Austria.

Notes and Comments column,* *The Political Quarterly* 25 (1954): 201–04. Editorial introduction to the article "What Prospect for the Labour Party?" by Donald Chapman, M. P. Woolf discusses Labour Party foreign and domestic policies.

"Liberalism and Socialism," Notes and Comments column,* *The Political Quarterly* 26 (1955): 1–3. Editorial on historical and present day aspects of Liberalism and Socialism. Political problems in Africa discussed within the context of Liberalism and Socialism in the latter part of this piece.

Book Review section, Shorter Notices,* *The Political Quarterly* 26 (1955): 98.** Reviews of *The Yearbook of the United Nations, 1953* (Stationary Office) and *The Constitution of Ceylon*, 3rd edition, by Sir Ivor Jennings (Oxford University Press).

Book Review section, Shorter Notices,* *The Political Quarterly* 26 (1955): 206.** Reviews of *The British Constitution*, 3rd edition, by H. R. G. Greaves (Allen & Unwin) and *Organizing for Peace* by Daniel S. Cheever and H. Field Haviland, Jr. (Stevens).

"Is There a Revolt Against Reason?" Notes and Comments column,* *The Political Quarterly* 26 (1955): 207–10. Editorial introduction to a special issue to examine the period from 1914 to 1955 for evidence of a "revolt against reason, science, and the ideas and ideals of the French Revolution." Articles in this issue deal with politics, the social sciences, science, religion, philosophy, and history.

"After Geneva," Notes and Comments column,* *The Political Quarterly* 26 (1955): 319–22. Editorial on the July 1955 Geneva Summit Conference of the United States, Britain, France, and the Soviet Union that dealt with German reunification, European security, disarmament, and East-West relations.

Book Review section, Shorter Notices,* *The Political Quarterly* 26 (1955): 418. Review of *Personalities and Powers* by Sir Lewis Namier (Hamilton).

"Trade Unions in a Changing World," **Notes and Comments column,*** *The Political Quarterly* 27 (1956): 1–5. Editorial introduction to a special issue on problems confronting trade unions at present and in the future. "The articles deal with matters of labour policy affecting wages and conditions of employment; with organization and leadership of the unions; with the position of the T. U. C.; with staff problems and finance; with strikes and inter-union disputes; with the outlook of the rank and file; with the attitude of the unions towards industrial democracy and greater productivity."

"Washington and Moscow," **Notes and Comments column,*** *The Political Quarterly* 27 (1956): 125–28. Editorial on the February 1956 Washington Conference of Britain and the United States when Prime Minister Anthony Eden and President Dwight Eisenhower issued a "Declaration of Washington" and on Premier Nikita Khrushchev's address to the 20th Congress of the Communist Party of the Soviet Union on February 14.

Book Review section, Shorter Notices,* *The Political Quarterly* 27 (1956): 232. Reviews of *The International Who's Who, 1955* (Europa) and *Geoffrey Dawson and Our Times* by John Evelyn Wrench (Hutchinson).

"Employers and Labour Problems," **Notes and Comments column,*** *The Political Quarterly* 27 (1956): 233–36. Editorial introduction to a special issue on "industrial relations and trade unions from the point of view of employers and management."

"The Suez Canal Crisis," **Notes and Comments column,*** *The Political Quarterly* 27 (1956): 361–65. Editorial on the Suez Crisis.

"The Middle East Aflame," **Notes and Comments column,*** *The Political Quarterly* 28 (1957): 1–4. Editorial on the continuation of the Suez Crisis.

"The Storm Centre," **Notes and Comments column,*** *The Political Quarterly* 28 (1957): 101–06. Editorial introduction to a special issue on "the fundamental issues in the Middle East problem" within the context of the Suez Crisis and the Cold War.

"Israel and the Middle East," **Notes and Comments column,*** *The Political Quarterly* 28 (1957): 209–13. Editorial on Israel and its relationship to the Arab states. Woolf draws on insights gained from a visit to Israel in 1957 and on his views of international order.

"Pressure Groups in Britain," **Notes and Comments column,*** *The Political Quarterly* 29 (1958): 1–4. Editorial introduction to a special issue on the role of pressure groups in public life. The issue includes articles on the following: trade associations, the National Farmers' Union, ex-servicemen's associations, the roads lobby, and the relationship between some pressure groups and political parties.

"Towards the Summit Conference," Notes and Comments column,* *The Political Quarterly* 29 (1958): 101–04. Editorial on the need for a summit conference of the United States and the Soviet Union to negotiate an arms control agreement and ease Cold War tensions.

"The Splendours and Miseries of Colonialism,"* *The Political Quarterly* 29 (1958): 209–14. Editorial introduction to a special issue on the transition of former African and Asian colonies into independent nation states. Woolf defines the issue's objective, in part, as follows: "Our object is to survey the present position in these countries which have already passed from colonial status to that of independent states, in those countries which are still undergoing the process, and in those in which the outcome of a struggle for liberation is still doubtful."

"Labour's Plan for Progress," Editorial,* *The Political Quarterly* 29 (1958): 317–22. Editorial on the Labour Party's draft policy statements, entitled *Plan for Progress*, which will be presented at the Labour Party Conference later in the year.

Book Review section, Shorter Notices,* *The Political Quarterly* 31 (1960): 415. Review of *Essays in Labour History. In Memory of G. D. H. Cole, September 25, 1889–January 14, 1959* edited by Asa Briggs and John Saville (Macmillan). The book contains recollections about Cole and his work and nine essays on subjects related to the history of Labour.

PART 3

Selected Titles on Political Subjects from the Library of Leonard Woolf

The entries below, in Part Three, are based on the original, annotated *Catalogue of Books from the Library of Leonard and Virginia Woolf* (Holleyman and Treacher Ltd., Brighton, 1975) at Washington State University. Z881.W3

Also recommended is use of a particularly valuable source to confirm location in the present-day library: "The Library of Leonard and Virginia Woolf: A Short-title Catalog" (Washington State University). The web address may be found on page 275, in "Related Collections and Resources" at the end of this volume.

1. Books Taken from Monks House, Rodmell, Sussex

Leonard Woolf's personal library had many classical volumes in it. The following items from it, though, are of interest on political subjects. Page references are from Holleyman and Treacher's catalogue, the side pertaining to the Monks House (MH) inventory.

MH, III, P. 15:

Stansky, P., and Abrahams, W. *Journey to the Frontier: Julian Bell and John Cornford: Their Lives and the 1930s*. 8vo cloth d. w. 1966. [Inserted in this book is a short note addressed to Leonard and signed "Philip."]

The Criminal Procedure Code. Ordinance No. 15 of 1898. By Authority. 8vo cloth. Colombo, Ceylon. [Inscription in ink on title page: "L. S. Woolf. December 1904"; also a few notes in ink in margins in Leonard's hand]

MH, IV, P. 1:

Bell, Julian. *Work for the Winter: More or Less for Christmas*. 8vo wrappers. [Recovered in coloured paper. Internal hinges repaired with tape. Handwritten label on spine by Leonard Woolf. Inscription in pencil on verso of title: "Leonard and Virginia from Julian"]

Woolf, Bella Sidney (Mrs. W. T. Southorn). *Eastern Star Dust*. 8 vo boards, 1922. [Inscription in ink on end paper: "To Virginia and Leonard With love from the Author Aug."—remainder of inscription erased.]

MH, V, P. 3:

Mill, John Stuart. *The Subjection of Women*. 8vo cloth. First edition, 1869.

MH, V, P. 4:

Forster, E. M. *The Government of Egypt.* Published by Labour Research Dept. (1919). 8vo wrappers, first ed.

MH, V, P. 10:

The British Civil Servant by eleven authors. Edited by W.A. Robson. 8vo cloth, 1937.

MH, V, P. 11:

Tawney, R. H. *Beatrice Webb* 1858–1943. (Reprinted from the Proceedings of the British Academy). 8vo wrappers, n.d., c. 1944.

MH, V, P. 12:

Taylor, Henry. *The Statesman,* intro. essay by H. J. Laski Reprint Series No. 2. 8vo cloth. Cambridge, 1927. Library No. 9938.
Morel, E. D. *Truth and the War.* 8vo wrappers. National Labour Press 1916 [in pencil—"penciled marks in margins of text, by L. Woolf?"].

MH, V, P. 16:

Toynbee, A. J. *The Conduct of British Empire Foreign Relations since the Peace Settlement.* 8vo. cloth, 1928. Library No. 14058.
Toynbee, A. J. *The World After the Peace Conference.* 8vo cloth 1925. Library No. 2518 [in pencil, notes by Leonard Woolf].

MH, V, P. 18:

Schapiro, L. *The Communist Party of the Soviet Union.* 8 vo wrappers, 1960. [Proof Copy, with "Publication April 21" written in front cover.]

MH, V, P. 20:

Webb Sidney and Beatrice. *English Local Government: Statutory Authorities for Special Purposes.* 8vo cloth, 1922.
Ritchie, Alice. *The Peacemakers.* 8vo cloth. Hogarth Press, 1928. [in pencil: Trekkie Parson's sister—"traveler for Hogarth Press]
Dennis, A. L. P. *The Foreign Policies of Soviet Russia.* 8vo cloth, 1924. Library No. 6464.

MH, V, P. 21:

Bernard, L. L. *An Introduction of to Social Psychology.* 8vo cloth, 1927. Library No. 7667. [WSU strikethrough of "of" and correction to "to" in green pencil]

Nicolson, Harold. *The Colonial Problem.* 8vo wrappers. Reprinted from "International Affairs," 1938. [Inscription in ink on cover "from Harold."]

Scott, A. P. *The Introduction to the Peace Treaties.* 8vo cloth. U.S.A., 1920.

MH, V, P. 22:

Pink, G. P. *The Conference of Ambassadors* (Paris 1920 and 1931; Geneva Studies Vol. 12 Nos. 4 and 5). 8vo wrappers, Geneva, 1942.

Davies, M. L. *The Woman's Co-Operative Guild 1883–1904.* 8vo cloth. Manchester, 1904.

Earle, E. M. "Turkey." *The Great Powers and the Bagdad Railway: A Study in Imperialism,* 8vo cloth, U.S.A., 1923.

Butler, N. M. *The International Mind.* 8vo cloth, New York, 1912.

Mann, H. H. *Land and Labour in a Deccan Village.* 8vo wrappers. University of Bombay. Economic Series. No. 1. 1917

Scott, J. B. *A Survey of International Relations Between the United States and Germany* August 1st, 1914 to April 6th, 1917. 8vo. cloth, N.Y., 1917.

MH, V, P. 23:

Hearnshaw, F. J. C. *Democracy at the Crossways.* 8vo. cloth, 1918.

Reed, John. *Ten Days That Shook The World.* 8vo cloth, U.S.A., 1919.

Corwin, E. S. *The President's Control of Foreign Relations.* 8vo cloth. U.S.A., 1917.

Bergson, H. *The Meaning of War.* 8vo cloth, 1915.

McCabe, J. *The Kaiser, His Personality and Career.* 8vo cloth, 1915 [in pencil: "Review Copy"].

Die Kommunistische International, Nos. 12, 13 and 16, German text. 8vo wrappers. Hamburg, 1920 1921

MH, V, P. 24:

International Conciliation No. 369. Text of H. R. 1776 An Act to Promote the Defence of the United States. 8vo wrappers. U.S.A. 1941.

Ossiannilsson, K. G. *Who Is Right in the World War?* 8vo cloth 1917.

MH, Section VI—Books with notes and references to text and on end papers in the hand of L. S. Woolf

MH, VI, p. 1:

Beaverbrook, Lord. *Men and Power, 1917 & 1918*. 8vo cloth, 1956.

Blake, Robert. *The Unknown Prime Minister: The Life and Times of Andrew Bonar Law 1858–1923*. 8vo cloth, 1955.

Borkenau, F. *The Totalitarian Enemy*. 8vo. cloth, 1940.

Burrow, George. *Celebrated Trials and Remarkable Cases of Criminal Jurisprudence from the Earliest Records to the Year 1825*. 8vo cloth, 1928.

Bullock, Alan. *Hitler*. 8vo cloth, 1952.

Butler, Harold. *The Lost Peace*. 8vo cloth, 1941.

MH, VI, p. 2:

Carr, E. H. *The Twenty Years Crisis 1919–39*. 8vo cloth, 1939.

Carr-Saunders, A. M., and P. S. Florence, R. Peers. *Consumer's Co-Operation in Great Britain*. 8vo cloth, 1938.

Chambers, F. P. *The War Behind the War 1914–18*. 8vo cloth, 1939. [In pencil: "complimentary copy."]

Charpentier, Armand. *The Dreyfus Case*. 8vo cloth, 1935.

Cobban, Alfred. *Edmund Burke and the Revolution Against the 18th Century*. 8vo cloth, 1929.

Cole, G. D. H. *British Working Class Politics 1832–1914*. 8vo cloth, 1941.

Cole, G. D. H. *A Century of Co-Operation*. 8vo cloth, 1944 [1945?].

Cole, Margaret. *The Story of Fabian Socialism*. 8vo cloth, 1961.

Cole, Margaret. *Beatrice Webb*. 8vo cloth, 1945.

Deutscher, I. *The Prophet Armed: Trotsky 1879–1921. The Prophet Unarmed: Trotsky 1921*. 2 vols. 8vo cloth, 1954.

MH, VI, p. 3:

Dicey, A. V. *The Statesmanship of Wordsworth: An Essay*. 8vo cloth, 1917.

Ensor, R.C.K. *England 1870–1914*. 8vo cloth, 1936.

Esher, Reginald (Viscount). *Journals and Letters of*. 4 vols. 8vo buckram, 1934.

Fabian Essays by Bernard Shaw, Sidney Webb etc. 8vo cloth, 1950.

Faguet, Emile. *Politicians and Moralists of the Nineteenth Century*. 8vo cloth, 1928.

Feiling, Keith. *The Life of Neville Chamberlain*. 8vo buckram, 1946. [In pencil: "Review copy"; also an erased pencil note: "Notes by Leonard Woolf."]

Garvin, J. L., and Julian Amery. *Life of Joseph Chamberlain*. 4vols. 8vo cloth, 1932–51.

Godwin, William. *An Enquiry Concerning Political Justice and Its Influence on Virtue and Happiness*. 2 vols. 8vo cloth. New York, 1926.

Gollin, Alfred M. *The Observer and J. L. Garvin 1908–1914*. 8vo cloth, 1960.

MH, VI, p. 4:

Gooch, G. P. *Recent Revelations of European Diplomacy.* 8vo cloth. Revised, 1940. [Erased note, in pencil: "notes on back end-paper by Leonard Woolf and also some pencil marks in margins of text."]

Halevy, Elie. *The Growth of Philosophic Radicalism.* 8vo cloth, 1928.

Hammond, J. L. *Gladstone and the Irish Nation.* 8vo cloth, 1938.

Harrod, R. F. *The Life of John Maynard Keynes.* 8vo cloth, 1951.

Hendrick, Burton J. *The Life of Andrew Carnegie.* 8vo buckram 1933.

Herrick, Christine Terhune, ed. *The Letters of the Duke of Wellington to Miss J. 1834-51.* 8vo boards cloth backed 1924. Woolf Library no. 6927.

Hinden, Rita. *Plan for Africa: A Report Prepared for the Colonial Bureau of the Fabian Society.* 8vo cloth, 1941.

Hitler, Adolf. *The Speeches of, April 1922-August 1939.* 2 vols. buckram, 1942.

Hobson, J. A. *Democracy.* 8vo cloth. 20th-Century Library, 1934.

Hobson, J. A. *Work and Wealth.* 8vo cloth 1914.

Holroyd, Michael. *Lytton Strachey.* Vol. 1 only. *The Unknown Years.* 1880-1910. Large 8vo cloth 1967.

MH, VI, p. 5:

Hone, Joseph. *The Life of Henry Tonks.* 8vo cloth, 1939. [Noted in green pencil in WSU catalogue: "notes by Roger Fry, not Leonard Woolf"—however, Fry died in 1934!]

Johnstone, J. K. *The Bloomsbury Group.* 8vo cloth, 1954.

Keynes, John Maynard. *Essay in Persuasion.* 8vo cloth, 1931. [A note in pencil: "L.W. Review of N.S. & N. Dec. 19, 1931) 2:788."]

Laski, Harold J. *Studies in Law and Politics.* 8vo cloth, 1932.

Lewis, Wyndam. *Paleface. The Philosophy of the "Melting Pot."* 8vo cloth. First Edition, 1929.

Lichnowsky, Prince. *Heading for the Abyss.* 8vo cloth, 1928. Library No. 13430. [Penciled in; also, erased: "notes and marks by Leonard Woolf].

Lindsay, A. D. *The Modern Democratic State.* Vol. 1, only. 8vo. cloth, 1943.

Macmillan, Harold. *Winds of Change 1914-39.* 8vo cloth, 1966.

MH, VI, p. 6:

Mann, Golo. *Secretary of Europe. The Life of Friedrich Gentz.* 8vo cloth. USA, 1946.

Martin, Kingsley. *Editor: A Second Volume of Autobiography 1931-45.* 8vo cloth, 1968.

Martin, Kingsley. *Harold Laski (1893-1950).* 8vo cloth, 1953.

Muggeridge, Kitty, and Ruth Adam. *Beatrice Webb: A Life 1858-1953.* 8vo wrappers, 1967.

Namier, L. B. *The Structure of Politics at the Accession of George III.* 2 vols. 8vo. cloth, 1929.
Newman, Bertram. *Edmund Burke.* 8vo cloth 1927. [Pencil note: "Resewn by Virginia?"]
Nicolson, Harold. *The Congress of Vienna: A Study in Allied Unity 1812–1822.* 8vo cloth, 1946.
Oppenheim, L. *The League of Nations and Its Problems. Three Lectures.* 8vo cloth, 1919.

MH, VI, p. 7:
Paoadatos, Peter. *The Eichmann Trial.* 8vo cloth, 1964.
Perham, M. *Lugard: The Years of Adventure.* Vol. 1: *1858–1898* 8vo cloth, 1956.
Petrov, V. *It Happens in Russia: Seven Years Forced Labor in the Siberian Gold Fields.* 8vo cloth, 1951.
Pinchbeck, Ivy. *Women Workers and the Industrial Revolution 1750–1850.* 8vo cloth, 1930.
Pink, M. Alderton. *The Defence of Freedom.* 8vo. cloth, 1935.
Prince Max of Baden. The Memoirs of. 2 vols. 8vo cloth, 1928.
Radhakrishnan, S. *An Idealist View of Life.* Being the Hibbert Lectures of 1929. 8vo cloth, 1932.
Ramsay, A. A. W. *Sir Robert Peel.* Makers of the Nineteenth Century series. 8vo cloth, 1928. [In pencil: "Woolf Library no. 12311."]
Raymond, E. T. *Disraeli: The Alien Patriot.* 8vo cloth. 1920.
Roberts, Stephen H. *History of French Colonial Policy 1870–1925.* 2 vols. 8vo buckram. 1928.
Russell, Bertrand. *The Basic Writings of 1903–59* (1961) 8vo cloth. 1961.
Russell, Bertrand. *Power: A New Social Analysis.* 8vo wrappers. 1938.
Russell, Bertrand. *Autobiography 1872–1967*, 3 vols. 8vo. 1967–69.

MH, VI, p. 8:
Shaw, Bernard. *Everybody's Political What's What.* 8vo cloth, 1944.
Sorel, Georges. *Reflections on Violence.* 8vo cloth. 1916.
Streit, Clarence K. *Union Now.* 8vo cloth. 1939.
Tawney, R. H. *The Attack and Other Papers.* 8vo cloth, 1953.
Taylor, A. J. P. *Bismarck.* 8vo buckram, 1955.
Temperley, Harold. *The Foreign Policy of Canning 1822–1827.* 8vo cloth. 1925.
Thompson, J. M. *Robespierre.* 2 vols. 8vo cloth. 1935.
The History of "The Times" 1785–1948. 4 vols. in 5. 8vo buckram, 1935–52.
Toynbee, Arnold J. *Survey of International Affairs 1935.* Vol. 1 only. 8vo cloth. 1936.
Toynbee, Arnold J. *A Historian's Approach to Religion.* 8vo cloth Oxford, 1956.

MH, VI, p. 9:
Trevelyan, G. M. *The Life of John Bright.* 8vo cloth. New Edition, 1925. [in pencil: Library No. 2434].
Trotsky, L. *Trotsky's Diary in Exile 1935.* 8vo cloth. 1959.
Tunstall, B. *Admiral Byng: and the Loss of Minorca.* 8vo cloth. 1928.
Unwin, Sir Stanley. *The Truth About Publishing.* 8vo cloth. 4th revised ed., 1946.
Villiers, Brougham, and W. H. Chesson. *Anglo-Amercan Relations 1861–1865.* 8vo cloth. 1919.
Webb, Beatrice. *The Diaries of 1912–1932,* 2 vols., 8vo cloth. 1952 and 1956.
Webb, Beatrice. *My Apprenticeship,* vol. 2 only. small 8vo. no wrappers. Pelican Books. 1938.
Webb, Beatrice. *Our Partnership,* 1948. 8vo cloth. 1948.
Wheeler-Bennett, John W. *John Anderson, Viscount Waverley.* 8vo cloth, 1962.
Woodward, E. L., and R. Butler. *Documents on British Foreign Policy 1919–1939.* Second series. Vols 1 and 3 only. 8vo cloth, 1946. 1948.

MH, VI, p. 10:
Woodward, W. E. *Lafayette: A Biography.* 8vo buckram, 1938 [in pencil: "Review copy"].
Young, G. M. *Victorian England: Portrait of an Age.* 8vo cloth. 1936.
Queen Victoria. *The Letters of.* 8vo cloth.
- First Series. Vols. 1 to 3 (small format).
- Second Series. Vols. 1 to 3 (large format), 1907–32.
- Third Series. Vols. 1 to 3 (large format).
- [Notes in Second Series Vols. 1 and 3 Leonard Woolf Bloomsbury style bookplate in Vols. 1 and 2. Second Series. Library No. 11392.]

Programme for Victory: A Collection of Essays Prepared for the Fabian Society by H. J. Laski, Herbert Read &c. 8vo boards, 1941.
Duggan, S. P., Editor. *The League of Nations: The Principle and the Practice.* 8vo cloth Boston, 1919.
Reinsch, P. S. *Secret Diplomacy: How far can it be eliminated?* 8vo cloth, 1922. Library No. 8196.
Tagore, Rabindranath. *Nationalism.* 8vo cloth. 1917.
Le Goffic, C. *General Foch at the Marne.* 8vo cloth, 1918. [Erased note: "Penciled marks, notes by Leonard Woolf" next to unerased "resewn binding by Virginia?"]
Dobbs, A. E. *Education and Social Movements 1700–1850.* 8vo cloth. 1919.
Kawakami, K. K. *Japan's Pacific Policy.* 8vo cloth. New York, 1922.

MH, VI, p. 11:
Hanson, Laurence. *Government and the Press 1695–1763.* Large 8vo quarto calf, 1936.

Stoddard, L. *The Revolt Against Civilization. The Menace of the Under-man.* 8vo cloth, 1922.

Addresses and Discussions at the Conference of Scientific Management. Held October 12, 13, 14, 1911 (Dartmouth College Conference). 8vo cloth. U.S.A., 1912.

Enforced Peace. Proceedings of the first annual national assemblage of the League to Enforce Peace, Washington May 26/27, 1916. 8vo cloth, n.d.

Bates, J. V. *Our Allies and Enemies in the Near East.* 8vo cloth. 1918.

Raven, C. E. *Christian Socialism 1848–1854.* 8vo cloth, 1920.

Butler, Sir Geoffrey. *A Handbook to the League of Nations.* 8vo cloth, 1919.

Levine, I. D. *The Russian Revolution.* 8vo cloth. 1917.

Van De Perre, A. *The Language Question in Belgium.* 8vo cloth. 1919.

Root, E. *The Military and Colonial Policy of the United States.* 8vo cloth. U.S.A., 1916.

Belloc, Hilaire. *The Jews.* 8vo cloth. First ed., 1922. Library no. 4396.

Bosanquet, H. *Social Work in London 1869–1912. A History of Charity Organization Society.* 8vo cloth, 1914.

Henderson, Arthur. *The Aims of Labour.* 8vo wrappers. N.d. (c. 1917). [Noted in pencil: "Review copy."]

Spargo, J. *Bolshivism.* 8vo. Cloth. 1919. Library no. 1409.

Ball, A. H. R., ed. *Ruskin as a Literary Critic.* Selection. 8vo cloth, 1928 Library No. 13593.

MH, VI, p. 12:

Yerta, G. and M. *Six Women and the Invasion.* 8vo cloth, 1917 [in pencil: "presentation copy" embossed on t.p.].

De Lanessan, J.-L. *Histoire De L'Entente Cordiale: Franco-Anglaise.* 8vo wrappers. Paris, 1916.

Carr, E. H. *The Bolshevik Revolutions 1917–1923.* Vol. 1. 8vo cloth. 1950.

Halevy, E. *A History of the English People.* Vol. 3: *1830–1841.* 8vo cloth, 1927. Library no. 11245.

Halevy, E. *A History of the English People.* Vol. 4: *1895–1905.* 8vo cloth, 1929. Library no. 1266.

Hammond, J. L. and B. *The Age of the Chartists. 1832–1854.* 8vo cloth. 1930.

Hammond, J. L. and B. *The Skilled Labourer 1760–1832.* 8vo cloth. 1919. Library No. 2347.

Wells, H. G. *In the Fourth Year. Anticipations of a World Peace.* 8vo cloth. 1st Edition, 1918. [in pencil: "Presentation copy" notation: "notes & marks" erased].

2. Books Taken from 24 Victoria Square, London

Page references are from the Holleyman and Treacher catalogue, parts pertaining to the Victoria Square (VS) inventory.

2.1. Items Belonging to or Presented to Leonard Woolf [Selections]

VS, III, p. 1:

Maurtua, Dr. Victor M. *The Questions of the Pacific*. (An Edition in English enlarged in 1901 by F.A. Pezet). 8vo wrappers. U.S.A., 1901. [Inscription in ink on title page "with compliments of the Author. / Victor M. Maurtua." In pencil: "to Leonard Woolf]

Russell, Bertrand. *Principles of Social Reconstruction*. 8vo cloth. 1st ed., 1916. [Inscription in pencil—front end page: "L.S.W. / Dec. 1916".]

Anson, W.R. *Principles of the English Law of Contract*. 8vo cloth. 8th Edition. 1898. [Inscription in ink on front end paper: "*A. R. Slater* Sept. 1899 / Columbo" // "To W. T. Southern / January 1904" [also there are some notes in pencil on back end paper].

Barnes, Leonard. *The Duty of Empire*. 8vo cloth 1935. [Inscription in ink on front end paper: "Leonard Woolf / from L. B. May 1935."]

Morel, E. D. *Africa and the Peace of Europe*. 8vo wrappers. National Labour Press Ltd., 1917. [Inscription in ink on front cover: "Mr. L. Woolf from the Author May 31 '18"]

Fraser, Robert. *What's What in Politics*. 8vo cloth. Labour Book Service, 1939. [Typewritten letter inserted. "3.3.39 / Dear Mr. Woolf, // Labour Book Service": "I am sending you a copy of the first set of books offered by the Labour Book Service. I hope you will like them.

With kind regards
Yours sincerely,
W. Surrey Dane [signed]"

VS, III, p. 2:

Fulani, Fulani Bin. *Africa and the Twentieth Century Reformation*. 8vo wrappers. 1920. [Inscription in ink on front cover: "Leonard Woolf from Fulani Bin Fulani / August 1920"]

Shaw, Bernard. *The Irrational Knot*. 8vo 1st Edition, 1905. [Inscription in ink on front end paper "L.S. Woolf / December 1905."]

Conrad, Joseph. *Under Western Eyes*. 8vo cloth. 2nd edition 1911 [Inscription in ink on front end paper: "L. S. Woolf". One note in pencil on back end paper in the hand of Leonard Woolf.]

Conrad, Joseph. *The Secret Agent*. 8vo cloth. 3rd edition 1907. [Inscription in pencil on front end paper: "L. S. Woolf"]

VS, III, p. 3:

Conrad, Joseph. *The Nigger of the Narcissus*. 8vo cloth. Popular Edition 1910. [Autograph in pencil on front end paper: "L. S. Woolf"; also some numbers penciled inside front and back cover in the hand of L. W.]

Woolf, Bella Sidney. *The Twins in Ceylon*. 8vo cloth 1st Edition. 1909. [Inscription in ink on front end paper "To Leonard with the Author's love. / October 1909"—Bella was Leonard Woolf's sister]

Reinsch, P. S. *Public International Unions. Their Work and Organization*. 8vo cloth 1911. [Inscription in ink on front end paper: "L.S. Woolf from/Hugh Richardson / The Gables / Elswick Road / Newcastle on Tyne / August 1919." Some notes in pencil on back and paper in the hand of Leonard Woolf. WSU Library staff has crossed out Woolf's name in the marked catalog and penciled in "Hugh Richardson / also notes in text." Also beside this has been penciled: "additional information on front end paper not shown by Holleyman."]

Darby, W. Evans. *International Arbitration—International Tribunals*. Addendum. 8vo cloth. 1899. [Inscription in pen on front end paper: "L.W. per H.H." [i.e. Hugh Richardson] [WSU staff notes Holleyman entry: "Bound with *The Peace Conference at the Hague: It's History, Work, and Results*. London: Peace Society, 1900.]

Justinian. *The Institutes of*: Translated into English by J. B. Moyle. 8vo cloth 3rd edition 1896. [Inscription in pencil on front end paper: "L. S. Woolf, June 1904"; also in ink in another hand: "Kemp V. Neville"; also in pencil: "Corpus Juris Civilis Institutiones."]

VS, III, p. 4:

Spinoza, Benedict de. *The Works of*: Vol. 2. *De Intellectus Emendatione—Ethica*. Trans. R.H.M. Elwes. 8vo cloth. 1903. [Inscription in pencil on front end paper: "L. Sidney Woolf / December 1903."]

VS, III, p. 5:

The Political Quarterly. Edited by Leonard Woolf and William A. Robson. 8vo January 1933–June 1939. 13 vols. This run has been bound by Virginia Woolf in 13 vols with morocco leather spines of various colours and with patterned paper sides, each one of a different colour and pattern. Paper labels in the hand of V. W. have survived in 10 volumes but on three of these the ink has almost completely faded out.

Addison, Joseph, and Richard Steele. *The Spectator*. A new edition edited by Henry Morley. 8vo cloth, 1888. [Inscription in ink on front end paper: "L. S. Woolf / Feb. 1898."]

VS, III, p. 6:

Kaeckenbeeck, G. *International Rivers*. Introductory note by H. Goudy. 8vo boards. Grotius Society Publication No. 1. 1918. [Inscription in ink on front end paper: "Leonard Woolf"; also notes in pencil on back end paper in the hand of Leonard Woolf]

VS, III, p. 7:

Justinian. *The Institutes of:* Translated into English by J. B. Moyle. 8vo cloth 3rd edition 1896. [Inscription in pencil on front end paper: "L. S. Woolf / June 1904"; also in pencil: "Corpus Juris Civilis Institutiones."]

Woolf, Leonard. *The War for Peace*. 8vo boards. The Labour Book Service. 1st edition. 1940.

VS, III, p. 8:

Stresemann, Gustav. *His Diaries, Letters and Papers*. Ed. & trans. by Eric Sutton, 3 vols. 8vo cloth 1935–40. Notes in pencil on back end papers of vols. 2 & 3 in the hand of Leonard Woolf. Also inserted a typewritten p.c. posted in Lewes, Sussex on September 15th, 1940, addressed to The Hogarth Press / 37 Mecklenburgh Square / London W.C. 1—dated 14/9/40: "I left some papers and some books for sale at the garage will you please get them. Among the books is one of *Gustav Stresemann* which I want to keep. All the others can be sold." Signed in ink Leonard Woolf. [Note in pencil by WSU Library staff in catalog: "a letter inserted in vol.3 addressed to the Literary editor advising that the introduction to the present edition is not by the translator but was part of the original German version. L.W. Review V. 1 PQ Jan–March '36, '37"]

Woolf, Leonard. *Socialism and Co-operation*. 8vo wrappers. The National Labour Press Ltd. I. L. P. Publication Dept. 1st edition. 1921.

Durbin, E. F. M. *The Politics of Democratic Socialism. An Essay on Social Policy*. 8vo boards. The Labour Book Service. 1st edition. 1940. [Inserted a typewritten letter dated 5th Feb. 1940 addressed to Leonard Woolf dealing with the publications of the re-organized Labour Book Service and signed by G. S. Bishop.]

Woolf, Leonard. *Empire and Commerce in Africa. A Study in Economic Imperialism*. 8vo quarto calf. Published by the Labour Research Dept. N.d. (c. 1920).

VS, III, p. 9:

Browne, W. J. *Civil Service Compendium for 1936*. Compiled by W. J. Browne, General Secretary Civil Service Clerical Association. 8vo rexine n.d. [Inscription in ink on front end paper: "With compliments from W. J. Browne / February 1938"; notation in pencil: "Civil Service Clerical Association."]

Various Authors. *Peace and the Colonial Problem*. 8vo. wrappers, 1935. [Typewritten letter inserted, headed Natural Peace Council / addressed to Leonard

Woolf Esq. asking for review and advice on distribution of this publication. Signed: Gerald Bailey, Directing Secretary, dated 10.12.35.]

VS, III, p. 10:
Sapru, Sir Tej Bahadur. *The Indian Constitution*. 8vo cloth. The National Secretaries Office. Madras, 1926. [Inserted is a typewritten letter headed The British Committee on Indian Affairs addressed to Leonard Woolf Esq. dated 16th November 1926 suggesting the book may be of interest to the recipient and that the author is "probably the greatest lawyer in India today". Signed by the Hon. Secretary Major D. Graham Pole.; note in pencil: shelved under India Constitution]

Woolf, Bella Sidney (Mrs. W. T. Southorn). *From Groves of Palm*. 8vo board, Cambridge 1925.

Poiret, Peter. *Bibliotheca Mysticorum Selecta*. 8vo calf. Amsterdam 1708. [Inscription in pencil on front end paper: "Leonard Sidney Woolf / Trin. Coll. Camb. Feb. 1901"; also in pencil on front end paper: "R. A. Vaughan"; followed by a note in another hand that the marginal notes in pencil throughout the book are by R.A. Vaughan. Autograph, p. 95: "August 8th 1850 / RAV"].

VS, III, p. 11:
Carr-Saunders, A. M., and P. S. Florence and R. Peers in consultation with M. I. Cole, Leonard Woolf & others: *Consumers Co-operation in Great Britain. An Examination of the British Co-operative Movement*. 8vo cloth. 1938. [Inscription in ink on front end paper: "Leonard Woolf / 1938"]

Trevelyan, Sir George. *Cawnpore*. 8vo cloth. 1910. [Inscription in ink on front end paper: "L. S. Woolf."]

Laski, Harold J. *The State In Theory and Practice*. 8vo cloth. 1st ed. 1935. [Inscription in pencil on front end paper: "Leonard Woolf" with notes in pencil on back end paper in the hand of Leonard Woolf.]

VS, III, p. 12:
Cromer, The Earl of. *Modern Egypt*. 2 vols. 8vo cloth. 1908. [Inscription in pencil on front end paper of Vol. 2: "L. S. Woolf / Dec. 1908."]

Eckel, Edwin C. *Coal, Iron and the War. A Study in Industrialism Past and Future*. 8vo cloth. "For Review" stamped on title page, 1921. [Enclosed a typewritten letter headed The Daily Herald Ltd. Addressed to Leonard Woolf Esq., Hogarth House, Paradise Road, Richmond Surrey. "Dear Woolf / If this book is worth reading, I / should be grateful for not more than / 300 words on it. / Yours sincerely, / W. S. Turner (signed) / Literary Editor"; also notes in pencil on back end paper in the hand of Leonard Woolf.]

VS, III, p. 13:
Wedgwood, Josiah C. *The Future of the Indo-British Commonwealth.* Preface by Viscount Haldane. 8vo cloth The Theosophical Publishing House, 1921. [Inscription in ink on front end paper. "To Leonard Sidney Woolf from his rival in the / good work / Josiah C. Wedgwood / 30.9.21."]

Osbourne, Sidney. *The Saar Question. A Disease Spirit in Europe.* 8vo cloth. 1923. [Typewritten letter enclosed. Headed "Trades Union Congress General Council and the Labour party Executive Committee. Joint Publicity Department." Addressed to: Mr. Leonard S. Woolf, Hogarth House, Richmond. "Dear Mr. Woolf, / I enclose a copy of 'The Saar / Questions' which has been sent for review in the Labour Magazine. / [New paragraph:] I should be obliged if you could spare time to write a short review of about 500 words for insertion in an early number of the Labour Magazine. / Yours sincerely, / W. W. Henderson (signed) / Secretary"; dated 1st November 1923.]

VS, III, p. 15:
Holmes, Oliver Wendell. *The Autocrat of the Breakfast Table*: Vol. 1 of *The Writings of.* Riverside edition in 13 vols. 8vo cloth. London, 1891.

Woolf, Leonard. *"From Geneva to the Next War."* Off-print from the *Political Quarterly* Vol. 4 No. 1 8vo wrappers 1933.

VS, III, p. 16:
Voltaire. *Oeuvres. Completes De L'Imprimerie De La Societe Litteraire—Typographique.* 70 vols. 8vo calf. 1784–1789. Vol. 52: *Racueil des Lettres de M. de Voltaire 1715–1737.* [Notes referring to text in pencil on back and papers in the hand of Leonard Woolf.]; Vol. 47 [Bookplate of Charles Edmund Rumbold inside front cover.] [This is the best and most complete of Voltaire's collected works. It was edited by Voltaire himself and later by Beaumarchais. Published by Kehl. The type used had been purchased from the Baskerville Press in England.] [This set of Voltaire was obviously one of Leonard's most prized possessions. It was the only literary work he took with him when he went to Ceylon in October 1904 and it came back to England with him in 1911. The four following references to this work are from Leonard Woolf's autobiography—]

[Woolf, Leonard,] Vol. II "Growing" Autobiography of the years 1904–11. p. 12. / "All that I was taking with me from the old life as a contribution to the new and to prepare me for my task of helping to rule the British Empire was 90 large, beautifully printed volumes of Voltaire [the 1784 edition printed in Baskerville type] and a wire-haired fox-terrier." // P. 23. "I spent a fortnight, which included Christmas, in Colombo and on January 1st or 2nd, 1905, now a Cadet in the Ceylon Civil Service on a salary of L300 a year, I set out for Jaffna with a Sinhalese servant, my dog, a wooden crate containing Voltaire, and an enormous tin-lined trunk containing clothes ." / P. 37. "A particular liability was my 90 large volumes of Voltaire. Socially and psychologically they did me no good, and materially throughout my years in Ceylon caused considerable difficulty when I was moved from one station to another and they suddenly had to be transported over hundreds of miles in country which sometimes was without a railway. I am a little proud of the fact that socially I lived down the 90 volumes and physically brought them back to England in fair condition, neither repudiating Voltaire spiritually and socially nor abandoning him materially." / P. 65 "He (Dutton) was extremely nervous and suspicious and for some time the interview and the conversation were awkward, but eventually, when he found that I had read as many books as he had — or even more — and that I did not think poetry funny, he agreed to take me in, and I and my Voltaire joined Dutton and his Home University Library." / [It is interesting to note that Leonard persistently quotes the wrong number of volumes, the set being in 70, not 90, volumes. / It is also interesting to observe that only one volume (Vol. 52) has notes on back end papers in the hand of Leonard Woolf. This need not however be significant as although almost all the books Leonard reviewed had his pencil notes at the end these reviewing activities were still many years ahead, and we need not infer therefore that any volume without notes had not been read by Leonard. / It may seem odd too that whereas a great many of the books he owned at school and at the university were signed by him, this work, his most treasured literary possession, was not signed. / At the time of Leonard's death about 20 of these volumes were in the library at Monk's House, the remainder being in the Victoria Square house, in London.]

VS, III, p. 17:
Woolf, Leonard. *After the Deluge. A Study of Communal Psychology.* Vol. 1. 8vo cloth. Published by Leonard and Virginia Woolf at the Hogarth Press 1931. [A few marginal textual corrections in the hand of Leonard Woolf, and referred to in notes on back end papers in his hand under the heading "Corrigenda." Correction made on p. 156 was missed by LW in his Corrigenda.]

2.2. Miscellaneous—Some with Slight Association with Leonard Woolf [Selections]

VS, V, p. 1:
Miller, D. H. *The Peace Pact of Paris. A Study of the Briand-Kellog Treaty.* Advance copy. 8vo cloth. USA 1928 Lib. No. 536.
Norton, Henry. *The Far Eastern Republic of Siberia.* 8vo cloth. Review copy, 1923. Lib. No. 1067.

Hyndman, H. M. *The Future of Democracy*. 8vo cloth. 1915.
Latham, J. G. *Australia and the British Commonwealth*. 8vo cloth. 1929. Lib. No. 3775.
Allen, W. E. D. *The Turks in Europe*. 8vo cloth. Review copy, 1919.
Petrovich, W. M. *Serbia. Her People, History and Aspirations*. 8vo cloth. Review copy, 1915.
Joseph, P. *Foreign Diplomacy in China 1894–1900*. 8vo cloth 1928. Lib. No. 14588.
Marx, Karl. *Critique of the Gotha Programme*. (Marxist and Leninist Library) 8vo cloth. U.S.S.R., n.d.
Luke, Sir Harry, and E. Keith-Roach. *The Handbook of Palestine and Trans-Jordan*. 3rd ed. 8vo. cloth. 1934.
Lawrence, T. J. *Handbook of Public International Law*. 11th ed. by P. H. Winfield. 8vo cloth, 1938.

VS, V, p. 2:
Cole, G. D. H. *Social Theory*. 8vo cloth. 1920.
Doyle, Phyllis. *A History of Political Thought*. 8vo cloth. 1933.
Blunt, Wilfred Scawen. *A Secret History of the English Occupation of Egypt*. 8vo cloth. (Review slip), 1907. Lib. No. 3286.
Webb, Sidney. *Towards Social Democracy. A Study of Social Evolutions During the Past Three-quarters of a Century*. 8vo wrappers. Fabian Society, 1916.
Martin, Kingsley. *Thomas Paine*. 8vo wrappers. Fabian tract No. 217, 1925.
Lipson, E. *Europe in the Nineteenth Century*. 8vo cloth. 1916.
Dillon, E .J. *The Eclipse of Russia*. 8vo cloth. 1918.
What Would Be the Character of a New War? Enquiry organized by the Inter-Parliamentary Union. Geneva. 8vo cloth. (Review slip), 1933.
Cerf, Barry. *Alsace-Lorraine Since 1870*. 8vo cloth. New York, 1919.
Jennings, W. I. *The Law and the Constitution*. 8vo cloth, 1938.
Cocks, F. S., ed. *The Secret Treaties and Understandings*. Text of the available documents. Preface by Charles Trevelyan. 8vo boards, n.d. (c. 1918).

VS, V, p. 3:
Marriott, J. A. R. *The Eastern Question. An Historical Study in European Diplomacy*. 8vo cloth (Review slip), 1924. Lib. No. 1065.
Adams, J. *Educational Theories*. 8vo wrappers (Benn's 6d. Library No. 170), 1927. Lib. No. 11346.
Cole, G. D. H. *Guild Socialism*. 8vo wrappers (Fabian Tract No. 192), 1920.
Laski, H. J. *The State in the New Social Order*. 8vo. wrappers (Fabian Tract No. 200), 1922.
Webb, Mrs. Sidney. *A New Reform Bill*. 8vo wrappers (Fabian Tract No. 236), 1931.

Enfield, A. Honora. *Guildswomen at Basle*. 8vo wrappers (Women's Co-operative Guild), 1921.

Counts, G. S. *Dare the School Build a New Social Order*. 8vo. wrappers. New York, 1932.

Barker, Ernest, ed. *The Future Government of Indian and the Indian Civil Service*. 8vo wrappers, 1919.

Geyer, C. and W. Loeb. *Gollancz in German Wonderland*. Translated from German by Ed. Fitzgerald. 8vo wrappers, 1942.

VS, V, p. 4:

Kikuyu Central Association. Memorandum presented to the Commission on the Administration of Justice in Criminal Matters in East Africa. 8vo wrappers, Niarobi, 1933.

Cole, G. D. H. *A Short History of the British Working Class Movement 1789–1937*. 3 vols. in 1. Complete edition with a supplementary chapter to 1937. 8vo cloth. (Review slip) 1937.

Porter, R. P. *Japan. The New World Power*. 8vo cloth, 1915. [Yellow review slip inserted with page numbers and notes by Leonard Woolf. Also sections marked in text.]

Webb, Sidney and Beatrice. *The Minority Report of the Poor Law Commission*. 2 vols. 1: *The Break Up of the Poor Law*. 2: *The Public Organization of the Labour Market*. 8vo cloth. 1st edition, 1909.

VS, V, p. 5:

The Brown Book of the Hitler Terror and the Burning of the Reichstag. Prepared by the World Committee for the Victims of German Fascism (Chairman: Einstein), 8vo cloth. 1933.

Barron, C. W. *The Mexican Problem*. 8vo cloth. (Review slip) USA, 1917.

Keynes, John Maynard. *Laissez-Faire and Communism*. 8vo wrappers. New York, 1926.

Wallas, Graham. *Human Nature in Politics*. 8vo cloth (Constables Miscellany), 1929. Library No. 371.

Lyall, Sir Alfred. *The Rise of the British Dominion in India*. 8vo cloth. 1st Edition, 1893.

Gheon, Henri. *Demos Esclav et Roi*. 4to wrappers, Paris, 1927.

Pearce, Major F. B. *Zanzibar, The Island Metropolis of Eastern Asia*. 8vo cloth. (Review slip) 1920.

Calvert, A. F. *The Cameroons*. 8vo cloth. (Review slip) 1917.

Faulkner, H. U. *A Short History of the American People*. Intro. H. J. Laski. 8vo cloth. (Review slip) 1938.

Anon. *The Problem of the Anglo-Japanese Alliance*. 8vo wrappers. Issued by the National Defence League, the Chinese League of Nations Society etc., n. d.

VS, V, p. 6:
Woo, T. C. *The Kuomintang and the Future of the Chinese Revolution.* 8vo cloth. (Review slip) 1928. Lib. No. 14056.
Fay, C. R. *Co-operations at Home and Abroad and Description and Analysis with Supplement on the Progress of Co-operation in the United Kingdom 1908–1918.* 8vo cloth, 1920.
Anon. *Proceedings of the Gibbon Commemoration 1794–1894.* 8vo wrappers. The Royal Historical Society, 1895. [Note in pencil: catalogued under Royal Historical Society, London, Proceedings.]
Gerig, Benjamin. *The Open Door and the Mandates System.* 8vo cloth, 1930. Lib. No. 4235.
Thomas, J. A. *The House of Commons 1832–1901.* 8vo cloth, Cardiff, 1939.
Barker, Ernest. *The Submerged Nationalities of the German Empire.* 8vo wrappers, 1915.
Willmore, J. S. *The Story of King Constantine. As Revealed in the Greek White Book.* 8vo wrappers. (Review slip) 1919.
Fox, Charles James. *Speeches During the French Revolutionary Period.* 8vo cloth. Everyman's Library, n.d. Lib. No. 7491.
Croce, B. *History of Europe in the Nineteenth Century.* Trans from Italian by Henry Furst. 8vo cloth, 1934.
Waddington, C. F. *Science and Ethics.* 8vo cloth. (Review slip) 1942.

VS, V, p. 7:
Bulow, Prince Bernhard von. *Imperial Germany.* 8vo cloth, 1914.
Evatt, H. V. *The King and His Dominion Governors.* 8vo cloth, 1936.
Polybius. *Greece Before the Conference.* 8vo cloth. (Review slip) n.d. [1919].
Eddy, J. P. *India's New Constitution. A Survey of the Government of India Act 1935.* 8vo cloth, 1938.
MacDonald, J. Ramsey. *The Socialist Movement.* 8vo cloth, n.d.
Guest, L. H. *The Labour Party and the Empire.* 8vo cloth. 1926. Lib. No. 7603.
Pigou, A. C. *Unemployment.* 8vo cloth, (H.U.L.) 1913.
Broz, Alexander. *The Rise of the Czechoslovak Republic.* 8vo wrapper, 1919.
Select Constitutions of the World. Prepared for presentation to Dail Eireann by order of the Irish Provisional Government 1922. 8vo wrappers. Dublin, 1922. Library No. 7339.

VS, V, p. 8:
Mallock, W H. *Democracy: Being an abridged edition of the Limits of Pure Democracy.* 8vo cloth, 1924. Lib. No. 5397.
Mendelssohn, Sidney. *The Jews of Africa. Especially in the 16th and 17th Centuries.* 8vo cloth, 1920. Lib. No. 1309.

Selected Political Titles from Leonard Woolf's Library 189

Willoughby, Westell W. *Foreign Rights and Interest in China.* 2 vols. 8vo cloth. (Review slip) The Johns Hopkins Press, Baltimore (USA), 1927. Lib. No. 8245.
Hannay, David. *The Great Chartered Companies.* 8vo cloth, 1926. Lib. No. 6985.
Disraeli, Benjamin. *The Letters of Runnymede.* 8vo cloth. The Abbey Classics. N.d. Lib. No. 1855.
Mann, Thomas. *The Coming Victory of Democracy.* Trans. from the German by A. E. Meyer. 8vo cloth, 1938.
Gouch, G. P. *Nationalism.* 8vo wrappers. "For Review" stamped on half-title page. 1920.
Brailsford, H. N. *Olives of Endless Age: Being a Study of the Distracted World and Its Need of Unity.* 8vo cloth. USA, 1928.

VS, V, p. 9:
Johnston, Sir H. H. *The Opening Up of Africa.* 8vo cloth. (H.U.L.) n.d.
Tagebuch Eines Halbwüch-Sigen Mädchens. 8vo boards Internationalen Psychoanalytischer Verlag. Leipzig 1919. [See under Hug-Hellmuth, Hermine Von, ed.]
Rousseau, J. J. *A Lasting Peace Through the Federations of Europe and the State of War.* Trans. C. E. Vaughan. 8vo cloth. "Presentation copy" embossed on title page. 1917.

VS, V, p. 10:
Morrell, W. P. *British Colonial Policy in The Age of Peel and Russell.* 8vo cloth. (Review slip) 1930.
Poincaré, Raymond. *How France Is Governed.* Trans. Bernard Miall. 8vo cloth, 1915. [Inscription in pencil under title on t.-page: "Ce que Demande la Cité" possibly in the hand of Leonard Woolf.]
Gavit, J. P. *Opium.* 8vo cloth. (Review slip) 1925. Lib. No. 3253.
Nicolson, Harold. *Byron: The Last Journey, April 1823–April 1824.* 8vo cloth, 1924. Lib. No. 5258.
Hamilton, General Sir Ian. *Compulsory Service. A Study of the Question in the Light of Experience.* 8vo cloth, 1911.
Jenks, Edward. *The Government of the British Empire (as at the End of the Year 1917).* 8vo cloth, "With Mr. Murray's Compliments" embossed on title page. 1918.

VS, V, p. 11:
Keith, A. B. *The Constitutional Law of the British Dominions.* 8vo cloth. (Review slip) 1933.
Martin, E. C. *The British West African Settlements 1750–1821. A Study in Local Administration.* 8vo cloth. (Imperial Studies No. 2) 1927. Lib. No. 10233.

Podmore, Frank. *Robert Owen*. A Biography. 2 vols. in 1. 8vo cloth, 1923. Lib. No. 5006.

Anon. *The Arbiter in Council*. 8vo cloth, 1906.

Cook, Sir Edward. *The Life of Florence Nightingale*. 8vo cloth, 1925. Lib. No. 3523.

Simpson, J. Y. *The Saburov Memoirs or Bismarck and Russia. Being Fresh Light on the League of the Three Emperors 1881*. 8vo cloth, 1929. Lib. No. 3119.

Various Jungle Tales. Blackwood. Tales from the Outposts. Vol. 8. 8vo cloth, 1933 [Note in pencil: "B. Southorn from H. B. L. D. 7/6/33"—catalogued under "Blackwood's Magazine."]

Massingham, H. W. *A Selection from the Writings of*. 8vo cloth, 1925. Lib. No. 2082.

VS, V, p. 12:

Maxwell, Herbert. *The Hon. Sir Charles Murray, K. C. B. A Memoir*. 8vo cloth, 1898.

Newton, Lord. *Lord Lyons, A Record of British Diplomacy*. 2 vols. 8vo cloth, 1913.

Alexander, Grand Duke of Russia. *Once a Grand Duke*. 8vo cloth, 1932. Lib. No. 2127?

Lieven, Princess. *The Unpublished Diary and Political Sketches of: Together with some of her Letters*. Edited by Harold Temperley. 8vo cloth, 1925. Lib. No. 2848.

Cobbett, William. *The Progress of a Ploughboy to a Seat in Parliament*. Edited by W. Reitzel. 8vo cloth. The Faber Library, 1933.

Maitland, F. W. *Selected Essays*. Edited by H. D. Hazeltine and Others. 8vo cloth, 1936.

VS, V, p. 13:

Ervine, St. John. *Parnell*. 8vo cloth, 1928. Lib. No. 11366.

Pollock, F. *Frederic William Maitland 1850–1906*. 8vo wrappers. Reprinted from the Proc. Of the British Academy. Vol. 2. n. d. (1905–06).

Smith, A. L. *Frederic William Maitland*. Two Lectures and a bibliography. 8vo boards, 1908.

VS, V, p. 14:

Pemberton, W. B. *Carteret. The Brilliant Failure of the 8th Century*. 8vo cloth, 1936.

Knight, W. S. M. *The Life and Works fo Hugo Grotius*. 8vo cloth. Grotius Society Publication No. 4. 1925. Lib. No. 3179.

Herzen, Alexander. *The Memoirs of*. Translated from Russian by J. D. Duff. 8vo cloth. Yale University Press, U.S.A., 1923. Lib. No. 3362.

Bailey, S. H. *The Framework of International Society.* 8vo cloth, 1932.
Florence, P. S. *Uplift in Economics.* 8vo quarter cloth. (Review slip) 1929. Lib. No. 3768.

VS, V, p. 15:
Angell, Norman. *Must Be War!* 8vo cloth, n.d.
Wells, H. G. *The Way to World Peace.* 8vo wrappers. 1st ed. 1930. Lib. No. 4171.
Spender, Stephen. *Forward to Liberalism.* 8vo cloth. 1st ed., 1937.
Laski, Harold J. *Karl Marx. An Essay.* 8vo wrappers. The Fabian Society, n.d.
Bailey, S. H. *The Anti Drug Campaign. An Experiment in International Control.* 8vo cloth, 1935.
Cosmos [i.e. Butler, Nicholas Murray]. *The Basis of Durable Peace.* 8vo cloth. New York, 1917.

VS, V, p. 16:
Zimmern, Alfred. *The Third British Empire. Being a Course of Lectures delivered at Columbia University, New York.* 8vo cloth. (Review slip) 1926. Lib. No. 6766.
Dawson, Thomas. *The Law of the Press.* 8vo cloth, 1927. Lib. No. 8074.
Woodward, E. L. *Three Studies in European Conservatism: Metternich, Guizot, The Catholic Church in the 19th Century.* 8vo cloth, 1929.
Laski, Harold J. *A Grammar of Politics.* 8vo cloth. (Review slip) 1938.
Hibbert, W. N. *International Private Law. Or the Conflict of Law.* 8vo cloth, "For Review" stamped on title page. 1918.

VS, V, p. 17:
Keith, A. B., ed. *Speech, and Documents on the British Dominions 9118-1931.* 8vo cloth. Worlds Classics, n.d.
Mowat, R. B. *Europe in the Age of Napoleon.* 8vo wrappers. Benn's 6d. Library. 1927. Lib. No. 11346.
Shaw, Bernard. *The Commonsense of Municipal Trading.* 8vo wrappers. 2nd edition. Fabian Socialist Series No. 5. 1912.
Webb, Mrs. Sidney and Miss B. L. Hutchins. *Socialism and National Minimum.* 8vo wrappers Fabian Socialist Series No. 6. 1909.
Lemonon, Ernest. *L'Europe et lat Politique Britannique 1882-1912.* 8vo wrappers Paris 1912.
Duncan, Ronald. *The Complete Pacifist.* 8vo wrappers, 1937.

VS, V, p. 19:
Angell, Norman. *The British Revolution and American Democracy. An Interpretation of British Labour Programmes.* 8vo cloth. New York, 1919.

VS, V, p. 20:
Smith, J. W. *The Law of Banker and Customer.* Revised by R. Borregaard. 8vo cloth (Review Slip) 1930. Lib. No. 2481.
Voltaire. *The Age of Louis XIV.* Translated by M. P. Pollack. 8vo cloth. Everyman Library. N.d.
Laski, H. J. *Political Thought in England from Locke to Bentham.* 8vo cloth. H.U.L., 1925.

VS, V, p. 22:
Dickinson, G. Lowes, ed. *Points of View. A Series of Broadcast Addresses by H. G. Wells, J. B. S. Haldane and Others.* 8vo cloth, 1930.
Curtis, L. *The Problem of the Commonwealth.* 8vo wrappers, 1916 [London: Macmillan].

VS, V, p. 23:
Abbott, G. F. *Greece and the Allies 1914–1922.* 8vo cloth, "presentation copy" stamped on title page. 1922. Lib. No. 31.
Temperley, Harold. *The Victorian Age in Politics, War and Diplomacy.* 8vo wrappers. (Review slip) 1928. Lib. No. 13603.
Engels: On Capital. Trans. L. E. Mins. 8vo cloth, n.d.

VS, V, p. 24:
Gueshoff, I. E. *The Balkan League.* 8vo cloth (Review Slip), 1915.
Jones, T. J. Editor. *Education in East Africa.* 4to cloth (Review Slip) U.S.A. N.d. (c. 1925).
Russell, Bertrand. *Power and New Social Analysis.* 8vo cloth. 1st edition, 1938 [WSU note in pencil: "Extensive annotation by Leonard Woolf"].
Olmstad, A. T. *History of Assyria.* 8vo cloth (Review Slip) 1928. Lib. No. 4326.
Howard-Ellis, C. *The Origin, Structure and Working of the League of Nations.* 8vo cloth (Review Slip) 1928. Lib. No. 14057.

VS, V, p. 25:
Stone, H. A., D. K. Price, and K. H. Stone. *City Manager Government in Nine Cities.* 8vo cloth. Published for the Committee on Public Administration of the Social Science Research Council. Chicago, 1940.
Macaulay, Lord. *Marginal Notes.* Selected and Arranged by Sir George Otto Trevelyan. 8vo cloth, 1907.
Howland, C. P. *Survey of American Foreign Relations 1928.* 8vo cloth (Review Slip) U. S. A., 1928. Lib. No. 1005.
Phillipson, Coleman. *Termination of War and Treaties of Peace.* 8vo cloth. "Presentation copy" embossed on title page. 1916. Lib. No. 1593. [WSU note: "Review slip."]

Wickwar, W. H. *The Struggle for the Freedom of the Press. 1819–1832.* 8vo cloth (Review Slip), 1938.

VS, V, p. 26:
Simon, Kathleen. *Slavery.* 8vo cloth. People's Library Edition, 1930.
Gettell, R. G. *History of Political Thought.* 8vo cloth. U.S.A. (Review Slip), 1924. Lib. No. 7379.

VS, V, p. 27:
Oldham, J. H. *White and Black in Africa. A Critical Examination the Rhodes Lectures of General Smuts.* 8vo wrappers (Review Slip), 1930. Lib. No. 4212.
Potter, Beatrice. *The Co-Operative Movement in Great Britain.* 8vo cloth, 1907. (Beatrice Potter later became Mrs. Sidney Webb). [A WSU note in pencil: "Autograph of J. F. Williams—a few notes in text. Address rubber stamped on front end paper: 'Moore Place, Stanford-Le-Hope, Essex.'"]
Haldane, J. B. S. *The Marxist Philosophy and the Sciences.* 8vo cloth. 1st ed. 1938.
Caillaux, Joseph. *Agadir. Ma Politique Exterieure.* 8vo wrappers. Paris, 1919.

VS, V, p. 28:
Harrison, Maire. *The Stolen Lands: A Study in Alsace-Lorraine.* 8vo cloth, 1918.
Beyens, Le Baron. *La Question Africaine.* 8vo wrappers Bruxelles et Paris, 1918.

VS, V, p. 29:
Buxton, Leland. *The Black Sheep of the Balkans.* 8vo cloth, 1920.
Eveleigh, William. *South-West Africa.* 8vo cloth "Presentation copy" embossed on title page, 1915.
Barnes, L. *Empire or Democracy. A Study of the Colonial Question.* 8vo cloth, 1939.
Mill, John Stuart. *The Autobiography of:* 8vo cloth. World Classics, 1924. Lib. No. 1298.

VS, V, p. 30:
Maxwell, Herbert. *The Life and Letters of George William Frederick 4th Earl of Clarendon.* 2 vols. 8vo cloth, 1913. [Note in pencil: "correction in pencil in text of Vol. 1. p. 296 in an unknown hand / both vols. have remains of a public library seal inside the front cover."]
Ponsonby, Arthur. *Falsehood in War Time.* 8vo wrappers, 1928. Lib. No. 12776.

VS, V, p. 31:
Hinde, H. *Some Problems of East Africa.* 8vo wrappers (Review Slip), 1926. Lib. No. 4531.

Hurgronje, Dr. C. Snouck. *The Holy War "Made in Germany."* 8vo cloth. New York, 1915.

VS, V, p. 32:
Lowe, B. E. *The International Protection of Labour.* 8vo cloth new edition, New York, 1935.
Callieres, Francois de. *The Practice of Diplomacy.* Being an English rendering of "De la maniere de Negocier avec les souverains." Presented with an introduction by A. F. Whyte. 8vo cloth "For Review" stamped on title page. 1919.

VS, V, p. 33:
Willoughby, W. W. *Opium as an International Problem. The Geneva Conferences.* 8vo cloth. Baltimore: Johns Hopkins University Press, 1925. Lib. No. 2615.

VS, V, p. 34:
Trotter, W. *Instincts of the Herd in Peace and War.* 8vo cloth, 1916. "Presentation copy" embossed on title page.

VS, V, p. 35:
Chamier, J. Daniel. *Fabulous Monster* (A Life of Kaiser Wilhelm 2nd). 8vo cloth (Review Slip), 1934.

VS, V, p. 36:
Lothian, Lord, C. E. M. Joad, et al. *Studies in Federal Planning.* Ed. by Patrick Ransom. 8vo cloth (Review Slip), 1943.
"Vigilantes" Inquest on Peace: An Analysis of the National Governments Foreign Policy. 8vo cloth 1935. ["Fabian Library / 11, Dartmouth Street, S. W. 1" / stamped inside front cover; with WSU notes in pencil in catalog as follows: "shelved under Zilliacus, Konni / {per?} p. 157. Fabian Library number 'U. 124a.'"]
Brailsford, H. N., Leonard Woolf, et al. *Fabian Colonial Essays.* Edited by Rita Hinden. 8vo cloth, 1945.
Mayer, J. P. *Max Weber and German Politics. A Study in Political Sociology.* 8vo cloth (Review Slip) 1944.
Huxley, Julian, H. J. Laski, et al. *When Hostilities Cease.* Papers on Relief and Reconstruction prepared for the Fabian Society with an Introduction by Leonard Woolf. 8vo cloth, 1943.
Laski, Harold J. *Reflections on the Revolution of Our Time.* 8vo cloth "With the Author's Compliments" slip. 1st ed., 1943.
Barker, R. E. *The Days are Long.* 8vo cloth. 1st ed. 1959. [Inscription in ink on front end paper: "This copy for Ian M. Parsons, who may recall something of the improbable manner in which the author chose to tell this tale and will

probably be more confused than ever by the time he has read it.... With all good wishes / Ronald Barker / 21st May 1959"]

VS, V, p. 37:
Brailsford, H. N. *Our Settlement with Germany.* 8vo wrappers. Penguin Special, 1944.
Brimble, L. J. F. and F. J. May. *Social Studies of World Citizenship. A Sociological Approach to Education.* 8vo cloth (Review Slip) 1943.
Childs, J. L. and G. S. Counts. *America Ratio and the Communist Party in the Post-War World.* 8vo cloth. New York, 1943. [Stamped inside front cover—"American Library, / London OW. 1." Which is written in ink—"Review copy cancelled"]
Vinogradoff, Paul. *Self-Government in Russia.* 8vo cloth. "Presentation copy" embossed on title page. 1915.

VS, V, p. 38:
Riddell, W. R. *The Constitution of Canada in Its History and Practical Working.* 8vo cloth. Yale University Press U.S.A. 1917.
Toynbee, A. J. (ed.). *British Commonwealth Relations.* 8vo cloth, 1934. [Note in pencil: "catalogued under Commonwealth Relations Conference."]
Mackay, Robert A. *Changes in the Legal Structure of the British Commonwealth of Nations.* 8vo wrappers. International Conciliation No. 272. September 1931.
Tallentyre, S. G. *The Friends of Voltaire.* 8vo cloth, 1906. [WSU notation: "pseud. catalogued under Hall, Evelyn Beatrice."]

VS, V, p. 39:
Mathieson, William Law. *Great Britain and the Slave Trade 1839-1865.* 8vo cloth, 1929. Lib. No. 2883.
Butler, A. J. *The Arab Conquest of Egypt and the Last Thirty Years of The Roman Domination.* 8vo cloth, 1902. [Inscription in ink on front end paper: "Herbert A. Hills / Ramb / 25 Dec. 1903."]
Nystrom, Anton. *Before, During and After 1914.* translated by H. G. de Walterstroff with an introduction by Edmund Gosse. 8vo cloth "Presentation copy" embossed on title page, 1915 [WSU note in pencil: "Review slip."]
Bury, J. P. T. *Gambetta and the National Defence, and Republican Dictatorship in France.* 8vo 1936.

VS, V, p. 40:
Fitzmaurice, Lord Edmond. *The Life of Granville, George Leveson Gower, Second Earl Granville K. G., 1815-1891.* 2 vols. 8vo cloth, 1905.

Lutz, Hermann. *Lord Grey and the World War.* Translated by E. W. Dickens. 8vo cloth, 1928. Lib. No. 11971.

Barbier, Edmund-Jean-Francois. *Chronique de la Regence et du Regne de Louis XV. 1718–1763 ou Journal de Barbier.* 8 vols. wrappers. Premiere Edition Complete, Paris, 1857.

VS, V, p. 41:

Trevelyan, G. M. *England under the Stuarts.* 8vo cloth. A History of England series. Edited by C. W. C. Oman, 1904.

Feiling, K. *A History of the Tory Party 1640–1714.* 8vo cloth (Review Slip), 1924. Lib. No. 6320.

Various Authors. *These Eventful Years. The 20th Century in the Making as told by Various of its Makers.* 2 vols. 8vo cloth. Encyclopaedia Britannica Co. 1924. [WSU note in pencil: "catalogued by title."]

Williams, Aneurin. *Co-Partnership and Profit Sharing.* 8vo cloth. H. U. L. 1913.

Voltaire. *Lettres Choisies.* 8vo wrappers. Classiques Larousse. Paris, 1937.

VS, V, p. 42:

Giles, Herbert A. *Chaos in China.* 8vo wrappers. Cambridge, 1924.

Tawney, R. H. *Religion and the Rise of Capitalism. A Historical Study.* Holland Memorial Lectures 1922. 8vo cloth, 1929. Lib. No. 2006.

Smith, Randolph Wellford. *Benighted Mexico.* 8vo cloth "Review Copy with John Lane's Compliments" embossed on title page. 1917.

Guenther, H. F. K. *The Racial Elements of European History.* Translated by G. C. Wheeler. 8vo cloth (Review Slip), 1927. Lib. No. 10994.

Sanger, C. P. and H. T. J. Norton. *England's Guarantee to Belgium and Luxemburg with the full text of the treaties.* 8vo cloth. 1915 [WSU note in pencil: "Review Slip."]

Anon. *The Historical Relations Between Japan and Saghalier.* 8vo wrappers (Review Slip), Tokyo, 1923.

VS, V, p. 43:

Various Authors. *Boxer Indemnity and Chinese Education.* (The Question on the Remission and Allocation of the British Share). 8vo wrappers (Review Slip) issued by the Chinese Association for the Promotion of Education, 1924. Lib. No. 5887

Pamphlets on Chinese Questions. Published for the Chinese National Defence League in Europe. 8vo wrappers. / No. 2 *The Relations Between China and Japan During the Last 25 Years* (Review Slip) 1919. / No. 3 Wang, Chung-Hui. *Law Reform in China* (Review Slip) 1919. [Note in pencil: "see Wang, Chung-Hui 1882–1952"] / No. 4 *The World Peace and Chinese Tariff Autonomy.* 1919 / No. 6 *China's Position in International Finance* (2 copies), n.d.

Strickland, C. F. *Co-Operation for Africa*. 8vo wrappers. Reprinted from "Africa Vol. 6 No. 1" n.d. (c. 1930).

Williamson, James A. *A Short History of British Expansion*. 8vo cloth "Presentation copy" stamped on the title page (Review Slip), 1922.

VS, V, p. 44:

Various Authors. *Readings in Recent Political Philosophy*. Selected, abridged and edited by Margaret Spahr. 8vo cloth New York, 1935. [WSU note in pencil: "catalogued under Spahr, Margaret."]

Summary of the Fulfilment of the First Five-Year Plan for the Development of the National Economy of the U.S.S.R. 8vo wrappers. State Planning Commission, Moscow, 1933. [WSU note in pencil: "catalogued under Russia (1923— USSR) Gosudarstvennaia Planovaia Komistia."]

Fay, S. B. *The Origins of the World War*. 2 vols. 8vo cloth. New York, 1929. Lib. No. 981.

White, Freda. *Mandates*. Foreword by Frederick Lugard. Published under the auspices of the League of Nations Union. 8vo cloth. 1926. Lib. No. 5142.

Cromer, The Earl of. *Abbas II*. 8vo cloth, 1915.

VS, V, p. 45:

Boswell, A. B. *Poland and the Poles*. 8vo cloth, 1919. "Presentation copy" stamped on title page.

Burns, C. D., Bertrand Russell, and G. D. H. Cole. *X—Symposium: The Nature of the State in View of its External Relations*. 8vo wrappers. Reprinted from the proceedings of the Aristotelian Soc., 1916

Steed, H. Wickham. *The Hapsburg Monarchy*. 8vo cloth. 2nd Ed. 1914.

Morel, E. D. *Ten Years of Secret Diplomacy. An Unheeded Warning* (Being a reprint of Morocco in Diplomacy.) 8vo wrappers, 1915. [Inscription in ink on front cover "International Agreements Committee."]

Fay, C. R. *The Corn Laws and Social England*. 8vo cloth, 1932.

VS, V, p. 46:

Kirk, John. *The Economic Aspects of Native Segregation in South Africa*. 8vo cloth. 1929.

Milton, John. *A Brief History of Moscovia and Other Less-Known Countries Lying Eastward of Russia as far away as Cathay*. With an introduction by Prince D. S. Mirsky. 4to buckram. The Blackamore Press, 1929. Lib. No. 3597.

Jeudwine, J. W. *Studies in Empire and Trade*. 8vo cloth. 1923. Lib. No. 787.

Vallentin, Antonia. *Stresemann*. Translated by Eric Sutton. Foreward by Prof. Albert Einstein. 8vo cloth. 1931.

Clementy, Sir Cecil. *A Constitutional History of British Guiana*. 8vo cloth, 1937.

Mills, Lennox A. *Ceylon under British Rule 1795–1932*. With an account of the East India Company's embassies to Kandy 1762–1795. 8vo cloth, 1933.

VS, V, p. 47:
Strachey, Ray. *A Quaker Grandmother Hanna Whitall Smith*. 8vo quarto cloth. U.S.A., 1914.
Gathorne-Hardy, G. M. *A Short History of International Affairs 1920–1934*. 8vo cloth, 1934. [WSU note in pencil: "Leonard Woolf's autograph on front end paper."]
Lenin, V. I., and Joseph Stalin. *The Russian Revolution. Writings and speeches from the February Revolution to the October Revolution 1917*. 8vo cloth, 1938.
Conwell-Evans, T. P. *The League Council in Action*. A study of the methods employed by the Council of the League of Nations to prevent War and to settle International Disputes. 8vo cloth, 1929. Lib. No. 3785.

VS, V, p. 48:
Furnivall, J. S. *Netherlands India. A Study of Plural Economy*. 8vo cloth, 1939.
McPhee, Allan. *The Economic Revolution in British West Africa*. 8vo cloth, 1926. Lib. No. 6843.
Strachey, Celia and J. G. Werner. *Fascist Germany Explains*. 8vo wrappers, 1934.
Humphrys, I. H. *A Short History of the French Revolution*. 8vo cloth, 1924. Lib. No. 5346.
Koo, V. K. Wellington and Cheng-Ting T. Wang. *China and the League of Nations*. 8vo wrappers Phamphlets on Chinese Questions, n.d.

VS, V, p. 49:
Leys, Norman. *Kenya*. With an Introduction by Prof. Gilbert Murray. 8vo cloth, 1924.
Holland, Bernard. *Imperium et Libertas. A Study in History and Politics*. 8vo cloth, 1901.
Anon. *Take Over the War Industries: A Reasoned Case for Public Ownership*. 8vo wrappers. Fabian Society Socialist Propaganda Committee. N.d. (c. 1941).

VS, V, p. 51:
Keltie, Sir John S. and M. Epstein, eds. *The Statesmen's Year Book for the Year 1919*. 8vo cloth, 1919. Lib. No. 1081. [WSU note in pencil: "1927 ed. came with M. H. JA/51/57/1927."]

VS, V, p. 52:
Bosanquet, Bernard. *The Philosophical Theory of the State*. 8vo cloth. "Presentation copy" embossed on title page and Review Slip. 3rd ed., 1920.
Wheeler-Bennett, J. W. *The Disarmament Deadlock*. 8vo cloth. Review Slip. 1934.

VS, V, p. 53:

Harris, John H. *Slavery or "Sacred Trust"?* Preface by Prof. Gilbert Murray. 8vo cloth, 1926.

Petrunkevitch, A., S. Northrup Harper, and F. A. Golder. *The Russian Revolution. The Jugo-Slav Movement* by R. J. Kerner. 8vo cloth. Harvard University Press, 1918.

Staley, Eugene. *Foreign Investment and War.* 8vo wrappers. Public Policy Pamphlet No. 18. University of Chicago Press, 1935. [Inscription: "With the Author's compliments" stamped on front cover.]

McNair, A. D. *Collective Security.* An inaugural lecture. 8vo wrappers, 1936.

Stalin, Joseph. *Three Speeches.* 8vo wrappers, 1935.

Temple, C. L. *Native Races and Their Rulers.* Sketches and studies of official life and administrative problems in Nigeria. 8vo boards. Cape Town, 1918.

VS, V, p. 54:

Pooley, A. M. *Japan's Foreign Policies.* 8vo cloth. Review Slip addressed to the New Statesman. 1st ed. 1920.

Ilbert, Sir Courtenay. *Parliament. It's History, Constitution and Practice.* 8vo cloth. H.U.L. n. d.

Price, M. P. *Germany in Transition.* 8vo cloth. Labour Publishing Co. Ltd., 1923. Lib. No. 4669.

U. S. S. R. Handbook. 8vo cloth, 1936.

Macaulay, Thomas Babington. *Critical and Historical Essays.* 2 vols. 8vo cloth. Everyman Library, 1907.

VS, V, p. 55:

Hirst, Francis W. *The Stock Exchange.* A short study of Investment and Speculation. 8vo cloth. H. U. L. n. d. (1911).

Anon. *Mr. Dooley in Peace and War.* 8vo cloth. 1899. [Inscription in ink on front end paper: "Sydney Turner" (Saxon Sydney Turner)] [WSU note in pencil: "shelved under Dunne, Finley Peter."]

VS, V, p. 57:

Various Authors. *Why the German Republic Fell and Other Studies of the Causes and Consequences of Economic Inequality.* Ed. by A. W. Madsen. 8vo wrappers (Review Slip). The Hogarth Press, 1941.

VS, V, p. 58:

Zimmern, Alfred. *The League of Natiions and the Rule of Law 1918–1935.* 8vo cloth (Review Slip), 1939.

Kennedy, W. P. M. and H. J. Schlosberg. *The Law and Custom of South African Constitution.* 8vo cloth, 1935.

Wheeler-Bennett, J. W. and F. E. Langermann. *Information on the Problem of Security (1917–1926)*. Introduction by H. A. L. Fisher. 8vo cloth, 1927. Lib. No. 7669.

Nearing, S. and J. Freeman. *Dollar Diplomacy. A Study in American Imperialism*. 8vo cloth, 1926. [Note in pencil: "Review Slip."] Lib. No. 5117.

Toynbee, A. J. *Nationality and the War*. 8vo cloth, 1915.

Paine, Thomas. *Political Writings During The American and French Revolutions*. Ed. by Hypatia Bradlough [sic] Bonner. 8vo wrappers. 1909. [Noted in pencil correction of spelling: "Bradlaugh"]

Angell, Norman. *The Great Illusion. A Study of the Relation of Military Power to National Advantage*. 8vo cloth, 1913.

VS, V, p. 59:

Laski, Harold J. *An Introduction to Politics*. 8vo cloth. 1st ed. 1931.

Kuczynski, R. R. *Colonial Population*. 8vo cloth. Published under the Royal Institute of National Affairs. 8vo cloth, 1937.

Lippmann, Walter. *Public Opinion*. 8vo cloth. 1st ed. 1922.

Pollard, A. F. *The Evolution of Parliament*. 8vo cloth. 2nd ed. revised. (Review Slip), 1926. Lib. No. 4568.

Fachiri, A. P. *The Permanent Court of International Justice: It's [sic] Constitution Procedure and Work*. 8vo cloth. 1st ed. 1925. Lib. No. 2514.

Webb, Sidney and Beatrice. *A Constitution for the Socialist Commonwealth of Great Britain*. 8vo cloth. 1st ed. 1920.

Lindley, M. F. *The Acquisition and Government of Backward Territory in International Law, Being a Treatise on the Law and Practice Relating to Colonial Expansion*. 8vo cloth (Review Slip). 1st ed. 1926. Lib. No. 5180.

Leang-Li, T'ang. *The Foundations of Modern China*. 8vo cloth, 1928. Lib. No. 14541.

Deslinieres, Lucien. *La France Nord-Africaine. Etude critique de la Colonization Anarchique Pratiquee Jusqu'a ce Jour*. 8vo wrappers. Paris, 1920.

VS, V, p. 60:

Dimitrov, G. *The People's Front Against Fascism and War*. 8vo wrappers, 1937.

Marx, Karl. *The Eighteenth Brumaire of Louis Bonaparte*. Trans. E. and C. Paul. 8vo wrappers. 1st English ed., 1926.

Coupland, R. *Kirk on the Zambesi: A Chapter of African History*. 8vo cloth. 1st ed., 1928. Library No. 205.

Mowat, R. B. *Select Treatise and Documents to Illustrate the Development of the Modern European States-System*. 8vo boards. Oxford pamphlets 1914–15 "Presentation Copy" embossed on title page. (Review sl;ip), 1915.

Vinacke, H. M. *Problems of Industrial Development in China: A Preliminary Study*. 8vo cloth. Princeton University Press, 1926.

Morel, E. D. *The Black Man's Burden*. 8vo boards (Review slip). The National Labour Press Ltd., 1920.

Breasted, J. H. *The Conquest of Civilization*. 8vo cloth. New York, 1926. Library No. 6761.

Archer, William. *The Thirteen Days July 23–August 4, 1914: A Chronicle and Interpretation*. 8vo cloth. "Presentation copy" embossed on title page. 1915.

VS, V, p. 61:

Thompson, Edward. *A History of India*. 8vo wrappers. Benn's 6d. Library, 1927. Library No. 10858.

Morel, E. D. *Red Rubber: The Story of the Rubber Slave Trade which flourished on the Congo for 20 years 1890–1910*. 8vo wrappers. New and revised ed. The National Labour Press Ltd., 1919.

Stanley, H. J. (Governor of Ceylon) et al. *Ceylon: Correspondence regarding the Constitution of Ceylon*. 8vo wrappers. Government White Paper. 1929. [WSU note: "catalogued under Great Britain, Colonial; Office."]

Olivier, Lord. *Imperial Trusteeship*. 8vo wrappers Fabian Tract No. 230. The Fabian Society, 1929.

Marburg, Theodore. *League of Nations: A Chapter in the History of the Movement*. 8vo boards. New York, 1917. Two additional letters inserted. [WSU pencil notation: "i.e. part of text" in reference to the letters.]

VS, V, p. 62:

Trevelyan, G. M. *The Two-Party System in English Political History: The Romanes Lecture*. 8vo wrappers. Oxford, 1926. Library No. 5297.

Clifford, Sir Hugh. *German Colonies: A Plea for the Native Races*. 8vo limp cloth. (Review slip), 1918.

Hearnshaw, F. J. C. *Conservatism in England: An Analytical, Historical and Political Survey*. 8vo cloth, 1933.

Hodgson, Margaret L. and W. G. Ballinger. *Britain in Southern Africa*. No. 2. Bechuanaland Protectorate. 8vo wrappers, n.d. (c. 1933).

Schneider, H. W. *Making the Fascist State*. 8vo cloth. New York, 1928. Library No. 838.

VS, V, p. 63:

Cramb, J. A. *Germany and England*. Preface by A. C. Bradley. 8vo cloth, 1914.

VS, V, p. 64:

Lucas, Sir. Charles. *The Story of the Empire*. 8vo cloth. "Review copy" embossed on title page. The British Empire Survey, 1924. Library No. 6193.

Angell, Norman. *The Foundations of International Polity.* 8vo cloth. Printed slip "With the Author's compliments." 1st ed. 1924. [Inscribed in ink on front endpaper: "Sidney Webb."]

Hill, R.L. *Toryism and the People 1832–1846.* 8vo cloth, 1929. Library No. 1262.

Various authors. *The Indian National Congress.* 8vo cloth (Review slip), 2nd ed. Madras n.d. (c. 1917). [WSU note: "catalogued by title."]

Flenley, R., and W. N. Weech. *World History: The Growth of Western Civilization.* 8vo cloth, 1936.

Redfern, Percy. *The New History of the C.W.S.* 8vo cloth, 1938.

Trevelyan, G. M. *Lord Grey of the Reform Bill, Being the Life of Charles, Second Earl Grey.* 8vo cloth. 2nd ed., 1929.

Allen, Clifford. *Labour's Future at Stake.* 8vo boards, 1932.

Stone, Julius. *International Guarantees of Minority Rights: Procedure of the Council of the League of Nations in Theory and Practice.* 8vo cloth, 1932.

Trowbridge, E. D. *Mexico Today and Tomorrow.* 8vo cloth. "Presentation copy" embossed on the title page. (Review slip). New York, 1919. [WSU notation: "postcard advertisement for the Globe-Werniche Co., Cincinnati."]

VS, V, p. 65:

Various authors. *Soviet Union 1936.* Ed. A. Fineberg. 8vo cloth, 1936. [WSU note: "catalogued by title."]

Boissier, Leopold, B. Mirkine-Guetzevitch, and J. LaFerriere. *Annuaire Interparlementaire. Premiere Annee.* 8vo cloth. Paris, 1931.

Earle, Edward Mead. *Turkey, the Great Powers, and the Bagdad Railway: A Study in Imperialism.* 8vo cloth. New York, 1923.

Hawtrey, R. G. *The Gold Standard in Theory and Practice.* 8vo cloth. 4th ed., 1939.

Keith, A. B. *Responsible Government in the Dominions.* 2 vols. 2nd ed. (revised to 1927). 8vo cloth, 1928. Library No. 11421.

VS, V, p. 66:

Perrin, Alice. *The Anglo-Indians.* 8vo wrappers. Tauchnitz edition. Leipzig, 1912.

Kruse, Vinding. *The Community of the Future.* 8vo cloth (Review slip). Copenhagen, 1950.

Clark, Grenville, and Louis B. Sohn. *World Peace through World Law.* 8vo cloth. 2nd ed. (rev.) Harvard University Press (Review slip), 1960.

VS, V, p. 67:

Elton, Godfrey. *Towards the New Labour Party.* 8vo boards (review slip), 1932.

Mill, John Stuart. *On Liberty.* 8vo cloth. New Universal Library. N.d.

Adair, E. R. *The Exterritoriality of Ambassadors in the 16th and 17th Centuries.* 8vo cloth. (Review slip), 1929. [WSU pencil note: "Woolfs' lib # 2667."]

Macartney, C. A. *National States and National Minorities*. 8vo cloth. Royal Institute of International Affairs, 1934.
Various authors. *Problems of a Socialist Government*. With preface by Sir Stafford Cripps. 8vo cloth, 1933.
Gooch, G. P. *Recent Revelations of European Democracy*. 8vo cloth. 4th impression with supplementary chapter on the revelations of 1928–29. 1930. Library No. 4137.
Hazen, Charles Downer. *Fifty Years of Europe 1870–1919*. 8vo cloth. "Presentation copy" embossed on the title page. 1919.

VS, V, p. 68:
Smith, Sir Frederick. *International Law*. 5th ed. (rev.). Ed. Coleman Phillipson. 8vo cloth, 1918. [WSU notation: "catalogued under Birkenhead, Frederick Edwin Smith."]
Strachey, Ray, and Oliver Strachey. *Keigwin's Rebellion (1683–4): An Episode in the History of Bombay*. 8vo cloth. Oxford Historical and Literary Studies, 1916.
Dewey, A. Gordon. *The Dominions of Diplomacy: The Canadian Contribution*. 2 vols. 8vo cloth. 1929.
Finlay, George. *History of the Byzantine Empire from DCCXVI to MLVII*. 8vo cloth. Everyman Library, 1906.
Fletcher, C. Brunsdon. *The New Pacific: British Policy and German Aims*. Preface by Viscount Bryce and foreword by W. M. Hughes. 8vo cloth. "Presentation copy" embossed on title page. (Review slip), 1917.
Pease, Edward R. *The History of the Fabian Society*. 2nd ed. with supplementary chapter. 8vo cloth, 1925.
Fabre-Luce, Alfred. *The Limitations of Victory*. Trans. Constance Vesey. 8vo cloth, 1926.
Wollstonecraft, Mary, and John Stuart Mill. *The Rights of Women and the Subjection of Women*. 8vo. Everyman Library, 1929. Library No. 759.

VS, V, p. 69:
Ewart, John S. *The Roots and Causes of the War (1914–1918)*. 2 vols. 8vo cloth. "With the publisher's compliments" stamped on the title page. (Review slip), 1925.
Stieve, Friedrich. *Isvolsky and the World War: Based on Documents Recently Published by the German Foreign Office*. Trans. E. W. Dickes. 8vo cloth, 1926. Library No. 4189.
Riches, Cromwell A. *The Unanimity Rule and the League of Nations*. 8vo cloth. (Review slip). Baltimore, 1933.
Denny, Ludwell. *We Fight for Oil*. 8vo cloth. (Review slip). New York, 1928.
La Motte, Ellen M. *The Ethics of Opium*. 8vo cloth. New York, 1924.

Hobbes, Thomas. *Behemoth or The Long Parliament.* Ed. Ferdinand Tonnies. 8vo wrappers, 1889. [WSU pencil notation: insertion: A review of Hobbes' *The Elements of Law, Natural and Politic,* ed. by F. Tonnies."]

VS, V, p. 70:
Anon. *Relations between China and Japan during the Last 25 Years.* 8vo wrappers. (Review slip). Published for the China National Defence League in Europe, 1919.
Burns, C. D. *A Short History of International Intercourse.* 8vo cloth, 1924. Library No. 5444.
Mitchison, G. R. *The First Workers Government; or New Times for Henry Dubb.* Introduction by Sir Stafford Cripps. 8vo cloth, 1934.
Arnold-Forster, W. *The Victory of Reason: A Pamphlet on Arbitration with a Letter by Benjamin Franklin.* 8vo cloth. Published by Leonard and Virginia Woolf at the Hogarth Press, 1926.
Pribram, A. F. *The Secret Treaties of Austria and Hungary 1879–1914. Texts of the Treaties and Agreements,* with translations by D. P. Myers & J. C. D'Arcy Paul. 2 vols. 8vo cloth. Harvard University Press, 1920 [vol. 1] and 1921 [vol. 2]. [Volume 2 bears publisher's review slip.]

VS, V, p. 71:
Bevan, Edwyn. *The World of Greece and Rome.* 8vo wrappers. Benn's 6d. Library. (Review slip), 1927. [WSU note: "—lists also Catholicism; Weather; Oliver Cromwell; Life of Christ; Russian Lit. (Benn Pubs.)."]
Seton-Watson, R. W. *Sarajevo: A Study into the Origins of the Great War.* 8vo cloth. (Review slip), 1925. Library No. 5280.
Wheeler-Bennett, J. W., and Maurice Fanshawe. *Information on the World Court 1918–1928.* With an introduction by Sir Cecil Hurst. 8vo cloth, 1929. Library No. 3098.
Livy, Titus. *The History of Rome.* Vols. 5 and 6 only. 8vo cloth. Everyman Library, n.d. Liubrary No. 7491.

VS, V, p. 72:
Moneypenny, W. F., and G. E. Buckle. *The Life of Benjamin Disraeli, Earl of Beaconsfield.* New and revised ed. in 2 vols. vol. 1: *1804–1859.* 8vo cloth, 1929. Library No. 2703. [See vol. 2 in the Monks House library.]
Oppenheim, L. *International Law: A Treatise in 2 volumes.* Vol. 1: *Peace.* 4th ed. Ed. A. D. McNair. Vol. 2: *Disputes, War and Neutrality.* 5th ed. Ed. H. Lauterpatch. 8vo cloth, 1928 and 1935. [WSU notation: "rev. by L.W. P.Q. A.-J. '36 p. 289."]

Keeton, G. W. *The Development of Extraterritoriality in China.* Vol. 1 (ex 2 vols.). 8vo cloth, 1928. Library No. 14427. [WSU note: "advertisement postcard inserted."]

Stowell, E. C., and H. F. Munro. *International Cases: Arbitrations and Incidents Illustrative of International Law as Practiced in Independent States.* Vol. 1: *Peace.* 8vo. cloth, 1916.

VS, V, p. 73:

Garvey, Marcus. The *Philosophy and Opinions of Marcus Garvey: Or, Africa for the Africans.* Compiled by Amy Jacques-Garvey. Vol. 2 only. 8vo cloth. U.S.A., 1926.

Debidour, A. *Histoire Diplomatique de l'Europe: Depuis le Congres de Berlin Jusqu'à nos Jours.* 2 vols. 8vo wrappers. 2nd ed. Paris, 1917–18.

Hanotaux, Gabriel. *Le Government de M. Thiers 1870–1873.* Vol. 2 only. New edition. 8vo wrappers. Paris, 1925. Library No. 2301.

Halevy, Elie. *Histoire du Peuple Anglais au XIX Siecle: Epilogue 1895–1914.* Vol. 1 [of this *Epilogue*]: *Les Imperialistes au Pouvoir (1895–1905)* (ex 9/<4> vols.). [WSU correction in pencil.] 8vo wrappers. Paris, 1926. Library No. 7164.

VS, V, p. 74:

Halevy, Elie. *A History of the English People in 1815.* Vol. 2: *Economic Life.* 8vo wrappers. Pelican Books, 1937.

Cory, G. E. *The Rise of South Africa: A History of the Origin of South African Colonization and Its Development towards the East from the Earliest Times to 1857.* Vol. 3 (ex 4 vols.). 8vo cloth. (Review slip), 1919.

Annual Register of World Events: A Review of Public Events at Home and Abroad for the Year 1928. Ed. M. Epstein. New series. 8vo cloth, 1929. Library No. 1777.

Trevelyan, G. M. *England under Queen Anne.* Vol. 1: *Blenheim.* Vol. 3: *The Peace and the Protestant Succession.* (ex 3 vols.) 8vo buckram. (Review slip [in vol. 3]), 1930 and 1934.

VS, V, p. 75:

Constitutional Year Book 1939. 53rd issue. 8vo cloth, 1939.

Cobbett, William. *Cobbetts Political Register.* Vols. 5, 7, 13, 14, 15, 20, and 22. 8vo half calf, 1804–1812.

Toynbee, A. J. *Survey of International Affairs.* 8vo cloth. The following items: 1920–23 [Library No. 2518], 1924 [Library No. 4662], 1925 [vol. 2 and Supplementary vol. Library No. 12225], 1927 [Library No. 7968], 1928, 1929 [Library No. 7204], 1931, 1932, 1934 [bearing notes on back end papers in hand of Leonard Woolf], 1935 [Vol. 2; see Monks House library for Vol. 1],

1936 [notes at end in hand of L.W.], 1937 [Part I—with notes at end in hand of L.W.], 1937 [Part II].

Documents on International Affairs. Various editors. 1928, 1929, 1931, 1935 (Part I). 8vo cloth. Library No. 1929 issue 7205. [WSU notation: "Lib. No 3948 on title page of vol. for 1928."]

Various authors. *L'Union des Associations Internationales.* 8vo wrappers. Bruxelles, 1912. [WSU pencil annotations: "catalogued under Union of International Associations", and "annotations by Roger Fry. / ?"]

VS, V, p. 76:

Political Quarterly, The. —Vol. 4, No. 3; Vol. 5, No. 4; Vol. 6, No. 4; Vol. 7, Nos. 1–3; Vol. 8, No. 2; Vol. 10, Nos. 3–4; Vol. 11, Nos. 1–3. 8 vo wrappers, 1933–40. [Contributors include Leonard Woolf, Bernard Shaw, Bertrand Russell, H. J. Laski, and others.]

Various authors. *German Diplomatic Documents 1871–1914.* Selected and trans. by E. T. S. Dugdale. Vols. 1–2 (ex 4 vols.). 8vo buckram, 1928–29. Library Nos. 2931 and 14096. [WSU notation correcting "Various authors": "Germany—Answartiges amt."]

Economic Journal (A Quarterly), The. —Nos. 134, 135, 144, 145, 156, 157, 160, 161, 164, 165, 166, 175, 205, 205. Ed. by J. M. Keynes. 8vo wrappers, 1924–42.

VS, V, p. 77:

Economic Journal (A Quarterly), The. (Index to Vols. 21–30) 1911–20 incl.). 8vo wrappers, 1922.

Economic History: A Supplement to the Economic Journal. Ed. by J. M. Keynes and others. Nos. 1, 5, 6, 7, and 9. 8vo wrappers, 1926–34.

Pierson, N. G. *Principles of Economics.* Trans. A. A. Wotzel. Vol. 1 (ex 2 vols.). 8vo cloth, 1902.

Hammond, J. L., and B. Hammond. *The Village Labourer 1760–1832: A Study in the Government of England before the Reform Bill.* (Part 1.) 8vo cloth. 4th ed., 1927.

McNair, A. D., and H. Lauterpacht (eds.). *Annual Digest of Public International Law Cases, for the Years 1925–1926.* 8vo cloth. (Contributions to International Law and Diplomacy), 1929.

VS, V, p. 78:

Lanson, Gustave. *Voltaire.* 8vo wrappers. Les grands ecrivains Francais. Paris, 1906.

Cochin, Augusten. *Les Societes de Pensee et la revolution en Bretagne 1788–1789.* Tome I only. *Histoire Analytique.* 8vo wrappers. Paris, 1923. Library No. 5575.

VS, V, p. 79:
International Conciliation. No. 127: *The Disclosures from Germany.* 8vo wrappers. American Association for International Conciliation, June 1918.
International Conciliation. No. 206: *The Japanese Law of Nationality and the Rights of Foreigners in Land under the Law of Japan.* By Tsunejiro Miyaoka. 8vo wrappers. Carnegie Endowment for International Peace, January 1925.
International Conciliation. No. 275: *Text of the Draft Convention for the Disarmament Conference.* 8vo wrappers. Carnegie Endowment for International Peace, December 1931.

2.3. Books with Notes and References on End Pages in Leonard Woolf's Handwriting
[Many of these books were reviewed by him.]

VS, VI, p. 1:
Kelsen, Hans. *La Democratic. Sa nature—Sa valeur.* 8vo wrappers. Paris, 1932.
Ernst, M. L. and W. Seagle. *To The Pure...A Study of Obscenity and the Censor.* 8vo cloth, 1929. Lib. No. 1297.
Muir, Ramsay. *The Expansion of Europe.* 8vo cloth, 1917.
Ostrerog, Count Léon. *The Turkish Problem.* Trans. from French by W. Stephens. 8vo cloth, 1919.
Postgate, R. W. *The Bolshevik Theory.* 8vo cloth, 1920.
Brailsford, H. N. *A League of Nations.* 8vo cloth, 1917.
Mathiez, Albert. *The French Revolution.* Trans. from French by C. A. Phillips. 8vo cloth, 1927. Library No. 14786 [WSU inscription: "bookmarks laid in p. 5, 51, 107, 136, 266. Review slip"].
Morgan, R. B., ed. *Readings in English Social History from Pre-Roman Days to A.D. 1837.* 8vo cloth 1923. Library No. 4600. ["Woolf rev. 19 Jan. 1924 N&A": this is a marginal notation in hand of Leila Luedeking in catalog.]
Koebel, W.H. *Paraguay.* The South American Series. 8vo cloth, 1917.
Smuts, J. C. *Africa and Some World Problems. Including the Rhodes Memorial Lectures 1929.* 8vo. cloth (Review slip), 1930.
Rai, Lajpat. *England's Debt to India. An Historical Narrative of Britain's Fiscal Policy in India.* 8vo cloth. New York, 1917.
Webster, C. K., and Sydney Herbert. *The League of Nations in Theory and Practice.* 8vo. cloth, 1933.
Laski, Harold J. *Liberty in the Modern State.* 8vo. cloth, 1930.

VS, VI, p. 2:
Delaise F. *Political Myths and Economic Realiteis.* 8vo cloth, 1925. Library No. 7570.

Grant A. J., and H. Lamperley. *Europe in the Nineteenth and Twentieth Centuries, 1789-1938.* 8vo cloth, 1939.

Vizetelly, E. A. *The True Story of Alsace-Lorraine.* 8vo cloth 1918. Library No. 140. [WSU note: "'Presentation copy' embossed on title page."]

Martin, Kingsley. *French Liberal Thought in the Eighteenth Century.* 8vo cloth, 1929.

Scholefield, G. H. *The Pacific—Its Past and Future. The Policies of the Great Powers from 18th Century.* 8vo. cloth. (Review slip) 1919. ["Review" corrected to "Compliments" in WSU copy.]

Fidel, M. Camille. *La Paige Coloniale Francaise.* 8vo wrappers. Paris, 1918.

Burns, C. Delisle. *Democracy. Its Defects and Additions.* 8vo cloth, 1929. Library No. 3560.

Harris, J. H. *Africa: Slave or Free.* Preface by Sir Sidney Olivier. 8vo cloth, 1919.

Webster, C. K. *The Foreign Policy of Castlereagh 1815-1822. Britain and the European Alliance.* 8vo cloth, 1925. Library No. 914.

Oakes, A., and R. B. Mowat, eds. *The Great European Treaties of the Nineteenth Century.* 8vo cloth, 1918.

Czernin, Count Ottokar. *Inn the World War.* 8vo. cloth, 1919.

Penman, John S. *The Irresistible Movement of Democracy.* 8vo cloth. "Presentation copy" embossed on title page. 1923. Library No. 4882.

VS, VI, p. 3

Morrison, C. C. *The Outlawry of War: A Constructive Policy in World Peace.* Forward by John Dawry. 8vo cloth, 1927. (Pencil scoring and notes in text.) [WSU note, in pencil, about the scoring and notes: "in unknown hand."]

Murray, D. H. *Disraeli.* 8vo cloth, 1927. Library No. 7927

Hobson, J. A. *Richard Cobden The International Man.* 8vo cloth. (Review slip) 1918.

Brailsford, H. N. *The War of Steel and Gold. A Study of the Armed Peace.* 8vo cloth. "Presentation copy" embossed on title page. 1914. [WSU catalog inscription, in pencil: "no notes / sections marked."]

Hannay, David. *Diaz.* 8vo cloth. "Presentation copy" embossed on title page. (Makers of the 19th Century) 1917. Library No. 498.

Poincaré, Raymond. *The Memoirs of Raymond Poincaré* (1912). Trans. by Sir George Arthur. 8vo cloth, 1926. Library No. 5354.

Murray, R. H. *Erasmus and Luther: Their Attitude to Toleration.* 8vo buckram, 1920. [In pencil, WSU note: "Review slip."]

Nietzsche, Fredrich. *Selected Letters of.* Translated by A.M. Ludovici. 8vo cloth. "Presentation copy" embossed on title page. 1921. Library No. 3783.

Best, Mary Agnes. *Thomas Paine. Prophet and Martyr of Democracy.* 8vo cloth. (Review slip) n.d. Library No. 9679.

Sandburg, Carl. *Abraham Lincoln. The Prairie Years.* 2 vols. 8vo cloth, 1926. Library No. 4908.
Guedalla, Philys. *Palmerson.* 8vo cloth, 1926.
Mazzini, Joseph. *Mazzini's Letters to an English Family 1844–1854.* Edited by E. F. Richards. 8vo. "Review copy" embossed on title page. 1920. Library No. 1730 ["?" — WSU question mark in pencil after library number.]

VS, VI, p. 4:
Champion, Piérre. *Louis XI.* Translated by W. S. Whale. 8vo cloth, n.d. Library No. 1245.
Clark, G. K. *Peel and the Conservative Party. A Study in Party Politics 1832–41.* (From unpublished material). 8vo. cloth, 1929. Library No. 1253.
Lascelles, E. C. P. *Granville Sharp and the Freedom of Slaves in England.* 8vo cloth, 1928. Library No. 13254.
Schirokauer, (Arno) Lassalle. *The Power of Illusion and the Illusion of Power.* Trans. by E. and C. Paul. 8vo cloth, 1931.
Sazonov, Serge. *Fateful Years 1909–1916. The Reminiscences of Serge Sazonov, Russian Minister from Foreign Affairs 1914.* 8vo cloth. Library No. 11746.
Anthony, Katherine. *Catherine the Great.* 8vo. cloth, 1926. Library No. 4524.
Nicolson, Harold. *Sir Arthur Nicholson. First Lord Carmock. A Study in the Old Diplomacy.* 8vo cloth, 1930.
Mayer, Gustav. *Friedrich Engels. A Biography.* 8vo cloth, 1936.
Maurice, Sir Frederick. *Haldane 1856–1928.* 2 vols. 8vo cloth, 1937 / 1939.
Dickinson, G. Lowes. *Causes of International War.* 8vo. wrappers. Swarthmore International Handbooks, 1920.
Webb, Sidney and Beatrice. *The History of Trade Unionism.* Revised Edition, extended to 1920. 8vo cloth, 1920. Library No. 3150.
Bourne, H. R. Fox. *Civilization in Congolaned: A Story of International Wrong Doing.* 8vo cloth, 1903. [WSU notation: "1295177" in pencil.]

VS, VI, p. 5:
Maddox, W. P. *Foreign Relations in British Labour Politics.* 8vo cloth. Harvard University Press, U.S.A., 1934.
Babbitt, Irving. *Democracy and Leadership.* 8vo cloth, 1924.
Murray, R. H. *Studies in the English Social and Political Thinkers of the Nineteenth Century.* 2 vols. 8vo cloth, 1929. [WSU notation: "Review slip"; also in pencil: "Bookmark."]
Angell, Norman. *Must Britain Travel the Moscow Road?* 8vo cloth. 1st Edition, 1926. Library No. 5599.
Zimmerman, Emil. *The German Empire of Central Africa.* 8vo wrappers. (Review slip) 1918.
Loftus, Pierse. *The Creed of a Tory.* 8vo cloth. (Review slip) 1926.

Conrad, Joseph. *Chance. A Tale in 2 parts.* 8vo cloth. 2nd Edition, 1914.
Conrad, Joseph. *Suspense.* 8vo cloth. 1st edition, 1925. Library No. 2985.
Conrad, Joseph. *The Rover.* 8vo cloth. 1st edition, 1923. Library No. 4427.
Ruskin, John. *Selections from.* Ed. by A. C. Benson. 8vo cloth, 1923. Library No. 3067.
Angell, Norman. *War Aims: A Need for a Parliament of the Allies.* 8vo quarter cloth. (Review slip) n.d. (c. 1918). [WSU notation in pencil: "Spine resewn by Virginia? Notes by Leonard."]
Coleman, Frederick. *The Far East Unveiled. An Inner History of Events in Japan and China in the Year 1916.* 8vo. cloth. "Presentation copy" embossed on title page. 1918.
Headlam, A. S. *The History of Twelve Days. July 24–August 4th, 1914.* 8vo cloth. "Presentation copy" embossed on title page. 1915.
Turberville, A. S. *The House of Lords in the XVIII Century.* 8vo. cloth, 1927. Library No. 10205.

VS, VI, p. 6:
Giordan, Paolo. *The German Colonial Empire. Its Beginning and Ending.* Translated by Mrs. Gustavus W. Hamilton. 8vo. cloth "Presentation copy" embossed on title page, 1916.
Ginsburg, B. W. *War Speeches 1914–1917. Collected by.* 8vo wrappers. "Presentation copy" embossed on title page. 1917.
Fay, C. R. *Life and Labour in the Nineteenth Century.* 8vo cloth, 1920.
Hobson, J. A. *Towards International Government.* 8vo. cloth, 1915.
Dukem, Jules. *The Question of Alsace-Lorraine.* Translated by R. Stawell. 8vo cloth. "For Review" stamped on h.-title page. 1918. Library No. 118.
Rai, Tajpat. *The Political Future of India.* 8vo cloth. New York, 1919.
Russell, Bertrand. *Which Way to Peace?* 8vo cloth. 1st edition, 1936.
Brailsford, H. N. *The Russian Workers Republic.* 8vo cloth, 1921. Library No. 2985.
Johnston, Sir H. H. *The Black Man's Part in the War.* 8vo wrappers, 1917.
Carr, E. H. *Michael Bakunin.* 8vo cloth, 1937.
Bright, John. *The Diaries of.* With a Forward by Philip Bright. 8vo cloth, 1930. Library No. 688.
Iswolsky, Alexander. *The Memoirs of.* (Formerly Russian Minister of Foreign Affairs and Ambassador to France. Ed. and trans. by C. L. Seeger. 8vo cloth. [Review slip: "With the Publishers Compliments" stamped on frontispiece.] 1920. Library No. 156 copy [used in column written by Leonard Woolf].

VS, VI, p. 7:
The Empire and the Future. A series of Imperial Studies Lectures delivered in the University of London. King's College. 8vo cloth. "Presentation copy" embossed on title page, 1916.

Selected Political Titles from Leonard Woolf's Library   211

Catherine the Great, Memoirs of. Translated by Katherine Anthony. 8vo cloth. U.S.A., 1927. Library No. 9575.

Bonjour, Felix. *La Démocratic Suisse.* 8vo wrapper. Lausanne, 1919.

Swift, Jonathan. *Gulliver's Travels.* 8vo cloth. World Classic, 1924.

Abbott, G. F. *Turkey, Greece and the Great Powers.* A study in friendship and hate. 8vo cloth. "Presentaiton copy" embossed on title page. 1916.

Webb, Sidney and Beatrice. *The Consumer's Co-operative Movement.* 8vo cloth. 1st edition, 1921.

Millard, Thomas F. *Democracy and the Eastern Question.* 8vo cloth, 1919.

Pollock, Sir Frederich. *The League of Nations.* 8vo cloth. (Review slip) 1920.

Tawney, R. H. *Equality.* The Halley Stewart Lectures. 1929. 8vo cloth, 1931.

Wallas, Graham. *The Art of Thought.* 8vo. 1926. Library No. 4969.

Ludwig, Emil. *Kaizer Wilhelm II.* Translated from the German by E.C. Mayne. 8vol. cloth, 1926. Library No. 6630.

Soltan, Roger. *French Political Though in the 19th Century.* 8vo. cloth, 1931. [WSU notation: "L.W. reviewed in N.S.&N. 2:580, 581."]

"*Vigilants.*" *The Road to War: Being an Analysis of the National Government's Foreign Policy.* With preface by C. R. Attler. 8vo. cloth. Published for the New Fabian Research Bureau, 1937. [WSU notations: "Shelved under title" and "Review slip" in pencil.]

Elliott, Hugh. *Herbert Spencer.* 8vo cloth. Makers of the 19th Century series. "Presentation copy" embossed on title page. 1917.

VS, VI, p. 8:

Moffat, R. U. *John Smith Moffat C.M.G., A Missionary. A Memoir.* 8vo cloth, 1921.

Lucas, Sir Charles. *The Partition and Colonization of Africa.* 8vo cloth, 1922.

Temple, William Johnston. *Diaries of: 1780–1796.* Edited with a memoir by Lewis Bettany. 8vo cloth, 1929. Library No. 2700.

Knowles, L.C.A. *The Economic Development of the British Overseas Empire.* 8vo cloth, 1924.

Loreburn, The Earl. *How the War Came.* 8vo cloth. "Presentation copy" stamped on title page, 1919.

Dutt, R.P. *Fascism and Social Revolution.* 8vo cloth, 1934.

Van Doren, Carl. *Benjamin Franklin.* 8vo cloth, 1939.

Worsfold, Basil, Sir Bartle Frere. *A Footnote to the History of the British Empire.* 8vo cloth. "For Review" stamped on h.-title page. 1923.

Von Eckardstein, Baron. *Ten Years at the Court of St. James' 1895–1905.* Translated and edited by Prof. George Young. 8vo cloth. "For Review" stamped on title page. 1921. Library No. 3236.

Clifford, Lady Anne. *The Diary of.* With an introductory note by V. Sackville-West. 8vo cloth, 1923. Library No. 4358.

Huizinga, J. *Erasmus*. 8vo cloth. Great Hollanders series. New York, 1924. Library No. 6186.

Hirst, F. W. *Early Life and Letters of John Morley*. 2 vols. 8vo cloth, 1927. Library No. 7647.

Franklin, Benjamin. *The Life of.... Written by himself.* Edited from his original manuscript by John Bigelow. 8vo cloth. World Classics, 1924. Library No. 6301.

VS, VI, p. 9:

Trevelyan, G. M. *Grey of Fallodon, Being the Life of Sir Edward Grey afterwards Viscount Grey of Fallodon*. 8vo cloth, 1937.

Greville, Charles C. F. *The Greville Diary Including Passages Hitherto Withheld From Publication*. Edited by Philip Whitwall Wilson. 2 vols. 8vo cloth, 1927. Library No. 10827.

Adams, Henry. *The Education of Henry Adams. An Autobiography*. 8vo cloth, 1928. Library No. 11460

Spender, J. A., and Cyril Asquith. *The Life of Herbert Henry Asquith, Lord Oxford and Asquith*. 2 vols. 8vo, 1932. [WSU notation: "L.W. reviewed N.S. & N. 4:485–86."]

Mayne, Ethel Colburn. *The Life and Letters of Anne Isabella, Lady Noel Byron*. From unpublished papers in the possession of the late Ralph, Earl of Lovelace. 8vo cloth, 1929. Library No. 2008.

Dickinson, G. Lowes. *The Choice Before Us*. 8vo cloth. 1st edition, 1917.

Roustan, M. *The Pioneers of the French Revolution*. Translated by Frederick Whyte. Introduction by H. J. Laski. 8vo cloth, 1926. Library No. 4078.

Piggott, Sir Francis. *The Declaration of Paris 1856. A Study Documented*. 8vo cloth. Law of the Sea series. Vol. 4. 1919.

Van Den Bruck, Mouller. *Germany's Third Empire*. Authorized English Edition (condensed) by E. O. Lorimer. 8vo. cloth (Review slip) 1934. ["Catalogued under Mouller van den Bruck, Arthur"—WSU note in pencil.]

Björnson, Björnstjerne. *Plays*. 2nd series. 8vo buckram. Translated by Edwin Bjorkman. "Presentation copy" perforated on title page. 1914.

Hazlitt, William. *Selected Essays*. Edited by George Sampson. 8vo quarter cloth, 1917.

Valentin, Veit. *1848 Chapters of German History*. 8vo cloth, 1940.

Clark, Cumberland. *Britain Overseas. the story of the foundations and development of the British Empire from 1495–1921*. 8vo cloth. (Review slip) 1924. Library No. 6373.

VS, VI, p. 10:

Russell, Bertrand. *The Problem of China*. 8vo. cloth. 1st edition, 1922.

Lovett, Sir Verney. *A History of the Indian Nationalist Movement*. 8vo cloth. (Review slip), 1920. [WSU note, striking out ""Review slip" in entry: "Compliments slip" in pencil.]

Barclay, Sir Thomas. *New Methods of Adjusting International Disputes and the Future*. 8vo cloth. "Presentation Copy" embossed on title page. 1917. [Label inside front cover: "Fabian Library. This book is the property of the Fabian Society, 25 Tothill Street, Westminster, London").

William II (ex-Emperor of Germany). *My Early Life*. Translated from the German. 8vo. cloth 1926. Library No. 6897.

Bosanquet, Bernard. *The Function of the State in Promoting the Unity of Mankind*. 4to wrappers, n.d. (c. 1916). [The following long note by L.L., in pencil: "Proof copy pub. in the proceedings of the Aristotelian Soc. n.s. Vol. XVII, 28–57. a rev. form of this is a chapter from the author's Social and Internationale Ideals Being Studies in Patriotism 1st pr. 1917. Rept. from a copy in NY Publ. Lib 1967."]

Hayes, C. J. H. *Essays on Nationalism*. 8vo. cloth. New York, 1926. Library No. 5546.

Gregory, J. W. *Human Migration and the Future: A Study of the Causes, Effects and Control of Emigration*. 8vo. cloth, 1928. Library No. 11920.

Wilte, Count. *The Memoirs of*. Translated from the original Russian Manuscript and edited by Abraham Yarmolinsky. 8vo cloth "Presentation copy" embossed on title page, 1921. Library No. 4332.

Allison, J. M. S. *Monsieur Thiers*. 8vo cloth, 1932.

Baker, P. J. Noel. *The Geneval Protocol for the Pacific Settlement of International Disputes*. 8vo cloth, 1925. Library No. 1281.

Eversley, Lord. *The Turkish Empire. Its Growth and Decay*. 8vo cloth. 1st edition, 1917.

VS, VI, p. 11:

Dickinson, G. Lowes. *The Internatioanl Hierarchy, 1904–1914*. 8vo cloth, 1926. Library No. 4323.

Kautsky, Karl. *Terrorism and Communism. A contribution to the natural history of revolution*. Translated by W.H. Kerridge. 8vo cloth, 1920. [Noted in pencil: "review slip."]

Brookes, E. H. *The History of Native Policy in South Africa from 1830 to the Present Day*. 8vo. 2nd edition revised. Pretoria, S.A., 1927. Library No. 9645.

Mathieson, W. T. *British Slavery and Its Abolition 1823–1838*. 8vo cloth. (Review slip) 1926. Library No. 6327.

Various Authors. *The Post Victorians*. Introduction by the very Revd. W. R. Inge. 8vo cloth, 1933. [In pencil—"catalogued by title."]

Mohr, Anton. *The Oil War*. Preface by Hartley Withers. 8vo cloth, 1925. Library No. 7623.

William of Germany (The ex-Crown Prince). *I Seek the Truth. A book on responsibility for war.* Translated from the German by Ralph Butler. 8vo cloth, 1926. Library No. 5495.

Various Authors. *The League of Nations Starts. An Outline by its Organizers.* 8vo cloth. "Presentation copy" embossed on title page. (Review slip) 1920. [In pencil—"catalogued under title."]

Percy, Lord Eustace, M.D. *Democracy on Trial. A preface to an Industrial Policy.* 8vo cloth, 1931.

Monckton Jones, M. E. *Warren Hastings in Bengal 1772-1774.* 8vo. cloth. (Review slip) Oxford Historical and Literary Studies, vol. 9. 1918.

Michels, Robert. *Political Parties. A Sociological Study of the Oligarchical Tendencies of Modern Democracy.* Trans. from the Italian by Eden and Cedar Paul. 8vo cloth, 1915.

VS, VI, p. 12:

Taylor, A. J. P. *Germany's First Bid for Colonies 1884-1885. A Move in Bismarck's European Policy.* 8vo. cloth, 1938.

Neff, Wanda Fraiken. *Victorian Working Women. An Historical Study of Women in British Industries and Professions 1832-1850.* 8vo. cloth. (Review slip). 1st. ed., 1929. Library No. 1765.

West, Julius. *A History of the Chartist Movement.* 8vo cloth. (Review slip addressed personally to L. Woolf, Esq.). 1st. edition, 1920. Library No. 1298.

Spengler, Oswald. *The Hour of Decision. Part 1: Germany and the World—Historical Traditions.* Translated from the German for the first time by C.F. Atkinson. 8vo cloth, 1934.

Laski, Harold J. *Parliamentary Government in England.* 8vo. cloth. 1st ed., 1938.

Curtis, Lionel. *Letters to the Peoples of India on Responsible Government.* 8vo. cloth. "Presentation copy" embossed on title page. (Review slip). 1st ed., 1918.

Lenin, V.I. *The Paris Commune.* 8vo boards, 1931.

Lewin, E. *The Resources of the Empire and their Development.* 8vo cloth. "Review copy" embossed on title page. 1924.

Beer, M. *A History of British Socialism.* Introduction by R.H. Tawney. 2 vols. 8vo cloth "Presentation copy" embossed on title page. 1919 Library No. 540, [WSU notation: "Vol. II—numbered 1554."]

Dawson, William Harbutt. *The Evolution of Modern Germany.* New and revised ed. 8vo cloth, 1919.

Tanner, J. R. *English Constitutional Conflicts of the Seventeenth Century. 1603-1689.* 8vo cloth. Cambridge, 1928.

de la Tramerye, Pierre L'espanol. *The World—Struggle for Oil.* Translated from the French by C. L. Leese. 8vo. cloth, 1923. Library No. 4856.

Phillipson, Coleman. *International Law and the Great War.* 8vo. cloth. 1st edition, 1915. [WSU notation, in pencil: "'Presentation copy' embossed on title page."]

Selected Political Titles from Leonard Woolf's Library 215

VS, VI, p. 13:

Laski, Harold J. *The Foundations of Sovereignty and Other Essays*. 8vo. cloth. 1st ed., 1921.

Ross, W. McGregor. *Kenya form Within. A short political history*. 8vo. cloth. 1st ed., 1927. Library No. 1049

Keith, A.B. *The Belgian Congo and the Berlin Act*. 8vo. cloth, 1919.

Graham, R. B. Cunningham. *The Conquest of the River Plate*. 8vo cloth. "Presentation copy" embossed on title page. 1st ed., 1924. Library No. 5620.

Angell, Norman. *The Political Conditions of Allied Success—A Plea for the Protection of the Democracies*. 8vo cloth. 1st ed., 1918. [WSU notation: "Marks and notes by Leonard Woolf."]

Barker, Ernest. *National Character and the Factors in Its Formation*. 8vo cloth. 1st ed., 1927.

Roxburgh, F. *Internation Conventions and Third States. A Monograph*. 8vo. cloth. 1st ed., 1917.

Fletcher, C. Brunsdon. *The Problem of the Pacific. Preface by Sir William MacGregor*. 8vo cloth. "Presentation copy" embossed on title page. 1919.

Hall, H. Duncan. *The British Commonwealth of Nations. A Study of its Past and Future Development*. 8vo cloth. "Presentation copy" stamped on title page. 1920.

Russell, Bertrand. *The Practices and Theory of Bolshevism*. 8vo quarter cloth. 1st ed., 1920.

Phillipson, Coleman, and Noel Buxton. *The Question of the Bosphorus and Dardanelles*. 8vo cloth, 1917.

Laski, Harold J. *Studies in the Problem of Sovereignty*. 8vo. cloth. Yale UP, USA, 1917.

Webster, C. K., ed. *British Diplomacy 1813–1815. Select documents dealing with the reconstruction of Europe*. 8vo. cloth 1921. Library No. 2816.

VS, VI, p. 14:

Laski, Harold J. *Democracy in Crisis*. 8vo cloth. 1st ed., 1933.

Peiris, M. V. P. *Ceylon. A Study of the Report of the Special Commission on the Constitution*. 8vo wrappers. (Review slip) 1929.

Haldane, Viscount. *Before the War*. 8vo. cloth "Presentation copy" embossed on title page. 1920.

Spengler, Oswald. *The Decline of the West*. 2 vols. Vol. 1: *Form and actuality*. Vol. 2: *Perspectives of World-History*. Trans. with notes by C. F. Atkinson. 8vo cloth, 1926–28. Library Nos. 5407 and 231. [WSU notation: "LW notes on back."]

Kerensky, A. F. *The Prelude to Bolshevism: The Krenilov Rebellion*. 8vo. cloth, 1919.

Woods, Maurice. *A History of the Tory Party in the Seventeenth and Eighteenth Centuries with a sketch of its development in the Nineteenth Century*. 8vo. cloth, 1924. Library No. 5979.

Agor, Herbert. *Pursuit of Happiness: The Story of American Democracy.* 8vol. cloth, 1939.

Heard, Gerald. *The Ascent of Humanity: An essay on the Evolution of Civilization.* 8vo cloth, 1929.

Wright, I. A. *The Early History of Cuba 1492–1586. Written from Original Sources.* 8vo cloth, New York, 1916.

Hayes, Carlton J. H. *A Political and Social History of Modern Europe.* 2 vols. 8vo cloth. "Presentation Copy." embossed on title page. New York, 1916.

Trevelyan, G. M. *History of England.* 8vo. cloth, 1926. Library No. 5421.

Joad, C. E. M. *Counter-Attack from the East. The Philosophy of Radhakrichnan.* 8vo cloth. (Review slip) 1933.

Laski, Herold J. *The Rise of European Liberalism: An Essay in Interpretation.* 8vo cloth. 1st Edition. 1936.

Pink, M. Alderton. *A Realist Looks at Democracy with a preface by Aldous Huxley.* 8vo cloth, 1930.

Robson, W.A. *Justice and Administration Law. A Study of the British Constitution.* 8vo cloth. (Review slip) 1928. Library No. 11769.

Greaves, H. R. G. *The League Committees and World Order. A study of the permanent expert committees of the League of Nations as an instrument of International Government.* 8vo buckram, 1931.

Angell, Norman. *The Dangers of Half-Preparedness. A Plea for a Declaration of American Policy.* 8vo. boards. USA, 1916.

Masaryk, T. G. *The Spirit of Russia. Studies in History Literature and Philosophy.* Trans. from German by Eden and Cedar Paul. 2 vols. 8vo cloth, 1919. Library No. 890.

Overlach, T.W. *Foreign Financial Control in China.* 8vo cloth. New York, 1919.

Page, William. *London: Its Origin and Early Development.* 8vo cloth, 1923. Library No. 2361. [WSU notation: "Review slip."]

Drinkwater, John. *Patriotism in Literature.* 8vo cloth. "Presentation copy" embossed on title page. HVL. 1st ed., 1924. Library No. 6157.

Abbott, Wilbur Cortez. *The Expansion of Europe. A history of the foundations of the modern world.* 2 vols. 8vo cloth. "Presentation copy" embossed on title page. 1919.

Baker, Ray Stannard. *Woodrow Wilson and World Settlement.* Written from his unpublished and personal material. 3vols. 8vo cloth. "Presentation copy" embossed on title pages. 1923.

Namier, L. B. *England in the Age of the American Revolution.* 8vo cloth, 1930.

Huxley, Elspeth, and Marjorie Purham [sic.]. *Race and Politics in Kenya: A Correspondence.* Introduction by Lord Lugard. 8vo cloth, 1944. [WSU note corrects "Marjorie" to "Margery" but fails to correct the misspelling of Parham's last name.]

Selected Political Titles from Leonard Woolf's Library 217

VS, VI, p. 16:

Orvis, Julia Swift. *A Brief History of Poland.* 8vo cloth. "Presentation copy" embossed on title page. 1919.

Menken, H. L. *Notes on Democracy.* 8vo cloth. 1st ed. London, 1927. Library No. 7813.

Enchen, Cecil C. *The People and Constitution.* 8vo cloth, 1933.

Finer, Herman. *Mussolini's Itlay.* 8vo cloth, 1935.

Huxley, Aldous. *On the Margin: Notes and Essays.* 8vo cloth. 1st ed., 1923. Library No. 1821.

Spender, J. A. *Fifty Years of Europe. A Study in Pre-War Documents.* 8vo cloth, 1933.

Reid, Rev. Gilbert. *China, Captive or Free? A Study of China's Entanglements.* 8vo cloth, 1922. [WSU notation: "Review slip inserted. Sections marked in text and notes on back end paper in hand of Leonard Woolf."]

Young, George. *The New Germany.* 8vo cloth. "Presentation copy" embossed on title page. 1920.

Dawson, William Harbutt. *Richard Cobden and Foreign Policy. A Critical Exposition, with Special References to our Day and Its Problems.* 8vo cloth. (Review slip) 1926. Library No. 7281.

Robertson, J. M. *A History of Free Thought in the Nineteenth Century.* 2vols. 8vo cloth. 1st ed., 1929.

Gayda, Virginio. *Modern Austria: Her Racial and Social Problems, with a Study of Italia Irredenta.* Trans. by Z. M. Gibson and C. A. Miles. 8vo cloth."Presentation copy" embossed on title page. (Review slip) 1915.

Pyke, H. Reason. *The Law of Contraband of War.* 8vo buckram, 1915.

Farjenel, Fernand. *Through the Chinese Revolution: My Experience in the South and North. The Evolution of Social Life. Interviews with party leaders. An unconstitutional loan—the coup d'etat.* Trans from French by M. Vivian. 8vo cloth. (Review stamp on title page) 1915.

VS, VI, p. 17:

Bland, J. O. P. *China, Japan and Korea.* 8vo cloth, 1923.

Wolff, Theodor. *The Eve of 1914.* Translated by E. W. Dickes. 8vo cloth, 1915.

Grey, Viscount of Fallodon. *Twenty-five Years 1892–1916.* 2vols. 8vo cloth. 1st ed. 1925. Library No. 3063. [WSU notation: "'For Review' stamped on both 1/2 titles."]

Theal, George McCall. *A History of South Africa 1795 to 1872.* 3 vols. (ex 5 vols.) 8vo cloth. 4th ed. (bearing review slip), 1915–16. [WSU pencil note: "Vol. 3, 3rd ed. 1916."]

Theal, George McCall. *A History of South Africa 1873–1884.* 2 vols. 8vo cloth 1919. Library No. 202.

Lee, Sir Sidney. *King Edward VII: A Biography.* Vol. 2 (ex. 2 vols). 8vo cloth. (Review Slip) 1927. Lib. No. 10306.

Gooch, G. P. *Before the War.* Vol. 2: *The Coming of the Storm* (ex 2 vols). 8vo cloth, 1938.

Dugdale, Blanch E. C. *Arthur James Balfour: 1st Earl of Balfour K.G.O.M., F.R.S. 1906–1930.* Vol. 2 (ex 2 vols.). 8vo cloth, 1936.

Noel-Baker, Philip. *The Private Manufacture of Armaments.* Preface by Viscount Cecil. Vol. 1 (ex 2 vols). 8vo cloth, 1936.

Poincare, Raymond. *The Memoirs of : 1914.* Vol. 3. Trans. by Sir George Arthur. 8vo cloth, 1929. Library No. 802.

Dawson, William Harbutt. *The German Empire 1867–1914 and the Unity Movement.* Vol. 2 (ex 2 vols). 8vo cloth, 1919.

House, Colonel. *The Intimate Papers of: Arranged as a Narrative by Charles Seymour.* Vols. 3 and 4 (ex 4 vols.) . 8vo cloth, 1928. Library No. 14002.

Paget, Walburga, Lady. *In My Tower.* Vol. 1 (ex 2 vols). 8vo cloth, "with publishers compliments" stamped on title page. 1924. Library No. 635.

Ronaldshay, The Earl of [cat. under Zetland]. *The Life of Lord Curzon: Being the Authorized Biography of George Nathaniel, Marquess of Kodleston K.G.* Vol 1 (ex 2 vols). 8vo buckram, 1928. Library No. 11961.

VS, VI, p. 18:

Curtis L., ed. *The Commonwealth of Nations. An enquiry into the Nature of Citizenship in the British Empire and into the Mutual Relations of the Several Communities Thereof.* Part 1 only. 8vo boards, 1916. Library No. 1248.

Lander, Walter Savage. *The Complete Works of: Edited by T. Earle Welby.* Vols. 1–11 (ex 16 vols.). Limited to 525 sets. 8vo buckram 1927–30. Library Nos. as follows:

Vol. 1. 10088 / Vol. 2 10088 / Vol. 3 10490 / Vol. 4 10490 / Vol. 5 11103 / Vol. 6 11345 / Vol. 7 11725 <3> / Vol. 8 12757 / Vol. 9 236 / Vol. 10 1748 / Vol. 11 4948 (2 Review slips) [strikethroughs and corrections here and above are entered in the WSU copy, in pencil, with the following addendum: "3 Publisher's Compliment slips."]

Moore, George. *"Hail & Farewell": A Trilogy.* Vol. 3 only—*Vale.* 8vo cloth. 1st ed. "Presentation copy" embossed on title page. 1914.

The Glass Palace Chronicle of the Kings of Burma. Trans. Pe Maung Tin and G.H. Luce. 8vo buckram, 1023. Lib No. 2550.

Acres, W. Marston. *London and Westminster in History and Literature.* 8vo cloth, 1923. Library No. 2064.

Index to Part 3 (by Author, Subject, and Title): Selected Titles on Political Subjects from the Library of Leonard Woolf

Based on the original *Catalogue of Books from the Library of Leonard and Virginia Woolf* (Holleyman and Treacher Ltd., Brighton, 1975) at Washington State University. Z881.W3

The section and page references are from Holleyman and Treacher's catalogue, for both the Monks House (MH), Sussex, or Victoria Square (VS), London, sides of the inventory, when provenance is definitely associated with Leonard Woolf.

Author, Subject, or Title   Location (Holleyman and Treacher)

1848 Chapters of German History. VS, VI, p. 9

Abbas II. VS, V, p. 44

Abbott, G. F. VS, V, p. 23; VS, VI, p. 7

Abbott, Wilbur Cortez. VS, VI, p. 14

Abraham Lincoln: The Prairie Years. VS, VI, p. 3

Abrahams, W. MH, III, p. 15

Acquisition and Government of Backward Territory in International Law, Being a Treatise on the Law and Practice Relating to Colonial Expansion. VS, V, p. 59

Acres, W. Marston. VS, VI, p. 18

Adair, E. R. VS, V, p. 67

Adam, Ruth. *Beatrice Webb: A Life 1858–1953.* MH, VI, p. 6

Adams, Henry. VS, VI, p. 9

Adams, J. VS, V, p. 3

Addison, Joseph. VS, III, p. 5

Addresses and Discussions at the Conference of Scientific Management (1911). MH, VI, p. 11

Admiral Byng: and the Loss of Minorca. MH, VI, p. 9

Africa and Some World Problems, Including the Rhodes Memorial Lectures 1929. VS, VI, p. 1

Africa and the Peace of Europe VS, III, p. 1

Africa and the Twentieth Century Reformation. VS, III, p. 2

Africa MH, VI, p. 4; MH, VI, p. 7; VS, III, p. 8; VS, V, p. 9; VS, VI, p. 1; VS, III, p. 2; VS, III, p. 3; VS, V, p. 4; VS, V, p. 5; VS, V, p. 8; VS, V, p. 24; VS, V, p. 27; VS, V, p. 29; VS, V, p. 31; VS, V, p. 43; VS, V, p. 46; VS, V, p. 48; VS, V, p. 49; VS, V, p. 53; VS, V, p. 58; VS, V, p. 59; VS, V, p. 60; VS, V, p. 61; VS, V, p. 62; VS, V, p. 73; VS, V, p. 74; VS, VI, p. 2; VS, VI,

p. 4; VS, VI, p. 11; VS, VI, p. 13; VS, VI, p. 14; VS, VI, p. 17

Africa: Slave or Free. VS, VI, p. 2

After the Deluge: A Study of Communal Psychology. **Vol. 1.** VS, III, p. 17

Agadir: Ma Politique Exterieure. VS, V, p. 27

Age of Louis XIV, The. VS, V, p. 20

Age of the Chartists: 1832–1854, The. MH, VI, p. 12

Agor, Herbert. VS, VI, p. 14

Aims of Labour, The. MH, VI, p. 11

Alexander, Grand Duke of Russia. VS, V, p. 12

Allen, Clifford. VS, V, p. 64

Allen, W. E. D. VS, V, p. 1

Allison, J. M. S. VS, VI, p. 10

Alsace-Lorraine Since 1870. VS, V, p. 2

American-British relations. MH, VI, p. 9; VS, V, p. 25

America Ratio and the Communist Party in the Post-War World. VS, V, p. 37

American (U.S.) foreign policy and general history. MH, V, p. 23; MH, VI, p. 4; MH, VI, p. 11; VS, V, p. 5; VS, V, p. 58; VS, VI, p. 14

American (U.S.) government. VS, VI, p. 14

Amery, Julian. MH, VI, p. 3

Angell, Norman. VS, V, p. 15; VS, V, p. 19; VS, V, p. 58; VS, V, p. 64VS, VI, p. 5; VS, VI, p. 13; VS, VI, p. 14

Anglo-American Relations 1861–1865. MH, VI, p. 9

Anglo-Indians, The. VS, V, p. 66

Annuaire Interparlementaire: Premiere Annee. VS, V, p. 65

Annual Digest of Public International Law Cases, for the Years 1925–1926. VS, V, p. 77

Annual Register of World Events: A Review of Public Events at Home and Abroad for the Year 1928. VS, V, p. 74

Anson, W.R. VS, III, p. 1

Anthony, Katherine. VS, VI, p. 4

Anti Drug Campaign: An Experiment in International Control. VS, V, p. 15

Arab Conquest of Egypt and the Last Thirty Years of The Roman Domination, The. VS, V, p. 39

Arbiter in Council, The. VS, V, p. 11

Arbitration. VS, V, p. 70

Archer, William. VS, V, p. 60

Arnold-Forster, W. VS, V, p. 70

Art of Thought, The. VS, VI, p. 7

Arthur James Balfour: 1st Earl of Balfour K.G.O.M., F.R.S. 1906–1930. VS, VI, p. 17

Ascent of Humanity: An essay on the Evolution of Civilization. VS, VI, p. 14

Asia. MH, VI, p. 11; VS, V, p. 3; VS, V, p. 5; VS, VI, p. 5; VS, VI, p. 18

Asquith, Cyril. VS, VI, p. 9

Assyria. VS, V, p. 24

Attack and Other Papers, The. MH, VI, p. 8

Australia and the British Commonwealth. VS, V, p. 1

Austria. VS, V, p. 70; VS, VI, p. 16

Autobiography [of Bertrand Russell] 1872–1967 MH, VI, p. 7

Autobiography [of Leonard Woolf... **Vol. II: Growing: Autobiography of the years 1904–1911.** VS, III, p. 16

Autobiography of John Stuart Mill. VS, V, p. 29

Autocrat of the Breakfast Table, The: VS, III, p. 15

Babbitt, Irving. VS, VI, p. 5
Bailey, S. H. VS, V, p. 14; VS, V, p. 15
Baker, P. J. Noel. VS, VI, p. 10
Baker, Ray Stannard. VS, VI, p. 14
Balfour, Arthur. VS, VI, p. 17
Balkan League, The. VS, V, p. 24
Balkans. VS, V, p. 24; VS, V, p. 29
Ball, A. H. R. (ed.) MH, VI, p. 11
Ballinger, W. G. VS, V, p. 62
Barbier, Edmund-Jean-Francois. VS, V, p. 40
Barclay, Sir Thomas. VS, VI, p. 10
Barker, Ernest (ed.). VS, V, p. 3
Barker, Ernest. VS, V, p. 6; VS, VI, p. 13
Barker, R. E. VS, V, p. 36
Barnes, L. VS, V, p. 29
Barnes, Leonard. VS, III, p. 1
Barron, C. W. VS, V, p. 5
Basic Writings of [Bertrand Russell] 1903–59 MH, VI, p. 7
Basis of Durable Peace, The. VS, V, p. 15
Bates, J. V. MH, VI, p. 11
Beatrice Webb 1858–1943. MH, V, p. 11
Beatrice Webb. MH, VI, p. 2
Beaverbrook, Lord. MH, VI, p. 1
Beer, M. VS, VI, p. 12
Before the War. VS, VI, p. 14
Before the War. Vol. 2: The Coming of the Storm. VS, VI, p. 17

Before, During and After 1914. VS, V, p. 39
Behemoth or The Long Parliament. VS, V, p. 69
Belgian Congo and the Berlin Act, The. VS, VI, p. 13
Belgium. MH, VI, p. 11; VS, V, p. 42
Bell, Julian. MH, IV, p. 1
Belloc, Hilaire. MH, VI, p. 11
Benighted Mexico. VS, V, p. 42
Benjamin Franklin. VS, VI, p. 8
Bergson, H. MH, V, p. 23
Berlin Act. VS, VI, p. 13
Bernard, L. L. MH, V, p. 21
Best, Mary Agnes. VS, VI, p. 3
Bevan, Edwyn. VS, V, p. 71
Beyens, Le Baron. VS, V, p. 28
Bibliotheca Mysticorum Selecta. VS, III, p. 10
Bismarck. MH, VI, p. 8
Björnson, Björnstjerne. VS, VI, p. 9
Black Man's Burden, The. VS, V, p. 60
Black Man's Part in the War, The. VS, VI, p. 6
Black Sheep of the Balkans, The. VS, V, p. 29
Blake, Robert. MH, VI, p. 1
Bland, J. O. P. VS, VI, p. 17
Bloomsbury Group, The. MH, VI, p. 5
Blunt, Wilfred Scawen. VS, V, p. 2
Boissier, Leopold, B. Mirkine-Guetzevitch. VS, V, p. 65
Bolshevik Revolutions 1917–1923. MH, VI, p. 12
Bolshevik Theory, The. VS, VI, p. 1

Bolshivism. MH, VI, p. 11

Bonjour, Felix. VS, VI, p. 7

Borkenau, F. MH, VI, p. 1

Bosanquet, Bernard. VS, V, p. 52; VS, VI, p. 10

Bosanquet, H. MH, VI, p. 11

Bosphorus and Dardanelles. VS, VI, p. 13

Boswell, A. B. VS, V, p. 45

Bourne, H. R. Fox. VS, VI, p. 4

Boxer Indemnity and Chinese Education. VS, V, p. 43

Brailsford, H. N. VS, V, p. 8; VS, V, p. 36; VS, V, p. 37; VS, VI, p. 1; VS, VI, p. 3; VS, VI, p. 6

Breasted, J. H. VS, V, p. 60

Brief History of Moscovia and Other Less-Known Countries Lying Eastward of Russia as far away as Cathay. VS, V, p. 46

Brief History of Poland. VS, VI, p. 16

Bright, John. VS, VI, p. 6

Brimble, L. J. F. VS, V, p. 37

Britain in Southern Africa. VS, V, p. 62

Britain Overseas: The story of the foundations and development of the British Empire from 1495–1921. VS, VI, p. 9

British Civil Servant, The. MH, V, p. 10

British Colonial Policy in The Age of Peel and Russell. VS, V, p. 10

British Commonwealth (also Empire). VS, V, p. 7; VS, V, p. 22; VS, V, p. 29; VS, V, p. 36; VS, V, p. 38; VS, V, p. 59; VS, V, p. 61; VS, V, p. 65; VS, VI, p. 7; VS, VI, p. 8; VS, VI, p. 12; VS, VI, p. 13; VS, VI, p. 18

British Commonwealth of Nations: A Study of its Past and Future Development. VS, VI, p. 13

British Commonwealth Relations. VS, V, p. 38

British Diplomacy 1813–1815.: Select documents dealing with the reconstruction of Europe. VS, VI, p. 13

British foreign policy. MH, VI, p. 8; MH, VI, p. 9; MH, VI, p. 12; VS, III, p. 1; VS, III, p. 13; VS, V, p. 12; VS, V, p. 16; VS, V, p. 23; VS, VI, p. 2; VS, VI, p. 3; VS, VI, p. 4; VS, VI, p. 5; VS, VI, p. 8; VS, VI, p. 16

British Guiana. VS, V, p. 46

British history. MH, III, p. 15; MH, V, p. 20; MH, VI, p. 2; MH, VI, p. 3; MH, VI, p. 6; MH, VI, p. 7; MH, VI, p. 10; MH, VI, p. 12; VS, III, p. 1 ; VS, V, p. 4; VS, V, p. 6; VS, V, p. 8; VS, V, p. 11; VS, V, p. 12; VS, V, p. 30; VS, V, p. 39; VS, V, p. 40; VS, V, p. 41; VS, V, p. 43; VS, V, p. 45; VS, V, p. 46; VS, V, p. 54; VS, V, p. 62; VS, V, p. 64; VS, V, p. 72; VS, V, p. 74; VS, V, p. 77; VS, VI, p. 1; VS, VI, p. 5; VS, VI, p. 6; VS, VI, p. 8; VS, VI, p. 12; VS, VI, p. 14; VS, VI, p. 16; VS, VI, p. 18

British Revolution and American Democracy: An Interpretation of British Labour Programmes. VS, V, p. 19

British Slavery and Its Abolition 1823–1838. VS, VI, p. 11

British West African Settlements 1750–1821: A Study in Local Administration. VS, V, p. 11

British Working Class Politics 1832–1914. MH, VI, p. 2

British-American relations. MH, VI, p. 9

Brookes, E. H. VS, VI, p. 11

Brown Book of the Hitler Terror and the Burning of the Reichstag, The. VS, V, p. 5

Browne, W. J. VS, III, p. 9

Broz, Alexander. VS, V, p. 7

Buckle, G. E. VS, V, p. 72

Bullock, Alan. MH, VI, p. 1

Bulow, Prince Bernhard von. VS, V, p. 7

Burma. VS, VI, p. 18

Burns, C. D. VS, V, p. 45; VS, V, p. 70

Burns, C. Delisle. VS, VI, p. 2

Burrow, George. MH, VI, p. 1

Bury, J. P. T. VS, V, p. 39

Butler, A. J. VS, V, p. 39

Butler, Harold. MH, VI, p. 1

Butler, N. M. MH, V, p. 22

Butler, R. MH, VI, p. 9

Butler, Sir Geoffrey. MH, VI, p. 11

Buxton, Leland. VS, V, p. 29

Buxton, Noel. VS, VI, p. 13

Byron: The Last Journey, April 1823–April 1824. VS, V, p. 10

Caillaux, Joseph. VS, V, p. 27

Callieres, Francois de. VS, V, p. 32

Calvert, A. F. VS, V, p. 5

Cameroons, The. VS, V, p. 5

Canada. VS, V, p. 38; VS, V, p. 68

Capitalism (see also "Communism," "Socialism," and "Economics"). VS, V, p. 42

Carr, E. H. MH, VI, p. 2; MH, VI, p. 12; VS, VI, p. 6

Carr-Saunders, A. M. MH, VI, p. 2; VS, III, p. 11

Carteret: The Brilliant Failure of the 8th Century. VS, V, p. 14

Catherine the Great. VS, VI, p. 4

Causes of International War. VS, VI, p. 4

Cawnpore. VS, III, p. 11

Celebrated Trials and Remarkable Cases of Criminal Jurisprudence from the Earliest Records to the Year 1925. MH, VI, p. 1

Censorship. MH, VI, p. 11; VS, V, p. 16; VS, V, p. 25; VS, V, p. 30; VS, VI, p. 1

Century of Co-Operation. MH, VI, p. 2

Cerf, Barry. VS, V, p. 2

Ceylon under British Rule 1795–1932. VS, V, p. 46

Ceylon. MH, III, p. 15; VS, III, p. 3; VS, V, p. 46; VS, V, p. 61; VS, VI, p. 14

Ceylon: A Study of the Report of the Special Commission on the Constitution. VS, VI, p. 14

Ceylon: Correspondence regarding the Constitution of Ceylon. VS, V, p. 61

Chambers, F. P. MH, VI, p. 2

Chamier, J. Daniel. VS, V, p. 35

Champion, Piérre. VS, VI, p. 4

Chance: A Tale in 2 parts. VS, VI, p. 5

Changes in the Legal Structure of the British Commonwealth of Nations. VS, V, p. 38

Chaos in China. VS, V, p. 42

Charpentier, Armand. MH, VI, p. 2

Chartist movement. VS, VI, p. 12

Chesson, W. H. MH, VI, p. 9

Childs, J. L. VS, V, p. 37

China and the League of Nations. VS, V, p. 48

China, Captive or Free? A Study of China's Entanglements. VS, VI, p. 16

China, Japan and Korea. VS, VI, p. 17

China. VS, V, p. 1; VS, V, p. 6; VS, V, p. 8; VS, V, p. 14; VS, V, p. 42; VS, V, p. 43; VS, V, p. 48; VS, V, p. 60; VS, V, p. 59; VS, V, p. 70; VS, V, p. 72; VS, VI, p. 5; VS, VI, p. 10; VS, VI, p. 16; VS, VI, p. 17

Choice Before Us, The. VS, VI, p. 9

Christian Socialism 1848-1854. MH, VI, p. 11

Chronique de la Regence et du Regne de Louis XV. 1718-1763 ou Journal de Barbier. VS, V, p. 40

City Manager Government in Nine Cities. VS, V, p. 25

Civil service (British). VS, III, p. 9

Civil Service Compendium for 1936. VS, III, p. 9

Civilization in Congoland: A Story of International Wrong Doing. VS, VI, p. 4

Civilization, history of. VS, V, p. 60; VS, V, p. 64; VS, VI, p. 14

Clark, Cumberland. VS, VI, p. 9

Clark, G. K. VS, VI, p. 4

Clark, Grenville. VS, V, p. 66

Clementy, Sir Cecil. VS, V, p. 46

Clifford, Lady Anne. VS, VI, p. 8

Clifford, Sir Hugh. VS, V, p. 62

Coal, Iron and the War. A Study in Industrialism Past and Future. VS, III, p. 12

Cobban, Alfred. MH, VI, p. 2

Cobbett, William. VS, V, p. 12; VS, V, p. 75

Cobbetts Political Register. VS, V, p. 75

Cochin, Augusten. VS, V, p. 78

Cocks, F. S. (ed.). VS, V, p. 2

Cole, G. D. H. MH, VI, p. 2; VS, V, p. 2; VS, V, p. 3; VS, V, p. 4; VS, V, p. 45

Cole, M. I. VS, III, p. 11

Cole, Margaret. MH, VI, p. 2

Coleman, Frederick. VS, VI, p. 5

Collective Security. VS, V, p. 53; VS, V, p. 58

Colonial Population. VS, V, p. 59

Colonial Problem, The. MH, V, p. 21

Coming Victory of Democracy, The. VS, V, p. 8

Commonsense of Municipal Trading, The. VS, V, p. 17

Commonwealth of Nations: An Enquiry into the Nature of Citizenship in the British Empire.... VS, VI, p. 18

Communism. MH, V, p. 18; MH, V, p. 23; MH, VI, p. 9; MH, VI, p. 11; MH, VI, p. 12; VS, V, p. 5; VS, V, p. 15; VS, V, p. 23; VS, V, p. 27; VS, V, p. 37; VS, VI, p. 1; VS, VI, p. 4; VS, VI, p. 11; VS, VI, p. 13; VS, VI, p. 14

Communist Part of the Soviet Union, The. MH, V, p. 18

Community of the Future, The. VS, V, p. 66

Complete Pacifist, The. VS, V, p. 17

Complete Works of Walter Savage Landor, The. VS, VI, p. 18

Compulsory Service. A Study of the Question in the Light of Experience. VS, V, p. 10

Conduct of British Empire Foreign Relations since the Peace Settlement, The. MH, V, p. 16

Conference of Ambassadors, The. MH, V, p. 22

Congress of Vienna: A Study in Allied Unity 1812-1822. MH, VI, p. 6

Conquest of the River Plate, The. VS, VI, p. 13

Conrad, Joseph. VS, III, p. 2; VS, III, p. 3; VS, VI, p. 5

Conservatism in England: An Analytical, Historical and Political Survey. VS, V, p. 62

Constitution for the Socialist Commonwealth of Great Britain. VS, V, p. 59

Constitution of Canada in Its History and Practical Working, The. VS, V, p. 38

Constitutional History of British Guiana. VS, V, p. 46

Constitutional Law of the British Dominions. VS, V, p. 11

Constitutional Year Book 1939. VS, V, p. 75

Consumer's Co-Operation in Great Britain. MH, VI, p. 2

Consumer's Co-operative Movement, The. VS, VI, p. 7

Contraband. VS, VI, p. 16

Conwell-Evans, T. P. VS, V, p. 47

Cook, Sir Edward. VS, V, p. 11

Co-Operation for Africa. VS, V, p. 43

Co-operations at Home and Abroad and Description and analysis with Supplement on the Progress of Co-operation in the United Kingdom 1908-1918. VS, V, p. 6

Co-Operative Movement in Great Britain, The. VS, V, p. 27

Co-operative movement. MH, V, p. 22; MH, VI, p. 2; VS, III, p. 8; VS, V, p. 6; VS, VI, p. 7; VS, V, p. 27; VS, V, p. 41

Co-Partnership and Profit Sharing. VS, V, p. 41

Corn Laws and Social England, The. VS, V, p. 45

Corvin, E. S. MH, V, p. 23

Cory, G. E. VS, V, p. 74

Cosmos [i.e. Butler, Nicholas Murray]. VS, V, p. 15

Counter-Attack from the East: The Philosophy of Radhakrichnan. VS, VI, p. 14

Counts, G. S. VS, V, p. 3; VS, V, p. 37

Coupland, R. VS, V, p. 60

Cramb, J. A. VS, V, p. 63

Creed of a Tory, The. VS, VI, p. 5

Criminal Procedure Code, The. (Ceylon) MH, III, p. 15

Critical and Historical Essays. VS, V, p. 54

Critique of the Gotha Programme. VS, V, p. 1

Croce, B. VS, V, p. 6

Cromer, The Earl of. VS, III, p. 12; VS, V, p. 44

Cuba. VS, VI, p. 14

Curtis L. (ed.). VS, VI, p. 18

Curtis, L. VS, V, p. 22

Curtis, Lionel. VS, VI, p. 12

Czechoslovakia. VS, V, p. 7

Czernin, Count Ottokar. VS, VI, p. 2

Dangers of Half-Preparedness: A Plea for a Declaration of American Policy. VS, VI, p. 14

Darby, W. Evans. VS, III, p. 3

Dare the School Build a New Social Order. VS, V, p. 3

Davies, M. L. MH, V, p. 22

Dawson, Thomas. VS, V, p. 16

Dawson, William Harbutt. VS, VI, p. 12; VS, VI, p. 16; VS, VI, p. 17

Days are Long, The. VS, V, p. 36

de la Tramerye, Pierre L'espanol. VS, VI, p. 12

De Lanessan, J.-L. MH, VI, p. 12

Debidour, A. VS, V, p. 73

Declaration of Paris 1856: A Study Documented. VS, VI, p. 9

Decline of the West, The. VS, VI, p. 14

Defence of Freedom, The. MH, VI, p. 7

Democracy and Leadership. VS, VI, p. 5

Democracy and the Eastern Question. VS, VI, p. 7

Democracy at the Crossways. MH, V, p. 23

Democracy in Crisis. VS, VI, p. 14

Democracy on Trial: A preface to an Industrial Policy. VS, VI, p. 11

Democracy, Its Defects and Additions. VS, VI, p. 2

Democracy. MH, VI, p. 4

Democracy. VS, V, p. 8

Democracy: Being an abridged edition of the Limits of Pure Democracy. VS, V, p. 8

Demos Esclav et Roi. VS, V, p. 5

Dennis, A. L. P. MH, V, p. 20

Denny, Ludwell. VS, V, p. 69

Deslinieres, Lucien. VS, V, p. 59

Deutscher, I. MH, VI, p. 2

Development of Extraterritoriality in China, The. VS, V, p. 72

Dewey, A. Gordon. VS, V, p. 68

Diaries of [Beatrice Webb] 1912–1932. MH, VI, p. 9

Diaries of John Bright, The. VS, VI, p. 6

Diaries of William Johnston Temple: 1780–1796. VS, VI, p. 8

Diary of Lady Anne Clifford. VS, VI, p. 8

Diaz. VS, VI, p. 3

Dicey, A. V. MH, VI, p. 3

Dickinson, G. Lowes (ed.). VS, V, p. 22

Dickinson, G. Lowes. VS, VI, p. 4; VS, VI, p. 9; VS, VI, p. 11

Die Kommunistische International. MH, V, p. 23

Dillon, E. J. VS, V, p. 2

Dimitrov, G. VS, V, p. 60

Disarmament Deadlock, The. VS, V, p. 52

Disraeli, Benjamin. VS, V, p. 8

Disraeli. VS, VI, p. 3

Disraeli: The Alien Patriot. MH, VI, p. 7

Dobbs, A. E. MH, VI, p. 10

Documents on British Foreign Policy 1919–1939. MH, VI, p. 9

Documents on International Affairs. VS, V, p. 75

Dollar Diplomacy. A Study in American Imperialism. VS, V, p. 58

Dominions of Diplomacy: The Canadian Contribution. VS, V, p. 68

Doyle, Phyllis. VS, V, p. 2

Dreyfus Case, The. MH, VI, p. 2

Drinkwater, John. VS, VI, p. 14

Drugs, the international control of (esp. Opium). VS, V, p. 10; VS, V, p. 15; VS, V, p. 33; VS, V, p. 69

Dugdale, Blanch E. C. VS, VI, p. 17

Duggan, S. P. (ed.). MH, VI, p. 10

Dukem, Jules. VS, VI, p. 6

Dulainse F. VS, VI, p. 2

Duncan, Ronald.

Durbin, E. F. M. VS, III, p. 8

Dutt, R.P. VS, VI, p. 8

Duty of Empire, The. VS, III, p. 1

Earle, E. M. MH, V, p. 22

Earle, Edward Mead. VS, V, p. 65

Early History of Cuba 1492–1586. VS, VI, p. 14

Early Life and Letters of John Morley. VS, VI, p. 8

Eastern Question: Historical Study in European Diplomacy, The. VS, V, p. 3

Eastern Star Dust. MH, IV, p. 1

Eckel, Edwin C. VS, III, p. 12

Eclipse of Russia, The. VS, V, p. 2

Economic Aspects of Native Segregation in South Africa, The. VS, V, p. 46

Economic Development of the British Overseas Empire, The. VS, VI, p. 8

Economic History: A Supplement to the Economic Journal. VS, V, p. 77

Economic Journal (A Quarterly), The. VS, V, p. 76; VS, V, p. 77

Economic Revolution in British West Africa, The. VS, V, p. 48

Economics. VS, V, p. 8; VS, V, p. 14; VS, V, p. 20; VS, V, p. 53; VS, V, p. 55; VS, V, p. 65; VS, V, p. 76; VS, V, p. 77; VS, VI, p. 8

Eddy, J. P. VS, V, p. 7

Editor: A Second Volume of Autobiography 1931–45 [Kingsley Martin]. MH, VI, p. 6

Edmund Burke and the Revolution Against the 18th Century. MH, VI, p. 2

Edmund Burke. MH, VI, p. 6

Education and Social Movements 1700–1850. MH, VI, p. 10

Education in East Africa. VS, V, p. 24

Education of Henry Adams. An Autobiography. VS, VI, p. 9

Education. MH, VI, p. 10; VS, V, p. 3; VS, V, p. 37

Educational Theories. VS, V, p. 3

Egypt. MH, V, p. 4; VS, V, p. 2; VS, III, p. 12; VS, V, p. 39

Eichmann Trial, The. MH, VI, p. 7

Eighteenth Brumaire of Louis Bonaparte, The. VS, V, p. 60

Elliott, Hugh. VS, VI, p. 7

Elton, Godfrey. VS, V, p. 67

Emigration. VS, VI, p. 10

Empire and Commerce in Africa.: A Study in Economic Imperialism. VS, III, p. 8

Empire and the Future: A series of Imperial Studies Lectures delivered in the University of London. King's College (1916). VS, VI, p. 7

Empire or Democracy: A Study of the Colonial Question. VS, V, p. 29

Enchen, Cecil C. VS, VI, p. 16

Enfield, A. Honora. VS, V, p. 3

Enforced Peace. MH, VI, p. 11

Engels: On Capital. VS, V, p. 23

England 1870–1914. MH, VI, p. 3

England in the Age of the American Revolution. VS, VI, p. 14

England under Queen Anne. VS, V, p. 74

England under the Stuarts. VS, V, p. 41

England's Debt to India: An Historical Narrative of Britain's Fiscal Policy in India. VS, VI, p. 1

England's Guarantee to Belgium and Luxemburg with the full text of the treaties. VS, V, p. 42

English Constitutional Conflicts of the Seventeenth Century. 1603–1689. VS, VI, p. 12

English Local Government: Statutory Authorities for Special Purposes. MH, V, p. 20

Enquiry Concerning Political Justice and Its Influence on Virtue and Happiness. MH, VI, p. 3

Ensor, R.C.K. MH, VI, p. 3

Epstein, M. VS, V, p. 51

Equality: The Halley Stewart Lectures, 1929. VS, VI, p. 7

Erasmus and Luther: Their Attitude to Toleration VS, VI, p. 3

Erasmus. VS, VI, p. 8

Ernst, M. L. VS, VI, p. 1

Ervine, St. John. VS, V, p. 13

Esher, Reginald (Viscount). MH, VI, p. 3

Essay in Persuasion MH, VI, p. 5

Essays on Nationalism. VS, VI, p. 10

Ethics of Opium, The. VS, V, p. 69

Europe in the Age of Napoleon. VS, V, p. 17

Europe in the Nineteenth and Twentieth Centuries, 1789–1938. VS, VI, p. 2

Europe in the Nineteenth Century. VS, V, p. 2

European conservatism. VS, V, p. 16

European history. MH, VI, p. 2; MH, VI, p. 4; MH, VI, p. 6; MH, VI, p. 12; VS, III, p. 17; VS, V, p. 2; VS, V, p. 6; VS, V, p. 17; VS, V, p. 20; VS, V, p. 42; VS, V, p. 49; VS, V, p. 60; VS, V, p. 67; VS, V, p. 73; VS, VI, p. 1; VS, VI, p. 2; VS, VI, p. 14; VS, VI, p. 16; VS, VI, p. 17

Evatt, H. V. VS, V, p. 7

Eve of 1914, The. VS, VI, p. 17

Eveleigh, William. VS, V, p. 29

Eversley, Lord. VS, VI, p. 10

Everybody's Political What's What. MH, VI, p. 8

Evolution of Modern Germany, The. VS, VI, p. 12

Evolution of Parliament, The. VS, V, p. 59

Ewart, John S. VS, V, p. 69

Expansion of Europe, The. VS, VI, p. 1

Expansion of Europe: A history of the foundations of the modern world. VS, VI, p. 14

Exterritoriality of Ambassadors in the 16th and 17th Centuries. VS, V, p. 67

Fabian Colonial Essays. VS, V, p. 36

Fabian Essays by Bernard Shaw, Sidney Webb etc. MH, VI, p. 3

Fabian Society, history of. VS, V, p. 68

Fabre-Luce, Alfred. VS, V, p. 68

Fabulous Monster (A Life of Kaiser Wilhelm 2nd). VS, V, p. 35

Fachiri, A. P. VS, V, p. 59

Faguet, Emile. MH, VI, p. 3

Falsehood in War Time. VS, V, p. 30

Fanshawe, Maurice. VS, V, p. 71

Far East Unveiled: An Inner History of Events in Japan and China in the Year 1916. VS, VI, p. 5

Far Eastern Republic of Siberia, The. VS, V, p. 1

Farjenel, Fernand. VS, VI, p. 16

Fascism and Social Revolution. VS, VI, p. 8

Fascism. MH, VI, p. 1; MH, VI, p. 11; VS, V, p. 5; VS, V, p. 48; VS, V, p. 60; VS, V, p. 62

Fascist Germany Explains. VS, V, p. 48

Fateful Years 1909–1916. The Reminiscences of Serge Sazonov, Russian Minister from Foreign Affairs 1914. VS, VI, p. 4

Faulkner, H. U. VS, V, p. 5

Fay, C. R. VS, V, p. 6; VS, V, p. 45; VS, VI, p. 6

Fay, S. B. VS, V, p. 44

Feiling, K. VS, V, p. 41

Feiling, Keith. MH, VI, p. 3

Fidel, M. Camille. VS, VI, p. 2

Fifty Years of Europe 1870–1919. VS, V, p. 67

Fifty Years of Europe: A Study in Pre-War Documents. VS, VI, p. 16

Finer, Herman. VS, VI, p. 16

Finlay, George. VS, V, p. 68

First Workers Government; or New Times for Henry Dubb. VS, V, p. 70

Fitzmaurice, Lord Edmond. VS, V, p. 40

Flenley, R. VS, V, p. 64

Fletcher, C. Brunsdon. VS, V, p. 68; VS, VI, p. 13

Florence, P. S. MH, VI, p. 2; VS, III, p. 11; VS, V, p. 14

Footnote to the History of the British Empire. VS, VI, p. 8

Foreign Diplomacy in China 1894–1900. VS, V, p. 1

Foreign Financial Control in China. VS, VI, p. 14

Foreign Investment and War. VS, V, p. 53

Foreign Policies of Soviet Russia, The. MH, V, p. 20

Foreign Policy of Canning 1822–1827. MH, VI, p. 8

Foreign Policy of Castlereagh 1815–1822: Britain and the European Alliance. VS, VI, p. 2

Foreign Relations in British Labour Politics. VS, VI, p. 5

Foreign Rights and Interest in China. VS, V, p. 8

Forster, E. M. MH, V, p. 4

Forward to Liberalism. VS, V, p. 15

Foundations of International Polity, The. VS, V, p. 64

Foundations of Modern China, The. VS, V, p. 59

Foundations of Sovereignty and Other Essays. VS, VI, p. 13

Fox, Charles James. VS, V, p. 6

Framework of International Society, The. VS, V, p. 14

Franco-Prussian relations. VS, III, p. 13; VS, VI, p. 9

Franklin, Benjamin. VS, VI, p. 8

Fraser, Robert. VS, III, p. 1

Frederic William Maitland 1850–1906. VS, V, p. 13

Frederic William Maitland. VS, V, p. 13

Freeman, J. VS, V, p. 58

French colonial policy. MH, VI, p. 7; VS, VI, p. 2

French government. VS, V, p. 10; VS, V, p. 39; VS, V, p. 40; VS, V, p. 58; VS, V, p. 60; VS, V, p. 65; VS, V, p. 73; VS, VI, p. 9; VS, VI, p. 12

French Liberal Thought in the Eighteenth Century. VS, VI, p. 2

French Political Thought in the 19th Century. VS, VI, p. 7

French Revolution, The. VS, VI, p. 1

French, military history. MH, VI, p. 2; MH, VI, p. 12; VS, V, p. 48; VS, V, p. 78

French-German relations. VS, V, p. 2; VS, V, p. 28; VS, VI, p. 2; VS, VI, p. 6

Friedrich Engels. A Biography. VS, VI, p. 4

Friends of Voltaire, The. VS, V, p. 38

From Geneva to the Next War. VS, III, p. 15

From Groves of Palm. VS, III, p. 9

Fulani, Fulani Bin. VS, III, p. 2

Function of the State in Promoting the Unity of Mankind, The. VS, VI, p. 10

Furnivall, J. S. VS, V, p. 48

Future Government of Indian and the Indian Civil Service, The. VS, V, p. 3

Future of Democracy, The. VS, V, p. 1

Future of the Indo-British Commonwealth, The. VS, III, p. 13

Gambetta and the National Defence, and Republican Dictatorship in France. VS, V, p. 39

Garvey, Marcus. VS, V, p. 73

Garvin, J. L. MH, VI, p. 3

Gathorne-Hardy, G. M. VS, V, p. 47

Gavit, J. P. VS, V, p. 10

Gayda, Virginio. VS, VI, p. 16

General Foch at the Marne MH, VI, p. 10

Geneval Protocol for the Pacific Settlement of International Disputes, The. VS, VI, p. 10

Gerig, Benjamin. VS, V, p. 6

German colonial affairs (esp. Pacific). VS, V, p. 68

German Colonial Empire: Its Beginning and Ending. VS, VI, p. 6

German Colonies: A Plea for the Native Races. VS, V, p. 62

German Diplomatic Documents 1871-1914. VS, V, p. 76

German Empire 1867-1914 and the Unity Movement. VS, VI, p. 17

German Empire of Central Africa, The. VS, VI, p. 5

German history MH, VI, p. 7; MH, VI, p. 8; VS, III, p. 8; VS, V, p. 3; VS, V, p. 5; VS, V, p. 6; VS, V, p. 7; VS, V, p. 11; VS, V, p. 31; VS, V, p. 35; VS, V, p. 45; VS, V, p. 54; VS, V, p. 57; VS, V, p. 62; VS, V, p. 63; VS, V, p. 76; VS, VI, p. 9; VS, VI, p. 12; VS, VI, p. 16

German-French relations. VS, III, p. 13; VS, V, p. 2; VS, VI, p. 28; VS, VI, p. 2; VS, VI, p. 6

German-U.S. relations. MH, VI, p. 8

Germany and England. VS, V, p. 63

Germany in Transition. VS, V, p. 54

Germany's First Bid for Colonies 1884-1885: A Move in Bismarck's European Policy. VS, VI, p. 12

Germany's Third Empire. VS, VI, p. 9

Gettell, R. G. VS, V, p. 26

Geyer, C. VS, V, p. 3

Gheon, Henri. VS, V, p. 5

Giles, Herbert A. VS, V, p. 42

Ginsburg, B. W. VS, VI, p. 6

Giordan, Paolo. VS, VI, p. 6

Gladstone and the Irish Nation. MH, VI, p. 4

Glass Palace Chronicle of the Kings of Burma, The. VS, VI, p. 18

Godwin, William. MH, VI, p. 3

Gold Standard in Theory and Practice, The. VS, V, p. 65

Golder, F. A. VS, V, p. 53

Gollancz in German Wonderland. VS, V, p. 3

Gollin, Alfred M. MH, VI, p. 3

Gooch, G. P. MH, VI, p. 4; VS, V, p. 8; VS, V, p. 67; VS, VI, p. 17

Government and the Press 1695–1763. MH, VI, p. 11

Government of Egypt, The. MH, V, p. 4

Government of the British Empire (as at the End of the Year 1917). VS, V, p. 10

Government, theory of. MH, VI, p. 11; VS, III, p. 11; VS, V, p. 3; VS, V, p. 7; VS, V, p. 25; VS, V, p. 59; VS, V, p. 66; VS, V, p. 69; VS, V, p. 75; VS, VI, p. 1; VS, VI, p. 10; VS, VI, p. 13

Graham, R. B. Cunningham. VS, VI, p. 13

Grammar of Politics. VS, V, p. 16

Grant A. J. VS, VI, p. 2

Granville Sharp and the Freedom of Slaves in England. VS, VI, p. 4

Great Britain and the Slave Trade 1839–1865. VS, V, p. 39

Great Chartered Companies, The. VS, V, p. 8

Great European Treaties of the Nineteenth Century, The. VS, VI, p. 2

Great Illusion: A Study of the Relation of Military Power to National Advantage. VS, V, p. 58

Greaves, H. R. G. VS, VI, p. 14

Greece and the Allies 1914–1922. VS, V, p. 23

Greece Before the Conference. VS, V, p. 7

Greece. VS, V, p. 6; VS, V, p. 7; VS, V, p. 23; VS, V, p. 71

Gregory, J. W. VS, VI, p. 10

Grey of Fallodon, Being the Life of Sir Edward Grey afterwards Viscount Grey of Fallodon. VS, VI, p. 9

Grey, Viscount of Fallodon. VS, VI, p. 17

Growth of Philosophic Radicalism. MH, VI, p. 4

Guedalla, Philys. VS, VI, p. 3

Guenther, H. F. K. VS, V, p. 42

Gueshoff, I. E. VS, V, p. 24

Guest, L. H. VS, V, p. 7

Guild Socialism. VS, V, p. 3

Guildswomen at Basle. VS, V, p. 3

Gulliver's Travels. VS, VI, p. 7

Hail and Farewell: A Trilogy. Vol. 3 only–Vale. VS, VI, p. 18

Haldane 1856–1928. VS, VI, p. 4

Haldane, J. B. S. VS, V, p. 22; VS, V, p. 27

Haldane, Viscount. VS, VI, p. 14

Halevy, E. MH, VI, p. 12

Halevy, Elie. MH, VI, p. 4; VS, V, p. 73; VS, V, p. 74

Hall, H. Duncan. VS, VI, p. 13

Hamilton, General Sir Ian. VS, V, p. 10

Hammond, B. MH, VI, p. 12; VS, V, p. 77

Hammond, J. L. MH, VI, p. 4; MH, VI, p. 12; VS, V, p. 77

Handbook of Palestine and Trans-Jordan, The. VS, V, p. 1

Handbook of Public International Law. VS, V, p. 1

Handbook to the League of Nations. MH, VI, p. 11

Hannay, David. VS, V, p. 8; VS, VI, p. 3

Hanotaux, Gabriel. VS, V, p. 73

Hanson, Laurence. MH, VI, p. 11

Hapsburg Monarchy, The. VS, V, p. 45

Harold Laski (1893-1950). MH, VI, p. 6

Harper, Northrup. VS, V, p. 53

Harris, J. H. VS, VI, p. 2

Harris, John H. VS, V, p. 53

Harrison, Maire. VS, V, p. 28

Harrod, R. F. MH, VI, p. 4

Hawtrey, R. G. VS, V, p. 65

Hayes, Carlton J. H. VS, VI, p. 10; VS, VI, p. 14

Hazen, Charles Downer. VS, V, p. 67

Hazlitt, William. VS, VI, p. 9

Heading for the Abyss. MH, VI, p. 5

Headlam, A. S. VS, VI, p. 5

Heard, Gerald. VS, VI, p. 14

Hearnshaw, F. J. C. MH, V, p. 23; VS, V, p. 62

Henderson, Arthur. MH, VI, p. 11

Hendrick, Burton J. MH, VI, p. 4

Herbert Spencer. VS, VI, p. 7

Herbert, Sydney. VS, VI, p. 1

Herrick, Christine Terhune (ed.). MH, VI, p. 4

Herzen, Alexander. VS, V, p. 14

Hibbert, W. N. VS, V, p. 16

Hill, R.L. VS, V, p. 64

Hinde, H. VS, V, p. 31

Hinden, Rita. MH, VI, p. 4

Hirst, F. W. VS, VI, p. 8

Hirst, Francis W. VS, V, p. 55

His [Gustav Stresemann's] Diaries, Letters and Papers. VS, III, p. 8

Histoire de l'Entente Cordiale: Franco-Anglaise. MH, VI, p. 12

Histoire Diplomatique de l'Europe: Depuis le Congres de Berlin Jusqu'a nos Jours. VS, V, p. 73

Histoire du Peuple Anglais au XIX Siecle: Epilogue 1895-1914. VS, V, p. 73

Historian's Approach to Religion, A. MH, VI, p. 8

Historical Relations Between Japan and Saghalier, The. VS, V, p. 42

History of "The Times" 1785-1948. MH, VI, p. 8

History of Assyria. VS, V, p. 24

History of British Socialism. VS, VI, p. 12

History of England. VS, VI, p. 14

History of Europe in the Nineteenth Century. VS, V, p. 6

History of Free Thought in the Nineteenth Century. VS, VI, p. 16

History of French Colonial Policy 1870–1925. MH, VI, p. 7

History of India. VS, V, p. 61

History of Native Policy in South Africa from 1830 to the Present Day. VS, VI, p. 11

History of Political Thought. VS, V, p. 26

History of Political Thought. VS, V, p. 2

History of Rome. VS, V, p. 71

History of South Africa 1795 to 1872. VS, VI, p. 17

History of South Africa 1873–1884. VS, VI, p. 17

History of the Byzantine Empire from DCCXVI to MLVII. VS, V, p. 68

History of the Chartist Movement. VS, VI, p. 12

History of the English People in 1815. VS, V, p. 74

History of the English People, A. MH, VI, p. 12

History of the Fabian Society. VS, V, p. 68

History of the Indian Nationalist Movement. VS, VI, p. 10

History of the Tory Party 1640–1714. VS, V, p. 41

History of the Tory Party in the Seventeenth and Eighteenth Centuries with a sketch of its development in the Nineteenth Century. VS, VI, p. 14

History of Trade Unionism, The. VS, VI, p. 4

History of Twelve Days. July 24–August 4th, 1914. VS, VI, p. 5

Hitler, Adolf. MH, VI, p. 4; VS, V, p. 5

Hitler. MH, VI, p. 1

Hobbes, Thomas. VS, V, p. 69

Hobson, J. A. MH, VI, p. 4; VS, VI, p. 3; VS, VI, p. 6

Hodgson, Margaret L. VS, V, p. 62

Holland, Bernard. VS, V, p. 49

Holmes, Oliver Wendell. VS, III, p. 15

Holroyd, Michael. MH, VI, p. 4

Holy War "Made in Germany", The. VS, V, p. 31

Hon. Sir Charles Murray, K. C. B., A Memoir. VS, V, p. 12

Hone, Joseph. MH, VI, p. 5

Hour of Decision. Part 1: Germany and the World-Historical Traditions. VS, VI, p. 12

House of Commons 1832–1901, The. VS, V, p. 6

House of Lords in the XVIII Century, The. VS, VI, p. 5

House, Colonel. VS, VI, p. 17

How France Is Governed. VS, V, p. 10

How the War Came. VS, VI, p. 8

Howard-Ellis, C. VS, V, p. 24

Howland, C. P. VS, V, p. 25

Hug-Hellmuth, Hermine Von (ed.). VS, V, p. 9

Huizinga, J. VS, VI, p. 8

Human Migration and the Future: A Study of the Causes, Effects and Control of Emigration. VS, VI, p. 10

Human Nature in Politics. VS, V, p. 5

Humphrys, I. H. VS, V, p. 48

Hungary. VS, V, p. 70

Hurgronje, C. Snouck. VS, V, p. 31

Hutchins, B. L. VS, V, p. 17

Huxley, Aldous. VS, VI, p. 16

Huxley, Elspeth. Parham, Margery. VS, VI, p. 14

Huxley, Julian. VS, V, p. 36

Hyndman, H. M. VS, V, p. 1

I Seek the Truth. A book on responsibility for war [by William of Germany]. VS, VI, p. 11

Idealist View of Life, An. MH, VI, p. 7

Ilbert, Sir Courtenay. VS, V, p. 54

Imperial Germany. VS, V, p. 7

Imperial Trusteeship. VS, V, p. 61

Imperium et Libertas: A Study in History and Politics. VS, V, p. 49

In My Tower [Lady Walburga Paget]. VS, VI, p. 17

In the Fourth Year: Anticipations of a World Peace. MH, VI, p. 12

In the World War. VS, VI, p. 2

India. VS, III, p. 9; VS, III, p. 13; VS, V, p. 3; VS, V, p. 7; VS, V, p. 48; VS, V, p. 61; VS, V, p. 64; VS, V, p. 66; VS, V, p. 68; VS, VI, p. 1; VS, VI, p. 6; VS, VI, p. 10; VS, VI, p. 11; VS, VI, p. 12; VS, VI, p. 14

India's New Constitution. A Survey of the Government of India Act 1935. VS, V, p. 7

Indian Constitution, The. VS, III, p. 9

Indian National Congress, The. VS, V, p. 64

Information on the Problem of Security (1917–1926). VS, V, p. 58

Information on the World Court 1918–1928. VS, V, p. 71

Instincts of the Herd in Peace and War. VS, V, p. 34

Intellectual history (political). VS, V, p. 2; VS, VI, p. 16

Internation Conventions and Third States: A Monograph. VS, VI, p. 13

International Arbitration–International Tribunals. **Addendum.** VS, III, p. 3

International Cases: Arbitrations and Incidents Illustrative of International Law as Practiced in Independent States. VS, V, p. 72

International Conciliation. MH, V, p. 24

International Conciliation. VS, V, p. 79

International government. VS, V, p. 14; VS, VI, p. 6; VS, VI, p. 11

International Guarantees of Minority Rights: Procedure of the Council of the League of Nations in Theory and Practice. VS, V, p. 64

International Hierarchy, 1904–1914. VS, VI, p. 11

International Law and the Great War. VS, VI, p. 12

International Law. VS, V, p. 68

International Law: A Treatise in 2 volumes. VS, V, p. 72

International Mind, The. MH, V, p. 22

International Private Law. Or the Conflict of Law. VS, V, p. 16

International Protection of Labour, The. VS, V, p. 32

International relations. MH, V, p. 22; MH, VI, p. 8; VS, V, p. 32; VS, V, p. 47; VS, V, p. 64; VS, V, p. 70; VS, V, p. 75

International Rivers. VS, III, p. 6

International unions. MH, VI, p. 12; VS, III, p. 3

Intimate Papers of Colonel House: Arranged as a Narrative by Charles Seymour. VS, VI, p. 17

Introduction to Politics, An. VS, V, p. 59

Introduction to Social Psychology. MH, V, p. 21

Introduction to the Peace Treaties, The. MH, V, p. 21

Ireland. MH, VI, p. 4; VS, V, p. 13; VS, VI, p. 18

Irrational Knot, The. VS, III, p. 2

Irresistible Movement of Democracy, The. VS, VI, p. 2

Isvolsky and the World War: Based on Documents Recently Published by the German Foreign Office. VS, V, p. 69

Iswolsky, Alexander. VS, VI, p. 6

It Happens in Russia: Seven Years Forced Labor in the Siberian Gold Fields. MH, VI, p. 7

Italy. VS, VI, p. 16

Japan. The New World Power. VS, V, p. 4

Japan. MH, VI, p. 10; VS, V, p. 4; VS, V, p. 5; VS, V, p. 42; VS, V, p. 54; VS, V, p. 70; VS, VI, p. 5; VS, VI, p. 17

Japan's Foreign Policies. VS, V, p. 54

Japan's Pacific Policy. MH, VI, p. 10

Jenks, Edward. VS, V, p. 10

Jennings, W. I. VS, V, p. 2

Jeudwine, J. W. VS, V, p. 46

Jews of Africa, Especially in the 16th and 17th Centuries, The. VS, V, p. 8

Jews, The. MH, VI, p. 11

Joad, C. E. M. VS, V, p. 36; VS, VI, p. 14

John Anderson, Viscount Waverley. MH, VI, p. 9

John Smith Moffat C.M.G., A Missionary: A Memoir. VS, VI, p. 8

Johnston, Sir H. H. VS, V, p. 9; VS, VI, p. 6

Johnstone, J. K. MH, VI, p. 5

Jones, T. J. (ed.). VS, V, p. 24

Joseph, P. VS, V, p. 1

Journals and Letters of Viscount Reginald Esher. MH, VI, p. 3

Journey to the Frontier: Julian Bell and John Cornford: Their Lives and the 1930s. MH, III, p. 15

Jurisprudence. MH, VI, p. 1; VS, VI, p. 14

Justice and Administration Law: A Study of the British Constitution. VS, VI, p. 14

Justinian. The Institutes of: VS, III, p. 3; VS, III, p. 7

Kaeckenbeeck, G. VS, III, p. 6

Kaiser Wilhelm II. VS, VI, p. 7

Kaiser, His Personality and Career, The. MH, V, p. 23

Karl Marx. An Essay. VS, V, p. 15

Kautsky, Karl. VS, VI, p. 11

Kawakami, K. K. MH, VI, p. 10

Keeton, G. W. VS, V, p. 72

Keigwin's Rebellion (1683–4): An Episode in the History of Bombay. VS, V, p. 68

Keith, A. B. VS, V, p. 11; VS, V, p. 65; VS, VI, p. 13

Keith, A. B. (ed.). VS, V, p. 17

Keith-Roach, E. VS, V, p. 1

Kelsen, Hans. VS, VI, p. 1

Keltie, Sir John S. VS, V, p. 51

Kennedy, W. P. M. VS, V, p. 58

Kenya from Within. A short political history. VS, VI, p. 13

Kenya. VS, V, p. 49

Kerensky, A. F. VS, VI, p. 14

Kerner, R. J. VS, V, p. 53

Keynes, J. M. (ed.). VS, V, p. 77

Keynes, John Maynard. MH, VI, p. 5; VS, V, p. 5

Kikuyu Central Association. VS, V, p. 4

King and His Dominion Governors, The. VS, V, p. 7

King Edward VII: A Biography. VS, VI, p. 17

Kirk on the Zambesi: A Chapter of African History. VS, V, p. 60

Kirk, John. VS, V, p. 46

Knight, W. S. M. VS, V, p. 14

Knowles, L.C.A. VS, VI, p. 8

Koebel, W.H. VS, VI, p. 1

Koo, V. K. Wellington. VS, V, p. 48

Korea. VS, VI, p. 17

Kruse, Vinding. VS, V, p. 66

Kuczynski, R. R. VS, V, p. 59

Kuomintang and the Future of the Chinese Revolution, The. VS, V, p. 6

L'Europe et lat Politique Britannique 1882-1912. VS, V, p. 17

L'Union des Associations Internationales. VS, V, p. 75

La Démocratic Suisse. VS, VI, p. 7

La Democratic. Sa nature–Sa valeur. VS, VI, p. 1

La France Nord-Africaine. Etude critique de la Colonization Anarchique Pratiquee Jusqu'a ce Jour. VS, V, p. 59

La Motte, Ellen M. VS, V, p. 69

La Paige Coloniale Francaise. VS, VI, p. 2

La Question Africaine. VS, V, p. 28

Labour Party (movement). MH, VI, p. 11; VS, V, p. 4; VS, V, p. 7; VS, V, p. 64; VS, V, p. 67; VS, VI, p. 5

Labour Party and the Empire, The. VS, V, p. 7

Labour's Future at Stake. VS, V, p. 64

Lafayette: A Biography MH, VI, p. 10

LaFerriere, J. VS, V, p. 65

Laissez-Faire and Communism. VS, V, p. 5

Lamperley, H. VS, VI, p. 2

Land and Labour in a Deccan Village. MH, V, p. 22

Landor, Walter Savage. VS, VI, p. 18

Langermann, F. E. VS, V, p. 58

Language Question in Belgium, The. MH, VI, p. 11

Lanson, Gustave. VS, V, p. 78

Lascelles, E. C. P. VS, VI, p. 4

Laski, H. J. VS, V, p. 3; VS, V, p. 20

Laski, H. J., et al. VS, V, p. 36

Laski, Harold J. MH, VI, p. 5; VS, III, p. 11; VS, V, p. 15; VS, V, p. 16; VS, V, p. 36; VS, V, p. 59; VS, VI, p. 1; VS, VI, p. 12; VS, VI, p. 13; VS, VI, p. 14

Laski, Herold J. [*sic*.] VS, VI, p. 14

Index to Part 3   237

Lasting Peace Through the Federations of Europe and the State of War. VS, V, p. 9

Latham, J. G. VS, V, p. 1

Lauterpacht, H. (ed.). VS, V, p. 77

Law and Custom of South African Constitution, The. VS, V, p. 58

Law and the Constitution, The. VS, V, p. 2

Law of Banker and Customer, The. VS, V, p. 20

Law of Contraband of War, The. VS, VI, p. 16

Law of the Press, The. VS, V, p. 16

Law, constitutional. MH, VI, p. 5; VS, V, p. 2; VS, V, p. 11

Law, international. MH, VI, p. 11; VS, III, p. 6; VS, V, p. 16; VS, V, p. 32; VS, V, p. 59; VS, V, p. 64; VS, V, p. 66; VS, V, p. 68; VS, V, p. 72; VS, V, p. 77; VS, V, p. 79; VS, VI, p. 10; VS, VI, p. 12

Lawrence, T. J. VS, V, p. 1

Le Goffic, C. MH, VI, p. 10

Le Government de M. Thiers 1870–1873. VS, V, p. 73

League Committees and World Order: A study of the permanent expert committees of the League of Nations as an instrument of International Government. VS, VI, p. 14

League Council in Action: A study of the methods employed by the Council of the League of Nations to prevent War and to settle International Disputes. VS, V, p. 47

League of Nations and Its Problems: Three Lectures. MH, VI, p. 6

League of Nations and the Rule of Law 1918–1935, The. VS, V, p. 58

League of Nations in Theory and Practice, The. VS, VI, p. 1

League of Nations Starts: An Outline by its Organizers. VS, VI, p. 11

League of Nations, A. VS, VI, p. 1

League of Nations, The. VS, VI, p. 7

League of Nations. MH, VI, p. 6; MH, VI, p. 10; MH, VI, p. 11; VS, V, p. 6; VS, V, p. 24; VS, V, p. 44; VS, V, p. 47; VS, V, p. 58; VS, V, p. 61; VS, V, p. 69; VS, VI, p. 1; VS, VI, p. 7; VS, VI, p. 11; VS, VI, p. 14

League of Nations: A Chapter in the History of the Movement. VS, V, p. 61

League of Nations: The Principle and the Practice. MH, VI, p. 10

Leang-Li, T'ang. VS, V, p. 59

Lee, Sir Sidney. VS, VI, p. 17

Lemonon, Ernest. VS, VI, p. 17

Lenin, V. I. VS, V, p. 47; VS, VI, p. 12

Leonard Woolf, et al. VS, V, p. 36

Les Societes de Pensee et la revolution en Bretagne 1788–1789. VS, V, p. 78

Letters of Runnymede, The. VS, V, p. 8

Letters of the Duke of Wellington to Miss J. 1834–51. MH, VI, p. 2

Letters to the Peoples of India on Responsible Government. VS, VI, p. 12

Lettres Choisies [de Voltaire]. VS, V, p. 41

Levine, I. D. MH, VI, p. 11

Lewin, E. VS, VI, p. 12

Lewis, Wyndam. MH, VI, p. 5

Leys, Norman. VS, V, p. 49

Liberty in the Modern State. VS, VI, p. 1

Lichnowsky, Prince. MH, VI, p. 5

Lieven, Princess. VS, V, p. 12

Life and Labour in the Nineteenth Century. VS, VI, p. 6

Life and Letters of Anne Isabella, Lady Noel Byron. VS, VI, p. 9

Life and Letters of George William Frederick 4th Earl of Clarendon. VS, V, p. 30

Life and Works of Hugo Grotius. VS, V, p. 14

Life of Andrew Carnegie. MH, VI, p. 4

Life of Benjamin Disraeli, Earl of Beaconsfield. VS, V, p. 72

Life of Benjamin Franklin. VS, VI, p. 8

Life of Florence Nightingale. VS, V, p. 11

Life of Granville, George Leveson Gower, Second Earl Granville K. G., 1815–1891. VS, V, p. 40

Life of Henry Tonks, The. MH, VI, p. 5

Life of Herbert Henry Asquith, Lord Oxford and Asquith. VS, VI, p. 9

Life of John Bright. MH, VI, p. 9

Life of John Maynard Keynes, The. MH, VI, p. 4

Life of Joseph Chamberlain. MH, VI, p. 3

Life of Lord Curzon: Being the Authorized Biography of George Nathaniel, Marquess of Kodleston K.G. VS, VI, p. 17

Life of Neville Chamberlain, The. MH, VI, p. 3

Limitations of Victory, The. VS, V, p. 68

Lincoln, Abraham. VS, VI, p.3

Lindley, M. F. VS, V, p. 59

Lindsay, A. D. MH, VI, p. 5

Lippmann, Walter. VS, V, p. 59

Lipson, E. VS, V, p. 2

Livy, Titus. VS, V, p. 71

Loeb, W. VS, V, p. 3

Loftus, Pierse. VS, VI, p. 5

London and Westminster in History and Literature. VS, VI, p. 18

London: Its Origin and Early Development. VS, VI, p. 14

Lord Grey and the World War. VS, V, p. 40

Lord Grey of the Reform Bill, Being the Life of Charles, Second Earl Grey. VS, V, p. 64

Lord Lyons, A Record of British Diplomacy. VS, V, p. 12

Loreburn, The Earl. VS, VI, p. 8

Lost Peace, The. MH, VI, p. 1

Lothian, Lord. VS, V, p. 36

Louis XI. VS, VI, p. 4

Lovett, Sir Verney. VS, VI, p. 10

Lowe, B. E. VS, V, p. 32

Lucas, Sir Charles. VS, V, p. 64; VS, VI, p. 8

Ludwig, Emil. VS, VI, p. 7

Lugard: The Years of Adventure. MH, VI, p. 7

Luke, Sir Harry. VS, V, p. 1

Lutz, Hermann. VS, V, p. 40

Luxembourg. VS, V, p. 42

Lyall, Sir Alfred. VS, V, p. 5

Lytton Strachey. Vol. 1: The Unknown Years. 1880–1910. MH, VI, p. 4

Macartney, C. A. VS, V, p. 67

Macaulay, Lord. VS, V, p. 25

Macaulay, Thomas Babington. VS, V, p. 54
MacDonald, J. Ramsey. VS, V, p. 7
Mackay, Robert A. VS, V, p. 38
Macmillan, Harold. MH, VI, p. 5
Maddox, W. P. VS, VI, p. 5
Maitland, F. W. VS, V, p. 12
Making the Fascist State. VS, V, p. 62
Mallock, W H. VS, V, p. 8
Mandates. VS, V, p. 44
Mann, Golo. MH, VI, p. 6
Mann, H. H. MH, V, p. 22
Mann, Thomas. VS, V, p. 8
Marburg, Theodore. VS, V, p. 61
Marginal Notes. VS, V, p. 25
Marriott, J. A. R. VS, V, p. 3
Martin, E. C. VS, V, p. 11
Martin, Kingsley. MH, VI, p. 6; VS, V, p. 2; VS, VI, p. 2
Marx, Karl. VS, V, p. 1; VS, V, p. 60
Marxist Philosophy and the Sciences, The. VS, V, p. 27
Masaryk, T. G. VS, VI, p. 14
Massingham, H. W. VS, V, p. 11
Mathieson, W. T. VS, VI, p. 11
Mathieson, William Law. VS, V, p. 39
Mathiez, Albert. VS, VI, p. 1
Maurice, Sir Frederick. VS, VI, p. 4
Maurtua, Victor M. VS, III, p. 1
Max Weber and German Politics: A Study in Political Sociology. VS, V, p. 36
Maxwell, Herbert. VS, V, p. 12; VS, V, p. 30
May, F. J. VS, V, p. 37

Mayer, Gustav. VS, VI, p. 4
Mayer, J. P. VS, V, p. 36
Mayne, Ethel Colburn. VS, VI, p. 9
Mazzini, Joseph. VS, VI, p. 3
Mazzini's Letters to an English Family 1844–1854. VS, VI, p. 3
McCabe, J. MH, V, p. 23
McNair, A. D. VS, V, p. 53
McNair, A. D. (ed.). VS, V, p. 77
McPhee, Allan. VS, V, p. 48
Meaning of War, The. MH, V, p. 23
Memoirs of Alexander Herzen, The. VS, V, p. 14
Memoirs of Alexander Iswolsky. VS, VI, p. 6
Memoirs of Catherine the Great. VS, VI, p. 7
Memoirs of Count Wilte, The. VS, VI, p. 10
Memoirs of Raymond Poincaré, The. VS, VI, p. 3
Memoirs of Raymond Poincare: 1914. Vol. 3. VS, VI, p. 17
Men and Power. MH, VI, p. 1
Mendelssohn, Sidney. VS, V, p. 8
Menken, H. L. VS, VI, p. 16
Mexican Problem, The. VS, V, p. 5
Mexico Today and Tomorrow. VS, V, p. 64
Mexico. VS, V, p. 5; VS, V, p. 42; VS, V, p. 64
Michael Bakunin. VS, VI, p. 6
Michels, Robert. VS, VI, p. 11
Middle East. VS, V, p. 1
Military and Colonial Policy of the United States, The. MH, VI, p. 11

Mill, John Stuart. MH, V, p. 3; VS, V, p. 29; VS, V, p. 67; VS, V, p. 68

Millard, Thomas F. VS, VI, p. 7

Miller, D. H. VS, V, p. 1

Mills, Lennox A. VS, V, p. 46

Milton, John. VS, V, p. 46

Minorca, military history. MH, VI, p. 9

Minority Report of the Poor Law Commission, The. VS, V, p. 4

Mitchison, G. R. VS, V, p. 70

Modern Austria: Her Racial and Social Problems, with a Study of Italia Irredenta. VS, VI, p. 16

Modern Democratic State, The. MH, VI, p. 5

Modern Egypt. VS, III, p. 12

Moffat, R. U. VS, VI, p. 8

Mohr, Anton. VS, VI, p. 11

Monckton Jones, M. E. VS, VI, p. 11

Moneypenny, W. F. VS, V, p. 72

Monsieur Thiers. VS, VI, p. 10

Moore, George. VS, VI, p. 18

Morel, E. D. MH, V, p. 12; VS, III, p. 1; VS, V, p. 45; VS, V, p. 60; VS, V, p. 61

Morgan, R. B. (ed.). VS, VI, p. 1

Morrell, W. P. VS, V, p. 10

Morrison, C. C. VS, VI, p. 3

Mowat, R. B. VS, V, p. 17; VS, V, p. 60

Mowat, R. D. (ed.). VS, VI, p. 2

Mr. Dooley in Peace and War. VS, V, p. 55

Muggeridge, Kitty. MH, VI, p. 6

Muir, Ramsay. VS, VI, p. 1

Municipal trading. VS, V, p. 17

Munro, H. F. VS, V, p. 72

Murray, D. H. VS, VI, p. 3

Murray, R. H. VS, VI, p. 3; VS, VI, p. 5

Mussolini's Italy. VS, VI, p. 16

Must Be War! VS, V, p. 15

Must Britain Travel the Moscow Road? VS, VI, p. 5

My [Beatrice Webb's] Apprenticeship. MH, VI, p. 9

My Early Life [Kaiser Wilhelm II of Germany]. VS, VI, p. 10

Namier, L. B. MH, VI, p. 6; VS, VI, p. 14

National Character and the Factors in Its Formation. VS, VI, p. 13

National States and National Minorities. VS, V, p. 67

Nationalism. VS, V, p. 8

Nationalism. MH, VI, p. 10

Nationalism. MH, VI, p. 10; VS, V, p. 6; VS, V, p. 8; VS, VI, p. 10; VS, VI, p. 13

Nationality and the War. VS, V, p. 58

Nationality. VS, V, p. 58; VS, V, p. 67

Native Races and Their Rulers [in Nigeria]. VS, V, p. 53

Nearing, S. VS, V, p. 58

Neff, Wanda Fraiken. VS, VI, p. 12

Netherlands India: A Study of Plural Economy. VS, V, p. 48

New Germany, The. VS, VI, p. 16

New History of the C.W.S., The. VS, V, p. 64

New Methods of Adjusting International Disputes and the Future. VS, VI, p. 10

New Pacific: British Policy and German Aims. VS, V, p. 68

New Reform Bill, A. VS, V, p. 3

Newman, Bertram. MH, VI, p. 6

Newton, Lord. VS, V, p. 12

Nicolson, Harold. MH, V, p. 21; MH, VI, p. 6; VS, V, p. 10; VS, VI, p. 4

Nietzsche, Fredrich. VS, VI, p. 3

Nigger of the Narcissus, The. VS, III, p. 3

Noel-Baker, Philip. VS, VI, p. 17

Norton, H. T. J. VS, V, p. 42

Norton, Henry. VS, V, p. 1

Notes on Democracy. VS, VI, p. 16

Nystrom, Anton. VS, V, p. 39

Oakes, A. (ed.). VS, VI, p. 2

Observer and J. L. Garvin 1908–1914, The. MH, VI, p. 3

Oeuvres: Completes De L'Imprimerie De La Societe Litteraire – Typographique (Voltaire). VS, III, p. 16

Oil (world competition). VS, VI, p. 11; VS, VI, p. 12

Oil War, The. VS, VI, p. 11

Oldham, J. H. VS, V, p. 27

Olives of Endless Age: Being a Study of the Distracted World and Its Need of Unity. VS, V, p. 8

Olivier, Lord. VS, V, p. 61

Olmstad, A. T. VS, V, p. 24

On Liberty. VS, V, p. 67

On the Margin: Notes and Essays. VS, VI, p. 16

Once a Grand Duke [Alexander of Russia]. VS, V, p. 12

Open Door and the Mandates System, The. VS, V, p. 6

Opening Up of Africa, The. VS, V, p. 9

Opium as an International Problem: The Geneva Conferences. VS, V, p. 33

Opium. VS, V, p. 10

Oppenheim, L. MH, VI, p. 6

Oppenheim, L. VS, V, p. 72

Origin, Structure and Working of the League of Nations. VS, V, p. 24

Origins of the World War, The. VS, V, p. 44

Orvis, Julia Swift. VS, VI, p. 16

Osbourne, Sidney. VS, III, p. 13

Ossiannilsson, K. G. MH, V, p. 24

Ostrerog, Count Léon. VS, VI, p. 1

Our [Sydney and Beatrice Webb] Partnership. MH, VI, p. 9

Our Allies and Enemies in the Near East. MH, VI, p. 11

Our Settlement with Germany. VS, V, p. 37

Outlawry of War: A Constructive Policy in World Peace, The. VS, VI, p. 3

Overlach, T.W. VS, VI, p. 14

Pacific [The]–Its Past and Future: The Policies of the Great Powers from 18th Century. VS, VI, p. 2

Pacifism. VS, V, p. 8; VS, V, p. 17

Page, William. VS, VI, p. 14

Paget, Walburga, Lady. VS, VI, p. 17

Paine, Thomas. VS, V, p. 58

Paleface. The Philosophy of the "Melting Pot." MH, VI, p. 5

Palmerson. VS, VI, p. 3

Pamphlets on Chinese Questions. VS, V, p. 43

Paoadatos, Peter. MH, VI, p. 7

Paraguay. VS, VI, p. 1

Paris Commune, The. VS, VI, p. 12

Parliament. It's History, Constitution and Practice. VS, V, p. 54

Parliamentary Government in England. VS, VI, p. 12

Parnell. VS, V, p. 13

Partition and Colonization of Africa, The. VS, VI, p. 8

Patriotism in Literature. VS, VI, p. 14

Peace (see also "Pacifism"). MH, V, p. 16; MH, V, p. 20; MH, V, p. 21; MH, VI, p. 1; MH, VI, p. 11; MH, VI, p. 12; VS, III, p. 7; VS, III, p. 9; VS, III, p. 15; VS, V, p. 1; VS, V, p. 8; VS, V, p. 9; VS, V, p. 15; VS, V, p. 25; VS, V, p. 34; VS, V, p. 36; VS, V, p. 37; VS, V, p. 47; VS, V, p. 52; VS, V, p. 55; VS, V, p. 66; VS, V, p. 68; VS, VI, p. 3; VS, VI, p. 6; VS, VI, p. 13; VS, VI, p. 14

Peace and the Colonial Problem. VS, III, p. 9

Peace Pact of Paris: A Study of the Briand-Kellogg Treaty. VS, V, p. 1

Peacemakers, The. MH, V, p. 20

Pearce, Major F. B. VS, V, p. 5

Pease, Edward R. VS, V, p. 68

Peel and the Conservative Party. A Study in Party Politics 1832-41. VS, VI, p. 4

Peers, R. MH, VI, p. 2; VS, III, p. 11

Peiris, M. V. P. VS, VI, p. 14

Pemberton, W. B. VS, V, p. 14

Penman, John S. VS, VI, p. 2

People and Constitution, The. VS, VI, p. 16

People's Front Against Fascism and War, The. VS, V, p. 60

Percy, Lord Eustace. VS, VI, p. 11

Perham, M. MH, VI, p. 7

Permanent Court of International Justice: It's [sic] Constitution Procedure and Work. VS, V, p. 59

Perrin, Alice. VS, V, p. 66

Petrov, V. MH, VI, p. 7

Petrovich, W. M. VS, V, p. 1

Petrunkevitch, A., S. VS, V, p. 53

Phillipson, Coleman. VS, V, p. 25; VS, VI, p. 12; VS, VI, p. 13

Philosophical radicalism. MH, VI, p. 4

Philosophical Theory of the State, The. VS, V, p. 52

Philosophy and Opinions of Marcus Garvey: Or, Africa for the Africans. VS, V, p. 73

Pierson, N. G. VS, V, p. 77

Piggott, Sir Francis. VS, VI, p. 9

Pigou, A. C. VS, V, p. 7

Pinchbeck, Ivy. MH, VI, p. 7

Pink, G. P. MH, V, p. 22

Pink, M. Alderton. MH, VI, p. 7; VS, VI, p. 14

Pioneers of the French Revolution, The. VS, VI, p. 9

Plan for Africa: A Report Prepared for the Colonial Bureau of the Fabian Society. MH, VI, p. 4

Plays [of Björnstjerne Björnson]. VS, VI, p. 9

Podmore, Frank. VS, V, p. 11

Poincaré, Raymond. VS, V, p. 10; VS, VI, p. 3; VS, VI, p. 17

Points of View. A Series of Broadcast Addresses by H. G. Wells, J. B. S. Haldane and Others. VS, V, p. 22

Poiret, Peter. VS, III, p. 10

Poland and the Poles. VS, V, p. 45

Poland. VS, V, p. 45; VS, VI, p. 16

Political and Social History of Modern Europe. VS, VI, p. 14

Political Conditions of Allied Success–A Plea for the Protection of the Democracies. VS, VI, p. 13

Political Future of India, The. VS, VI, p. 6

Political Morality of the Nineteenth Century. MH, VI, p. 3

Political Myths and Economic Realities. VS, VI, p. 2

Political Parties. A Sociological Study of the Oligarchical Tendencies of Modern Democracy. VS, VI, p. 11

Political philosophy. MH, VI, p. 7; MH, VI, p. 11; VS, III, p. 4; VS, V, p. 36; VS, V, p. 44; VS, V, p. 52; VS, V, p. 59; VS, VI, p. 2; VS, VI, p. 3; VS, VI, p. 4; VS, VI, p. 5; VS, VI, p. 9; VS, VI, p. 14

Political Quarterly, The. VS, III, p. 5

Political Quarterly, The. VS, V, p. 76

Political thought (history). VS, V, p. 2; VS, V, p. 5; VS, V, p. 20; VS, V, p. 24; VS, V, p. 26; VS, V, p. 75

Political Thought in England from Locke to Bentham. VS, V, p. 20

Political Writings During the American and French Revolutions. VS, V, p. 58

Politics of Democratic Socialism: An Essay on Social Policy. VS, III, p. 8

Pollard, A. F. VS, V, p. 59

Pollock, F. VS, V, p. 13

Pollock, Sir Frederick. VS, VI, p. 7

Polybius. VS, V, p. 7

Ponsonby, Arthur. VS, V, p. 30

Pooley, A. M. VS, V, p. 54

Porter, R. P. VS, V, p. 4

Post Victorians, The. VS, VI, p. 11

Postgate, R. W. VS, VI, p. 1

Potter (later Webb), Beatrice. VS, V, p. 27

Power and New Social Analysis. VS, V, p. 24

Power of Illusion and the Illusion of Power, The. VS, VI, p. 4

Power: A New Social Analysis. MH, VI, p. 7

Practice of Diplomacy, The. VS, V, p. 32

Practices and Theory of Bolshevism, The. VS, VI, p. 13

Prelude to Bolshevism: The Krenilov Rebellion. VS, VI, p. 14

President's Control of Foreign Relations, The. MH, V, p. 23

Pribram, A. F. VS, V, p. 70

Price, D. K. VS, V, p. 25

Price, M. P. VS, V, p. 54

Prince Max of Baden: The Memoirs of. MH, VI, p. 7

Principles of Economics. VS, V, p. 77

Principles of Social Reconstruction. VS, III, p. 1

Principles of the English Law of Contract. VS, III, p. 1

Private Manufacture of Armaments, The. VS, VI, p. 17

Problem of China, The. VS, VI, p. 10

Problem of the Anglo-Japanese Alliance, The. VS, V, p. 5

Problem of the Commonwealth, The. VS, V, p. 22

Problem of the Pacific: Preface by Sir William MacGregor. VS, VI, p. 13

Problems of a Socialist Government. VS, V, p. 67

Problems of Industrial Development in China: A Preliminary Study. VS, V, p. 60

Proceedings of the Gibbon Commemoration 1794–1894. VS, V, p. 6

Programme for Victory: A Collection of Essays Prepared for the Fabian Society by H. J. Laski, Herbert Read &c. MH, VI, p. 10

Progress of a Ploughboy to a Seat in Parliament, The. VS, V, p. 12

Prophet Armed: Trotsky 1879–1921: The Prophet Unarmed: Trotsky 1921, The. MH, VI, p. 2

Public International Unions. Their Work and Organization. VS, III, p. 3

Public Opinion. VS, V, p. 59

Publishing. MH, VI, p. 9

Pursuit of Happiness: The Story of American Democracy. VS, VI, p. 14

Pyke, H. Reason. VS, VI, p. 16

Quaker Grandmother: Hanna Whitall Smith. VS, V, p. 47

Queen Victoria. The Letters of. MH, VI, p. 10

Question of Alsace-Lorraine, The. VS, VI, p. 6

Question of the Bosphorus and Dardanelles, The. VS, VI, p. 13

Questions of the Pacific, The. VS, III, p. 1

Race and Politics in Kenya: A Correspondence. VS, VI, p. 14

Racial Elements of European History, The. VS, V, p. 42

Radhakrishnan, S. MH, VI, p. 7

Rai, Lajpat. VS, VI, p. 1

Rai, Tajpat. VS, VI, p. 6

Ramsay, A. A. W. MH, VI, p. 7

Raven, C. E. MH, VI, p. 11

Raymond, E. T. MH, VI, p. 7

Readings in English Social History from Pre-Roman Days to A.D. 1837. VS, VI, p. 1

Readings in Recent Political Philosophy. VS, V, p. 44

Realist Looks at Democracy with a preface by Aldous Huxley. VS, VI, p. 14

Recent Revelations of European Democracy. VS, V, p. 67

Recent Revelations of European Diplomacy. MH, VI, p. 4

Red Rubber: The Story of the Rubber Slave Trade which flourished on the Congo for 20 years 1890–1910. VS, V, p. 61

Redfern, Percy. VS, V, p. 64

Reed, John. MH, V, p. 23

Reflections on the Revolution of Our Time. VS, V, p. 36

Reflections on Violence. MH, VI, p. 8

Reid, Rev. Gilbert VS, VI, p. 16.

Reinsch, P. S. MH, VI, p. 10; VS, III, p. 3

Relations between China and Japan during the Last 25 Years. VS, V, p. 70

Religion and the Rise of Capitalism: A Historical Study. VS, V, p. 42

Resources of the Empire and their Development, The. VS, VI, p. 12

Responsible Government in the Dominions. VS, V, p. 65

Revolt Against Civilization. The Menace of the Under-man. MH, VI, p. 11

Richard Cobden and Foreign Policy: A Critical Exposition, with Special References to our Day and Its Problems. VS, VI, p. 16

Richard Cobden, The International Man. VS, VI, p. 3

Richard Steele. VS, III, p. 5

Riches, Cromwell A. VS, V, p. 69

Riddell, W. R. VS, V, p. 38

Rights of Women and the Subjection of Women, The. VS, V, p. 68

Rise of European Liberalism: An Essay in Interpretation. VS, VI, p. 14

Rise of South Africa: A History of the Origin of South African Colonization and Its Development towards the East from the Earliest Times to 1857. VS, V, p. 74

Rise of the British Dominion in India, The. VS, V, p. 5

Rise of the Czechoslovak Republic, The. VS, V, p. 7

Ritchie, Alice. MH, V, p. 20

Robert Owen: A Biography. VS, V, p. 11

Roberts, Stephen H. MH, VI, p. 7

Robertson, J. M. VS, VI, p. 16

Robespierre. MH, VI, p. 8

Robson, W. A. (ed.). MH, V, p. 10

Robson, W.A. VS, VI, p. 14

Robson, William A. VS, III, p. 5

Roman history. VS, III, p. 3; VS, III, p. 7; VS, V, p. 68; VS, V, p. 71

Ronaldshay, The Earl of [cat. under Zetland]. VS, VI, p. 17

Root, E. MH, VI, p. 11

Roots and Causes of the War (1914-1918), The. VS, V, p. 69

Ross, W. McGregor. VS, VI, p. 13

Rousseau, J. J. VS, V, p. 9

Roustan, M. VS, VI, p. 9

Rover, The. VS, VI, p. 5

Roxburgh, F. VS, VI, p. 13

Ruskin as a Literary Critic. MH, VI, p. 11

Ruskin, John. VS, VI, p. 5

Russell, Bertrand. MH, VI, p. 7; VS, III, p. 1; VS, V, p. 24; VS, V, p. 45; VS, VI, p. 5; VS, VI, p. 6; VS, VI, p. 10; VS, VI, p. 13

Russian history. MH, VI, p. 7; VS, V, p. 2; VS, V, p. 11; VS, V, p. 12; VS, V, p. 37; VS, V, p. 46; VS, VI, p. 4; VS, VI, p. 7; VS, VI, p. 14

Russian Revolution, The. MH, VI, p. 11; VS, VI, p. 6

Russian Revolution. Writings and speeches from the February Revolution to the October Revolution 1917, The. VS, V, p. 47

Russian Revolution: The Jugo-Slav Movement. VS, V, p. 53

Russian Workers Republic, The. VS, VI, p. 6

Saar Question. A Disease Spirit in Europe, The. VS, III, p. 13

Saburov Memoirs or Bismarck and Russia, Being Fresh Light on the League of the Three Emperors 1881. VS, V, p. 11

Sandburg, Carl. VS, VI, p. 3

Sanger, C. P. VS, V, p. 42

Sapru, Sir Tej Bahadur. VS, III, p. 9

Sarajevo: A Study into the Origins of the Great War. VS, V, p. 71

Sazonov, Serge. VS, VI, p. 4

Schapiro, L. MH, V, p. 18

Schirokauer, (Arno) Lassalle. VS, VI, p. 4

Schlosberg, H. J. VS, V, p. 58

Schneider, H. W. VS, V, p. 62

Scholefield, G. H. VS, VI, p. 2

Science and Ethics. VS, V, p. 6

Scientific management MH, VI, p. 11

Scoot, A. P. MH, V, p. 21

Scott, J. B. MH, V, p. 22

Seagle, W. VS, VI, p. 1

Secret Agent, The. VS, III, p. 2

Secret Diplomacy: How far can it be eliminated? MH, VI, p. 10

Secret History of the English Occupation of Egypt. VS, V, p. 2

Secret Treaties and Understandings, The. VS, V, p. 2

Secret Treaties of Austria and Hungary 1879-1914: Texts of the Treaties and Agreements. VS, V, p. 70

Secretary of Europe. The Life of Friedrich Gentz. MH, VI, p. 6

Select Constitutions of the World. VS, V, p. 7

Select Treatise and Documents to Illustrate the Development of the Modern European States-System. VS, V, p. 60

Selected Essays [of F. W. Maitland]. VS, V, p. 12

Selected Essays [of William Hazlitt]. VS, VI, p. 9

Selected Letters of Fredrich Nietzsche. VS, VI, p. 3

Selection from the Writings of H. W. Massingham. VS, V, p. 11

Selections from John Ruskin. VS, VI, p. 5

Self-Government in Russia. VS, V, p. 37

Serbia. Her People, History and Aspirations. VS, V, p. 1

Seton-Watson, R. W. VS, V, p. 71

Shaw, George Bernard. MH, VI, p. 3; MH, VI, p. 8; VS, III, p. 2; VS, V, p. 17

Short History of British Expansion. VS, V, p. 43

Short History of International Affairs 1920-1934 VS, V, p. 47

Short History of International Intercourse. VS, V, p. 70

Short History of the American People. VS, V, p. 5

Short History of the British Working Class Movement 1789-1937. VS, V, p. 4

Short History of the French Revolution. VS, V, p. 48

Simon, Kathleen. VS, V, p. 26

Simpson, J. Y. VS, V, p. 11

Sir Arthur Nicholson: First Lord Carmock: A Study in the Old Diplomacy. VS, VI, p. 4

Sir Robert Peel. MH, VI, p. 7

Six Women and the Invasion. MH, VI, p. 12

Skilled Labourer 1760-1832, The. MH, VI, p. 12

Slavery or "Sacred Trust"? VS, V, p. 53

Slavery. VS, V, p. 26

Slavery. MH, VI, p. 7; VS, V, p. 26; VS, V, p. 39; VS, V, p. 53; VS, V, p. 61; VS, VI, p. 4; MH, VI, p. 7

Smith, A. L. VS, V, p. 13

Smith, J. W. VS, V, p. 20

Smith, Randolph Wellford. VS, V, p. 42

Smith, Sir Frederick. VS, V, p. 68

Smuts, J. C. VS, VI, p. 1

Social psychology. MH, V, p. 21; MH, V, p. 22; VS, V, p. 34; VS, VI, p. 13

Social Studies of World Citizenship. A Sociological Approach to Education. VS, V, p. 37

Social Theory. VS, V, p. 2

Social Work in London 1869–1912: A History of Charity Organization Society. MH, VI, p. 11

Socialism and Co-operation. VS, III, p. 8

Socialism and National Minimum. VS, V, p. 17

Socialism. MH, VI, p. 2; MH, VI, p. 4; MH, VI, p. 11; VS, III, p. 8; VS, V, p. 2; VS, V, p. 3; VS, V, p. 7; VS, V, p. 11; VS, V, p. 17; VS, V, p. 36; VS, V, p. 67; VS, V, p. 68; VS, V, p. 70; VS, VI, p. 12

Socialist Movement, The. VS, V, p. 7

Sohn, Louis B. VS, V, p. 66

Soltan, Roger. VS, VI, p. 7

Some Problems of East Africa. VS, V, p. 31

Sorel, Georges. MH, VI, p. 8

South-West Africa. VS, V, p. 29

Soviet Union 1936. VS, V, p. 65

Soviet Union. MH, V, p. 18; MH, V, p. 20; MH, V, p. 23; MH, VI, p. 2; VS, V, p. 1; VS, V, p. 44; VS, V, p. 47; VS, V, p. 53; VS, V, p. 54; VS, V, p. 65

Spargo, J. MH, VI, p. 11

Spectator, The. VS, III, p. 5

Speech, and Documents on the British Dominions 1918–1931. VS, V, p. 17

Speeches During the French Revolutionary Period. VS, V, p. 6

Speeches of Adolf Hitler, April 1922–August 1939. MH, VI, p. 4

Spender, J. A. VS, VI, p. 9; VS, VI, p. 16

Spender, Stephen. VS, V, p. 15

Spengler, Oswald. VS, VI, p. 12; VS, VI, p. 14

Spinoza, Benedict de. VS, III, p. 4

Spirit of Russia: Studies in History Literature and Philosophy. VS, VI, p. 14

Staley, Eugene. VS, V, p. 53

Stalin, Joseph. VS, V, p. 47; VS, V, p. 53

Stanley, H. J. (Governor of Ceylon) et al. VS, V, p. 61

Stansky, P. MH, III, p. 15

State in the New Social Order, The. VS, V, p. 3

State in Theory and Practice, The. VS, III, p. 11

Statesman, The. MH, V, p. 12

Statesmanship of Wordsworth: An Essay. MH, VI, p. 3

Statesmen's Year Book for the Year 1919, The. VS, V, p. 51

Steed, H. Wickham. VS, V, p. 45

Stieve, Friedrich. VS, V, p. 69

Stock Exchange: A Short Study of Investment and Speculation. VS, V, p. 55

Stoddard, L. MH, VI, p. 11

Stolen Lands: A Study in Alsace-Lorraine. VS, V, p. 28

Stone, H. A. VS, V, p. 25

Stone, Julius. VS, V, p. 64

Stone, K. H. VS, V, p. 25

Story of Fabian Socialism, The. MH, VI, p. 2

Story of King Constantine: As Revealed in the Greek White Book. VS, V, p. 6

Story of the Empire, The. VS, V, p. 64

Stowell, E. C. VS, V, p. 72

Strachey, Celia. VS, V, p. 48

Strachey, Oliver. VS, V, p. 68

Strachey, Ray. VS, V, p. 47; VS, V, p. 68

Streit, Clarence K. MH, VI, p. 8

Stresemann, Gustav. VS, III, p. 8

Stresemann. VS, V, p. 46

Strickland, C. F. VS, V, p. 43

Structure of Politics at the Accession of George III. MH, VI, p. 6

Struggle for the Freedom of the Press, 1819–1832, The. VS, V, p. 25

Studies in Empire and Trade. VS, V, p. 46

Studies in Federal Planning. VS, V, p. 36

Studies in Law and Politics. MH, VI, p. 5

Studies in the English Social and Political Thinkers of the Nineteenth Century. VS, VI, p. 5

Studies in the Problem of Sovereignty. VS, VI, p. 13

Subjection of Women, The. MH, V, p. 3

Submerged Nationalities of the German Empire, The. VS, V, p. 6

Summary of the Fulfillment of the First Five-Year Plan for the Development of the National Economy of the U.S.S.R. VS, V, p. 44

Survey of American Foreign Relations 1928. VS, V, p. 25

Survey of International Affairs 1935. MH, VI, p. 8

Survey of International Affairs. VS, V, p. 75

Survey of International Relations Between the United States and Germany. MH, V, p. 22

Suspense. VS, VI, p. 5

Sutton, Eric (ed). VS, III, p. 8

Swift, Jonathan. VS, VI, p. 7

Switzerland. VS, VI, p. 7

Tagebuch Eines Halbwüch-Sigen Mädchens. VS, V, p. 9

Tagore, Rabindranath. MH, VI, p. 10

Take Over the War Industries: A Reasoned Case for Public Ownership. VS, V, p. 49

Tallentyre, S. G. VS, V, p. 38

Tanner, J. R. VS, VI, p. 12

Tawney, R. H. MH, V, p. 11; MH, VI, p. 8; VS, V, p. 42; VS, VI, p. 7

Taylor, A. J. P. MH, VI, p. 8; VS, VI, p. 12

Taylor, Henry. MH, V, p. 12

Temperley, Harold. MH, VI, p. 8; VS, V, p. 23

Temple, C. L. VS, V, p. 53

Temple, William Johnston. VS, VI, p. 8

Ten Days That Shook the World. MH, V, p. 23

Ten Years at the Court of St. James' 1895–1905. VS, VI, p. 8

Index to Part 3

Ten Years of Secret Diplomacy: An Unheeded Warning. VS, V, p. 45

Termination of War and Treaties of Peace. VS, V, p. 25

Terrorism and Communism. A contribution to the natural history of revolution. VS, VI, p. 11

The Conquest of Civilization. VS, V, p. 60

Theal, George McCall. VS, VI, p. 17

These Eventful Years.: The 20th Century in the Making as told by Various of Its Makers. VS, V, p. 41

Third British Empire: Being a Course of Lectures delivered at Columbia University. VS, V, p. 16

Thirteen Days July 23–August 4, 1914: A Chronicle and Interpretation. VS, V, p. 60

Thomas Paine. VS, V, p. 2

Thomas Paine: Prophet and Martyr of Democracy. VS, VI, p. 3

Thomas, J. A. VS, V, p. 6

Thompson, Edward. VS, V, p. 61

Thompson, J. M. MH, VI, p. 8

Three Speeches [of Joseph Stalin]. VS, V, p. 53

Three Studies in European Conservatism: Metternich, Guizot, The Catholic Church in the 19th Century. VS, V, p. 16

Through the Chinese Revolution. VS, VI, p. 16

To The Pure...A Study of Obscenity and the Censor. VS, VI, p. 1

Tory Party. VS, V, p. 41; VS, V, p. 64; VS, VI, p. 14

Toryism and the People 1832–1846. VS, V, p. 64

Totalitarian Enemy, The. MH, VI, p. 1

Towards International Government. VS, VI, p. 6

Towards Social Democracy: A Study of Social Evolutions During the Past Three-quarters of a Century. VS, V, p. 2

Towards the New Labour Party. VS, V, p. 67

Toynbee, A. J. MH, V, p. 16; VS, V, p. 58; VS, V, p. 75

Toynbee, A. J. (ed.). VS, V, p. 38

Toynbee, Arnold J. MH, VI, p. 8

Trade unionism. VS, VI, p. 4

Trevelyan, G. M. MH, VI, p. 9; VS, V, p. 41; VS, V, p. 62; VS, V, p. 64; VS, V, p. 74; VS, VI, p. 14; VS, VI, p. 9

Trevelyan, Sir George. VS, III, p. 11

Trotsky, L. MH, VI, p. 9

Trotsky's Diary in Exile 1935. MH, VI, p. 9

Trotter, W. VS, V, p. 34

Trowbridge, E. D. VS, V, p. 64

True Story of Alsace-Lorraine, The. VS, VI, p. 2

Truth About Publishing, The. MH, VI, p. 9

Truth and the War. MH, V, p. 12

Tunstall, B. MH, VI, p. 9

Turberville, A. S. VS, VI, p. 5

Turkey, Greece and the Great Powers: A study in friendship and hate. VS, VI, p. 7

Turkey, the Great Powers, and the Bagdad Railway: A Study in Imperialism. VS, V, p. 65

Turkey. The Great Powers and the Bagdad Railway: A Study in Imperialism. MH, V, p. 22

Turkey. MH, V, p. 22; VS, V, p. 1; VS, V, p. 65; VS, VI, p. 1; VS, VI, p. 7; VS, VI, p. 10

Turkish Empire. Its Growth and Decay, The. VS, VI, p. 10

Turkish Problem, The. VS, VI, p. 1

Turks in Europe, The. VS, V, p. 1

Twenty Years Crisis 1919–39, The. MH, VI, p. 2

Twenty-five Years 1892–1916. VS, VI, p. 17

Twins in Ceylon, The. VS, III, p. 3

Two-Party System in English Political History: The Romanes Lecture. VS, V, p. 62

U.S.S.R. Handbook. VS, V, p. 54

Unanimity Rule and the League of Nations, The. VS, V, p. 69

Under Western Eyes. VS, III, p. 2

Unemployment. VS, V, p. 7

Union Now. MH, VI, p. 8

Unknown Prime Minister: The Life and Times of Andrew Bonar Law 1858–1923, The. MH, VI, p. 1

Unpublished Diary and Political Sketches of Princess Lieven, Together with Some of Her Letters. VS, V, p. 12

Unwin, Sir Stanley. MH, VI, p. 9

Uplift in Economics. VS, V, p. 14

Valentin, Veit. VS, VI, p. 9

Vallentin, Antonia. VS, V, p. 46

Van De Perre, A. MH, VI, p. 11

Van Den Bruck, Mouller. VS, VI, p. 9

Van Doren, Carl. VS, VI, p. 8

Various Jungle Tales. VS, V, p. 11

Victorian Age in Politics, War and Diplomacy. VS, V, p. 23

Victorian England: Portrait of an Age. MH, VI, p. 10

Victorian Working Women: An Historical Study of Women in British Industries and Professions 1832–1850. VS, VI, p. 12

Victory of Reason: A Pamphlet on Arbitration with a Letter by Benjamin Franklin. VS, V, p. 70

Vigilantes—Inquest on Peace: An Analysis of the National Governments Foreign Policy. VS, V, p. 36

Vigilants. The Road to War: Being an Analysis of the National Government's Foreign Policy. VS, VI, p. 7

Village Labourer 1760–1832: A Study in the Government of England before the Reform Bill. VS, V, p. 77

Villiers, Brougham. MH, VI, p. 9

Vinacke, H. M. VS, V, p. 60

Vinogradoff, Paul. VS, V, p. 37

Vizetelly, E. A. VS, VI, p. 2

Voltaire. VS, III, p. 16; VS, V, p. 20; VS, V, p. 38; VS, V, p. 41

Voltaire. VS, V, p. 78

Von Eckardstein, Baron. VS, VI, p. 8

Waddington, C. F. VS, V, p. 6

Wallas, Graham. VS, V, p. 5

Wallas, Graham. VS, VI, p. 7

Wang, Cheng-Ting T. VS, V, p. 48

War Aims: A Need for a Parliament of the Allies. VS, VI, p. 5

War Behind the War 1914–18, The. MH, VI, p. 2

War for Peace, The. VS, III, p. 7

War of Steel and Gold: A Study of the Armed Peace, The. VS, VI, p. 3

War Speeches 1914–1917. VS, VI, p. 6

War. MH, V, p. 12; MH, V, p. 23; MH, V, p. 24; MH, VI, p. 2; MH, VI, p. 7; MH, VI, p. 10; MH, VI, p. 12; VS, III, p. 12; VS, III, p. 15; VS, V, p. 2 ; VS, V, p. 9; VS, V, p. 15; VS, V, p. 23; VS, V, p. 25; VS, V, p. 30; VS, V, p. 31; VS, V, p. 34; VS, V, p. 39; VS, V, p. 40; VS, V, p. 44; VS, V, p. 47; VS, V, p. 49; VS, V, p. 53; VS, V, p. 55; VS, V, p. 58; VS, V, p. 60; VS, V, p. 68; VS, V, p. 69; VS, V, p. 71; VS, VI, p. 3; VS, VI, p. 4; VS, VI, p. 5; VS, VI, p. 6; VS, VI, p. 8; VS, VI, p. 11; VS, VI, p. 13; VS, VI, p. 14; VS, VI, p. 16; VS, VI, p. 17

Warren Hastings in Bengal 1772–1774. VS, VI, p. 11

Way to World Peace, The. VS, V, p. 15

We Fight for Oil. VS, V, p. 69

Webb, [Beatrice] Mrs. Sidney. MH, V, p. 20; MH, VI, p. 6; VS, V, p. 3; VS, V, p. 4; VS, V, p. 17; VS, V, p. 59; VS, VI, p. 4; VS, VI, p. 7

Webb, Sidney. MH, V, p. 20; MH, VI, p. 3; VS, V, p. 2; VS, V, p. 4; VS, V, p. 59; VS, VI, p. 7

Webster, C. K. VS, VI, p. 1; VS, VI, p. 2

Webster, C. K. (ed.). VS, VI, p. 13

Wedgwood, Josiah C. VS, III, p. 13

Weech, W. N. VS, V, p. 64

Wells, H. G. MH, VI, p. 12; VS, V, p. 15; VS, V, p. 22

Werner, J. G. VS, V, p. 48

West, Julius. VS, VI, p. 12

What Would Be the Character of a New War? VS, V, p. 2

What's What in Politics. VS, III, p. 1

Wheeler-Bennett, J. W. MH, VI, p. 9; VS, V, p. 52; VS, V, p. 58; VS, V, p. 71

When Hostilities Cease. VS, V, p. 36

Which Way to Peace? VS, VI, p. 6

White and Black in Africa: A Critical Examination the Rhodes Lectures of General Smuts. VS, V, p. 27

White, Freda. VS, V, p. 44

Who Is Right in the World War? VS, V, p. 24

Why the German Republic Fell and Other Studies of the Causes and Consequences of Economic Inequality. VS, V, p. 57

Wickwar, W. H. VS, V, p. 25

William II (ex-Emperor of Germany). VS, VI, p. 10

William of Germany (The ex-Crown Prince). VS, VI, p. 11

Williams, Aneurin. VS, V, p. 41

Williamson, James A. VS, V, p. 43

Willmore, J. S. VS, V, p. 6

Willoughby, W. W. VS, V, p. 33

Willoughby, Westell W. VS, V, p. 8

Wilte, Count. VS, VI, p. 10

Winds of Change 1914–39. MH, VI, p. 5

Wolff, Theodor. VS, VI, p. 17

Wollstonecraft, Mary. VS, V, p. 68

Woman's Co-Operative Guild 1883–1904, The. MH, V, p. 22

Women Workers and the Industrial Revolution 1750–1850. MH, VI, p. 7

Women's suffrage (working women). MH, V, p. 3; MH, VI, p. 7; VS, V, p. 47; VS, V, p. 68; VS, VI, p. 12

Woo, T. C. VS, V, p. 6

Woodrow Wilson and World Settlement. VS, VI, p. 14

Woods, Maurice. VS, VI, p. 14

Woodward, E. L. MH, VI, p. 9; VS, V, p. 16

Woodward, W. E. MH, VI, p. 10

Woolf, Bella Sidney (Mrs. W. T. Southorn). MH, IV, p. 1; VS, III, p. 3; VS, III, p. 9

Woolf, Leonard (ed.). VS, III, p. 5

Woolf, Leonard. VS III, p. 7; VS III, p. 8; VS, III, p. 11; VS, III, p. 15; VS, III, p. 16; VS, III, p. 17

Work and Wealth. MH, VI, p. 4

Work for the Winter: More or Less for Christmas. MH, IV, p. 1

Works of Benedict de Spinoza: Vol. 2. *De Intellectus Emendatione–Ethica.* VS, III, p. 4

World After the Peace Conferences, The. MH, V, p. 16

World Committee for the Victims of German Fascism (Chairman: Einstein). VS, V, p. 5

World Court. VS, V, p. 71

World events and history. VS, V, p. 74

World History: The Growth of Western Civilization. VS, V, p. 64

World of Greece and Rome, The. VS, V, p. 71

World Peace through World Law. VS, V, p. 66

World-Struggle for Oil, The. VS, VI, p. 12

Worsfold, Basil, Sir Bartle Frere. VS, VI, p. 8

Wright, I. A. VS, VI, p. 14

X—Symposium: The Nature of the State in View of its External Relations. VS, V, p. 45

Yerta, G. MH, VI, p. 12

Yerta, M. MH, VI, p. 12

Young, G. M. MH, VI, p. 10

Young, George. VS, VI, p. 16

Yugoslavia. VS, V, p. 71

Zanzibar, The Island Metropolis of Eastern Asia. VS, V, p. 5

Zetland, see Ronaldshay, Earl of. VS, VI, p. 17

Zimmerman, Emil. VS, VI, p. 5

Zimmern, Alfred. VS, V, p. 16; VS, V, p. 58

APPENDICES A–D

APPENDIX A

Notes on *The Nation and Athenaeum* Archival Records[1]

by Janet M. Manson

The weekly periodical *The Nation and Athenaeum* is an enormously useful instrument for scholars attempting to piece together the intellectual interests and activities of Leonard and Virginia Woolf and others whose contributions made this slim serial an important index of political and literary progressive opinion in the 1920s. So, naturally, the marked files and related papers of this journal should be of great value for their wealth of information on the authorship of unsigned articles and reviews of books, musical and theatrical performances, lectures, even contemporary phonograph records. Leonard Woolf was an early advocate of an international peace maintained by a collective security organization authorized to use force, if necessary, to keep "rogue nations" in line and bore the responsibilities of the literary editorship of *The Nation and Athenaeum* between 1921 and 1929 (see Appendix B, below). While researching a book on Woolf's political activities, especially his work to promote international collective security organizations such as the League of Nations (precursor to our United Nations), a tip from a researcher on another subject led me to City University, London, temporary home of the periodical's extant archives. I came to appreciate the enormous task involved in reconciling these materials with those dispersed or lost—a job for a real sleuth! The files (actually bound volumes containing annotated issues of *The Nation and Athenaeum*) were used by the journal's editors, including Maynard Keynes and Leonard Woolf, to note authorship and to commission payments for unsigned contributions. Authorship, at best recorded briefly in an annotation such as "L. Woolf" for Leonard Woolf, is not documented scrupulously for all unsigned contributions. Even so, I found the files indispensable in recovering a sense of Woolf's intellectual milieu—one that gave him a philosophical basis for his work and a place among the English intelligentsia, persons who stimulated his activism with their own.

At present, one will find a six-volume partial set of *The Nation and Athenaeum* at London's City University—specifically, volumes 35 (issues of April 5–September 27, 1924), 37 (issues of April 4–September 26, 1925), 38 (issues of October 3, 1925–March 27, 1926), 43 (issues of April 7–September 29, 1928), 45 (issues of April 6–September 28, 1929), and 47 (issues of April 5–September

27, 1930). In searching for articles written by Leonard Woolf, one will of course find a number of short items designated "Mrs. Woolf" (Virginia Woolf). As it turns out, authorship is occasionally ambiguous in the case of the Woolfs because the "L" or "Mrs" or forename preceding "Woolf" in the margins was written indistinctly or cropped in binding, and in some cases the authorship has been given simply as "Woolf." The fact that writers associated with Bloomsbury (Winifred Holtby, Vera Brittain, and Ray Strachey, for instance) wrote for the journal confirms our thesis that they tended to work closely with one another in various fields of endeavor. Vera Brittain, in particular, began a regular column on feminist issues shortly after Virginia Woolf's A Room of One's Own appeared in October 1929 and stirred up discussion in the Letters to the Editor column.

At this writing, City University holds on deposit the editorial correspondence of *The Nation and Athenaeum*. Leonard Woolf's correspondence with the editor of the *New Statesman* from 1915 to 1919, formerly at City University but now at the University of Sussex (see Sotheby's sale catalogue of December 12, 1991, lot 122, and Pat Coyne, "Under the Hammer," *New Statesman and Society*, November 29, 1991) must necessarily be compared with those letters among his papers at the University of Sussex (I.H.1.) and is frequently revealing. For example, an exchange between Woolf and his editor regarding James Strachey's unemployment simultaneously demonstrates the cohesiveness of the Bloomsbury network and provides insight into pacifist issues. When James Strachey lost his position at *The Spectator* because he, like most of his draft-age relatives and Bloomsbury friends, became a conscientious objector (noted by Chapman in his article about Alix Strachey in *Women in the Milieu*), Woolf finessed this point in his letter to *New Statesman* editor Clifford Sharp, even though Strachey's views were well-known because Keynes and others supported his case before the Military Tribunal. Woolf wrote to Sharp requesting employment for his friend: "I believe you know James Strachey. He has been for 6 years on *The Spectator*, & has now had to leave owing to the Editor's scruples about men of military age. He would, I know, like to write for the *New Statesman* if any opportunity at which you could use him occurred" (folio 145, L. S. Woolf to Sharpe [sic], November 28, 1915). Sharp admitted knowing Strachey but unfortunately could not offer him employment though Sharp acknowledged that one of James's brothers (presumably Lytton) sometimes wrote for the journal (see folio 145, [Sharp] to L. Woolf, November 30, 1915). James Strachey later found employment at *The Athenaeum* through the intercession of his family. See Virginia Woolf, *The Letters of Virginia Woolf*, eds. Nigel Nicolson and Joanne Trautmann, vol. 2: 1912–1922 (London and New York: Harcourt Brace Jovanovich, 1976), 341; Virginia Woolf to Vanessa Bell, March 23, 1919. Moreover, when John Middleton Murry, husband of Katherine Mansfield, became editor of *The Athenaeum* in 1919, the Stracheys persuaded him to take on James as drama critic. The correspondence files have since found a home in the archival collection at the University of Sussex Library.

The whereabouts of the complete marked files of *The Nation and Athenaeum* has intrigued researchers for some time and remains a mystery. The location of marked issues of *The Nation* published during H. W. Massingham's editorship, roughly 1907 to 1921, was the subject of a brief exchange between Ken Blackwell and Leonard Woolf in the spring of 1968. (Letters from Ken Blackwell to Leonard Woolf, May 7 and June 12, 1968, and; Leonard Woolf to Ken Blackwell, May 15, 1968, Leonard Woolf Papers, I.I.4., University of Sussex Library.) Woolf referred Blackwell to the Keynes Papers, King's College, Cambridge (because he knew Keynes had an unbound set of partially marked numbers of *The Nation and Athenaeum* but did not know this to be located in the Marshall Library, apart from the main body of papers), and to the *New Statesman* offices, which became the repository for the marked files of *The Nation* and subsequently related papers. Blackwell was unable to locate *The Nation*'s files during Massingham's editorship, although he did find at the *New Statesman*'s offices the partial set of marked files of *The Nation and Athenaeum* (1924–1931) later moved to City University. In fact, Keynes's odd, unbound issues of the latter paper have proven a valuable means of supplementing the record available at City University for some 28 issues between November 17, 1923 and January 14, 1933, partly filling the lacunae of volumes 34, 36, 39–42, and 44, or nearly 60% of Leonard Woolf's editorial tenure.

According to B. J. Kirkpatrick, virtually all extant sets of *The Nation and Athenaeum* marked files, along with those of the *New Statesman* and *New Statesman and Nation*, were at the *New Statesman* offices at Great Turnstile, London, in the 1960s. However, when the journal moved to a new location, there was no longer space for all the files. An incomplete set of *The Nation and Athenaeum* marked files (noted above) and the publication's editorial letter-files were then placed on deposit at City University, which also lacks space and staff to permanently accommodate a sizeable research collection. The fate of the missing seven marked volumes is unknown since Kirkpatrick viewed the existing records at the Great Turnstile offices some thirty years ago and recently inventoried all of the files for us at the offices of *The New Statesman and Society*. Because the present staff is inadequate to maintain files of the antecedent papers, such volumes are not kept in order. She finds, however, that the three sets of the *New Statesman and Nation* she used in compiling *A Bibliography of Virginia Woolf* (3rd edition, 1980) are still worth consulting. Two of these sets are bound in red, and the third, an apparently unmarked set, in blue. Both red sets are annotated—of course, the most useful of which is marked as described above. The second red set, designated the Audit Day Book, reports payments for advertisements and, as such, could be of great interest to economic and business historians. Scholars remain indebted to Kirkpatrick for her able sleuthing and concern for the fate of these files—a fate not certain and all the more unfortunate because it involves almost fifty years of distinguished journalism, from *The New Statesman* (vols. 1–35, April 1913 through October 1930) to the *New Statesman and Nation* (vols. 1–59, February 1931 through June 1960, save for volumes 26, 44, 47, 50, 52–53, 55, and 57, which might still have been overlooked in the general disorder of these materials in the *New Statesman and Society* office). At this writing, however, an understanding between the management of the *New Statesman and Society* and the University of Sussex Library should result in the fortunate transfer of these valuable records after library renovations are complete in 1999. The revised 4th edition of Kirkpatrick's bibliography, assisted by Stuart Clarke, was published by Oxford University Press in 1997.

Note

1. Appendix A first appeared in *Women in the Milieu of Leonard and Virginia Woolf: Peace, Politics, and Education*, ed. Wayne K. Chapman and Janet M. Manson (New York: Pace University Press, 1998) and then incorporated as a hyperlink into the first and second editions of our *Annotated Guide to the Writings and Papers of Leonard Woolf* (2005, 2006), courtesy of Pace University Press.

APPENDIX B

COLLABORATIVE REVIEWING BY LEONARD AND VIRGINIA WOOLF[1]

by Wayne K. Chapman

John Maynard Keynes gave Leonard Woolf the job of literary editor of *The Nation and Athenaeum* (hereafter *N&A*); and, with volume 33, issue 5 (Saturday, May 5, 1923), Woolf signed his first column in that capacity. "The World of Books," as it was called, had been a regular feature of *The Athenaeum* before that journal merged with *The Nation*, joined together (on 19 February 1921) yet largely unassimilated in common issues with separate tables of contents. Under Leonard Woolf's stewardship and some direct managing by Keynes, *The Nation & The Athenaeum*, as the amalgamation had been dubbed initially, became a unified publication (simplified in title by deletion of the climactic definite article); and, until mid-1930, Woolf maintained a rigorous output in this and other columns as well as individual reviews, both signed and unsigned. His departure from the staff anticipated his co-editorship of the *Political Quarterly* in 1931 and, in the same year, the merger of *The New Statesman* and the *N&A*—afterwards *The New Statesman and Nation: A Weekend Review*, *The New Statesman: A Weekend Review*, and, finally, *The New Statesman and Society*. As Leila Luedeking notices on checking B. J. Kirkpatrick's meticulous *Bibliography of Virginia Woolf*, 3rd ed. (Oxford: Clarendon Press, 1980): "Virginia [Woolf] increased her writing for periodicals while LW [Leonard Woolf] was Literary Editor of the *Nation & Athenaeum*" ("Leonard Woolf and the book review" in Leila Luedeking and Michael Edmonds, *Leonard Woolf: A Bibliography* [Winchester, UK: St Paul's Bibliographies; New Castle, DE: Oak Knoll Books, 1992], 286). The observation partly mistakes number for quantity and needs to appreciate the fact that a great number of Virginia Woolf's contributions to the *N&A* were mere paragraphs written with her husband and others in virtual community efforts such as the columns "From Alpha to Omega" and "Books in Brief," which Leonard edited. Moreover, individual authority seems a mirky form of both shadow and substance when one considers the issue of canon in light of Virginia Woolf's activity as an *ex officio* but paid auxiliary writer for the *N&A* from at least February 1924 to December 1928. (See my review of Kirkpatrick reprinted in Appendix D, below.) Recent research discovers a serious problem the remediation of which might yet identify a significant amount of writing by both Leonard and Virginia Woolf, not to mention other Bloomsbury figures.

Because the archival record of the *N&A* is incomplete (see Appendix A, above), we may never know fully the extent of the Woolfs' unsigned writings in the paper. Roughly 400 such pieces identified by Manson became part of the Luedeking/Edmonds bibliography before discrepancies could be rechecked. Because authority for these pieces is assigned on the basis of only 6 of 16 volumes of the marked files for the period of Leonard Woolf's editorship, it follows that over 600 other writings actually by him remain "anonymous." Some of these may be identified following inspection of the 28 odd unbound issues of *N&A* in the Keynes Papers, Marshall Library of Economics, Cambridge University (not to be confused with the Keynes Papers in King's College Library). Kirkpatrick drew on the Marshall Library materials in her bibliography of E. M. Forster, and it provided her (according to her private account) with approximately a third of the 82 unsigned reviews and paragraphs in the *N&A* that she attributed to Virginia Woolf. At this rate, an estimated 350-item supplement to the Leonard Woolf bibliography might be recovered at Cambridge. However, fortune will be smiling on whoever locates the missing bound volumes of the *N&A* archive. Barring the possibility that they have been pulped or shredded, these documents might give us, one day, as many as 50 writings for Andrew McNeillie's comprehensive work-in-progress, *The Essays of Virginia Woolf* (1986–). This would be equal to the boon of 44 unsigned *TLS* reviews Kirkpatrick recently brought to light (in *Modern Fiction Studies* 38.1 [1992] 279–83, published January 1993).

In essence, part of Virginia Woolf's canon achieves clarity as the immense *oeuvre* of Leonard Woolf is worked out.[2] Thus additions might be made to her bibliography—though they include trifles such as her curt endorsement of Auction Bridge in the "Books in Brief" column in *N&A* 43 (5 May 1928): 152, 154. Introduced between her longer review of A. T. Schofield's *Behind the Brass Plate* and Leonard's review of G. S. Tomkinson's bibliography of *Principal Modern Presses, Public and Private, in Great Britain and Ireland*, the notice rounded out a column written almost entirely by the two Woolfs in an indistinguishable voice. (Schofield's writing was found to be "extremely clear, so that there is no excuse for the most muddle-headed to misunderstand.") In other cases, reviews might be downgraded to the status of Kirkpatrick's "Doubtful and Untraced Contributions" (e.g., C246.31) because trimmed margins have reduced the reviewer's name to an ambiguous "Woolf" (cf. "[Au]stin Clarke" and "[Forr]est Reid" near C246.31). Or some such classifications might be promotions, as in the case of Virginia's probable "Books in Brief" paragraph on Katharine Tynan's *Memories* (reviewed above C246.31 in N&A 35 [June 7, 1924]: 332). In yet other cases, Virginia Woolf's authorship seems plainly contested, as one finds in Kirkpatrick's C246.6 and C249.1, both definitely logged as by "L. Woolf" in the bound volume 35 of the marked files, though the files are clearly fallible if the draft of the former, a review of the autobiography of Robert Smith Surtees—a review composed among holograph pages of *Mrs Dalloway*—is not a work of dictation (see McNeillie's Editorial Note in *The Essays of Virginia Woolf*, vol. 3 [1988], p. xxv).

It is true that the authors of ephemeral paragraphs published in the *N&A* had little thought of the literary value of work that appeared unsigned—and they did sign a great deal more significant (meaning longer) work in the paper. The McNeillie project and the bibliographies of Kirkpatrick and Luedeking/Edmonds, however, do convey a sense of significance to every slight work they incorporate. This impression is perhaps the inevitable cost of important scholarly objectives. But, since these resources produce a monophonic rather than a polyphonic survey of writings (dedicated, as each is, to one writer), they do not convey very well the corporate context of pieces never actually conceived to be complete works by themselves. Leonard Woolf's weekly responsibilities were considerable, and he did not spend full time in the office. Naturally, he would enlist the aid of his wife (since they would financially profit thereby) and numerous other writers to maintain production. Though not a regular contributor, Virginia Woolf thus wrote much more for the journal than the occasional feature reviews and articles that *N&A* succeeded in deterring from her vehicle-of-preference, *The Times Literary Supplement*, between 1924 and 1928. She sometimes contributed oddments to the general column "From Alpha to Omega" (see Kirkpatrick, C245.1, C253.1, and C262.1), always with Leonard but sometimes with others, too (see Luedeking/Edmonds, C0441, C0497, and C0539). And she more frequently joined him in writing equally anonymous critiques for "Books in Brief," a regular section of the serial that usually followed his often hefty notice of books received, called "On the Editor's Table." Their collaboration in "Books in Brief" is reflected in the conjunction of 23 unsigned contributions by her and 40 by him in 18 different issues between June 7, 1924 and July 14, 1928. These numbers include 7 omissions in Luedeking/Edmonds and adjust for two reviews mistakenly attributed to Leonard Woolf. The collations here testify, then, to the Woolfs' joint labor at various times:

N&A (by date)	Kirkpatrick (VW)	Luedeking/Edmonds (LW)
7 June 1924	C246.31	C0462 (2 items)[3]
21 June 1924	C246.4, C246.6 (see above)	C0467 (3 items)
11 Apr. 1925	C260.2, C260.3	C0533 (1 item)
9 May 1925	C262.3	C0545 (3 items)
16 May 1925	C262.5	C0549 (1 item)
15 Aug. 1925	C265.4	omits *The History of Mathematics* (J.W.N. Sullivan) & *Concerning the Habits of Insects* (F. Balfour-Browne)

17 Oct. 1925	C268.2	C0621 (6 items)
26 Dec. 1925	C269.4	C0645 (2 items, omitting *The Diary of a Young Lady of Fashion in the Year 1764–65*)
30 Jan. 1926	C270	C0664 (4 items)
6 Feb. 1926	C271.1	C0668 (3 items)
6 Mar. 1926	C272.1	omits *The Augustan Books of Modern Poetry* (F. W. Harvey, E. Gosse, W. Whitman, A. Lang, and S. Sassoon), *Karl Marx's "Capital"* (A. D. Lindsay) and *Burke's Peerage* [etc.]
20 Mar. 1926	C272.2, C272.3, C272.4	C0686 (1 item)
27 Mar. 1926	C272.5	C0690 (1 item)
7 Apr. 1928	C298.1	C0818 (1 item)
28 Apr. 1928	C301.1	C0826 (1 item)
5 May 1928	C301.2 (and *Auction Bridge*, see above)	C0828 (1 item)
30 June 1928	C301.4	C0855 (1 item)
14 July 1928	C301.5	C0864 (2 items)

In the end, one returns to the fact that documentary evidence at present can only tell about 40 percent of the whole story. Fortunately, a sample of this size is large enough to be significant and reliable for inferences about the collaboration. First, when there were other hands at work in these columns, Leonard and Virginia Woolf dominate the majority of those columns on which they worked together, at least until 1927. Second, an editorial intelligence (Leonard's) is at work organizing the columns: that is, paragraphs written separately on disparate topics were arranged according to a logic. (While both of the Woolfs were interested in biography, for instance, Virginia critiqued biographical works as a rule, undoubtedly given choice books to read as Leonard maintained the more perfunctory chore work, exercising his responsibilities rather more than his privileges as literary editor. Hence biographical and literary topics were given priority in arrangement over politics and other "practical" ones, which, though sometimes more numerous, were not as fully treated as were the biographical and literary. 56 percent of the time, too, he led with his wife's work as compared with the mere 11 percent of the time that "Books in Brief" began with a critique of his own.) And in the spirit of collective journalism, finally, the intelligence that organized the humble "works" of this feature exercised its station as an agency of synthesis and cohesion. Since the rule of both columns was to stimulate with variety, counterpointing became the means of integration as the editor reworked the constituent parts to achieve the desired effect. Particularly in "From Alpha to Omega" Leonard Woolf proved himself to be adept at cooperative enterprise. He would write about a recent theater performance, an exhibition of caricatures by Max Beerbohm, or "things to see or hear in the coming week" while his wife recorded her impressions of the pleasures of walking on a country road, a night out at one of London's music halls, or a demonstration of a color film process. The staff pitched in accounts of their own activities—indeed, writing most of the column and hoaxing the public by impersonating the editor in first-person voice. Corporate adoption of the editorial "I" was then a commonplace in British journalism, of course, and therefore a precedent known to professional writers who, like Virginia Woolf, would later call for "men and women [to] work...together" to prevent war and rescue civilization from the forces of egoism and barbarity (*Three Guineas* [1938], 155). Bloomsbury, in short, manifested itself as an example in the *N&A* during Leonard Woolf's term as literary editor and possibly Virginia Woolf's seven finest years as both essayist and novelist.

Notes

1. Appendix B first appeared in *Women in the Milieu of Leonard and Virginia Woolf: Peace, Politics, and Education*, ed. Wayne K. Chapman and Janet M. Manson (New York: Pace University Press, 1998) and then incorporated as a hyperlink into the first and second editions of our *Annotated Guide to the Writings and Papers of Leonard Woolf* (2005, 2006), courtesy of Pace University Press.
2. The reader is hereafter directed to the respective bibliographies.
3. Luedeking and Edmonds give Kirkpatrick's C246.31 to LW as well as the adjoining review of Katharine Tynan's Memories. See above.

APPENDIX C

VIRGINIA WOOLF'S CONTRIBUTIONS TO ANONYMOUS, COMPOSITE REVIEWS IN *THE NATION AND ATHENAEUM* 1924–1928

by Wayne K. Chapman

This paper[1] makes a comparative accounting of 22 short, unsigned compositions by Virginia Woolf which contributed to 18 articles written jointly with other persons in the weekly paper *The Nation and Athenaeum* (*N&A*) between June 7, 1924, and July 14, 1928, during Leonard Woolf's tenure as literary editor. All of these pieces are listed in B. J. Kirkpatrick's *A Bibliography of Virginia Woolf*, 3rd edition (1980), but, as I will show, their listings are subject to revision in the projected 4th edition because they are discrepant with archival material, requiring that some of the pieces should be moved into the category of questionable attributions or to the canon of her husband, more than half of whose journalism as editor was unsigned.

Let me begin by speaking somewhat anecdotally about the circumstances that bring me to this topic, which is a convenient one because, for a number of years, laying the bibliographic foundation for a study of Leonard Woolf's political development has required keeping up with similar work on Virginia Woolf, principally with Brownlee Kirkpatrick. Naturally, separate lines of inquiry involving the same methodology, much the same resources, and similar interests will intersect and promote collaboration, just as it did when the Woolfs and various *N&A* staff writers joined to write those columns. The opening of the offices of the *TLS* to Brownlee's personal review of its archives greatly increased the store of titles attributed to Virginia Woolf. Six years ago, before publishing in *Modern Fiction Studies* (Spring 1992) her report on the 44 unrecorded reviews recovered in those offices, my wife and I had begun editing a book now called *Women in the Milieu of Leonard and Virginia Woolf* for which I tried to solicit Brownlee's essay but succeeded, instead, in winning her cooperation and countless hours rechecking archival materials she had studied nearly fifty years ago. These included the problematic remains of the editor's "marked files" of the *Nation and Athenaeum* at City University, London. ("Marked files" are sets of printed issues annotated to record the authors of unsigned contributions and sometimes the amount paid for them.) With Brownlee at work answering questions on Leonard Woolf affecting the Virginia Woolf bibliography, the "C" section of *Leonard Woolf: A Bibliography* by Leila Luedeking and Michael

Edmunds hastened to incorporate the findings that my wife, Janet Manson, had assembled from marked files of the *Nation and Athenaeum*. Although making acknowledgment in their introduction, Luedeking and Edmonds have not acknowledged that the information they published in 1992 as if *bona fide* was even then being cross-checked against the body of data on Virginia Woolf's canon because of several contradictions of which they were evidently unaware. Nevertheless, on her knees and up on ladders looking for still missing volumes of the record, Brownlee Kirkpatrick will soon pay us all dividends, assisted by Stuart Clarke, in her new revised edition of *A Bibliography of Virginia Woolf*, possibly the last we'll see in a long while.

To estimate the scope of Virginia Woolf's overall contributions to periodicals, one might start with what was known in 1980—that 532 signed and unsigned pieces are listed in Kirkpatrick's bibliography in its 3rd edition, to which are added 11 doubtful and 36 untraced items. Her 1992 inventory of additional, unsigned *TLS* reviews would add 44, as mentioned above, and confirm one previously listed as "Doubtful or Untraced." If all speculations were verified, including the latter case, the total number of "essays" credited to Virginia Woolf would stand at 623. Though I prefer "pieces," "items," or "contributions" to the word "essays" (since scores of those published in the *Nation and Athenaeum* were mere paragraphs and some of those not self-standing), "essays" is the term conferred upon all of them in the projects of Andrew McNeillie and Elizabeth Steele.

Any way you cut it, the body of Woolf's discursive shorter works is a huge creature. Generally speaking, *The Times Literary Supplement* remained her preferred vehicle as essayist and reviewer, as one concludes by taking into account the relative insignificance of the ephemera printed in the *Nation and Athenaeum* between June 1924 and mid-1928. Steele counts 246 essays published in the *TLS* over a thirty-two-year period (4), to which 44 are now added to obtain a total of 290, more than half the output in all. However, there was a demonstrable curtailment of *TLS* contributions during Leonard's tenure at the *N&A*. The range of textual evidence begins with the *N&A* volume 33 on May 5, 1923, and concludes with volume 47 in mid-1930, encompassing Leonard Woolf's term as literary editor. Because the surviving six volumes of the marked files (vols. 35, 37, 38, 43, 45, 47) show that Virginia Woolf contributed no unsigned pieces in the last two volumes (45 and 47), it follows that Virginia Woolf's contributions of this kind largely ended after she gave 9 unsigned pieces to volume 43 between April 7 and September 29, 1928. The marked files attribute 16 items to her in both volumes 35 and 37, with 13 items in volume 38, suggesting a peak in activity from 1924 to 1926. Kirkpatrick's sources for the succeeding gap in the record confirm a tapering off after March 1926. Yet I believe the curve projected for the missing volumes 39–42, based on the distribution of 65 unsigned pieces in volumes 35 through 38 of the marked files,² would allow that perhaps 50 more unsigned contributions in that period are still to be identified. In point of fact, Virginia Woolf produced *at least* 82 unsigned items and possibly more for her husband's editing while, at the same time, publishing only about a dozen articles in *TLS*.

One point of such exercises is that numbers tell a story; another is that, inevitably, numbers are deceptive because the vast majority of Virginia Woolf's unsigned *Nation and Athenaeum* efforts were exceedingly short. Leonard published a number of longer, signed works by her, too, but usually to establish copyright in England when the work was also to appear in an American newspaper such as *The New Republic*. The practical matter before us, though, is to consider the logic and method of 22 minor instances in which her work, not just presented anonymously, yielded itself to the corporate authority of collaborative writing. Her contributions to delegated staff efforts fell under the rubric of two regular columns, "From Alpha to Omega" and "Books in Brief," both assembled by Leonard Woolf, with the assorted paragraph-reviews of "Books in Brief" following his own column of notices, "On the Editor's Table," his feature column "The World of Books," and signed individual reviews by various contributors including Virginia Woolf.

Her contributions to "From Alpha to Omega" are the easiest to summarize because she only participated in three of them so far as we know. The first time it sounded like this:

> I was given the opportunity to see a demonstration of a new colour film process by Mr. Friese-Greene. The inventor's results probably compare favourably with other colour films, but they are very uneven in merit. The quiet-coloured scenes of English country are much the most successful; anything like a bright colour tends immediately to produce an oleographic effect. This is, of course, not peculiar to Mr. Friese-Greene's process. It almost looks as if nature's brighter colours which harmonize pleasingly when seen in three dimensions acquire an unpleasantly garish quality when represented in two. (N&A 5 Apr. 1924: 16)

The whole thing, five sentences, gives an impression and, written in first-person voice, might be mistaken for Leonard Woolf, who wrote the paragraph above it also in first-person, recalling an amusing production at the Comedy Theatre. Two paragraphs on an art lecture and an exhibition conclude the column in third person and by other hands. Though hardly an essay, Virginia's paragraph was determined to fit with Leonard's, and it is possible that the "opportunity" to which she alludes was one way they subsidized their outings. Certainly, her second contribution to "From Alpha to Omega," reflects a drive in the country, the thesis being that "the cheapening of motor-cars is another step towards the ruin of the country road" (N&A 27 Sept. 1924: 777). In her last venture with such writing, it is she who writes the account of Madame Lopokova's dancing at the Coliseum, a London music hall in which the wife of Maynard Keynes "bewitched the audience" with a "performance as effortless and as gay as the tossing of a bunch of spring flowers from the stage to the stalls"; and it is Leonard who flanks this impression with one of his own on Max Beerbohm's caricatures at the Leicester Galleries (N&A 25 Apr. 1925: 105). Two paragraphs by others were joined to these before Leonard concluded the column with the calendar, "Things to see or hear in the coming week," and affixed as the corporate signature "Omicron," the 15th letter of the Greek alphabet.

The "Books in Brief" columns had their own logic. But, when several hands were at work there, the Woolfs dominated most of those on which they worked together, at least until 1927. "Books in Brief" consisted of a miscellany of miniature reviews, never more than a paragraph apiece. When both of the Woolfs contributed to this column, biography became the emphasis although Leonard often addressed other topics. Because nearly all of Virginia's contributions critiqued biographical works and Leonard led with her work 56% of the time, their dominance tended on those occasions to position most of the weight of the column on individual lives rather than on political economy, the history of the Fabian Society, the habits of insects, co-operative storekeeping, travel, geography, and sport—to name but a few examples of subjects otherwise treated, often by Leonard Woolf. In a paragraph, there is, at most, opportunity to issue an impression and a verdict, and Virginia's paragraphs were sometimes keen sketches of the subject of a book. The best I can do in this short paper, unfortunately, is to gloss those paragraphs chronologically, citing revisions in Kirkpatrick's bibliography when necessary.

The first, probably, were critiques of Katharine Tynan's *Memories* and an autobiography, *Marie Elizabeth Townsley: a Memoir*, constituting the entire "Books in Brief" column of June 7, 1924. The former is a new item for the bibliography's list of "Doubtful" contributions, and the latter has been demoted to that status due to cropping in the marked copy that has sheared a presumed "Mrs." from the name "Woolf" in the left margin. Tynan's memoir draws from Virginia an elliptical allusion to similar work by Jane Barlow, reviewed earlier and elsewhere by Virginia Woolf,[3] touching on the Yeats circle in its Victorian habitat: "Gay and gifted and a little superficial they appear, in this pleasant testimony to the incredible remoteness of the 'eighties" (332). Structured similarly, her paragraph on the Townsley memoir first notes an interesting woman's life in a brilliant world and then concludes: "The story is told simply, if with too much insistence upon coats of arms and noble pedigrees" (332).

These and Woolf's next two mini-reviews, in the *Nation and Athenaeum* of 21 June 1924, of Cosmo Hamilton's *Unwritten History* and Stephen Graham's *The Life and Last Words of Wilfrid Ewart*, were light on two accounts. They were uncharacteristically under 20 lines and epigrammatically playful. Hamilton's was the kind of "stout, much illustrated…kind of book that the late King Edward would have enjoyed in his bath," "read[ing] like a gramophone record of good club talk" (392). Ewart, a "brilliant journalist" whom "a stray bullet wandering about Mexico" discovered before Graham's readers quite know what the journalist might have become, is nonetheless rendered in "a vivid record of possibilities" and "an eager and transparent sentimentality which is very readable" (392). Two paragraphs attributed to "LW" in the marked files for June 21 and July 5, 1924, on reminiscences by Robert Smith Surtees and B. de Sales La Terrière, naturally have been expunged from the Virginia Woolf bibliography.[4]

From 1925 to 1927, Virginia Woolf's paragraph contributions almost double in length to an average of about 30 lines, as a rule longer than those of other contributors and invariably longer than those written by Leonard Woolf, who had evidently decided to grant more space to her whenever she wanted it. (Both benefitted because their income grew by the increase in the number of column inches either gave to their journalism.) Her slightly longer reviews of Una Taylor's *Guests and Memories* ("an impression rather than a biography") and Stewart Ellis's *Mainly Victorian* (and "Mainly Victorian the book certainly is") in the 11 April 1925 "Books in Brief" have been confirmed, as have the other attributions cited in Kirkpatrick, 3rd edition, though, when he was alive, Leonard Woolf has had to arbitrate certain contradictions in the record.[5] For the remainder of 1925, we can positively identify Virginia Woolf's significantly longer paragraph responses to Herbert Garland's translation of *The Tragic Life of Vincent Van Gogh* by Louis Piérard (*N&A* 9 May: 182), Herman Berstein's *Celebrities of Our Times* (*N&A* 16 May: 214), John Gloag's non-biographical design book *Time, Taste, and Furniture* (*N&A* 15 Aug.: 604), the artist Louise Jopling-Rowe's *Twenty Years of My Life* (*N&A* 17 Oct.: 126), and W. Lanceley's *From Hall-Boy to House-Steward* (*N&A* 26 Dec.: 476). The last "makes out a good case for the life of a servant," but Woolf notices that the author's "vivacity steadily diminishes as he climbs higher" in the book.

The marked files show that she is very active in the column from January 30 to March 27, 1926 before a gap in the record gives no authority for her contributions until the record resumes in April 1928. In five issues, she sees 7 of her miniature reviews published; in fact, in the "Books in Brief" of March 20, 1926, her 3 reviews, together, are half again longer than those by all other contributors combined. Women's lives have the edge in the count, including *Mary Elizabeth Haldane, a Record of a Hundred Years* (*N&A* 30 Jan.: 624), *Queen Alexandra the Well-Beloved* by Elizabeth Villiers (*N&A* 6 Feb.: 654), *Reminiscences of Mrs.*

Comys Carr (*N&A* 20 Mar.: 870), and *The Flurried Years* by Violet Hunt (also 20 Mar. issue, same page). Other subjects emphasized place, time, and extraordinary perspectives of London and included Harry Furniss's *Paradise in Piccadilly* (*N&A* 6 Mar.: 780), Arthur Hayward's *The Days of Dickens* (*N&A* 20 Mar.: 870), and William Larkins's inartistic but thrilling *Steeple-Jacks and Steeple-jacking* (*N&A* 27 Mar.: 906), which carried the moral that, "once you get used to it, climbing a steeple is no whit more dangerous than sitting at a desk." Seldom one to pass up an opportunity to close with a punch-line, since that was part of the formula, she was quick to add: "But the reader, being green to the work, will get enough thrills from Mr. Larkins's story to break his neck a dozen times over."

In 1928, she made 5 contributions to as many "Books in Brief" columns and ended her involvement in these collaborations so far as marked copies of the *Nation and Athenaeum* tell. The first two of these last pieces, to gainsay all but slightest approval of their subjects, *Stalky's Reminiscences* by Major-General L. C. Dunsterville, C.B., C.S.I (*N&A* 7 Apr.: 22) and *Behind the Scenes with Cyril Maude* by Cyril Maude (*N&A* 28 Apr.: 120), are mere notices of the sort she had not written since her earliest contributions. Perhaps the chore had become tedious. In her longer paragraph on A. T. Schofield's *Behind the Brass Plate* (*N&A* 5 May: 152) she seems mainly diverted by an amusing description of Lady Ashburton connected with Carlyle's life: "We have seldom read a more vivid and accurate account of the vagaries of a great lady of the Victorian age.... [O]ne can see by what spells...she captivated the peasant of genius and nearly ruined his life." Woolf found similar isolated scenes of "picturesque power" but not a real writer in George Arliss's *On the Stage: an Autobiography*, "which vacillates in the strangest manner from an actor's scrap book to a genuine autobiography" (*N&A* 30 June: 436) and failed to hold her interest beyond the first chapter on Bloomsbury in 1880. Her last effort—and I will close on this—is written in the high spirit of her efforts of 1926. Published in the 14 July 1928 "Books in Brief," her 246-word panegyric on a statuesque singer blends easily with a critique of Winifred Ponder's performance as a writer in *Clara Butt: Her Life Story*. For it is to the biographer's credit that her reader "feel[s] that Miss Butt is a great deal bigger than the ordinary human being" because the writing bears with it "a strain of adulation which is fitted for a giantess" (506). Woolf says that Butt "is obviously a woman of gigantic vitality" but sees that she will also serve a review as a comic butt. The biographer stresses her subject's relation to the Empress of Germany, seldom mentioning music, while the reviewer applies the human touch to a verdict: "She seems possessed not only of the height but of the temper of the Gods....Few people could have sung `Abide with me,' as she did, with a fly stuck in her throat."

I wager that there are scores of gems like these yet to be detected in the unsigned writings of Virginia Woolf.

Notes

1. Appendix C first appeared in *Virginia Woolf and Her Influences: Selected Papers from the Seventh Annual Conference on Virginia Woolf*, ed. Laura Davis and Jeanette McVicker (New York: Pace University Press, 1998), 63–69. Courtesy of Pace University Press.
2. Volume 36, which is missing in the marked files would seem to be, for the most part, accounted for in the 11 unsigned contributions Kirkpatrick has been able to trace.
3. See Kirkpatrick, *A Bibliography* (3rd ed.), 178; an unsigned review of Barlow's *By Beach and Bogland* in *The Guardian* 22 Mar. 1905: 507–08.
4. In the bibliography (3rd ed.), these are C246.6, a review of *Robert Smith Surtees (Creator of "Jorrocks") 1803–1864* by Surtees and E. D. Cuming, and C249.1, a review of *Days that are Gone* by B. de Sales La Terrière, which appear, respectively, in the *N&A* on 21 June 1924 (392) and on 5 July 1924 (454).
5. The cropping of the bound edge, necessarily led to questions that Kirkpatrick posed to Leonard Woolf, such as when the notation "Woolf" remains beside reviews either he or Virginia might have written or, in some cases, as in that of a notation beside a short notice of *Auction Bridge* bracketed with Virginia's review of A. T. Schofield's *Behind the Brass Plate* (Kirkpatrick C301.2; in *N&A* 5 May 1928: 152), when the attribution in the marked copy seemed in error.

Works Cited

Chapman, Wayne K., and Janet M. Manson, eds. *Women in the Milieu of Leonard and Virginia Woolf: Peace, Politics, and Education*. New York: Pace University Press, 1998.

Kirkpatrick, B. J. *A Bibliography of Virginia Woolf*. 3rd ed. Oxford: Clarendon, 1980. [4th ed., rev., assisted by Stuart Clarke, was published in late 1997.]

———. "Virginia Woolf: Unrecorded *Times Literary Supplement* Reviews." Modern Fiction Studies 38.1 (Spring 1992): 279–301. [Published in January 1993.]

Luedeking, Leila, and Michael Edmonds. *Leonard Woolf: A Bibliography*. Winchester, UK: St Paul's Bibliographies, 1992; New Castle, DE: Oak Knoll Books, 1992.

McNeillie, Andrew, ed. *The Essays of Virginia Woolf*. 3 vols. To date. New York: Harcourt, 1986- .

Steele, Elizabeth. *Virginia Woolf's Rediscovered Essays: Sources and Allusions*. New York: Garland, 1987.

APPENDIX D

GRIST AND RAINBOW

B. J. Kirkpatrick and Stuart N. Clarke, *A Bibliography of Virginia Woolf*, Fourth Edition. (Oxford: Clarendon P; New York: Oxford UP, 1997) Pp. xiv, 472. $135.

Reviewed by Wayne K. Chapman, Clemson University.[1]

All major authors such as Virginia Woolf become industries for scholarly grist provided that someone sets down first a foundation on which to begin the milling process. To sustain other forms of scholarship, the bibliographer must identify texts and map the canon, a rainbow in this case. The nature of the process may seem as evanescent as that of its subject. In forty years, we have witnessed four times the expansion of the Woolf industry's foundation since Brownlee Kirkpatrick first published her indispensable bibliography in 1957. In January 1993, with delayed publication of *Virginia Woolf: Modern Fiction Studies* 38.1 (Spring 1992), the latest edition became necessary when she brought to light 45 unrecorded *TLS* and *Times* reviews by Virginia Woolf, temporarily entrusting Andrew McNeillie to deal with certain apocryphal attributions in his multi-volume edition of *The Essays of Virginia Woolf*. By July 1994, however, she joined forces with Stuart Clarke, editor of *Orlando: The Original Holograph Draft* (1993), to bring out a fourth edition of No. IX of The Soho Bibliographies, the second and third ones having been published in 1967 and 1980. She will be remembered for her bibliographies of E. M. Forster, Edmund Blunden, and Katherine Mansfield in the same series. But there the Kirkpatrick/Clarke bibliography has no peer, unless it will be the long-awaited fourth edition of Allan Wade's *A Bibliography of the Writings of W. B. Yeats*, which for years has been in preparation by Colin Smythe. Such works are classics that support an enormous weight in dependent scholarship.

I have written elsewhere about the importance of work now incorporated into this bibliography. Especially relevant to this review are my notes "Collaborative Reviewing by Leonard and Virginia Woolf" (in *Women in the Milieu of Leonard and Virginia Woolf*, eds. Wayne K. Chapman and Janet M. Manson, 1998) and, particularly, "Virginia Woolf's Contributions to Anonymous, Composite Reviews in the *Nation and Athenaeum*, 1924–1928" (in *Virginia Woolf and Her Influences*, eds. Laura Davis and Jeanette McVicker, 1998), which relate to the scope of findings that Kirkpatrick and Clarke bring to light here with the humility of dedicated bibliographers. (See Appendices B and C, above.) By their count on the dust jacket, "Section A, Books and Pamphlets, has increased from 54 to 79 items [from 3rd to 4th editions]; Section AA, Composite Editions, is a new section with nine items; Section C, Contributions to Periodicals, has increased by 78 items, including 56 unsigned reviews; Section D, Translations, has increased from 207 to 557 items; Section F, Letters, is new in that it now itemizes only uncollected letters." Section G, Manuscripts, is significantly expanded from 10 to 22 collections listed, each more detailed than previously.

The first section, "A. Books and Pamphlets," carries on from A55 to A77 with titles first published after the 3rd edition went to press in 1980. This includes Volume 3 of the *Diaries* (1980; A55) onward, Volume 6 of the *Letters* (1980), Susan Dick's edition of *The Complete Shorter Fiction* (1985), Volumes 1–4 of McNeillie's edition of *The Essays* (1986–94), and Mitchell Leaska's edition of *A Passionate Apprentice: The Early Journals 1897–1909* (1990), with various later printings—English, American, and Canadian—to 1996 and several light confections selected usually from Woolf's shorter works in recognition of her popularity and market in England at the brink of her short-lived post-copyright period, in 1991. (Julia Briggs's perspective of the Woolf industry in the 1990s, published in the special "Virginia Woolf International" issue of *The South Carolina Review* 29.1 [Fall 1996] is here strongly recommended.) Also indicative of market forces and popularity are the new editions of Woolf's major titles since 1980: 6 of 7 for *The Voyage Out* (including *Melymbrosia*) appearing since 1990; 4 of 5 for *Night and Day* since 1990; 2 of 3 *Jacob's Room* since 1990; 7 of 10 for *Mrs. Dalloway* since 1990; 8 of 16 for *To the Lighthouse* since 1990; 7 of 7 for *Orlando: A Biography* since 1990; 5 of 7 for *A Room of One's Own* since 1991; 5 of 5 for *The Waves* since 1990; 2 of 6 for *The Years* since 1990; 3 of 5 for *Between the Acts* since 1990; and 2 new editions each, in 1984 and 1986, for the *Common Reader* series of 1925 and 1932. There are surprises, too, in the bibliographic landscape, in contrast to the popularity of these 11 titles. For example, despite its lightheartedness and the phenomenal success of its sister work *Orlando*, *Flush: A Biography* has seen no new editions since 1977. For that matter, there has been but one photo-offset reprint of *Three Guineas* from that time, in 1986, introduced by Hermione Lee to acknowledge the book's importance to Woolf's reputation as a political writer. Since 1979, Diane Gillespie's critical edition for the Shakespeare Head Press gives the English-speaking world the only new (now definitive) text of this work. As elsewhere, Kirkpatrick and Clarke are good to notice marked differences between initial and reset stock of the 1940 American edition, with respect to several pages of gossip on J. P. Morgan and his mistresses. Furthermore, ephemera such as the booklet of Woolf's notes on Roger Fry (edited by Diane Gillespie for Cecil Woolf, 1994) would be easily lost were they not fittingly recorded.

Section "AA. Composite Editions" is a new division but not wholly new in matter. AA1, the combined First and Second Series of *The Common Reader*

(1948), and AA2, the combined *Jacob's Room* and *The Waves* (1960), formerly occupied the designated A18e and A6e spaces in the bibliography. Of the remaining 7 items in the new section, 6 show how the big presses leaped at opportunity once held by the Hogarth Press as, from 1992 to 1994, Oxford University Press, Penguin, Macmillan, and Chancellor Press (Great Classic Library) began issuing quickly cheap, compact editions for students and "the home library."

Section "B. Contributions to Books and Pamphlets (Excluding Selections Reprinted in Anthologies) and Books Translated by Virginia Woolf" does not get a word on the dust jacket but is really quite different from its state in the 3rd edition, where Leonard Woolf's five volumes of autobiography were listed presumably because of the extent to which he quoted from her. These books are no longer listed and have, in fact, been deleted from the index and the volume entirely. The item numbers are reassigned; the only former ones adhered to and thus giving the section some resemblance to that of the preceding edition are B1–11, where B4b, a 1969 photo-offset reprint of the 1923 *Talks with Tolstoi*, is the only amendment. Thereafter, items published in 1980 or later are listed, including *Virginia Woolf's Reading Notebooks* by Brenda Silver (1983) and *The Sisters' Arts* by Diane Gillespie (1988; noted for illustrations by Virginia Woolf), to cite but the most significant works. An item on "English Youth," a fragmentary portrait of Octavia Wilberforce that Evelyn Haller and I prepared as an appendix for *Women in the Milieu of Leonard and Virginia Woolf* (loc. cit.), might have appeared had there had been time to do more than acknowledge it in the Preface with other works forthcoming when the bibliography went to press.

The "C" section of the book is where the really significant changes have taken place and, to my mind, the most interesting. Not only is this where the 45 unrecorded *TLS* and *Times* reviews have gone into the accounting, but also 14 new items that were first published in periodicals in 1979 or later. Overall, 56 unsigned reviews have been added to the bibliography. However, with *Woolf Studies Annual* publishing primary work such as Beth Rigel Daugherty's transcription of Woolf's "How Should One Read a Book?" (in *WSA* 4 [1998]), from Berg Collection holographs not listed in section "G. Manuscripts," section C is already falling behind. Indeed, as I suggest elsewhere, there is probably a vast amount of work to do to identify scores of still unrecorded mini-reviews that Virginia Woolf wrote when her husband was literary editor of the *Nation and Athenaeum* in the 1920s, particularly for missing volumes 39–42 of the marked files. But correcting their own work is where Kirkpatrick and Clarke prove most worthy of our praise. Comparing Kirkpatrick's "a" and "b" lists of "Doubtful" and "Untraced" items in the 3rd edition with the 4th edition's three lists—Ca, Cb, and Cc, the third being works previously attributed but now regarded "not by VW"—we see that the challenge remains for us to find 31 of 36 untraced pieces we know Woolf wrote or have reason to believe she wrote. Five have been found since 1980 and moved into the "C" section proper. One new lead has been added to the list as Cb20.1. The new list Cc (works "not by VW") includes 9 items for which the bibliographers correct the 3rd edition, fulfilling Kirkpatrick's intention as outlined in her 1992 article on the newly discovered *TLS* reviews.

Sections D and E, respectively "Translations into Foreign Languages" and "Foreign Editions in English and Miscellaneous Material," will be the greatest use to scholars interested in Woolf from international perspectives, of which many are represented. Beyond the English-language editions published outside England, the U.S., and Canada—several of these in Japan and, lately, Korea—one needn't be a linguist to perceive the universality of Woolf's appeal to her uncommon readers in thirty-six languages. Just review the 204 titles! All I can add to this account is the suggestion that users might give context to several foreign audiences by considering the secondary scholarship addressed in *Virginia Woolf International: The South Carolina Review*, especially that of post-war Germany (by Vera and Ansgar Nünning) and pre- and post-Maoist China (by Melba Cuddy-Keane and Kay Li), to which extensive bibliographies are appended.

Finally, as everywhere else an indication of increased demand and growth in Woolf scholarship, the last two sections of this solid book have increased by 150% and 250%, respectively, the number of "Books and Articles Containing Uncollected Letters and Extracts..." (F) and the manuscript collections (G) on which this thriving industry increasingly turns nowadays. As Kirkpatrick and Clarke seem to acknowledge in their preface, much of the last section was obsolete on publication because of the appearance of *Major Authors on CD-ROM: Virginia Woolf* (Primary Source Media), which, attached electronically to Mark Hussey's comprehensive reference book *Virginia Woolf: A to Z*, includes all of Woolf's "published works and most of the manuscript holdings" (ix) in two main collections: the Monk's House Papers at the University of Sussex and the Berg Collection of the New York Public Library. Section F has become, since the 3rd edition, a useful index of sales advertisements from Sotheby's, among other things. And section G, for the 22 collections recorded, is only 8 pages—not exactly a census of manuscripts considering what inevitably gets omitted (for instance, the holographs of "How Should One Read a Book?") and no substitute for the on-site conspectus that those archives will provide to their readers. The advantage of having information on manuscripts is that such information is now one with Woolf's printed works and thoroughly, even painstakingly, cross-referenced.

In short, *A Bibliography of Virginia Woolf* constitutes a foundation on which scholarship flourishes. Heaven knows where the bibliography will go when the print-on-paper medium gives place to the more transitory electronic forms of publication. With the University of Sussex putting its Woolf holdings on the World Wide Web, the art of bibliography will have to adapt. This book is no exception. It will simply go on creating sections for the new, compounding, recasting, and emending successive states of itself as necessary to keep the mill-wheel turning. The Woolf industry shows no sign of slackening.

Note

1. This review first appeared in *The South Carolina Review* 31.1 (fall 1998): 204–07, and is reproduced here courtesy of Clemson University Press. A longer version was published in *Woolf Studies Annual* Volume 5 (New York: Pace University Press, 1999): 161–66.

Related Collections and Resources

Washington State University Libraries, Manuscripts, Archives, and Special Collections (Selected Collections, e.g., The Leonard and Virginia Woolf Collection and The Hogarth Press Collection)
<https://libraries.wsu.edu/masc/rare-books>

The Library of Leonard and Virginia Woolf: A Short-title Catalog (Washington State University)
<ntserver1.wsulibs.wsu/masc/onlinebooks/woolflibrary/woolflibraryonline.htm>

Bloomsbury Collections (University of Sussex Library Special Collections)
<http://www.thekeep.info/bloomsbury-collections/>

Leonard Woolf Papers (University of Sussex Library Special Collections)
<http://www.thekeep.info/collections/leonard-woolf-papers/>

New Statesman Archive (University of Sussex Library Special Collections)
<http://www.thekeep.info/collections/getrecord/GB181_SxMs60>

The Nation and Athenaeum Collection (City University, London)
<https://www.city.ac.uk/library/resources/special-collection>

About the *Athenaeum* (City University, London)
<smcse.city.ac.uk/doc/cisr/web/athenaeum/aboutath.html>

Archives of the Hogarth Press (1917–1955) (University of Reading Library)
<https://www.reading.ac.uk/special-collections/collections/sc-hogarth.aspx>

Virginia Woolf Collection (Harry Ransom Humanities Research Center, University of Texas at Austin)
<http://norman.hrc.utexas.edu/fasearch/results.cfm?name=woolf>

Lytton Strachey Collection (Harry Ransom Humanities Research Center, University of Texas at Austin)
<http://norman.hrc.utexas.edu/fasearch/results.cfm?name=strachey>

The Henry W. and Albert A. Berg Collection of English and American Literature (NY Public Library; some Berg Collection items online via NYPL's Digital Collections)
<https://www.nypl.org/about/divisions/berg-collection-english-and-american-literature>

The Papers of John Maynard Keynes (at the King's College Modern Archives, Cambridge University)
<https://janus.lib.cam.ac.uk/db/node.xsp?id=EAD%2FGBR%2F0272%2FPP%2FJMK>

Location Register of 20th-Century Manuscripts and Letters (University of Reading Library)
<https://www.reading.ac.uk/library/about-us/projects/lib-location-register.aspx>

FURTHER RESOURCES

The International Virginia Woolf Society
<http://sites.utoronto.ca/IVWS/>

The Virginia Woolf Society of Great Britain
<http://www.virginiawoolfsociety.co.uk/index.html>

Pace University Press (including *Woolf Studies Annual*)
<http://press.pace.edu/woolf-studies-titles/>

Virginia Woolf Selected Papers (monographic series at Clemson University Press)
<https://www.clemson.edu/centers-institutes/press/books/virginia-woolf.html>

Virginia Woolf Website at SCSU (Southern Connecticut State University)
<http://woolf-center.southernct.edu/>

www.ingramcontent.com/pod-product-compliance
Lightning Source LLC
Chambersburg PA
CBHW020640230426
43665CB00008B/259